LATIN AMERICA
IN DEBATE

A BOOK IN THE SERIES

LATIN AMERICA IN TRANSLATION / EN TRADUCCIÓN / EM TRADUÇÃO

Sponsored by the Duke–University of North Carolina Program in Latin American Studies

LATIN AMERICA
IN DEBATE

Indigeneity, Development,
Dependency, Populism

MARISTELLA SVAMPA

Translated by Alejandro Reyes

Duke University Press   *Durham and London*   2025

Project Editor: Liz Smith
Designed by Courtney Leigh Richardson
Typeset in Garamond Premier Pro and Knockout by Westchester
Publishing Services

Library of Congress Cataloging-in-Publication Data
Names: Svampa, Maristella author | Reyes, Alejandro, [date] translator
Title: Latin America in debate : indigeneity, development, dependency,
populism / Maristella Svampa ; translated by Alejandro Reyes.
Other titles: Latin America in translation/en traduccion/em traducao
Description: Durham : Duke University Press, 2025. | Series: Latin
America in translation / en traduccion / em traducao | Includes
bibliographical references and index.
Identifiers: LCCN 2024050764 (print)
LCCN 2024050765 (ebook)
ISBN 9781478031949 (paperback)
ISBN 9781478028710 (hardcover)
ISBN 9781478060918 (ebook)
Subjects: LCSH: Political culture—Latin America | Populism—Latin
America | Indigenous peoples—Latin America—Social conditions |
Social movements—Latin America | Latin America—Social conditions
| Latin America—Politics and government | Latin America—Economic
conditions
Classification: LCC HN110.5.A8 S936 2025 (print) | LCC HN110.5.A8
(ebook) | DDC 306.098—dc23/eng/20250519
LC record available at https://lccn.loc.gov/2024050764
LC ebook record available at https://lccn.loc.gov/2024050765

Cover art: Map courtesy PrintingSociety/Adobe Stock. Texture
courtesy Nadejda/Adobe Stock.

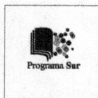

Programa Sur

This work has been published within the framework of the Sur
Translation Support Programme of the Ministry of Foreign Affairs,
International Trade and Worship of the Argentine Republic. [Obra
editada en el marco del Programa Sur de Apoyo a las Traducciones del
Ministerio de Relaciones Exteriores, Comercio Internacional y Culto de
la República Argentina.]

In memory of Norma Giarracca

Dogma allows a course, a geographic map: it is the only guarantee of not, under the illusion of advancing, covering the same ground twice, and of not landing in an impasse because of bad information. . . . Dogma is not an itinerary but a compass on the journey. To think with freedom, the first condition is to abandon the preoccupation of absolute liberty. Thought has a strict need for direction and objective. Thinking well is, in large part, a question of direction or orbit.—JOSÉ CARLOS MARIÁTEGUI, *Defensa del marxismo*

Contents

Acknowledgments

This book was read in parts by friends and colleagues. Among them, my special thanks to Rubén Lo Vuolo, Pablo Stefanoni, and Pablo Ospina. Their comments certainly improved this text, even though this does not make them responsible for the final result.

My gratitude to all participants and students of the "Latin American Debates" series at the Faculty of Humanities and Social Sciences of the National University of La Plata (Universidad Nacional de La Plata; UNLP) from 2010 to 2015. This book is dedicated to them, the youngest, in whom I hope to have awakened a passion for thinking with a global perspective but with their feet well planted in Latin America. My special thanks to Florencia Puente, who accompanied me with a Latin American head and heart during all these years of academic work. My thanks to Susana Savioa for her advice and friendship.

My thanks to Fernando Fagnani for his priceless support, and to the entire production team at Edhasa.

Finally, my gratitude to Carlos Janin, for his readings and support. I know the task was not easy for him, for in all these years this book has grown in challenges and writings, more so than expected. However, I believe that regardless of the results, it was a worthwhile endeavor.

—BUENOS AIRES, OCTOBER 28, 2015

Acknowledgments

Introduction

One of the major problems of Latin American social theory is a deficit of accumulation, resulting not only from occasional and cyclic erasures caused by dictatorships and exile but also from a recurrent depreciation and neglect of our own production in these latitudes—that is, a disdain for the conceptual contributions, debates, and topics examined by theoretical and social reflection in Latin America. There is therefore an internal difficulty in building a legacy, related to a very significant weakness of academic and extra-academic transmission, not only in regional terms but also across generations, aggravated by the tendency of many Latin American scholars and intellectuals to exercise tabula rasa—in tune with political shifts and epistemological turns—thus discarding, through a dialectic without a synthesis, debates and categories that in other times were an important part of critical thought.

On the other hand, that deficit of accumulation is also related to Latin American culture's anthropophagical vocation, historically expressed in an urge to incorporate other lexicons, other philosophical and political vocabularies. Nothing foreign is strange to us, which, as the Brazilian Oswald de Andrade pointed out in 1928, illustrates our capacity to devour all things foreign and incorporate them, thus creating a complex, new, and constantly changing identity. However, the flip side of this restless and omnivorous intellectual spirit, of this constitutive hybridity and this artistically, culturally, and intellectually cosmopolitan vocation, is greater intellectual dependence.

The processes of epistemic expropriation should also be underscored. In this regard, it is worth recalling an anecdote. At the World Social Forum in Tunisia in March 2015, as I awaited my turn to speak, a Brazilian colleague and I listened to a renowned French economist speak of globalization and its critics. During his talk, the good man spoke of dependency theory and stated without hesitation that its founders were Samir Amin and Andre Gunder Frank. My Brazilian colleague and I looked at each other with surprise; there is no doubt that the African thinker Samir Amin is *not* one of the founders of dependency theory (although he adopted its hypotheses), and while it is true that the German Frank is one of its representatives, there are many others—all of them Brazilian—who have played a central role in it (Fernando H. Cardoso, Theotônio dos Santos, Ruy Mauro Marini, and Vânia Bambirra, among others). But what cannot be denied, in addition to the Latin American character of dependency theory, is its importance in the debates of a whole era in the subcontinent, as well as its capacity to radiate to other parts of the world. And yet the French economist ignored these origins and placed them elsewhere, omitting other authors, naming—en passant—only those who were not Latin American. I have no doubt that behind this omission there was an act of epistemic appropriation, a gesture naturalized in the dominant academic habitus.

Before continuing, I would like to clarify that I do not intend to shut myself off in a sort of chauvinist vindication on a regional scale, nor to give in to essentialist temptations so strongly associated with the Latin American essay. I merely wish to underscore that in my many years in academia and militant spaces in several latitudes, I have observed that many intellectuals and scholars from central countries have participated in that omission, which, rather than building avenues for a North-South dialogue of knowledges, contributes to epistemic expropriation and the consolidation of asymmetries.

Finally, both the invisibility of Latin American theoretical production and the process of epistemic expropriation strengthen the notion that there are no general theories in Latin America but rather a "specific gaze," a sort of "local production." In other words, the concepts that compose Latin American philosophy and social sciences, rather than being generally applicable or comprising theories with a certain universal relevance, are encapsulated in the specific, a discourse about and from the margins, characterized by a local color and an obsession with identity and case studies. Latin American social sciences, especially those currents or perspectives related to popular thought, are thus confined, as Alcira Argumedo argues, to the "suburbs of reflection, where viscous and irrelevant eclecticisms are examined" (2009, 10).[1]

Several authors have recently attempted to examine and reconstruct these intricacies of Latin American social theory. For example, in his history of Latin American thought, Chilean author Eduardo Devés Valdés (2003) argues that it wavers between the search for identity and an urge for modernization, which has led to the emergence of different cycles and spirals, fads, generations, and schools in the past two centuries of Latin American culture. Based on this alternating movement, the author draws a line that separates Sarmiento from José Martí, Rodó from José Carlos Mariátegui, the Economic Commission for Latin America and the Caribbean (Comisión Económica para América Latina y el Caribe; CEPAL) from the advocates of dependency theory, neoliberals from decolonial thinkers. This, however, does not imply that there is a cosmopolitan pole and a particularist or Americanist pole. Devés Valdés's second—and most interesting—thesis is that many thinkers who defend one dimension do not radically deny the other; rather, they have (often unsuccessfully) attempted to reconcile both sides. Furthermore, throughout their lives, many authors have adopted different options with different emphases. In other words, without implying a contradiction, Latin American thought can be understood as a history of the explicit and implicit attempts to reconcile that ever-desperate urge for modernization with an unwavering obsession with identity.

On the other hand, Argentine sociologist Marcos Roitman (2008b, 5–10) argues in *Pensar América Latina: El desarrollo de la sociología latinoamericana* (Thinking Latin America: The development of Latin American sociology) that we Latin Americans have tended to "define ourselves negatively." We have therefore tended to read our reality in relation to Europe and have thus concluded that that which is most characteristic of Latin America is its deficit, its shortfalls, its incompleteness. Latin American reality is therefore accursed because it was part of colonial capitalism and because we have an ingrained frustration about not being European, about not having European virtues and grandeur, about remaining outside of history, about being marginal in that sense. "We have been incapable of making history" (8). This sentence is the quintessence of the notion of deficit. Latin America is therefore reflected on as a sort of appendix of a central body basically consisting of Europe and the United States. The curse thus defines our condition as subaltern, and our modernity as forever incomplete.

This feeling of inferiority permeates Latin American philosophy in particular. The latter has traditionally been founded on an awareness of our insufficiency and rupture and has been devoted to the search for Latin America's singularity in the context of epistemic dependency. Several authors have re-created the original core of this philosophical outlook, among them the Mexican Leopoldo Zea and Argentinean Arturo Roig. While Zea (1965), a great historian of ideas, proposed a recurrent reflection on the search for singularity, Roig ([1981] 2009) preferred to insist on the foundational role of the experience of rupture in Latin American thought. But both of them believe that the point of departure of Latin American philosophy is an inquiry into the concrete, the peculiar, that which is original to America, the very possibility of philosophy, revealing in this roundabout way an awareness of the fact that its existence is a marginal and mestizo consciousness. From this standpoint, the great topic of American thought is the specific—and not universal—subject of American culture (Zea 1965, 48). There is no question that, in its essay version, philosophy has asked questions about our historic specificity with an excessive emphasis on the other's gaze, on how the other names us, which has deeply influenced the process of constructing Latin American thought, marked by an awareness of our marginality, our rootlessness, and thus our obsession with reflexivity.

Different from philosophy, sociology commits other sins related to the classical normative heritage. The weight of the normative model is such that, conceptually, Latin American political reality is stuck halfway, thus constituting a recurrent example of an "anomaly." To understand this, it suffices to think of the ways populism has been defined. Yet it is not only modernity and democracy that appear as lacking and unfinished but also the social subjects themselves. So much so that, in general, Latin American sociology has found it difficult to reflect on the diversity of social players as full social actors. The bourgeoisie, the working class, and the middle classes are considered "only halfway" players in the context of the structural conditions of peripheral societies and the reality of dependency, but also that of the heterogeneity of Latin America's social universe—in terms of origin—where other categories of people who are not considered full actors abound, including indigenous people, peasants, informal workers, and the unemployed.[2] In a renowned article on social classes, Brazilian sociologist Florestan Fernandes (1973) suggested that these classes are no different in Latin America; what differs is the way in which capital materialized itself and irradiated historically as a social force. This "difference," he argued, explains why Latin America has neither the "conquering bourgeois" nor the "restless peasant" nor the "rebellious worker."

Few things are as characteristic of Latin America's sociological outlook as the will to inscribe interpretation in broad sociopolitical models that nonetheless are permanently imbued with both an excess and an interpretative deficit. One such excess: these sociopolitical models conceal what is probably one of the main particularities of peripheral modernity, that is, the fact that analyses of the principles of the political rarely (and always partially) coincide with the actors' lived experience. One such deficit: Inscribing action in significant totalities obliterates the analysis of political experience, whose main role is to interpret the nature of the links established by individuals with the political system (Martuccelli and Svampa 1997).

2.

In recent decades, Latin American critical thought has examined the issue of epistemic dependency in depth. I would like to highlight three of these critical perspectives, which share the same elective affinities. First, the subaltern and postcolonial perspective questioned the national or nationalist and Marxist paradigms and proposed thinking the subaltern as such, as something that cannot be reduced and whose voice we cannot fully grasp, in a context in which identities are always migrating and changing.[3] Not only are the popular sectors heterogeneous, but there is a multiplicity of different universes ("motley societies," according to René Zavaleta Mercado), often refractory (in terms of ontological necessity) to being interconnected—the peasant world, indigenous people, formal and informal workers, the unemployed, and so on. In other words, there is in fact a popular, subaltern, migrating, and ever-changing subject defined in the plural, who must be approached in its diversity, without, however, depriving it of its own voice. This historical and anthropological current, which sought to identify the moments when the subaltern has emerged in the various historical cycles in Latin America, can make significant contributions when analyzing self-proclaimed progressive governments, examining the avatars of the dialectic between the emergence of the subaltern and the processes of re-subalternization. The work of Bolivian theorist and historian Silvia Rivera Cusicanqui stresses these very aspects, focusing once again on the issue of internal colonialism, understood as a form of domination internalized in subjectivity (Rivera Cusicanqui and Santos 2015, 83). Examined in the long term, internal colonialism is conceptualized as a "structural framework of identities" (León Pesantez 2013, 140).

The second critical current is the decolonial perspective, condensed in the concept of *coloniality of power* proposed by Peruvian sociologist Aníbal Quijano, which underscores the economic/political dimension of coloniality as a pattern of general domination with an ethnic/racial character derived from colonial heritage. Revisiting this definition in a widely read book published in 2000, Edgardo Lander coined the concept of "coloniality of knowledge" as an extension of the former, based on the epistemological dimension: Our social sciences have thus naturalized the concepts and categories of the social sciences that developed with the expansion of colonialism. Furthermore, this naturalization of the various dimensions of modernity is founded on the defeat of our traditional and popular or plebeian cultures and the triumph of a new (capitalist) reality that organized time and territories in a different manner. Examples of this are the naturalization of the idea of progress, with its entire hierarchy of peoples, stages, nations, historical experiences, and continents; the naturalization of the very idea of human nature as derived from Europe's liberal experience; the naturalization of the process of social differentiation; and, as a consequence, the naturalization of the superiority of some forms of knowledge over others. This process of naturalization has been aggravated with the professionalization of the social sciences. The ideas of civilization, development, and modernization thus gradually configure a paradigm of normality (Lander 2000, 9–11). Lander's proposal is part of a long search "for perspectives of non-Eurocentric knowledge," which recovers valuable contributions by authors such as José Martí and José Carlos Mariátegui, as well as more recent ones by Aníbal Quijano, Walter Mignolo, Enrique Dussel, and Catherine Walsh, among others (5). In short, coloniality has two faces—colonialism not only is a historical fact but also expresses itself in the denial of different realities and of the knowledge produced by those realities. To these two dimensions, Colombian author Santiago Castro Gómez (2012) adds the "coloniality of being," understood not as yet another dimension of the process of coloniality but emphasizing the existence of three distinct axes that allude to a diversity of logics. There is therefore not one single pattern but different dimensions: economic/political, epistemological, and ontological, which refer to how capitalism has become the way of life of millions of people.

Finally, in this line of thought, it is important to highlight the contributions of *Epistemologies of the South*, by Portuguese essayist Boaventura de Sousa Santos, who has maintained a constant dialogue with Latin America, its struggles, and its intellectual spaces for decades.[4] According to Santos, "the epistemologies of the south point to the search for knowledge and criteria for the validity of knowledge that give visibility and credibility to the cognitive practices of classes, peoples, and social groups that have historically been victimized, exploited, and oppressed by colonialism and capitalism" (2009b, 12). The author aims at replacing the indolent Reason of hegemonic knowledge, whose temporal conception is founded on a contraction of the present and an expansion of the future, with a cosmopolitan Reason that expands the present (in order to understand and value the current social experience) and contracts the future and that must be founded by means of three meta-sociological procedures: the sociology of absences, the sociology of emergences, and the task of translation (100–101). The premises of *Epistemologies of the South* are therefore the ecology of knowledges and intercultural translation. While the ecology of knowledges is "a horizontal dialogue between different knowledges, including scientific knowledge, but also peasant, artistic, indigenous, popular, and many other knowledges that are dismissed by traditional scholarship," intercultural translation is a procedure that enables the creation of a reciprocal understanding between the various experiences of the world. For Santos, knowledge is constructed in the context of struggles, and concepts and theories are developed in the process of such struggles, often by the social movements themselves. It is therefore a matter of constructing not only an ecology of different knowledges, shedding light on those knowledges that have been suppressed—vernacular knowledges or those produced by indigenous peoples—but an epistemological proposal, a way of conceiving knowledge production in the context of social struggles.

3.

This book was born as a political, intellectual, and pedagogical challenge slightly over seven years ago when I participated in a roundtable discussion during a sociology conference at the National University of La Plata (Universidad Nacional de La Plata; UNLP) (in December 2008, before becoming a professor at that university), and I wrote an article on the current state of certain Latin American debates in Latin America's political scene at the time. In it, I referred to three central debates with a long and rich history in the region, located at the porous border between the intellectual and political fields. The first one alluded to the advancement of indigenous struggles and inquired into the place of indigenous peoples and the communal matrix in the process of nation building; the second one examined the revival of populism in several Latin American regimes and inquired into the meaning and interpretation of this line of historical accumulation; the third one referred to the full-fledged return of a borderline concept of Latin American thought, development, through the expansion of various forms of extractivism, and inquired into the return of a certain "developmentalist illusion" (Svampa 2010a).

In the same article, I argued that the epochal change observed since 2000, based on the denaturalization of the relationship between globalization and neoliberalism, had led to a transitional situation that exhibited a clear trend toward a reconfiguration of the relationship between the populist tradition and neo-developmentalist extractivism. From that standpoint, I wondered how these three trends could or did coexist or, more simply stated, what would happen with indigenous peoples' project of autonomy, expressed in the challenge of creating a plurinational state and the rise and proliferation of collective resistances of an eco-territorial nature.

I presented that introductory paper at various academic meetings and spaces, including in a short course I taught at the PhD program in Latin American studies at the National Autonomous University of Mexico (Universidad

Nacional Autónoma de México; UNAM) in 2010, which convinced me that if I really wanted to achieve a certain conceptual density and narrative consistency in those debates, I had to dive into the history of Latin American thought and social sciences. I attempted to do so in the course Latin American Debates, which I started teaching that year at the Faculty of Humanities and Social Sciences of the UNLP, which was part of the sociology program and which I continued teaching with the new title of Latin American Social Theory until 2021.

It is worth noting that in 2009 I also had the opportunity of participating with other Latin American colleagues in an encounter at the University of Costa Rica devoted to "Latin American sociology today." Some of the questions posed were: Can we speak of a *Latin American sociology*? Does *Latin American sociology* have certain specificities? What is the role of sociologists and the discipline of sociology in Latin America today? Of what use is sociology in our region? That encounter was unquestionably one of the triggers for this research.[5]

The years I have been teaching that course at UNLP convinced me that I had to deal with three major challenges. The first and fundamental one is that there is an immense number of archives and libraries on the topic of indigenous people in Latin America. It suffices to travel to countries like Mexico, Guatemala, Bolivia, Peru, or Ecuador, to cite only a few, to understand the magnitude of the contributions from different disciplines, the incommensurate multidimensionality of the topic, its unavoidable complexity in regional terms, the wealth of the history of struggles and generations, visible both in organizational experience and in social, philosophical, and literary reflections present in books, declarations, manifestos, and articles, as well as the important contributions of Latin America's oral tradition. I therefore had to make certain choices regarding the work of historical reconstruction and to justify the selection of certain countries over others. As I explain in chapter 1, the result of this effort was to focus on four countries when examining the indigenous question: Mexico, Bolivia, Peru, and Argentina.

At this point, I would like to speak of my personal trajectory. Although I am a native of Patagonia, I stepped into the indigenous universe the first time I visited Argentina's Northeast in 2000, to teach a course, Modernity and Social Theory, at the National University of Jujuy. The following years I conducted a series of research studies and wrote several books on social movements in Argentina, especially on unemployed people's organizations, which also allowed me to engage in the world of popular resistances and plebeian struggles, while redefining myself as an amphibian intellectual (Svampa 2008).

Starting in December 2003, after the fall of President Gonzalo Sánchez de Lozada, I took a road of no return toward insurgent Latin America, toward indigenous and anti-neoliberal struggles, through recurrent visits to Bolivia, which allowed me to reflect on and experience other rationalities and political relationalities through intense indigenous mobilizations and, years later, the discussion of novel concepts such as the plurinational state, autonomies, and Good Living (*Buen Vivir*). Visits to other Latin American countries such as Mexico, Ecuador, and Peru further fueled my interest in writings and debates on the place of indigenous people in the Americas.

However, many of these debates are unknown in Argentina, a country that constructed a narrative on national identity based on the original genocide (Lenton 2011) and the denial of all things indigenous. "The fear of being ourselves," as Rodolfo Kush (1976) put it, translated into the stereotype of the racial melting pot that aimed the spotlight at the immigrants who descended from the ships, leaving in the dark all those who, in the name of Progress—and with a Remington in hand—had been dismissed and swept over by state power. Indigenous people, as David Viñas (1982) added, thus became "our first disappeared persons" . . .

The second challenge I had to deal with was to accept the necessarily incomplete and arbitrary nature of such reconstructions, not in terms of depth regarding each of the debates examined, but in relation to other equally important debates throughout the region's history and present in today's political scenario. In this respect, I made the decision to exclude some of them, such as the campesino question—a topic with an unquestionably specific importance in Latin American history. Its extraordinary breadth and evident complexity led me to that decision, even as I am aware that we can learn something from it through its connection—at some points—with the indigenous question and the issue of populism. However, I do realize that this unforgivable absence is a matter still to be examined, especially considering my own rural family origins—or perhaps because of them. I also chose to include another classical debate, that of dependency. There is no doubt that in spite of the emergence of a Latin American space; in spite of the existence of a "new defiant regionalism" (Jaime Preciado Coronado's [2013] beautiful expression)—clearly illustrated by the events at the Summit of the Americas in Mar del Plata in 2005, when Latin American countries turned their back on the Free Trade Area of the Americas (FTAA); in spite of the proliferation of Latin Americanist and progressive blocs (Bolivarian Alliance for the Peoples of our America [Alianza Bolivariana para los Pueblos de Nuestra América; ALBA]) and the Community of Latin American and Caribbean States (Comunidad de Estados Latinoamericanos y Caribeños; CELAC), among others); in spite of the deployment of a strongly anti-imperialist and emancipatory discourse, structural dependency is—and, more important, as everything indicates, will continue to be—an integral part of our future as peripheral nations. That is why I decided to include the debate on dependency, a category and approach that—as has been repeatedly stated—had a significant theoretical and political impact in the 1960s, in order to examine its relevance in present-day Latin America.

The third challenge was material, regarding my access to the literature. Unlike Mexico, Argentina does not stand out for cultivating a Latin Americanist tradition, and this is reflected in our public and university libraries as well as our bookstores. For that reason, visiting other countries in the region and speaking to Latin American friends and colleagues were essential to gain access to the literature. Particularly productive were my feverish visits to the extraordinary used bookstores on Donceles Street in Mexico City's historic downtown near the Zócalo Plaza, where I found some of the books cited in this research. Another important part of the texts consulted is available on the internet, and, finally, a small number of books that at some point I believed inaccessible were provided to me by friends, or I was able to purchase them online.

The resulting book is structured in two parts that examine four essential debates, in the following order: the indigenous question, the issue of development, the question of dependency, and the question of populism. The first part, "Latin American Debates and History," as its title indicates, proposes a voyage through and a historical reconstruction of each of the debates in four chapters. The second part, entitled "Scenarios, Contemporary Debates, and Disputed Categories," consisting also of four chapters, provides a personal interpretation of the relevance of each of these debates in today's Latin American scene.

Beginning with the indigenous question is not arbitrary; furthermore, coloniality is the framework that allows us to understand and integrate the rest of the—more canonical—debates on Latin America. I argue that these nodal questions have been present in an important part of Latin American humanities and social sciences, regardless of the various theoretical and methodological traditions and argumentative styles. The debates present in this book are located at the intersection of several theoretical fields, especially those of social theory, the history of ideas, and Latin American social thought. For that reason, they include a broad range of disciplines, such as political economy, political sociology, anthropology and history, philosophy, and cultural studies.

Finally, as Roberto Briceño León and Heinz Sontag argue, "Two trends have oriented social science in Latin America: to respond to the people and their society in their singularity and their urgent needs; or to respond to the times, to the requirements of scientific rigor and universal knowledge. The great promise of Latin American thought was summarized a century ago by José Martí when he wrote that both trends should be attended to and that [social scientists] should be persons of their time and their people" (1998, 246). There is no doubt that Latin American critical thought derives its topics, theoretical approach, and potency from the social and political conflicts of its time and the analysis of the dynamics of capital accumulation and the forms of social, racial, territorial, and gender inequalities in our societies. This book belongs to that critical tradition of Latin American thought, which seeks to reconcile a global outlook and a concrete analysis, associated with the notion of a public and political intellectual committed to change.

In short, the different modes that coloniality of knowledge (Quijano, Lander) or internal colonialism (in Silvia Rivera's terms) has assumed have tended to erase and render invisible local theoretical production and other ways of seeing and interpreting the world that question the notion of a single or universal form of modernity. Thus, "epistemic blindness" (Machado Aráoz 2012), intellectual dependency, colonial heritage, the difficulties of institutionalization, the thematic diasporas related to the various forms of national development, and political ruptures explain this difficulty in consolidating a tradition of regional thought that can be passed on to different generations and countries. This book seeks to combat those erasures and constant attempts to subalternize local theoretical production and its main debates. It is an attempt to explore certain lines of historical/conceptual accumulation in the construction of a Latin American critical tradition in terms of ideas and theories, critical concepts, and horizon-concepts immersed in intense theoretical and political debates. It is therefore an attempt to accomplish what Boaventura de Sousa Santos (2009b) called "a sociology of absences" and "a sociology of emergences"—a contribution that seeks to recover and shed light on certain lines of accumulation of critical thought that once again speak to us as Latin Americans, at the ever-porous borders of the intellectual and political fields.

PART I

Latin American Debates and History

1

The Debate on the
Indigenous and *Indianidad*

As many authors remind us, in colonial times, "indigenous" was a political/ administrative category. Indigenous people had to be counted because they paid tribute or performed forced labor, especially in the mines, as was the case in Bolivia (Lavaud and Lestage 2009, 14). But the indigenous category soon became more complex, adopting a racial (or racialist) and cultural dimension defined by markers such as language, clothing, and rural origins (Barragán 1992; de la Cadena 2000), which always pointed to its inferiority relative to the nonindigenous.

In demographic terms, in 2011 the indigenous population of Latin America and the Caribbean was estimated at between 40 and 50 million people out of a total of 480 million inhabitants. For organizations such as UNICEF, according to the official censuses conducted between 2000 and 2008, the indigenous population in Latin America corresponded to 6 percent of the total population. Other estimates, however, set it at 10 percent of the total population (according to the United Nations Development Programme) (Sichra 2009). According to more recent data from the Economic Commission for Latin America and the Caribbean (CEPAL 2014, 36), Mexico and Peru are the countries with the largest indigenous population in the region, with almost 17 million and 7 million, respectively. Next come the Plurinational State of Bolivia and Guatemala, with a population of around 6 million people; Chile and Colombia, with more than 1.5 million; Argentina, Brazil, and Ecuador, with around 1 million people each; the Bolivarian Republic of Venezuela, with slightly over 700,000; Honduras and Nicaragua, with over 1.5 million; and Panama, with around 400,000. Of the countries that have included the category of indigenous population in their censuses, those with the smallest numbers are Costa Rica and Paraguay, with slightly over 100,000, and Uruguay, with almost 80,000. If we examine the proportion of the indigenous population relative to the national total, according to the estimates, the largest numbers correspond to Bolivia (62.2 percent),[1] Guatemala (41 percent), Peru (24 percent), and Mexico (15 percent). Panama (12 percent), Chile (11 percent), and Ecuador make up the second block of countries with the largest relative indigenous population. Finally, there is a third group of countries with a relative indigenous population between 0.5 percent (Brazil) and 3 percent (Argentina and Uruguay, with 2.4 percent) (CEPAL 2014, 43, table 2, based on data from 2012).

Likewise—the report continues—the 2010 results show a total growth of 49.3 percent of the indigenous population in one decade, which corresponds to an average annual growth rate of 4.1 percent. "This is a 'demographic recovery' of significant magnitude, especially considering that over the same period the population of Latin America increased by 13.1%, at an average annual rate of 1.3%. This rebound is likely due not only to the demographic dynamic of indigenous peoples . . . , but also to an increase in self-identification" (CEPAL 2014, 36). In effect, the process of ethnification and recognition of originary peoples has led to an increase in identification as indigenous people, with both an objective side (attribution by institutions) and a subjective side (belonging, self-identification).

On the other hand, there is a vast diversity of indigenous peoples in each country. As early as the 1970s, Guillermo Bonfil Batalla (1972) observed in a well-known article that, as a colonial category, there is only one Indian, but internally it subdivides into multiple local units. "Colonial society is dual in its basic structure and plural in the colonized sector," says Luis Beltrán, quoted by Bonfil Batalla (1972, 8). Thus, the Constitution of the Plurinational State of Bolivia recognizes the existence of thirty-six indigenous groups. In Mexico there are seventy-eight, while in Peru there are eighty-five, and in Argentina, thirty-two. Furthermore, as a result of the processes of revaluation of ethnic identity and a growing social and political protagonism by indigenous peoples, today we can count 826 peoples in Latin America (CEPAL 2014, 38).[2]

There are also significant regional differences. In countries like Bolivia and Peru, the existing tensions transcend a binary opposition (Indian/white-mestizo), revealing an internal plurality among subaltern indigenous sectors. There are therefore indigenous peoples that were and continue to be considered inferior to others. For example, some indigenous peoples from the Bolivian lowlands are often viewed as "savages" or *chunchos* ("uncivilized" inhabitants of the jungle region) relative to indigenous peoples from the highlands, believed to be culturally superior. The same thing happens in Peru, where, in addition to the traditional division between the coast (white-mestizo) and the mountains (indigenous-mestizo), there is the Amazon region (indigenous). In this respect, the repression of Bagua on June 5, 2009, which took the lives of some thirty inhabitants of the Amazon region and ten police officers and resulted in an undetermined number of missing indigenous people, compelled not only Peru but also the rest of the continent to discover the Amazonian peoples, historically considered "savage" and "backward."[3]

Now that such diversity has been established, I would like to begin by acknowledging that any attempt to synthesize long-term processes is fated to be incomplete. As a result, one of the concerns in the present chapter is how to account for the complexity of the political/cultural debates that characterize the history of some Latin American countries without simplifying them in such a way that we end up merely enumerating the various currents or perspectives on the topic. In an attempt to overcome this difficulty and to contribute to understanding the debates regarding the place of indigenous peoples in Latin America, the approach proposed here contains three axes.

The first one, which constitutes the core of my proposal, refers to what I call "tension fields," which configure and problematize the various categories related to the so-called indigenous question. These tension fields emerge from long-term processes and undergo changes in response to political and social dynamics. I argue that the political/cultural debates and perspectives regarding the indigenous and *indianidad* are traversed by epochally delimited fields/spaces in which different conceptual categories regarding the indigenous alternate and coexist, associate and dissociate, interrelate and stand in opposition, depending on the period: race and its hierarchies, the peasant, the mestizo, the rural, the urban, social class, ethnic identity and diversity, and, more recently, *indigenismo* and *indianismo*. These tension fields are dynamic and are often structured in the form of antinomies involving different categories: for example, indigenous and mestizo; indigenous and peasant; race and social class; rural and urban; ethnic and social belonging; and, finally, multiculturalism and autonomy. These dichotomies traverse the various political/cultural perspectives on the indigenous and tend to interrelate in the form of oppositions or mutually exclusive alternatives, thus configuring a magnetic and multipolar field that structures and polarizes the debates.

Thus, the mestizo category is constructed separate from and often in opposition to the indigenous category, even though the former is not always understood in negative terms. In this regard, the anthropologist Rosana Barragán (1992, 21) demonstrates that in the case of Bolivia, the stigmatization of mestizos in the late nineteenth and early twentieth centuries gave way in the 1940s to a revaluation that served as a means to legitimize and construct the desired nation. Something different occurs with the peasant category, which arises in association with the indigenous category (it is one of its fundamental markers, since the indigenous category implies rural origins) but gradually distances itself from the latter, without, however, becoming (entirely) opposed to it. Furthermore, even though they are associated in certain periods, the indigenous category only partially applies to the peasant category (since there are urban Indians) and vice versa (since there are mestizo and nonindigenous peasants). *Indigenismo* and *indianismo* become opposite categories in the 1970s with the crisis of the populist/integrationist model. The rural and the urban interact in different ways depending on the period: At first, the opposition marks the difference between indigenous and nonindigenous people (indigenous people being associated with rural settings), but beginning in the 1970s, with the expansion of the ethnic frontier, the rural and the urban are no longer conceived as a rigid opposition but as a bridge that contributes to understanding the processes of miscegenation through the phenomenon of contemporary urbanization, while also revaluing ethnic identity (whereby some people can conceive themselves as mestizo Indians).

This structure and conceptualization in terms of tension fields is inspired by what anthropologists Claudia Briones and Rita Segato call "national formations of alterity," which, according to the former, "not only produce categories and criteria for identification/classification and belonging but—by managing sociocultural hierarchies—regulate different conditions of existence for the internal others who are recognized as historical or recent members of the society over which the nation-state extends its sovereignty" (Briones 2008, 16). The notion of "national formations of alterity" speaks of a system "whose regularities and particularities are the result—and an evidence—of complex interactions between economic systems, social structures, legal/political institutions, and ideological apparatuses that prevail in the respective countries" (Briones 2008, 16). According to Segato's definition, "these are hegemonic representations of a nation that produce realities" (2007, 28–29). Thus, the conceptualization I propose in terms of tension fields aims at examining some of these formations of alterity, borrowing from the valuable work of both authors.

Given the enormous breadth of the topic, the second axis of my presentation has to do with the scope of the study that I adopted. To account for the tension fields that long-term memory has established regarding the indigenous, I chose four countries as references: Bolivia, Mexico, Peru, and Argentina. This selection, however, is not entirely arbitrary. On one hand, those four countries include at least three great geographic areas of study on indigenous people: Mesoamerica, the Andes, and the Amazon. On the other hand, two of those countries have a high percentage of indigenous population (Bolivia and Peru), and another has an indigenous population that has a smaller relative weight but is quite considerable in absolute terms (Mexico). In addition, Mexico stands out for its contributions to the history of theorizations about the indigenous. Finally, the fourth country of reference, Argentina, has a significantly smaller population of indigenous people than the other three, in addition to a genocidal past that has resulted in systematic attempts to deny its indigenous roots. This choice will allow us to make interesting comparisons, while also revealing common trends in terms of the devices employed in the construction of alterity. In spite of the significant demographic, national, and regional differences, and in spite of the diversity of truly existing matrices of alterity, Latin American countries exhibit certain common trends, evident in the configuration of different perspectives and debates regarding the place of indigenous peoples in the construction of the nation.

The third axis I propose is diachronic and responds to the title of the present chapter, for it reflects two different cycles in the constitution of those tension fields: the *indigenista* phase and the *indianista* phase. *Indigenismo* encompasses different perspectives, including racialist positivism, romantic *indigenismo* or the discourse of the autochthonous, social *indigenismo*, and especially state-integrationist *indigenismo*. The watershed between these two phases is the crisis of the hegemonic integrationist model (state-driven *indigenismo*) around 1970, associated with populist/developmentalist states, which inaugurates a new historical cycle that shifts the perspective regarding who asks the question about indigeneity, thus challenging the monocultural view promoted by integrationist and state-driven *indigenismo*. This second phase inaugurates a period that Chilean historian José Bengoa (2009) characterizes as one of "indigenous emergence." In other words, the transition from one cycle to the next signals the passage from Indians understood as a minority to Indians with status as indigenous peoples and nations (Briones 2008, 10) and their constitution as autonomous political actors who speak by and for themselves, who are no longer "ventriloquized" by nonindigenous political and intellectual elites. This second moment includes different perspectives and paradigms, often conceived as contradictory, such as multiculturalism and autonomy. I will therefore examine some of the most influential cultural and political interpretations that have been elaborated on the indigenous question (first moment) and on the issue of *indianidad* (second moment) in Latin America.

It is worth noting that in part 2 of this book, I reexamine this later historical cycle when dealing with the present-day politics of these debates in contemporary Latin America. Under different terms, what is debated today are not issues related to integrationist *indigenismo* but those related to the idea of indigenous people as full-fledged political actors, together with categories such as ethnic identity, autonomy, territoriality, the plurinational state, and collective rights, which have been incorporated into the mobilizing language of indigenous resistances and movements in various Latin American countries since the 1970s, and with greater emphasis in the past twenty years.

We shall therefore embark on a long journey that will diachronically immerse us in different tension fields and matrices of production of alterity: the way in which the indigenous is related to the mestizo; the increasingly complex relationship between the indigenous and the peasant, between race and social class, between the urban and the rural; even more so, a broadening of ethnic frontiers and the gradual emergence of an ethnic citizenship together with the international recognition of collective rights. And finally, the opposition between *indigenismo* and *indianismo* shall guide us through the various debates on the indigenous and indigeneity in Latin America.

Finally, it is worth noting that nothing is linear in this history: Tension fields are dynamic; they provide doorways, and sometimes they lock those doors to preclude any possibility of contact between presumably antagonistic categories. And yet, in tune with social, legal, and economic transformations, that is, epochal changes, new pathways emerge that eventually lead to the creation of new bridges between seemingly incompatible categories, establishing other dynamics of opening and closure in the very process of resignification and struggle. We will also observe, through the successive configurations of these tension fields that denote different dominant discourses and practices, how the indigenous appears politically, culturally, and socially inscribed in the sphere of subalternity/alterity.

Part 1: The Debate on *Indigenismo* (1900–1960)

The Question of Race, the Indigenous, and Mestizaje: *Positivism and the Discourse of the Autochthonous*

One of the central categories that traverse and define the tension fields regarding the indigenous is that of race, at least until the end of World War II (1945). The category of race is a historical/social construction, to a significant extent the product of the violent annexation of the Americas to the order imposed by the Spanish and Portuguese conquest. As Peruvian sociologist Aníbal Quijano argues, "The production of the category of 'race' based on the phenotype is relatively recent, and its full incorporation as a means to classify people in power relations is only 500 years old—it begins with the Americas and the globalization of the pattern of capitalist power" (2007, 119). As a result, when we speak of race, we are referencing European history, that is, the way of conceiving and representing difference elaborated by Europe as it related to other cultures or civilizations, in particular colonial America.

Race is also a relational category that develops within the framework of a hierarchical and classifying matrix. According to Rita Segato, "it is a sign, the inscription of a history on the subject that establishes a position for it and endows it with the heritage of dispossession" (2007, 23). Furthermore, race, the process of racialization, and racism are intimately related. In Latin America, in the name of scientism, a Darwinist understanding of races led to the naturalization of social inequalities between white, indigenous, Black, and mestizo people, attributing such inequalities to phenotypical differences—that is, to biology. As Peruvian anthropologist Marisol de la Cadena argues, the category of race is relatively empty, but "far from diminishing its history, its emptiness makes it take root in specific genealogies and acquire multiple pasts, many conceptual memories that provide it with structural texture and open it to local subjectivities" (2000; 2004, 14).[4] As a result, it is not the concept's relational or dialogical nature but its very emptiness that endows it with a great articulating capacity, a chameleonic potential applicable to different contexts. On the other hand, the notion of race establishes a tension field that is revealing in terms of the way we understand politics and the limits of democracy. In this respect, politics was not conceived as a space that indigenous people could occupy. For the elite and intellectuals, "Indians organized disorder, simple revolts, always resulting from external conditions that exceeded their age-old patience. Their claims were not considered expressions of political ideas, although there were always warnings regarding their potentially dangerous consequences such as a race war" (2004, 26).

As a result, for a long time and from different perspectives—academic, scientific, political—indigenous people were considered objects of study for the various sciences and even scientific patrimony (in Bolivia people spoke of "Indiology"), which inevitably brought them closer to nature and distanced them from being considered social and political subjects.[5] The Argentine case after the genocide committed by the nation-state against the indigenous people of Patagonia and the North in the late nineteenth century reflects this line of thought, undoubtedly in an extreme manner. It suffices to recall the collection of indigenous remains that was exhibited for decades at the Museum of Natural Sciences of La Plata (Museo de Ciencias Naturales de La Plata). "After the Conquest of the Desert, indigenous people were brought to the museum of La Plata and were employed as cleaners. When they died, their bodies were sent to the laboratories at the Medical School, where their brain, their hair, and their bones were removed, and the remains were sent back to the museum. They were still considered the museum's 'patrimony.' They were Objects, not Human Beings!" (Rex González, in Colectivo Guías 2010, 45).

POSITIVISM AND RACIALISM

In the book *La construcción de la aymaridad* (The construction of Aymara identity; 2009), Bolivian author Verushka Alvizuri recalls the 1899 Massacre of Mohoza in the Altiplano area. The massacre occurred at the time of the federal war, and in it the Indians murdered around 130 soldiers of the liberal army after the latter were attracted to the church, where mass was taking place. At the priest's request, the soldiers entered unarmed, but when the former raised the host, the Aymara Indians of Pablo Zárate Willca's army locked them up and, in a clear inversion of the ritual, forced them to dress like Indians and murdered them, going as far as committing acts of anthropophagy. A long trial followed. The minutes of the Mohoza trial are indicative, says Alvizuri, of the way in which positive sciences legitimized a moral discourse based on nature and reason. The argument set forth by the lawyer Bautista Saavedra, an avid Cesare Lombroso reader, emphasized "the degenerate condition and psychological and social structure of Aymara Indians" (Alvizuri 2009, 70).[6] Saavedra was convinced that Aymara Indians were naturally inclined to violence and criminality, something that not even schooling could change, and framed the crime as a typical case of collective transgression. But since collective crime was not recognized in the Penal Code of the time, Saavedra's recommendation, based on Gustave Le Bon, the renowned author of *Psychology of Crowds*, was to combat it the same way that popular uprisings (worker, anarchist, and socialist strikes) were, "removing the causes, preventing opportunities" (Alvizuri, 2009, 70). An entire people was tried: In a period of four years, about two hundred people were prosecuted, and thirty-two were sentenced to death. The defense counsel's argument was based on "the theory of mass insanity," thus illustrating the positivist views of the time, associated with criminalistics, which assumed that the accused were barbaric and decadent and conceived them as "uncivilized" and "members of an inferior race that must disappear" (70).

As an intellectual trend, positivism enjoyed significant interpretative and political success in Latin America. It had the advantage of synthesizing two intimately related dimensions: On one hand, its vision was in tune with the biologistic determinism of the time; on the other hand, such determinism reflected a liberal and evolutionist conception of society, which could be employed as an essential tool against conservative social forces contrary to the process of secularization. But between the racialist and the liberal wings of positivism, it was undoubtedly the former that had the greatest influence in the political and intellectual fields, since it was common sense at the time that humanity was divided into inferior and superior races. This racialist reading was so powerful that we could say that there were authors with positivist traits who "were positivists without knowing it" (Piñeiro Iñiguez 2006, 57).

In this regard, French researcher Marie D. Demélas points out that in the Bolivian case, "from about 1880 to 1910, social Darwinism was the common trait of those leaders who attempted to apply scientific laws to society, especially those of the struggle for existence and natural selection through the 'survival of the fittest.' . . . Bolivian positivism is a conventional way of uniting the *Criollo* elites' interest in the exact sciences, liberalism, and some anticlerical whims under the same term" (1981, 56). Thus, between 1890 and 1920, several essays were published about the "diseased continent" (Stabb 1968).[7] By questioning Latin America's potential to enter modernity in the same way as Europe and the United States, positivism implied a disquieting outlook, a sort of moral pessimism based on a continental reading of the "endemic ills": first and foremost, race, where biology and mass psychology converged; and, second, Latin American caudillismo, another great evil, in which biology, sociology, and politics converged.

As the various liberal nation-states were consolidated, positivism also provided a first conception of the opposition between civilization and barbarism. This was expressed in several historical/sociological works whose leitmotif was the analysis of "Latin American ills" from a biologist perspective.[8] Race explained the peoples' psychological characteristics, which were steadily and faithfully inherited. Authors such as Herbert Spencer, Charles Darwin, Gustave

Le Bon, and Hippolyte Taine were the bases for this racialist paradigm, which described the various expressions of the "national soul." This is evident in two emblematic works of the time: *Nuestra América, ensayo de psicología social* (Our America: Essay on social psychology; [1903] n.d.), by the Argentinean Carlos O. Bunge, and *Pueblo enfermo* (Sick people; [1909] 1999), by Bolivian author Alcides Arguedas. The former examines the continent, and the latter describes and diagnoses the ills of the Bolivian Altiplano, but both coincide in many ways in their characterization of both indigenous people and mestizos.

One of the main approaches employed by both authors was to compare Indians and mestizos to Europeans, that is, not to define them positively but in comparison. Along these lines, historians Patricia Funes and Waldo Ansaldi, revisiting the French author Étienne Balibar, argue that "raciological hermeneutics implies two basic operations: classification and hierarchization" (2006, 452). These are basic operations of naturalization, since hierarchization assumes a low end (animal nature) and a high end (humanity, incarnated in white Europeans). There are, however, nuances in this classification and hierarchization. For Bunge, the collective soul of indigenous people expresses itself in Oriental fatalism, sadness, and revenge. Arguedas employs similar adjectives to describe Altiplano Indians, who are presumably assimilated by or fused into the local geography.

Social Darwinism predicts the disappearance of the "weaker races." Bunge, speaking from Argentina, which at the time was receiving large numbers of European immigrants, argued that "pure Indians who live deep in their forests are in the process of disappearing, ashamed, cast out, dazed, annihilated by civilization. . . . This explains why pure Indians have little or no relevance in American sociology. Such is not the case with mestizos of indigenous and European descent" ([1903] n.d., 126). Arguedas in turn speaks of their sacrificial fate related to war: "For every white man who lost his life in Chaco, one hundred Indians died . . . legions and legions of Indians" ([1909] 1999, 70).

Racialist positivism seemed to be less concerned with indigenous people as a "problem"—since it considered them defeated, morally degraded, and in the process of extinction—than with the fast ascent and reproduction of mestizos, the foremost emerging players in the new national context. It was with regard to miscegenation that positivist writings became most virulent and demeaning—whether it was the mestizo, the *cholo*, the mulatto, mixtures of Indian, Black, or white, hybridity was always negative. Positivism thus exacerbated Darwinist theory, which maintains that all mixtures produce backward and degenerate beings. All the vices of the original races and none of their virtues were present in mestizos. "All physical mestizos, no matter who their father or mother is, are moral mestizos," writes Bunge in *Nuestra América*, where he dedicates only nine pages to describing the typical traits of indigenous psychology, four to the "African ethnic factor," and almost twenty to the different forms of miscegenation, as an illustration of the "phenomenon of degenerate semi-sterility of human hybrids" ([1903] n.d., 143–44). Arguedas devotes fewer pages to the mestizo (in Bolivia, Indians entailed the risk of a "race war"), but his diagnosis is similar. For example, the *cholo*, a mixture of Indian and criollo, is harshly criticized. "Think wrong and you'll guess right, says the proverb, which in the case of *cholos* expresses most precisely their conception of human experience regarding man's relations with his fellow men." Lacking ideals, coveting political prominence, and flaunting titles or wealth, if they had them, characterized *cholos*, who sought nothing but momentary success (Arguedas [1909] 1999, 72–73).

In short, the positivist outlook inscribes its analysis in the tension field between indigenous people and mestizos, in comparison to white Europeans, believed to be the unquestionably superior race regardless of the evident national differences (e.g., between Saxons and Hispanics) or the various forms of miscegenation (*cholos*, *zambos* [mixture of African and Indian], mulattoes, and their successive mixtures). The conclusion was that Indians were being increasingly displaced by mestizos as the predominant element of American reality. The meticulously described indigenous psychological traits and their collective soul, assimilated into the ancient landscape and the mineral geography of the Altiplano (the "bronze race"), associated with the ills and weaknesses of the Indian race, subdued both by Spanish superiority and by the sacrificial call of war, are a thing of the past. Compared to the social emergence of mestizos, Indians are a residual racial structure. But mestizos exhibit other levels of psychological and social complexity given their fickleness, their growth, their utilitarian view of the world, and, worse yet, their growing and profuse vitality. This is evident in the dominant political system, that is, caciquismo, caudillismo, and other variants of criollo politics. Thus, for the oligarchy and intellectual elites of the time, the "ethnic problem" did not so much apply to Indians, whose downfall was deemed inevitable, as to mestizos, who were perceived as the new political and social threat.

It is commonly believed that after World War II, once the Nazi genocide against Jewish populations in the name of racial differences/superiority became known, the category of race was discredited and expelled from the academic/scientific community and from democratic political discourse. Nonetheless, not only does racism remain alive, but the very concept of race, in spite of being discredited, seems to be one of those zombie categories that never die entirely and always return.

The foundational interpretative framework for the indigenous question in modern Argentina was Domingo Faustino Sarmiento's dichotomy between civilization and barbarism (Tamagno 2009; Svampa 1994), which sentenced the presumably barbaric races (rebellious Indians, *montoneros* [an Argentine Peronist guerrilla organization], gauchos, and rebel caudillos) to exclusion and extermination. The opposition between the two concepts materialized in the military campaigns conducted in the south and north of Argentina, as well as the violent end of a long cycle of civil wars, which concluded with the defeat and death of the last provincial caudillos.

The anthropologist Liliana Tamagno (2009) reminds us that from 1810 to 1816, official discourse acknowledged the significant participation of indigenous people in the struggle against the Spanish and considered them "free citizens." "Our countrymen, the Indians" is a famed phrase attributed to the consensual hero of the Argentine nation, José de San Martín. It is therefore not surprising that Argentina's 1816 Declaration of Independence was translated into Quechua and Aymara (Martínez Sarasola 2011). For a considerable part of the nineteenth century, the south of the country was controlled by indigenous peoples, toward which the new Argentine state deployed a policy that alternated war and conflict with negotiation and coexistence. The same thing happened on the Chilean side beyond the Bío Bío River, where various Araucanian peoples lived. It was only from 1861 to 1883 that the Chilean government undertook a campaign of acculturation and occupation through military means, euphemistically known as the "Pacification of the Araucanía." In Argentina it was in the late 1870s that the political elite opted for an exclusively military approach with the Conquest of the Desert, a name that manifested the conceptual framework implicit in its reading of the issue.

In both countries, the space occupied by indigenous people was understood as a "desert," an "empty space," or, to freely apply David Viñas's image, "the contradiction of that which is empty and must be filled" (1982, 73). In Argentina the desert metaphor instituted a certain idea of the nation that had deeply obsessed the 1837 generation: Rather than a nation for the desert, it was a matter of constructing a desert that justified the nation's expansion. In the case of Chile, the nation-state adopted the doctrine known as terra nullius, which maintains that "territories are discovered by the states when no other recognized state claims its sovereignty over them, denying any people previously occupying such territories any right of legitimate possession" (Durán Pérez et al., quoted by Impemba 2013, 59).

In Argentina the expansion of agrarian capitalism and the consolidation of the nation-state (through territorial control and the consolidation of the border with Chile) were accomplished through genocidal violence against indigenous populations in a series of military campaigns in Patagonia and the North between 1879 and 1885. This violence had a devastating effect on the different indigenous peoples. Yet they were not exterminated. According to Guillermo David (2008), the Conquest of the Desert in northern Patagonia lasted six months and resulted in 1,300 people dead, 1,200 indigenous warriors imprisoned, and about 10,000 prisoners—elders, women, and children—enslaved. The indigenous historian Mariano Nagy (2013), who studied the fate of the families who survived the Conquest of the Desert, asserts, "One of the characteristics is dispersion, migration, and circulation in a context of self-invisibility, proletarianization, and, in the best case, individual or family relocation to marginal zones in the new urban centers." Many indigenous people were deported to Martín García Island and other concentration camps (Valcheta and Malargüe, among others), where many died of smallpox without medical attention. Others were handed over to "good families" from Buenos Aires and La Plata. Carlos María Ocantos's novel *Quilito* narrates how captured indigenous people were delivered to prominent families of the criollo oligarchy, describing harrowing scenes where—as in a great slave market—husband and wife, brothers and sisters, and, "even more monstrous, more inhumane, more barbaric, children and their mother" (1891, 10) were separated.[9]

The subjugation of the surviving Indians, cornered in reserves far from the territories that capital deemed valuable at the time, auctioned off in the market or handed over to "good families," in the process of proletarianization, or incorporated in plantations as a cheap labor force, signals a long and endless journey for indigenous people in Argentina, which combines invisibility and denial. Thus, the originary genocide as a central milestone of the foundation of Argentina's modern nation-state (Lenton 2011) was followed by the expulsion of indigenous people from the nation's imaginary and the denial of their very existence: With immigrants arriving in large numbers, with the large-scale export of meat and cereals, with the criollo elite well established, Argentina soon became known as a white country devoid of Indians. The 1895 census determined that 80 percent of the country's population belonged to the white race of European origin. José Ingenieros (1913, quoted in Svampa 1994, 162) proudly wrote, "The issue of race, so relevant in the United States, no longer exists in the Argentine Republic."

The existing anthropological literature has made a number of critical readings of the place of indigenous people and their historical avatars in the Argentine nation.[10] I do not intend to synthesize that literature but rather to underscore that all of those interpretations coincide in their tendency to render indigenous people invisible in the nation's imaginary once the foundational genocide and their subsequent marginalization in the new social structure were accomplished. Thus, Gastón Gordillo and Silvia Hirsch argue, "Indigenous people became a sort of ever-present absence in national subjectivities at different levels. . . . The heritage of the Conquest of the Desert confined indigenous people to the backstage of the nation's imaginary" (2010, 16).

Indigenous people were associated with a violent past (symbolized by the surprise raids known as *malón*). This "invisibility did not erase them entirely but rather transformed them into a latent and invisible presence, culturally constitutive of hegemonic forms of nationality." This foundational device has become so hegemonic in Argentina's representation as a white and European nation that even many Argentineans who decried the Conquest of the Desert have engaged in that invisibility, contributing to perpetuating the idea that indigenous people are no longer part of the nation (Gordillo and Hirsch 2010, 20–21).

In another line of argument, the anthropologist Mónica Quijada argues that although the war resulted in death owing to violence and disease, no extermination occurred but rather a "social reclassification of indigenous people." This was accompanied by a collective conviction that Indians had disappeared as a result of the military conflict, which became an essential dimension of the construction of national identity (2004, 428). According to the author, this reclassification was undertaken by means of a "strategy to transform indigenous people into citizens through different means," where what mattered was a territorial understanding of the nation. Once indigenous people were subjected to the central power, they became citizens as natives of the national territory. Of course, this strategy of transforming indigenous people into citizens was far from having a happy end: People were displaced, and their incorporation into society took place at the lowest and poorest levels; the promises of land concessions went unfulfilled, and they remained unprotected from the brutal territorial takeover after the Conquest of the Desert. The notions of disappearance and extermination were thus consolidated, when in fact the strategy was to reclassify indigenous people as "Argentine citizens" at other levels of subalternity (Quijada 2004, 433).

Furthermore, unlike in other Latin American countries, even the concept of mestizo was absent from official discourse—a double invisibility that characterized Argentina for decades. Claudia Briones, who examines the construction of the "internal others" who constitute the basis for the national formation of alterity in Argentina, analyzes its main myth regarding the "racial melting pot," that is, the idea of a homogeneous nation based on a white and civilized Argentina linked to its generic European origins. In this regard, she argues that "unlike in other Latin American countries, miscegenation in Argentina has tended to be defined by a logic of hypo-descendance, which leads the marked category (the indigenous, in this case) to absorb the mixed category, therefore defining the mestizo category as closer to the indigenous than to the nonindigenous" (2005, 26). Morita Carrasco adds, "While no one would call the child of Euro-Argentineans a 'mestizo,' those who have an indigenous father or mother more clearly bear the stereotype of 'Indian' as an indelible mark that confirms the racialized and foundational asymmetry that gave rise to national society, symbolically legitimizing a relation of domination that affects the everyday life of indigenous peoples" (2002, 6).

Finally, the relationship established in the foundational period among science, genocide, and power is most disturbing, as illustrated by the Museum of Natural Sciences of La Plata, founded at that time. Although few people remember the museum's history, the fact is that the remains of indigenous people murdered during the Conquest of the Desert and others who died at the museum itself were on display until 2006.[11] Likewise, from the late nineteenth to the early twentieth century, the dissemination of photographs of indigenous people reinforced the hegemonic discourse of the criollo elites, which portrayed Indians as savages and barbarians, impervious to civilization, although these photographs were also employed for a more moralizing undertaking, that is, as an example of assimilation.

In short, what happened at the Museum of Natural Sciences of La Plata (replicated at a smaller scale in other provincial museums) is indicative of how the 1880 generation, which founded modern Argentina, read the indigenous question from the perspective of racialized positivism—indigenous people were not considered human beings but specimens of a primitive and inferior race that had to be "scientifically" studied (with medicine and anthropology joining forces), photographed as "examples of assimilation," and displayed as "relics," together with some of their utensils, in a showcase of a museum devoted to the natural sciences.

The Discourse of the Autochthonous

Culture shall once again descend from the Andes.—LUIS VALCÁRCEL, *Tempestad en los Andes* (Tempest in the Andes), 1927

Between the late nineteenth and early twentieth centuries, Andean countries and Mexico underwent a process of reassessment of indigenous peoples whereby the civilizations that existed prior to the conquest were considered the birthplace or the foundation of nationality. An antipositivist uprising began, which aimed at rethinking the role of indigenous people in the nation, especially in the context of the first centennial of the young South American republics. In addition, in Bolivia and Peru, reflections on the nation were also characterized by the need to foresee the nation's future in the context of both countries' defeat by Chile during the War of the Pacific (1879–83), which resulted in a very significant loss of life and a considerable territorial reduction.[12]

This first *indigenista* moment is known as "the discourse of the autochthonous" in Latin American historiography. This discourse, however, rather than relating to real indigenous people, deployed a romantic view of their telluric nature and fed from a glorification of the great pre-Hispanic cultures and empires—Aztec, Mayan, and Incan—by the criollo political and cultural elites. As Peruvian historian Cecilia Méndez (1996) proposes, this process of exaltation of the indigenous past can be synthesized in the slogan "Incas, yes; Indians, no." This process entails a glorification of the ideal—pre-Hispanic— Indian, while the real Indian is materially and morally demeaned in the new independent republics. This led to very significant changes in the tension field between the indigenous and the mestizo, because, while revaluing the autochthonous by idealizing indigenous people as something of the past was a common trait in all countries, there were significant differences regarding *mestizaje* (miscegenation) and its contribution to the process of nation building.

In philosophical terms, the discourse of the autochthonous feeds from European vitalistic theories that inherited a romantic and historicist understanding of culture (*volk*), which emphasized "social energy" and its role in nation building.[13] In both Bolivia and Argentina, Count Keyserling, a traveling intellectual well received by his South American peers, was quite influential. As Pablo Stefanoni (2010a) observes, after visiting Buenos Aires at the invitation of *Sur* magazine, created and directed by Victoria Ocampo, in 1929 Count Keyserling traveled to Bolivia, where he gave a series of lectures with a strong telluric content: "Bolivia is the very image of America, and America can take pride in having the most creative force of all continents. Bolivia is probably the most ancient part of humanity, and there is no better promise of a future than a very remote past, because time knows no end" (quoted in Stefanoni 2010a, 53).

One of the questions of greatest concern at the time was to what extent was it possible to "regenerate the race," especially in countries with a significant indigenous presence. The common response of the political and cultural elites was to undertake an educational and cultural reform capable of combating the backwardness of the "race" (its condition as untilled land, as was expressed at the time) and to thus contribute to regenerating it. Such was the case in Bolivia and Peru but also in Argentina, where, once indigenous people were marginalized, the criollo elites attempted to control the immigrants flowing from Europe.

In 1900 the Bolivian liberal government sent a mission to France, Germany, and other countries, assuming that there were universally valid pedagogical criteria that could be applied equally to all countries. The Bolivian intellectual Franz Tamayo vehemently rebutted this positivist policy, debating with Felipe Segundo Guzmán, who participated in the educational mission and was secretary of the Ministry of Education at the time. Throughout 1910 Tamayo wrote a series of editorials in the La Paz daily *El Diario* criticizing positivist views, which were later republished as *Creación de la pedagogía nacional* (The creation of national pedagogy; in Tamayo 1979). Guzmán replied to the criticism also in the written press.

The debate between the advocate of positivism on the government's side and the advocate of the autochthonous revealed antagonistic standpoints regarding the place of indigenous people, although there were certainly points in common. Regarding the antagonisms, it is worth underscoring that Tamayo (a serious reader of German vitalism) believed that indigenous people were "the true holders of the nation's energy" (Tamayo 1910) and that Bolivia should not copy European models but should turn to the country's own vital forces instead; Guzmán in turn argued from a liberal/positivist standpoint that indigenous people were an obstacle to national modernization, and he therefore proposed to broaden instruction, which he believed was the correct avenue leading to white civilization—the superior race—which Indians should assimilate to or face extinction (Martínez 2010, 261). Furthermore, for Tamayo, Bolivia was not ill; rather, by seeking foreign models, it was being untrue to itself (Stefanoni 2010a). It was not through instruction (external factors) or education (internal factors) that the race's energy—that national character that neither whites nor, of course, mestizos had—would be awakened. Closed off within themselves, Indians appeared as pure will, resisting both the environment they inhabited and the onslaught of civilization (Sanjinés 2005, 54).

The first point in common was the fact that Tamayo and Guzmán shared a uniform view of indigenous people. These people constituted the "national problem," which had to be elucidated and described in all its specificity, and yet, paradoxically, the arguments of both thinkers were devoid of anything that spoke of their culture, the group to which they belonged, their language, their habits, or their customs. The political and cultural elite turned indigenous people into an archetype (reduced to the Aymara) with very general qualities or vices (Martínez 2010, 258). The second assumption they shared was their criticism of the *cholo*, the Indianized mestizo, in tune with positivist beliefs. Guzmán believed that miscegenation with the privileged race should be promoted—that is, Indians with whites. Thus, the ideal mestizo was a Westernized mestizo, while the *cholo*, who had all the defects of the original races and none of their virtues, was expelled from Bolivia's national imaginary. This was therefore a de-Indianizing project whereby the value of miscegenation depended on whether the Indian or the white race prevailed. In short, as Jorge Sanjinés argues, in Bolivia, "the discourse of the autochthonous led to very ambivalent racial feelings—of pride, nostalgia, and fascination over the indigenous, but rejecting anything that criollo/mestizo consciousness could not rationalize and maintain under its strict control" (2005, 36). Such a project aimed at establishing a position and preventing the transformation of Indians into *cholos*, that is, into Indianized urban mestizos rather than criollo-like or Westernized mestizos, in a social context where the indigenous revolt of Chayanta still reverberated in people's minds.

There was also a reassessment of indigenous people underway in Peru in the same period, but differently from Bolivia, since the autochthonous was considered part of a distant "national" glory that aestheticized Inca culture while simultaneously employing it as a means for Cuzco to stand out culturally in its struggle against Lima's centralism. According to Carlos Degregori (1995) and Marisol de la Cadena (2000), Cuzco's mestizo criollos attempted to appropriate the Inca imperial heritage for themselves in order to stand apart from the dominant criollo elite established in Lima. Thus, rather than a "battle of the races," Cuzco's dispute with Lima's criollo and Hispanicizing elite was over the birthplace of Peruvianness, by vindicating Quechua culture and language. This idealization signals the birth of a sort of *indigenismo* without Indians, whereby Indians are discussed by and from the perspective of the mestizo elite, identifying them with the past and the local geography.

Transformed into Incaism, the discourse of the autochthonous in Peru materialized both in the city's monuments and in the Inca theater developed by the cultural elite. For Cuzco's elite, speaking Quechua was a highly prized sign of distinction even in other South American countries. For that reason, an Inca art company was created, whose tour in several southern countries staging *Ollantay*, one of the most celebrated plays of Inca theater, was quite successful (Pacheco Medrano 2007). One of the champions of this self-representation was Cuzco native Luis Valcárcel, quoted in the epigraph, whose *Tempestad en los Andes* (Tempest in the Andes), a very radical book about indigenous people published in 1927, associated *indigenismo* and agrarianism, which was a central topic of social *indigenismo*. The book's prologue was written by José Carlos Mariátegui, and its afterword by Luis Alberto Sánchez, two intellectuals who would later engage in a public debate about the indigenous and the mestizo in Peru.

It is worth examining whether, as in other countries in the region, in Argentina there was a reassessment of the autochthonous at the time of the first centennial. The discourse of the autochthonous in that country took place in the context of the confrontation between Buenos Aires and provincial elites regarding the flow of immigrants. Differently from other Latin American countries, where the percentage of immigrants in the total population was not so significant, in Argentina external immigration was perceived as a possible threat that could change the nation's physiognomy. As a result, immigrants, who had been welcomed with open arms, soon became the object of suspicion: Their distortion of the language and their combative unions imbued with "foreign ideologies" made them gradually lose their status as a paradigm of progress, becoming a social threat instead. Thus, the conflicts brought about by the construction of a modern country based on an agro-export model and overseas immigration soon revealed the inadequacy of the foundational motto of "Civilization versus Barbarism" as a means to understand the ills that afflicted the "new" society, resulting in a reorganization of the concepts involved. Together with the emergence of the "social question," immigrants represented a "denationalizing" barbarism that was countered by a representation of the nation that somehow rescued the image of the gaucho and, through him, the foundational criollo.

The first centennial was thus immersed in a reconfiguration of the original alterity device, reflecting the elites' disenchantment with immigrants, and as in other countries in the region, a national tradition was (re)invented in Argentina based on a reassessment of "the autochthonous." This operation was crowned by a revival of the mythological gaucho undertaken by the poet Leopoldo Lugones in his work *El payador* (The minstrel; [1913] 1980), definitively transformed into a legendary character by Ricardo Güiraldes in *Don Segundo Sombra* (1926). As Carlos Altamirano and Beatriz Sarlo (1983) argue, in a series of lectures at the Odeón Theater in Buenos Aires in 1913, Lugones instituted José Hernández's *El gaucho Martín Fierro* (The gaucho Martín Fierro) as the foundational poem of Argentine nationality, definitively consolidating the gaucho as the nation's mythical foundation, precisely at the time when real gauchos were in the process of extinction. Just like the Indian glorified by Cuzco's elite at the time, the gaucho revisited by Argentina's criollo elite is entirely romanticized—a domesticated gaucho whose symbolic presence is presumably part of the Pampa's landscape and who does not challenge the paternalist/authoritarian political model proposed by the elite for subaltern sectors.

Argentina's version of the discourse of the autochthonous therefore employs a relational device to read alterity similar to those employed by other Latin American countries but different in the way the internal oppositions are presented. It is not the Indian who is revisited but the mestizo in the form of the gaucho. At the same time, as in other countries, the discourse of the autochthonous served two purposes: It set a limit to the inevitable sociopolitical rise of certain social groups (especially immigrants, many of whom were identified with socialism and anarchism) and created a fracture among political elites (a dispute between the regional or provincial elites and the central power in their reconceptualization of "deep Argentina").

In short, the tension field between the indigenous and the mestizo had different national expressions: While in Bolivia the discourse was founded more on a telluric association between the Altiplano's landscape and indigenous people, materialized in the form of the "Andean massif" as a synthesis of Bolivia by Jaime Mendoza in 1925 (Lorini 2006, 95), both of them resistant to change and therefore a nearly unaltered source of national energy, in Peru romantic *indigenismo* expressed something more, a swift (and consistent) political appropriation by Cuzco's mestizo elite in its political/symbolic struggle against the coastal region, characterized as mestizo and pro-Spain. On the other hand, in Bolivia the discourse of the autochthonous differed from the positivist view of the indigenous on a fundamental point—the scope and contents of the educational reform. Regardless of the differences, however, just like positivism, both *indigenismos* rejected the mestizo, albeit for different reasons. While in Peru this first attempt at a political/symbolic appropriation of the indigenous provided a means for mestizos to gradually acquire an indigenous identity through different mechanisms of self-definition, in Bolivia the tension between the indigenous and the mestizo remained an important arena of political and cultural production until the 1940s.

On the other hand, in Argentina, while the mestizo gaucho was upheld in opposition to ungovernable immigrants who threatened the elite's stability with their economic success and their growing social demands, indigenous people were excluded—their place was a "nonplace" where alterity and pure exteriority blended. It was in the 1920s that the indigenous emerged as part of the process of American miscegenation in the work of nationalist writer Ricardo Rojas, "blending European consciousness and Indianness" (Volmer 2009, 12). This is what Rojas calls *Eurindia* , an aesthetic and cultural doctrine considered by the author to be the key to both Argentine and American identity: "*Eurindia* is the name of a myth created by Europe and the Indies, but that no longer belongs to either Europe or the Indies, even though it is constituted by both," he wrote in the book's prologue (1924, 12). *Eurindia* is therefore a neologism created by Rojas to promote a model that fuses Europe with the American continent (Volmer 2009, 12). However, in a country where the elite imagined itself as descending from ships, while simultaneously belonging to a mythical criollo origin, indigenous people remained stigmatized. It is therefore not surprising that Rojas's more aesthetic miscegenation proposal was met with little political and social enthusiasm.[14]

Indigenismo *and Social Class: The Truncated Ways*
of Latin American Marxism

The race problem is not common to all Latin American countries nor does it present the same proportions and characteristics in all those who suffer it. In some Latin American countries, it is a regional matter and does not significantly affect the social and economic problem. But in countries like Peru and Bolivia, most of the population is indigenous; indigenous demands are the dominant popular and social demands.—JOSÉ CARLOS MARIÁTEGUI, "El problema de las razas en la América Latina" (The problem of the races in Latin America), (1928) 1994

Early twentieth-century Latin America was characterized by intense labor mobilizations demanding better working conditions and wages. They were massive strikes that were considered a serious threat by the governing elites and ended in bloodshed: the massacre of Iquique, Chile, 1907; the Tragic Week of Buenos Aires, 1919; the worker massacre in Guayaquil, Ecuador, 1922; the miner massacre in Uncía, 1923; and the massacre of Magdalena in the banana-growing region of Colombia, 1928; among others.

In rural areas, there were also frequent indigenous and peasant revolts, although usually disconnected from urban worker struggles and with little support from other social sectors. In Peru, for example, peasant/indigenous movements operated on a local level, and as Alberto Flores Galindo (1977) argues, they had no ambitions as national struggles; however, they were indicative of the unbearable exploitation experienced by peasants and indigenous people at the time of the oligarchic/liberal republic. In Bolivia one of the most relevant revolts was the rebellion of rural communities and colonists against landowners in Chayanta in 1927, which shed light on the problem of advancing haciendas and required the intervention of then President Hernando Siles (Hylton 2003). The Russian Revolution of 1917 in turn had a strong impact in Latin America, demonstrating the success of "the first experiment at establishing a socialist state: the USSR" (Mariátegui 2010, 264). If Latin American elites, and in particular those of Andean countries, had long feared indigenous uprisings, after the Russian Revolution they also had to contend with the phantom of communism, whose threat seemed to include both urban and rural areas.

According to Adolfo Sánchez Vázquez, the Marxism that arrived in Latin America between the late nineteenth century and the first two decades of the twentieth century was the one promoted by the Second Socialist International, dominated by German social democracy, which had undertaken a revision of Karl Marx's writings. In the Southern Cone, Marxism arrived with Spanish and Italian immigrants, who created the first socialist parties. However, the Russian Revolution implied a break with more reformist postures and led to the emergence of the Third Communist International (Comintern) in 1919, which the various communist parties emerging in Latin America would follow (Sánchez Vázquez 1999, 126–28), closing the door to national diversity. As a result, albeit for a short time, the Comintern offered a new framework for national revolution in the most backward societies or countries as part of a more global process in the anti-imperialist struggle.

It is in this new context that social *indigenismo* arises in Latin America, whose political reflection underscores the importance of indigenous peasant struggles and their relation with the national question. Of course, indigenous people continued to be discussed from the outside by intellectuals and activists who embraced Marxist ideals. However, the questions formulated early on by this current pointed to fundamental issues, among them the need to reflect on the political specificity of national realities in Latin America, a continent where the urban working class was rather marginal. Neither Marx's response to Vera Zasulich's letter nor his writings on the Asiatic mode of production, and certainly not "late Marxism's" interest in the Russian rural commune, were known at the time (*Ethnological Notebooks*).

Latin American revolutionary social *indigenismo* first developed in this period with Peruvian José Carlos Mariátegui and Bolivian Tristán Marof. Far from proposing education or development plans as a panacea or strategy to solve the "indigenous problem," these authors promoted the class struggle, underlining the relationship between the miserable condition of indigenous people and the problem of land in the hands of political chiefs or large landowners. Social *indigenismo* rejected a racialist approach that viewed indigenous people as inferior and naturalized social and cultural inequalities, as well as the romanticized view of those who defended a strategic and archaeological *indigenismo* that rescued the great pre-Hispanic cultures but disdained real Indians. At this stage, social *indigenismo* of Marxist inspiration created ties and engaged in debates with the Comintern, prior to the political/ideological closure that would characterize Marxism as hegemonized by Soviet communism (Stalinism) in the following decades. As a result, that perspective displaced the indigenous problem to another tension field, in an attempt to view indigenous people as social and political actors relevant to the national question.

One of the first people to assume the challenge of rethinking the nation in relation to the issue of indigenous peoples' marginalization in postindependence liberal societies was the Peruvian Manuel González Prada, a teacher of generations, in the context of the first Centennial of the Independence and after Peru's and Bolivia's defeat by Chile in the War of the Pacific. In 1904 he wrote a brief and unfinished, yet highly influential, text called *Nuestros indios* (Our Indians), where he proposes a series of fundamental theses on the subject. One of them rejects the artifice of race, insisting on the idea that social issues must be explained socially. González Prada thus rejects the deterministic view of positivism, which considered indigenous people inferior by nature, and, citing Émile Durkheim, he argues that "we know of no social phenomenon which can be placed under the undeniable dependency of race" (1989, 220–21).

One fundamental question present in his writings, later revisited by Mariátegui, is the comparison of indigenous peoples' situation in the liberal republic and under Spanish rule. González Prada argues that rather than improving, their situation worsened. The republic, which followed the viceroyalty's traditions, was partly to blame. This made it clear that the indigenous question was not a racial or pedagogical matter but a social issue directly related to the regime of liberal domination and the conditions to which indigenous people were subjected.

Finally, González Prada proposes avoiding all paternalism, for nothing could be expected in terms of humanizing those who oppress indigenous people. Even though González Prada himself was a nonindigenous criollo, he argued that indigenous people's liberation could only be carried out by themselves: "One should not preach meekness and resignation to Indians but pride and rebelliousness. What have they gained from three or four hundred years of conformity and patience? The fewer authorities they have to endure, the more they are free from harm. There is a revealing fact: there is greater well-being in the communities that are most distant from haciendas, and those that are less frequented by authorities enjoy greater order and peace. In sum, Indians shall free themselves through their own effort, and not through their oppressors' humanity" (1989, 220–21).

Of special interest in Bolivia is the work of Tristán Marof, a pseudonym of Gustavo Navarro, an activist of Marxist origins who lived in Europe for several years as a diplomat and was later persecuted, imprisoned, and exiled a number of times (Mexico, Argentina).[15] In *La justicia del inca* (Justice of the Inca), Marof coined the famed phrase that would later synthesize the project of revolutionary nationalism: "Land to Indians, mines to the state" (1926, 27). This formula placed the indigenous question at the center, associated with the issue of land, as well as the nationalization of underground resources. Rather than proposing a return to the Inca past, which he admired for its organization, morality, justice, and agrarian laws, which had guaranteed the life of every member of the collectivity, Marof aimed at developing—as González Prada had done earlier and Mariátegui would underscore—a comparative approach in order to expose the shortfalls of the republic, under which millions of Indians lived and died under miserable conditions. *La tragedia del Altiplano* (The tragedy of the highland) (1935) speaks precisely of the feudal exploitation endured by indigenous people throughout their entire lives.[16] Marof's approach therefore aimed at transcending the literary/culturalist approach, introducing a purely materialist perspective on the indigenous question. In *La tragedia*, he did not speak of races but identified two social classes—the proletariat and the bourgeoisie. Indians, but also *zambos* and mestizos, were part of the unmeasurable army of the dispossessed. Their shortcomings were not the result of some sort of racial inferiority but of the miserable conditions of their lives. His ideal is "a free Indian, technically educated, with a feeling of dignity and class." "But to arrive at this, feudal society must be brought down by the Indians themselves, in alliance with all those who are affected by it: urban artisans, students, and miners. Indians must strengthen their communal organizations, coordinate alliances, establish contacts between the North and the South, between Quechuas and Aymaras, elect their representatives to worker congresses, and act in a unified manner" (Marof 1935, 60).[17] Indigenous people's liberation thus depended on two things: their desire to organize and take the land and the breakdown of the dominant class. But a fundamental element is the emergence of an indigenous vanguard capable of making alliances with other social sectors.

It was Mariátegui's innovative work, however, which served as a turning point that marked a before and after of what could have been a promising road in the construction of a revolutionary alternative based on Latin American Marxism, rooted in the national society and the indigenous question. In his short life, Mariátegui engaged in intense cultural and political activity through journals such as *La escena contemporánea* (The contemporary scene) and, especially, *Amauta*, founded in 1926, in which he gave visibility to the indigenous question.

Mariátegui's political and intellectual proposal was far from limited to a tolerant eclecticism. He aimed at relating Marxist socialism to indigenous vanguardism and at building a revolutionary *indigenismo*. We revisit here this latter concept, proposed by Mariátegui and developed by Fernanda Beigel (2003), understood as the result of the intersection between the political dimension, related to indigenous claims, their rights, and their place in Peruvian society, on one hand, and the cultural dimension, related to artistic *indigenismo* and to the Inca past, which endows the socialist project with a mythical dimension. Although his views on the indigenous question can be found in many articles, it is in his 1928 *Seven Interpretive Essays on Peruvian Reality* and in "El problema de las razas en la América Latina" (The problem of the races in Latin America; [1928] 1994), a paper read at the VI Congress of the Communist International (CI) in June 1929 in Buenos Aires, that we find his fundamental ideas on the topic.

Mariátegui adopted some of the conclusions previously set forth by González Prada as his point of departure. Four hypotheses are thus present in *Seven Interpretive Essays*: first, the importance of the indigenous question, since it affected a third of Peru's population; second, the idea that there is no possible redemption of indigenous people through education or the action of caudillos, since the conditions established by the republic aggravated their situation; third, the permanence of the agrarian community and its defense, not for abstract but for concrete reasons; and, finally, the hypothesis that without indigenous people, who are the foundation of nationality, Peruvianness would be impossible.

At the same time, as he proposed in "El problema de las razas," for Mariátegui the indigenous problem was feudal exploitation of the natives by large latifundia. "In 90 percent of the cases, Indians are not proletarians but serfs" (2010, 68). Agriculture therefore subsisted under a feudal or semifeudal regime that subjected Indians to slave labor in the most isolated places. Indigenous claims thus instinctively focused on land. All revolutionaries should cooperate with political propaganda and union movements, endowing those claims over land with an organized, systematic, and defined character (81, 109). *Indigenista* literature plays an important role in this, since it appears to serve the same function as "Muzhik" literature had in prerevolutionary Russia. "Indians themselves are beginning to demonstrate a new consciousness" (Mariátegui 1971; [1928] 1988, 48). The solution to the indigenous problem should therefore be the work of indigenous people themselves. The problem was not racial but social and economic, though race played a part in its solution, since only militants with an indigenous background could have an influence over their peers, thanks to their mentality and language (Mariátegui 2010, 111). This leads us to view the *congresos indigenales* as a historical feat, even though they were adulterated and lacked a national program or had few connections at the national level.[18]

On the other hand, one of Mariátegui's most innovative hypotheses is to think of agrarian communities as a factor of resistance and extraordinary persistence. It is in them that we can see the socialization of land and the habit of cooperation. In spite of republican laws, Indians did not become individualist, not because they are impervious to progress, but because communism remains their only defense (Mariátegui 1971; [1928] 1988, 83). According to Mariátegui, the community's defense is based not on abstract principles but on concrete issues related to the economic and social order, from the *minga* (collective work) to relations of cooperation and reciprocity in access to land and water. This does not imply equating socialism with agrarian communism but instead implies, as Flores Galindo (1980) argued, that there are "elements of practical socialism" in the community. In his essay on Mariátegui, the renowned Peruvian anthropologist argues, "This and only this understanding allows us to propose socialism as a viable alternative in a backward and peasant country, with a small working class and an incipient industry. Peasants could assume the socialist idea and merge it with their messianic aspirations, because in their everyday life they were able to maintain and defend the old Andean collectivism. Paradoxical as it may be, Mariátegui found the necessity and justification for socialism in the very backwardness of Peruvian society" (Flores Galindo 1980, 50).

This novel perspective, which sought to articulate Marxism, *indigenismo*, and vitalism, implicated Mariátegui in two famed controversies, one with the emerging *Aprista* nationalism (American Popular Revolutionary Alliance; Alianza Popular Revolucionaria Americana [APRA]) and the other one with the Third Communist International. The former took place in 1927, mainly in Lima's *Mundial* magazine, with Luis Alberto Sánchez, one of Peru's most outstanding intellectuals, and involved *indigenismo* and *mestizaje*. In a detailed reconstruction of the debate, Eugenio Chang Rodríguez (2009), in an attempt to explain Sánchez's accusation of a "foolish desire to destroy" by the "prevailing *Indiolatry*," traces its origins to the rhetoric of some *indigenismos*. Among other things, he criticized Mariátegui for confronting colonialism with *indigenismo* and for penning various works that drifted from his own ideology and contradicted his own proposal in the presentation of the *Amauta* magazine. Throughout the debate Mariátegui attempted to demonstrate that authentic *indigenismo* involved economic work and a policy of vindication, not of restauration or resurrection, and that since the indigenous question was of an economic nature, like all other problems in the country, it would be solved by the socialist revolution (Chang Rodríguez 2009, 107). Sánchez in turn advocated for all exploited people, including the *cholo* or mestizo—not a casual occurrence for him, as he would later embrace the popular nationalism proposed by the Peruvian Aprista Party (APRA), which defended the thesis of *mestizaje*.

On the other hand, even though Mariátegui had supported APRA in its beginnings, the differences between Mariátegui and APRA founder Víctor Raúl Haya de la Torre were profound. They disagreed regarding "Inca communism" and the role that the indigenous community, as a surviving element of Inca communism, would play in the revolutionary process. While Haya de la Torre viewed the agrarian problem in the context of capitalist development and saw its solution as lying in a form of state capitalism, Mariátegui saw the agrarian and indigenous problem as "part of the socialist project of reorganizing the entire Peruvian society" (Quijano 2014b, 400). Thus, Haya de la Torre defined the problem in terms of national exploitation exercised by imperialism toward Indo-America, illustrated by Central America and the Caribbean, which led him to conclude that a multiclass and nationalist front was necessary as the basis for a democratic revolution capable of confronting imperialism. Mariátegui in turn believed that imperialist exploitation was classist, since foreign capital, in alliance with the haute and petty bourgeoisie, ruled over peasants and proletarians. A democratic revolution was therefore impossible with such elements. Democratic reforms, Mariátegui proposed, should be implemented in the process of building socialism, which was the only way to destroy both the feudal and the capitalist orders.

The second controversy was with the Third Communist International in the context of the First Latin American Communist Conference, held in Buenos Aires in 1929, and it continued after Mariátegui's death, resulting in the censorship and expulsion of "Mariateguism," considered "deviationism" and later "populism."[19] We should recall that around 1928 the Third Communist International, already under Joseph Stalin and Nikolai Bukharin's iron-fisted control, with Trotskyism defeated, "discovered" Latin America, as expressed by its own leaders. Until that moment, the Comintern had rarely been interested in Latin America. The change took place after the Sixth Communist Congress, held from July to September 1928, when it was believed that a revolutionary situation was imminent as a result of the world crisis (Flores Galindo 1980, 22). The First Latin American Communist Conference was then planned, to take place in Buenos Aires in June 1929.

For communist leaders, Latin American countries were not yet ready for a proletarian revolution—as Marx had argued, they first had to undergo a bourgeois revolution. However, after the failure in China with the Kuomintang, the Comintern began to consider the colonial and semicolonial bourgeoisie as counterrevolutionary, that is, unsuited to undertake the required bourgeois revolution. Thus, the strategy of building a front or alliance of classes was abandoned and replaced with that of "class against class" (the bourgeoisie against the proletariat), in a context of increasing social and political polarization (Stefanoni 2014). Latin American reality thus motivated a number of debates regarding the way in which communists should position themselves to fight over those processes with the liberal petty bourgeoisie in favor of a worker/peasant revolution.

The text presented at the First Congress was entitled "The Problem of the Races" and consisted of two parts: The first was written entirely by Mariátegui, and the second by Hugo Pesce. It was the latter who defended the text in Buenos Aires, since Mariátegui was ill and could not travel. The thesis was discussed in the session of June 8, 1929. Hugo Pesce, representing the Peruvian trade union group and Mariátegui, inaugurated the session with these words: "Comrades, this is the first time that an International Congress of Communist Parties pays such broad and specific attention to the issue of race in Latin America" (Mariátegui 2010, 66–67).

While for the Comintern's spokespersons there was no need to reflect on the specificity of the Communist Party in Peru, since there was no reason for Peru's reality to differ from that of Mexico or Argentina, for Mariátegui, socialism in Peru could not do without the communities or destroy them, nor could it do without indigenous people. Thus, in the paper presented by Pesce, the notion of the proletariat included urban masses (workers) and rural masses (Indians/peasants). There were also interpretive differences regarding imperialism and the feudal character of Latin American societies, which according to the Comintern were similar to European feudalism. On the other hand, for the Third International, the peasant/Indian problem should be understood from the standpoint of nations' self-determination, including their right to separation and the creation of nations such as the Aymaras and Quechuas.[20]

For Mariátegui, the Peruvian case demonstrated both the failure of the capitalist regime (since the free labor regime was far from broadly applied) and the coexistence of a mixed regime: feudal (related to latifundia and serfdom) and communal (related to the community's survival). Mariátegui's controversy with the Comintern is emblematic of the discrepancy between the so-called indigenous question and Marxism, which attempted to inscribe the indigenous category in that of social class through an economicist reading. As José Fernández Fernández (2009) argues, the economicist approach conceives Latin American society as molded by two coexisting modes of production—a capitalist mode and a precapitalist or feudal mode. From this standpoint, the indigenous problem is explained by their backwardness and precarious conditions, related to the feudal productive structure. This backwardness could only be overcome by incorporating indigenous people into the capitalist mode of production following the European model, which would imply their incorporation into the universe of social classes, whether as proletarians (in the cities) or as peasants (in the countryside). Their transformation into peasants therefore served as a transition, facilitating indigenous people's advancement away from marginality and backwardness and their insertion in a modern productive system. Ethnic/cultural issues and their solution were thus subordinated to issues of class exploitation.[21]

As Agustín Cueva ([1972] 2007, 181–82), a renowned Ecuadorian intellectual with ties to the Communist Party, acknowledges, one of Mariátegui's great merits was therefore to have related Marxist discourse to Latin America's reality, thus performing a sort of "nationalization of Marxism." The later marginalization of Mariátegui's work implied an important regression in the emergence and consolidation of Latin American Marxist thought, in regard to not only the indigenous question but the national question in general. As José Aricó argued in his influential book *Mariátegui y los orígenes del marxismo latinoamericano* (Mariátegui and the origins of Latin American marxism), one of the consequences of this turn was the end of the search for originality in social studies on the country, since the revolution was understood more as a "model" to be applied than as "national pathways to be traversed" (1978, xxxix). Trapped in the web of Stalinist communism, Marxism as a political/ideological dogma was understood more as a (fixed, closed) itinerary than as a compass. In a posthumous book, *Defensa del marxismo* (Defense of marxism), Mariátegui, anticipating communism's attempts to impose such rigid readings, wrote: "Dogma allows a course, a geographic map: it is the only guarantee of not, under the illusion of advancing, covering the same ground twice, and of not landing in an impasse because of bad information. . . . Dogma is not an itinerary but a compass on the journey. To think with freedom, the first condition is to abandon the preoccupation with absolute liberty. Thought has a strict need for direction and objective. Thinking well is, in large part, a question of direction or orbit" (1972b, 67).

Integrationist Indigenismo *as a Dominant Paradigm*

Our indigenous problem does not reside in preserving Indians as "Indians," nor in Indianizing Mexico, but in Mexicanizing Indians. Respecting their blood, apprehending their emotions, their love of land and their unyielding tenacity, a national feeling will be more deeply rooted and enriched with moral virtues that shall strengthen the national spirit, consolidating Mexico's personality.—LÁZARO CÁRDENAS, "Discurso del Presidente de la República en el Primer Congreso Indigenista Interamericano," 1940

You will not awaken spontaneously. You require friendly hearts to labor for your redemption.—MANUEL GAMIO, *Forjando patria* (Nation building), 1916

For decades, the hegemony of the *indigenista* paradigm in Latin America was undeniable. In an attempt to define *indigenismo* in terms of a doctrine or current, many specialists resort to Henri Favre, who argued, "*Indigenismo* is a position held by non-Indians regarding Indians and is found specifically in Latin America"

(1998, 7). It is therefore "an inquiry into Indianness by non-Indians reflecting the concerns and objectives of the latter" (Favre 1976, quoted in Fernández Fernández 2009). Another often-cited definition is that of Alejandro Marroquín (1977, 13), who characterizes *indigenismo* as "a policy deployed by American states to respond to and solve the problems faced by indigenous populations in order to integrate them into the corresponding nationality."

In effect, *indigenismo* gradually became a paradigm that proposed a solution to the "indigenous problem" from a perspective of integration, whereby indigenous people were spoken and thought of by nonindigenous people. Although there are prior elements that point in that direction, it was the Mexican Revolution and the subsequent foundational period, with its state institutions and public policies, which served to revisit miscegenation as a racial and cultural process and to rethink the "indigenous problem" from the standpoint of national integration and linguistic homogenization. According to this line of thought, Indians were objects of study and interpretation by others, in order to be integrated into Mexican society (Kourí 2010) as part of a national political project.

The elements that define *indigenismo* are the establishment of *mestizaje* as the nation's foundation and the proposal of a solution to the "indigenous problem" through a series of public policies aiming at their integration into national society. Thus, *indigenismo* considers the existence of a significant indigenous population in Latin America, divided into different cultures and languages, an obstacle to integration and national unity in the continent and the nation's progress (Stavenhagen 2018). Miscegenation is consistently at the heart of the project of the modern nation as an avenue toward progress and "purification" of the indigenous through racial and cultural mixture.

In order to examine some of the dimensions of integrationist *indigenismo* and shed light on those tensions, I propose analyzing two topics. The first is the "thesis of *mestizaje*" developed by Mexican intellectuals, especially from the standpoint of anthropology; the second looks at the role played by *indigenista* congresses as a space to rework the indigenous question on a continental scale. In both cases, we underscore the connection with public policies at the national and regional scales.

The most outstanding advocates of integrationist *indigenismo* in Mexico were the writer José Vasconcelos and the anthropologist Manuel Gamio, who served in postrevolutionary governments, especially in areas related to education and culture.[22] As Ramón Máiz (2008) argues, *mestizaje* as a Latin American founding myth is based on three premises. First, the thesis of the racial melting pot as the central axis of the national project proposes a fusion of European and indigenous culture and tradition. Second, there is the thesis of the disappearance of indigenous cultures once they have concluded their contribution to the process (myth) of miscegenation. It should be noted that *indigenismo* coincides with the discourse of the autochthonous in its vindication of an ideal Indian (the pre-Columbian golden age of the great indigenous cultures, now extinct, yet visible through archaeological remains). Acculturation emerges as the key concept that points to the elimination of the great sources of backwardness represented by living Indians, who presumably constitute an obstacle to progress and national development. Third, the theory of *mestizaje* is accompanied by the myth of cultural homogeneity (which should be linguistic) imposed by political and cultural elites from above.

It was José Vasconcelos, the author of *The Cosmic Race/La raza cósmica* ([1925] 1997), who most zealously celebrated miscegenation, arguing that it was not racial purity but the fusion of races that leads to plenitude.[23] Revisiting the same arguments that rejected miscegenation from different standpoints—such as positivism—and inverting them, Vasconcelos argued that the mixture of races resulted in a superior synthesis that was the expression of the Arielist/spiritualist mission to be carried out by the Americas, contrary to the Saxon race, based on segregation and materialism.[24] In this opposition between the Latin and Saxon races, indigenous people are seen as a "good bridge for miscegenation," applicable to both Mexico and Latin America. Vasconcelos believed that as the days of pure white people ("today's winners") were numbered, so were those of pure Indians, who were now "Hispanicized, Latinized, like the environment is" (Piñeiro Iñiguez 2006, 553). Education thus emerges as the fundamental tool for Indians to overcome their backwardness. For that reason, Vasconcelos had little patience with pro-indigenous positions, which he considered a mere intellectual construction removed from the realities of pre-Columbian American societies (Piñeiro Iñiguez 2006, 553). Also, although Vasconcelos repeatedly refers to race, the latter is an idea based on the opposition between Latinxs and Saxons. As Patricia Funes observes, while the concept is devoid of biological connotations, it is excessively broad, employed erratically to mean "people," "civilization," "culture," "common customs," or "Ibero-Americanism" (2006, 76).

The icon of the integrationist paradigm, however, was Manuel Gamio. Educated in the United States with the renowned anthropologist Franz Boas, he conducted important work as an archaeologist and anthropologist, teaching and researching, and as the first director of the Inter-American Indigenista Institute for two decades. Some of Boas's influence on Gamio is evident in his idea that "anthropological research on human groups must feed from ethnography, archaeology, linguistics, and history, which this Mexican anthropologist called the 'integral research method'" (G. Ramírez 2013, 2).

In 1916 Gamio wrote *Forjando patria* (Nation building), which summarizes his project for the Mexican nation and the role of "the mixture of races" and "indigenous groups" in that project. He proposed that the main challenge is the nation's unity, that is, that there cannot be several nationalities as separate entities but that they must be integrated into a single nation. Unlike the positivist standpoint, in his view indigenous people's problem was not their presumed racial inferiority but their cultural backwardness—"certain historical factors and unique social, biological, geographic, and other conditions of their environment have made them incapable of receiving and assimilating European culture" (Gamio 1916, 38). Education and linguistic unification are the main mechanisms whereby they shall "assimilate European culture" (38–39). According to Gamio, indigenous people were a "poor and bereaved race" who had been oppressed by various fanaticisms—their priestly caste, Christian fanaticism, that of the conquerors. "Indian redemption" could not emerge from indigenous people and their rebellions but through their incorporation—or "regeneration," as was said at the time—to which anthropology, and especially ethnology, would contribute greatly. Finally, it is important to note that Gamio acknowledged the existence of three social groups in Mexico: Indians, mestizos, and the immediate or distant descendants of foreigners, "whose blood has mixed little with that of the middle class and not at all with that of Indians" (174). Heterogeneity was at the very heart of the "cultural schism" between indigenous and Western civilizations, but in order to build a nation, only the middle (mestizo) class, in spite of its shortcomings and inevitable distortions, emerged as the basis for a national culture, "[the class] of the future, which shall prevail once the population is ethnically homogeneous and is thus capable of feeling and understanding it" (174–75).

In short, Gamio's ideas on a revolutionary potential leave little room for indigenous people or cultural and linguistic diversity, even for indigenous groups separate or distant from the national state, such as the Lacandones in Chiapas. For Gamio, it was imperative to understand those Indians, to research their needs, and to establish the conditions for their incorporation. The great objective was therefore to "civilize" indigenous people and incorporate them, recognizing their contribution to the nation's foundation, welcoming their art and traditional culture, but also recognizing the backwardness of pre-Hispanic knowledge relative to Western culture, into which it should be incorporated through miscegenation and linguistic unification.

In consonance with this view, *indigenismo* spread throughout the continent at that time thanks to *indigenista* congresses, which started to outline specific policies based on general guidelines and recommendations. According to Henri Favre (1998, chap. 5), it was the laicization of the states that forced

Latin American governments to take a position on the "indigenous problem," which had deliberately been left in the hands of the Catholic Church. In 1918 the First International Convention of Teachers, held in Buenos Aires, recommended "incorporating indigenous people into modern culture" (Favre 1998, chap. 5). In 1933 the Seventh Pan-American Convention on Education, held in Mexico, finally approved the creation of a "continental Congress to study the problem of indigenous people in Latin American countries" (Stavenhagen 2018, 106). The watershed was the Indigenista Congress of Pátzcuaro, held in 1940 in Michoacán, where the groundwork for an *indigenista* policy on a continental scale was established and the creation of the Inter-American Indigenista Institute was planned through an international convention ratified by seventeen states. Mexico's president, Lázaro Cárdenas (1940), said at the opening session in Pátzcuaro that the indigenous problem "does not reside in preserving Indians as 'Indians,' nor in Indianizing Mexico, but in Mexicanizing Indians," as cited in the epigraph.

An institutional phase thus begins, expressed in the minutes and resolutions of the various *indigenista* congresses; in the creation of the Inter-American Indigenista Institute (III), an executive body of inter-American *indigenista* policy in charge of implementing the congresses' resolutions; and in the foundation of national *indigenista* institutes. The functions of the III were the following: "to create permanent links between governments regarding indigenous problems; to carry out scientific polls to serve as the bases for national *indigenista* programs; to train specialized personnel in indigenous matters; to promote the creation of national *indigenista* institutes" (Santoul 1988, 23). The recommendations emerging from the Pátzcuaro congress addressed the various aspects of the indigenous question, including education, economics, labor, legal issues, and culture, and suggested that anthropologists "preoccupied with the well-being of indigenous people" play a leading role implementing those programs (Santoul 1998, 24).

In Mexico the National Indigenista Institute (Instituto Nacional Indigenista; INI) was created in 1948. Its purpose was to coordinate the various government actions in indigenous regions (economic stimulus, education, basic infrastructure), but the core of institutional *indigenismo* would be the coordinating centers, the first one inaugurated in San Cristóbal de Las Casas, Chiapas (Korsbaek and Sámano Rentería 2007, 203). In Bolivia the National Indigenista Institute was created in 1941; in Ecuador, in 1942; and in Peru, in 1946. However, in his assessment of *indigenismo*, Marroquín (1977) observes that thirty years after joining the Inter-American Indigenista Institute, some countries had not even created a national institute. In short, after the Pátzcuaro congress in 1940, state policies regarding the indigenous population institutionalized an assimilationist approach that accentuated the redemptive and regenerative effects of the expected and inevitable integration of indigenous people into the national society, that is, into the hegemonic culture.

BETWEEN THE INDIAN AND THE PEASANT: POPULISM, MISCEGENATION, AND AGRARIAN REFORM

A third tension field emerged from the association between *indigenismo* and populism, which led to profound changes in the relationship between the indigenous and the peasant. Indigenous and peasant are in fact contiguous but not identical categories that operated in unison for a long time but that gradually dissociated, as policies and strategies to assimilate/incorporate indigenous people into the nation-state were deployed. In this section, we examine the close relationship between state-driven *indigenismo*, peasants, and agrarian reform, proposed by different populist experiences at three different moments: Mexico with Lázaro Cárdenas in the 1940s, Bolivia with the Nationalist Revolutionary Movement (Movimiento Nacional Revolucionario; MNR) in the 1950s, and Peru in the late 1960s under the military government of Juan Velasco Alvarado.

It is important to recall that in some Latin American countries, the break with oligarchic rule was the result of an intense revolutionary process. Such was the case of Mexico, which in the 1910s experienced a turbulent period of rupture with the traditional order, followed by long conflicts between different factions, with their caudillos and peasant masses fighting for power. Such was also the case of Bolivia in the 1950s, when oligarchic rule was overturned by an armed worker/peasant uprising that defeated the army and placed the government in the hands of an alliance of miner unions, urban middle classes, and peasant/indigenous masses.

However, in both Mexico and Bolivia, these complex political processes of revolutionary uprising and construction did not lead to socialism but to populism as the foundational regime. These governments assumed the challenge of reestablishing the social contract, creating new political/institutional frameworks, in order to homogenize and integrate the population into the national society. They therefore developed a modernizing program based on the conjunction of three main premises: a strategy of nationalization that included underground resources (oil and mining), up to then in the hands of foreign corporations; the inclusion of formal workers, through the establishment of labor rights (urban workers, miners), and of peasants/Indians as citizens through universal suffrage (Bolivia); and the implementation of agrarian reform programs for the peasant and indigenous sectors. In spite of their differences in terms of state structures, both Mexico's populist regime led by Lázaro Cárdenas (1934–40) and that of Bolivia with Víctor Paz Estenssoro and Hernán Siles Suazo (1952–64) tended to incorporate the rural sectors under the generic category of peasants. Finally, the populist regimes promoted an integrationist narrative that stressed the thesis of national homogenization through miscegenation.

The Mexican Revolution had a strong impact on Latin America. According to Adolfo Gilly ([1971] 2006), it was a great mass movement centered on the struggle for power and land, with an important peasant and indigenous base. With the revolution's institutionalization, peasants were included in the 1917 Constitution with a specific status and rights: They appeared under the general form of the right to land of peasants and "communities." The social and agrarian reforms implemented by the populist/corporatist state resulted in important changes in the processes of identification of collective subjects in rural areas, understood as peasants. As Máiz argues, "A double process was produced: on one hand, the Indians of central Mexico were identified as peasants, more specifically as poor peasants on their way to becoming proletarians; on the other hand, *indigenista* policies were designed, starting with Cárdenas, as a means of *Mexicanization*—incorporation into the market, corporative social policies for peasants, programs for linguistic and cultural assimilation, etc." (2004, 134).

Under Lázaro Cárdenas, the agrarian reform was strongly promoted, with more land distributed during his administration than in all previous ones (see Bravo Ahuja Ruiz et al. 1994, 310–17). Cárdenas, who had a personalist style and was inclined to make direct contact with the populations, promoted the collective ejido to justify the expropriations (Knight 1998, 206).[25] Later, in 1946, the party's various sections—labor, peasant, people's, and military—were institutionalized, and the party was renamed the Institutional Revolutionary Party (Partido Revolucionario Institucional; PRI), whereby the Mexican model adopted a clearly corporatist form. The labor and peasant sections—organized in the Confederation of Mexican Workers (Confederación de Trabajadores de México) and the National Peasant Confederation (Confederación Nacional Campesina)—were the most important.

In the Bolivian case, it was a lost war, this time in the Chaco (1932–35), that led people to question the oligarchic state, summoning the various social sectors that had participated in the war to rethink the Bolivian nation. During the administration of Gualberto Villaroel (1943–46), in a short-lived alliance with the MNR, the theory of *mestizaje* took root, adopting the Cochabamba *chola* as a sort of synthesis of Bolivian nationality (Gotkowitz 2007; 2011, 235–36). Finally, in April 1952 the Bolivian insurrection took place, with the solid participation of the workers' militias but also the peasant militias. The insurrection thus inaugurated the first and most radical phase of the Bolivian Revolution, with a government shared between the MNR and the Bolivian Central Workers' Union (Central Obrera Boliviana), when several important structural reforms were implemented, such as the nationalization of the mines, universal suffrage, agrarian reform, and educational reform (aimed at achieving a true mass education). Silvia Rivera called this phase "active subordination" of indigenous peasants to the state, under the aegis of Cochabamba trade unionism (Rivera Cusicanqui [1984] 2003, 139).

A second phase of the Bolivian Revolution began in 1964 that entailed a change in the social base, from the mining sectors to the indigenous peasant masses, thanks to universal suffrage. This phase also marked an ideological shift: "the passage from the ideological debate between bourgeois democratic revolution and socialist revolution to the struggle between nationalism and communism" (Mayorga 2003, 249). The clearest expression of this reactionary shift was the Campesino Military Pact (1964) between the armed forces led by René Barrientos and the agrarian unions. For others, it expressed the internal contradictions of the state project and the alignment of peasant syndicalism with sectors of the bureaucracy and right-wing fractions of the MNR (Rivera Cusicanqui [1984] 2003, 139).[26]

On the other hand, the agrarian reform had a significant impact, destroying the bases of oligarchic power: It abolished rural servitude, created the conditions to eliminate the hacienda regime, and distributed land among the landless—especially in the Andean region and the valleys of Cochabamba, where peasant militias were organized and haciendas were expropriated—and the former tenant farmers became owners.[27] However, even though it did away with most of the rural latifundio structure, the agrarian reform distributed land according to a liberal and individualist logic. As Esteban Ticona Alejo (2003, 289) observes, it did not attempt to apply socialist or communal criteria but aimed to subdivide land with a liberal approach. Furthermore, it was ambiguous regarding the ayllus and indigenous communities, which did not benefit from the law.

The centrality of the peasant in the populist model was reflected in the rise and expansion of agrarian, rural, or peasant unions. In both Mexico and Bolivia, a corporate representation structure emerged in the form of "agrarian unions," which aimed at integrating rural players mobilized through a participation model under state tutelage. In the Bolivian case, the 1953 agrarian reform introduced the agrarian union as a grassroots political organization of the communities: The former colonists transformed into communal farmers joined the union, as did the indigenous communities. As Álvaro García Linera and colleagues (2004, 109) point out, peasant unions resonated with "communal forms," since, beyond the specific demands for land and colonist rights, "they articulated the organizational logic, memory, and mechanisms for action accumulated over centuries of indigenous peasant resistance." Such was the case of the emblematic Unified Syndical Confederation of Peasant Workers of Bolivia (Confederación Sindical Única de Trabajadores Campesinos de Bolivia; CSUTCB), one of the major players in Bolivian politics, which emerged from peasant unionism in Cochabamba and spread throughout the nation after the 1952 nationalist revolution. Beginning in the 1970s, the CSUTCB became the most complete expression of the intersection among communal structure, *indianista* discourse, and union action, which gave rise to "the most important political proposals for indigenous emancipation by Bolivian communal unionism" (García Linera 2004, 130).

The 1952 revolution consecrated Tiwanaku—already consolidated as the source of the nation since 1930—as the source of Bolivian nationality and adopted the symbols of the great pre-Hispanic cultures.[28] But in the symbolic realm, it actively promoted miscegenation as the heart of the nation's identity: Thus, the predominant form under which the nation was conceived was the *indomestizo*—mestizos of indigenous descent. As early as 1942, the MNR condemned Arguedas's work, which denigrated indigenous and mestizo Bolivians, rejecting the idea that miscegenation was dangerous (Gotkowitz 2007; 2011, 235). However, the key to revaluing miscegenation was not the notion of "fusion" (as was the case in Mexico) but the issue of "historical struggles." Among the nationalist theoreticians who most influenced this symbolic construction of miscegenation was Carlos Montenegro with his book *Nacionalismo y colonialje* (Nationalism and colonialism), published in 1944 (2005), which offered a new way of reading the Bolivian nation in clearly populist terms (Nation/Anti-nation), "where anti-colonial struggles brought Indians and mestizos together" (Gotkowitz 2011, 236).

In a recent book, Vincent Nicolas and Pablo Quisbert (2014, 27) analyze how, during the MNR's government, the topic of miscegenation was present in official history, even reaching colonial art through the discovery of a "mestizo baroque," as it was called at the time.

PERU'S TRUNCATED POPULISM AND THE CLASS DISCOURSE

Although there was a political and cultural discourse on miscegenation in Peru, it did not evolve into a clear state policy, as was the case in other Latin American countries with populist governments. Paradoxically, although APRA was the first populist party in Latin America, it was unable to reach power, and its main leader, Víctor Raúl Haya de la Torre, was exiled in his own country, living in the Mexican embassy for years. Even though he proposed the name Indo-America, Haya de la Torre was an advocate of miscegenation; moreover, in his youth he was a disciple and secretary of José Vasconcelos, with whom he shared the thesis of *mestizaje* and the need to integrate or assimilate indigenous people into national society. This set him apart from José Carlos Mariátegui, who understood the indigenous question as intimately related to the issue of land.

Populism finally arrived in Peru—in an incomplete and military form—in 1968, when the leaders of the military coup adopted a view of the country whereby the nation's main problem was the lack of a leading group capable of maintaining a process of national and political integration of Peruvian society. The military government of Velasco Alvarado (1968–74) implemented a series of measures that had been advocated by APRA since the 1930s, such as nationalization of foreign corporations, guaranteed worker participation in property ownership, agrarian reform, and a number of processes that became part of the military's institutional consensus (North 1985), including a distrust of civilian politicians, a clear technocratic penchant, the perceived need for reforms to consolidate internal security, and a nationalism basically founded on military patriotism. This consensus, in spite of certain discrepancies, united Peru's armed forces around the project of creating a "social democracy with full participation" from the top down (Martuccelli and Svampa 1998).

The military government implemented an agrarian reform through measures such as expropriating sugar and cotton haciendas, which became large co-ops. It was a radical agrarian reform: Not only did it dismantle the oligarchic hacienda, but after expropriating the large haciendas, it maintained them as collective property through large productive units, thus inaugurating a period of state capitalism. Overall, however, the reform failed—peasants rejected the associative model, which did not imply self-management, since it was proposed from above, nor prosperity, since the government subordinated rural production in order to feed the urban poor.

In 1969 Velasco Alvarado instituted Peasant's Day by decree, substituting the word *Indian* for *peasant* after the Agrarian Reform Law was enacted. Overnight, indigenous communities legally became "peasant communities" and "Andean communities." Many researchers believe that this name change aimed at leaving behind the depreciatory terms *Indian* and *indigenous* (de la Cadena 2000; Yrigoyen Fajardo 2002). According to Raquel Yrigoyen Fajardo (2002), this process of identification as peasants, promoted by both the Velasco administration and the trade unions, was quickly adopted by the Andean peasant communities and allowed for a positive re-creation of popular identity. In this context, in 1974 the National Agrarian Confederation (Confederación Nacional Agraria;

CNA) was created, which fought over representation and political spaces in rural areas with the Campesino Confederation of Peru (Confederación Campesina del Perú; CCP), a communist association. But after Velasco Alvarado's ousting, the CNA became the main organizational instrument of the associative enterprises and rural organizations that defended the agrarian reform. On the other hand, the reform's interruption resulted in migration to the cities.

The new government created a legal corpus to regulate the (Andean) peasant and (Amazonian) indigenous communities, which protected their communal territory and their internal organization. The Native Communities Law (1974) recognized some forms of local community justice and declared indigenous communal land inalienable, imprescriptible, and unseizable. The law remained in place until 1993, when Alberto Fujimori's government implemented a constitutional reform that set a number of neoliberal measures in motion and dismantled those land rights.

In short, both Peruvian peasant confederations (CNA and CCP) deployed a class discourse centered on the peasant that displaced ethnic demands. As a result, as Marisol de la Cadena points out, "in the 1960s, the word 'Indian' no longer played a significant role in political campaigns, but was employed when Indians were tortured or as a way to humiliate indigenous leaders. The former Indians identified themselves as peasants and addressed each other as *compañeros*, an identity that strengthened their political capacity and represented a challenge to the dominant taxonomies that had turned them into inferior beings" (2000; 2004, 212).[29] Their assimilation to the condition of poor peasants, synonymous with serfdom and even illiteracy, further hindered the process of self-identification as Indians. In the 1970s several authors pointed out the difficulty in identifying "Indians" in Peru; that is, Andean peasants were uninclined to recognize themselves as such because of the derogatory connotation of the terms *Indian* and *indigenous* (Salazar Soler 2014, 80).

ARGENTINA: THE BLIND SPOTS OF PERONISM

The first Peronism was a watershed in twentieth-century Argentine history. Its arrival led to a political and social polarization that characterized national politics for decades. The representation of the two Argentinas, the dichotomous or binary discourse employed by both Peronists and anti-Peronists, penetrated the social, political, and cultural fields, becoming a sort of grand narrative, a reading that deployed a totalizing view of history and of the vicissitudes of Argentina's political life. Peronism thus brought about new conflictive displacements in the nation's process of construction of alterity, regarding the "internal other." Claudia Briones argues that three main logics permeate the construction of alterity in Argentina: "the arrival of progress through the port and the eviction of 'obstacles' through the service door, a logic related to another one of selective Argentinization and foreignization of alterities; both logics in turn coexist with one of denial and internalization of the color lines" (2005, 22). Indeed, during the foundation of the modern state, the first logic (exclusion of Indians) was applied; at the time of the first centennial, it was replaced by the logic of selectivity, foreignizing rowdy immigrants—portraying them as exotic and implementing concrete measures such as the Social Defense Law and the Residence Law (Svampa 1994); in the Peron era, a dividing line between the center and the periphery was consolidated through images of a mestizo and plebeian invasion, a raid on Buenos Aires from the deep interior (the *cabecitas negras*, "black heads").[30]

What happened, then, in Peronist Argentina after 1945 regarding the indigenous question? What political and symbolic transformations took place in that regard? Is it possible to speak of an integrationist policy, as was the case in other Latin American countries with populist regimes? There was a policy to turn the working class into citizens by expanding social and labor rights, but this policy was far from translating into an *indigenista* policy comparable to that of other countries such as Mexico and Bolivia, nor was there an agrarian reform that aimed at distributing land among poor peasants. However, the first Peronist government increased social rights, especially for rural laborers, which improved their working conditions and thus also benefited indigenous laborers (Gordillo and Hirsch 2010). Likewise, the 1949 constitutional reform eliminated Clause 15 of Article 67, which established that the National Congress was to "provide border security, maintain peaceful relations with Indians, and convert them to Catholicism."[31]

But the event that marked the Peronist period regarding the indigenous population was the Malón de la Paz in 1946, during the first year of Juan Domingo Perón's administration, which mobilized about two hundred Qulla indigenous peasants from Salta and Jujuy in a march from La Quiaca (on the border with Bolivia) to Buenos Aires, demanding their ancestral lands. As historians and anthropologists point out, the government was not pleased with the march, but Perón and the National Congress nonetheless received it with great pomp. Photographs of that time show indigenous leaders carrying portraits of Perón, in a march that was covered at every stage by the major media. After they were received by Peron and housed, coincidentally, in the famed Hotel de los Inmigrantes, before the impossibility of responding favorably to their demands, twenty-five days after their arrival in the capital, they were forcefully evicted by the police in the middle of the night, locked up in two trains, and sent directly back to Puna.[32] In spite of the humiliating outcome of the event, indigenous organizations understood the Malón de la Paz as a historic milestone that marked the beginning of their struggles on a national level (Gordillo and Hirsch 2010, 25).[33]

The issue of the National Identity Document, which allowed indigenous people to vote for the first time, thus effectively recognizing them as Argentine citizens, is also often cited. However, as anthropologist Morita Carrasco argues, "Although many Indians were pleased with the measure, asserting that 'Perón made us people,' the right to elect their representatives did not free indigenous people from state tutelage; on the contrary, it consolidated paternalism through one of its most perverse practices: political clientelism" (2002).

One year after the Malón de la Paz, the greatest massacre of indigenous people in twentieth-century Argentina took place in Rincón Bomba, in the province of Formosa, where around five hundred Indians from Toba, Pilagá, and Wichí communities were murdered between October 10 and 30 by troops of the National Gendarmerie (Gendarmería Nacional). Unarmed men, women, and children who carried portraits of Perón and Evita perished during that great repression.[34]

Thus, in spite of the genuine expectations elicited by Peronism among indigenous people, it did not explicitly vindicate them; rather, its policies were highly ambiguous, as demonstrated by its reaction to the Malón de la Paz and its passivity when faced with the Rincón Bomba massacre. In its integrationist and homogenizing dimension, Peronism could see the mestizo roots of the Peronist people (the rural "black heads") and, in the interstices of that mestizo representation of subalternity, indigenous faces of a different Argentina, but it was incapable of representing a diverse and multilingual indigenous Argentina. For that reason—as was evident with the Malón de la Paz march—Peronism exhibited discomfort and distrust. Such discomfort was evident in a little-known episode related to a sculpture of Eva Perón commissioned by the government from an Argentine artist. In 1950 the director of the National Museum of Decorative Arts (Museo Nacional de Arte Decorativo), Ignacio Pirovano, visited the sculptor Sesostris Vitullo, who had been living in France for decades and was recognized for his archetypical and telluric works, even though he was a marginal artist. In the name of the government, Pirovano commissioned a sculpture of Eva Perón, who died two years later, in 1952. Vitullo, who used to research the subject matter before beginning the work, began inquiring into Eva Perón's life. In one of the letters addressed to Pirovano, he wrote, "I understand everything now. Eva Perón is an *Archetypical Symbol*. A liberator of the oppressed races of America. I see her as a figurehead surrounded by laurels." When he completed the work in 1952, he enthusiastically wrote, "It is made of stone, two faces surrounded by laurels: a profile of Evita and another one almost Indian. There is no gloating, complacency, or demagogy" (PROA, n.d.). That was his summary of the metaphor of Eva that the artist materialized in *Arquetipo Símbolo*, as he named the sculpture.

In December that same year, a few months after Eva Perón's death, Vitullo exhibited his works at the Museum of Modern Art in Paris, *Arquetipo Símbolo* among them. Before taking it to the room where it would be put on display for the public, the artist showed the work to the delegation from the Argentine embassy that sponsored the exhibit; however, the authorities were not particularly enthusiastic about Vitullo's work. Before the opening night, the work was taken to the embassy's basement without being exhibited. In May 1952 Vitullo died, forgotten and poor, without receiving a response from the embassy, which neither paid for the work nor returned it to its creator.[35]

I do not mention this interesting episode to denigrate the first Peronism but because it serves to illustrate its ambiguities regarding indigenous people. The embassy's rejection of and inability to understand the American and indigenous Evita proposed by Vitullo was in tune with the times, that is, with the political and symbolic framework through which indigenous people were viewed. Populist Peronism had an explicitly working-class and plebeian foundation, which of course included the rural masses (the "black heads" who arrived in the city), but this did not imply vindicating indigenous people or even peasants. Thus, on one hand, Peronism sought to include indigenous peoples marginally in the name of the working class through social and labor policies; on the other hand, from a political and symbolic standpoint, it found it very difficult to conceive indigenous reality, at a time when different indigenous communities attempted to make their demands visible.

In the 1960s Argentine developmentalism attempted to pave the way for an incipient integrationist policy that aimed at converting Indians into "active subjects of their own integration, through acculturation policies," which often required expert advice (Carrasco 2002). This resulted in Law 3998 of 1965 (DIP 1991), which established the First National Indigenous Census, which estimated a population of 165,000 Indians out of a total population of twenty-three million, a conservative number according to Gordillo and Hirsch (2010), employing markers such as language and excluding indigenous people who lived in urban centers, precisely at a time when the first generation of migrants from the countryside to the great industrial centers had been consolidated.[36]

Representations of alterity are always relational. According to F. Mallon (cited in Máiz 2008), in countries like Peru and Bolivia, which have a greater indigenous presence, they are bipolar constructions that establish an opposition between whites/mestizos and Indians. Sometimes these oppositions have a geographic parallel, as is the case in Peru (coast, sierra, and jungle); in other cases, such as in Mexico, the mestizo is central, and the indigenous is peripheral. It is not by chance that it was in that country that a theory of *mestizaje* developed that posited the mestizo as the total social subject (Vasconcelos's "cosmic race").

In contrast, in Argentina white people are at the center, and mestizos in the periphery, in a binary representation that sometimes appears as symmetrical and sometimes not, while Indians are relegated to the periphery of the periphery, occupying a sort of nonplace far removed even from mestizos (the "black heads"). Two renowned Argentine anthropologists argue that indigenous people inhabit Argentina's history as an "absent presence" (Hirsch and Gordillo 2010). We are therefore faced with national contexts with varying levels of complexity, where indigenous people, their relationship to mestizos, and their place in the nation are understood differently according to the different national modalities of alterity.

On the other hand, since the mid-1940s, a hegemonic paradigm was gradually consolidated in the region: integrationist *indigenismo*, which aims at homogenizing the nation by incorporating Indians as peasants. While the integrationist paradigm spread throughout the continent, it did so in an unequal and heterogeneous manner, with different time frames and nuances, and with a close relationship to the populist/developmentalist model. First Mexico, where we find the political and academic apotheosis of *mestizaje*, and later Bolivia, where miscegenation emerges as the symbolic core of the nation, perfectly illustrate this integrationist paradigm, albeit with their specific differences. It is not by chance that the indigenous emergence of the 1970s stood against this integrationist model (its broken promises, its shortcomings, its intentions to acculturate indigenous people and dissolve them into the peasant).

In short, Latin American populism consolidated a certain worker/peasant matrix as paradigmatic figures of subalternity, in opposition to the dominant elite and its national and foreign allies. The peasant sector, through its evergrowing national agrarian confederations and even its class language, illustrated the subaltern pole in the rural context, conceived as separate from the devalued figure of the indigenous.

Part 2: The Reinvention of *Indianidad*:
Toward New Paradigms (1960–2000)

The Turn of the 1970s and the New Tension Fields

National frustration has its origins in the Quechua and Aymara cultures, which have always suffered a systematic attempt to destroy them.... We do not want to lose our noble ancestral virtues for the sake of pseudo-development. We fear this false "developmentalism" imported from abroad because it is fictitious and does not respect our deep values. We want to overcome stale paternalism and to stop being considered second-class citizens. We are foreigners in our own country.—FIRST TIWANAKU MANIFESTO, Bolivia, 1973

In the 1970s a new political cycle began, which gradually centered on the reinvention of *indianidad*. A number of events are at the origin of this novel turn of the discourse on the indigenous.[37] First, there was significant disappointment with reformist political models. In spite of the policies to turn indigenous people into citizens during the first populism of the 1940s and 1950s, by the 1970s there was an increase in (social, gender, and of course ethnic) inequalities; in spite of the developmentalist policies in vogue, the limits of socioeconomic integration and import substitution industrialization became evident, as illustrated by the expansion of irregular settlements in urban peripheries of large Latin American cities, which sociology and political economy at the time understood as "marginality."

Second, revolutionary feelings were stirring in Latin America with the triumph of the Cuban Revolution. Cuba's conversion to Marxism-Leninism, the spread of *foquismo*, and the various guerrilla movements in the region created a favorable context to make radical demands for social change. Furthermore, the decolonization process initiated in Asia and Africa pointed to the marks left by imperialism and the persistence of domination in society, carried out now by the national elites. As Frantz Fanon ([1961] 1963) argued, the liberated societies were divided between those that inherited the legacy of colonial domination and those that inherited the legacy of autochthonous peoples. In this context, a new space emerged to denounce not only dependency but also the colonial nature of indigenous people's condition. Hence, theses on internal colonialism were developed in the mid-1960s by Pablo González Casanova ([1965] 1970) and Rodolfo Stavenhagen (1967). According to González Casanova, "Today's indigenous problem is essentially a problem of internal colonialism. Indigenous communities are internal colonies. Indigenous communities are colonies located within national borders. Indigenous communities have the characteristics of a colonized society" ([1965] 1970). Internal colonialism exists wherever there are indigenous communities, and it takes on different economic, political, and cultural forms that delineate a colonial structure often related to phenomena of social breakdown: a predominantly subsistence economy, deficient agriculture and cattle raising, backward exploitation techniques, low productivity, lower standards of living than in nonindigenous rural regions, severe lack of services, promotion of prostitution and alcoholism, a magical/religious culture, and economic and political manipulation (106–7). The indigenous problem—that is, internal colonialism—is a national problem: It defines how the nation operates.

Third, the importance of nonindigenous strategic allies must be emphasized (Albó 2002, 2008; Martí i Puig 2004), among them, the new organizational networks (nongovernmental associations [NGOs], environmental associations) and churches. Thus, on one hand, the Catholic Church assumed a new role after the Second Vatican Council and the Latin American Conference of Medellin (1968). In this context of ideological radicalization, liberation theology emerged, which was the basis for the development of the indigenous pastoral. For example, in 1974 the Diocese of San Cristóbal de Las Casas organized the first Indigenous Congress, where the representatives spoke in their respective languages of problems such as land, health, trade, and education. On the other hand, in the 1970s "the World Council of Churches (of Protestant affiliation) financed the transport of indigenous leaders from the remotest communities in the jungle—especially in Brazil—to the locations of the encounters" (Martí i Puig 2004, 18–20).

Fourth, there was an expansion of the ethnic frontier. In this regard, José Bengoa (2009) argues that for a long time, scholars believed that indigenous people lived in communities and therefore could be studied as isolated groups and communities. As a result, the category excluded those who lived in cities, thus circumscribing ethnicity to the association between community and rurality. However, with the processes of urbanization and migration to the cities, the ethnic frontiers expanded, leading to the emergence of the concept of "indigenous peoples," which encompasses "all the inhabitants of the ethnicized territory, from mestizos to Indians living in communities, [who] feel they belong to the indigenous identity" (Bengoa 2009, 13). The ethnicization process thus poses an important challenge, since it inserts this dynamic in the heart of the cities, where those who conceived themselves as mestizos can also assume an indigenous identity, as was the paradigmatic case of the city of El Alto in the Bolivian highlands.

In this new context, several changes take place in the tension field between the indigenous/peasant and race/social class categories. On one hand, not only is integrationist *indigenismo* questioned but also the orthodox Marxist interpretation scheme, which tends to reduce the indigenous problem to a class issue (understanding indigenous people as peasants), thus despoiling it of its cultural dimensions and reducing it to an economic problem (misery, exploitation). The cultural dimension thus gradually became central in the process of political construction and empowerment, without this implying a return to the category of race. On the contrary, as the notion of race declines, the new tension field emerges linked to the notion of ethnicity.[38] This is no doubt also a polysemic notion. The interpretations of ethnicity, as well as the use that indigenous movements make of it, are in a permanent state of flux and unavoidable tension, whether their starting point is a political action whereby an identity prior to the nation-state (even pre-Hispanic) is vindicated, or whether they are based on a language of rights sustained by the extensive international and national regulations, or both simultaneously. It is worth noting, however, that both uses of ethnicity are generally disqualified by the hegemonic groups (the state, political parties, pressure groups, economic corporations)—either indigenous people are accused of fundamentalism and communal essentialism (primordialism), or, on the contrary, it is all a matter of (self-)construction of identity, and thus they are accused of deploying a purely strategic (instrumental) action in order to gain access to land and rights.

Questioning Marxism's economicist perspective in turn led to a more complex understanding of the relationship between ethnicity and social class in an attempt to transcend the culture/economy dichotomy. They were thus gradually perceived not so much as antithetical but as complementary categories—if social class refers to socioeconomic conditioning factors, and ethnicity refers to matters of a cultural nature, they are both different and intertwined, since they express "two types of inequalities" (Díaz Polanco 1991, 146). The new ethnic struggles reflect a "socioculturally heterogeneous national matrix" (146). Or, as one of the currents of Katarism expressed it, racial (cultural) and socioeconomic claims cannot be separated; they necessarily complement each other to serve as an instrument of liberation and national vindication.[39] This process was accompanied by an important qualitative change related to the irruption of vast ethnic conglomerates in the political scene, whether or not they were articulated with other social organizations, successful or not, that sought to carry out transformations on a national scale (Díaz Polanco 1991, 112).

New indigenous organizations thus arose throughout the subcontinent, interacting with other social actors, especially humanitarian NGOs and others related to the environment and human rights. The organizations that emerged in the context of these changes rejected an exclusive identification as peasants and positioned themselves as Indians. A series of declarations and manifestos by the various national indigenous confederations spread throughout the continent, from Mexico to Argentina.[40] This process included the Amazonian peoples, traditionally marginalized and seen as "jungle people." This was the case of the Shuar Federation in Ecuador, created in 1964, which spearheaded the creation of the Confederation of Indigenous Nationalities of the Amazon (Confederación de Nacionalidades Indígenas de la Amazonía Ecuatoriana; CONFENIAE) in 1980. A similar process began in the Peruvian jungle in 1968, which a decade later gave rise to the Interethnic Association for the Development of the Peruvian Rainforest (Asociación Interétnica de Desarrollo de la Selva Peruana; AIDESEP) (Albó 2002, 184–85). In Bolivia, in addition to the highland Quechuas and Aymaras organized since 1971 in the aforementioned CSUTCB, people in the lowlands organized in the Indigenous Confederation of Indigenous Peoples of the Bolivian East (Confederación de Pueblos Indígenas del Oriente Boliviano; CIDOB), founded in 1981. The counterfestivities of the five-hundred-year anniversary of the Spanish conquest (1992) represented a moment of "great symbolic significance" (employing Xavier Albó's expression)—two years before the Zapatista uprising in Chiapas (1994), one of the poorest and most neglected regions of Mexico.

In short, a cycle of gradual empowerment of indigenous organizations began, which politically translated into *indianismo* as a perspective, and the vindication of autonomy as a paradigm. Thus, the crisis of integrationist *indigenismo* was accompanied by a tension field that set *indigenismo* and *indianismo* in opposition. The difference between them has to do with how the indigenous is spoken of—whether "ventriloquized by the elites" (employing the expression coined by Silvia Rivera Cusicanqui [1984] 2003), spoken about from above or from the outside (by mestizos or white criollos), or spoken about from below by indigenous people themselves as political subjects. This position reflects the progressive empowerment of indigenous people through their words and actions, their social and political struggles, the international recognition of their rights, and their symbolic processes of visibility.

THE WAYS OF SELF-CRITICISM: *INDIGENISMO* AND KATARISM

That Indians organize and lead their own liberation movement is essential, or it ceases to be liberating. When non-Indians pretend to represent Indians, even on occasion assuming the leadership of the latter's groups, a new colonial situation is established. This is yet another expropriation of the Indian populations' inalienable right to determine their future.—DECLARATION OF BARBADOS, 1971

Academically speaking, the 1970s saw a realignment of the social and human sciences in a critical direction, especially in Mexico and Bolivia. In the former, critical anthropology (or critical *indigenismo*) emerges, which questions the dominant *indigenismo*, proposes an epistemological revision of anthropological language, and opens the doors to the recognition of ethnic diversity and a reflection on the autonomy of indigenous peoples. One of its antecedents is the Barbados Conference (1971), convened by the World Council of Churches in Berne, which gave rise to a critical declaration that brought together twelve renowned anthropologists, including Miguel Alberto Bartolomé, Darcy Ribeiro, and Guillermo Bonfil Batalla.[41]

The declaration expressed strong support for the processes of indigenous liberation and argued that indigenous people continued to be the subject of colonial domination, holding the state and its public policies, religious missions, and anthropology responsible for serving as instruments of such colonial domination. The document stated that *indigenista* policies had failed "both by error and omission," thus perpetuating genocide and ethnocide. The declaration concluded with a section entitled "The Indian as an Agent of His Own Destiny," where it stressed the need to incorporate them into national society while respecting their sociocultural specificities, regardless of their numbers, and emphasized that they should be the authors of their own history.

Another important event was the UNESCO meeting on ethno-development and ethnocide held five years later, in 1976, which was attended by indigenous organizations from several Latin American countries. The meeting insisted on the double nature of domination—economic and cultural—to which Indians were subjected. In the case of cultural domination, it blamed *indigenista* integration and acculturation policies, through the formal education system and the mass media. It therefore argued for the need for them to create their own political organization in order to achieve liberation.

One of the most emblematic representatives of critical anthropology was the Mexican Bonfil Batalla, author of a famed text cited above, "El concepto del indio en América: Una categoría de la situación colonial" (The concept of the Indian in America: A category of the colonial situation) published in 1972.[42] In it, Bonfil Batalla argues that the term *Indian* can be translated as *colonized*, a supra-ethnic category of the colonial order that implies recognizing two opposite poles: the colonized and the colonizer. He also proposed distinguishing between the colonial category of Indian and that of ethnicity, which is more descriptive and accounts for cultural diversity. Thus, for Bonfil Batalla, "the liberation of the colonized—breaking with the colonial order—implies the Indian's disappearance; but the Indian's disappearance does not imply suppressing ethnic units; on the contrary, it creates the possibility for them to regain control of their own history" (1972, 123).

In Bolivia in 1973, the Tiwanaku Manifesto, signed by a group of mainly Aymara indigenous organizations, criticized developmentalism and its unfulfilled promises and questioned political parties (which claimed to represent indigenous people) and peasant trade unionism, which had participated in the pact with the military. The manifesto concluded with a call to construct "a powerful autonomous peasant movement" (Primer Manifiesto de Tiahuanaco 1973).

The Katarist movement thus emerged at the time—a powerful political, trade union, and intellectual current that revisits the relationship between ethnicity and social class together with ethnic claims. According to Silvia Rivera Cusicanqui, the Katarists had the great idea to revisit the legacy of Tupac Katari, who was portrayed as an innocent precursor of the struggles for independence, and redefine him as a hero of the indigenous cause. The Katarist movement established itself as an ideological current capable of synthesizing cultural issues, political projections, and struggles for demands, both rural and urban (Rivera Cusicanqui [1984] 1987). On the other hand, while it questioned the mestizo and integrationist imaginary of the 1952 revolution, Katarism had the virtue of shortening the distance between the two poles of the tension established between the indigenous and the peasant, adopting the broader concept of *campesinado indio* (indigenous peasantry). The movement also expressed a deep distrust of both the right and the left, which saw Indians as a manipulable mass. It thus questioned the notion of Bolivia as a "mestizo nation" but did not abandon the idea of a Bolivian nation, critically revisiting the legacy of peasant unionism (Nicolas and Quisbert 2014, 40).

Bolivian political scientist and philosopher Luis Tapia argues that the emergence of Katarism was the main reason for the change in Bolivia's self-image— that is, the passage from a mestizo and more or less culturally united nation to a multicultural and multilingual Bolivia, not "as a mere ethnographic fact but as a product of the politicization of the peoples who had previously been excluded from the definition of what Bolivia is in political terms" (2006, 416).

In this regard, in a well-known article entitled "Marxismo e indianismo: El desencuentro entre dos razones revolucionarias" (Marxism and *indianismo*: The disparity between two revolutionary rationales; 2007), García Linera argues that Katarism is based on a denouncing and questioning discourse that reexamines history in its approach to the peasant/indigenous world.[43] It also redefined the "trade union" form, a legacy of the 1952 revolution, as a body of the new autonomous power. According to the author, there were three different lines of Katarism. First, there was trade unionism, illustrated by CSUTCB, which sealed the rupture with the trade union movements of the nationalist state and with the peasant military pact. Second, there was party politics, with two different expressions: the Tupac Katari Revolutionary Movement (Movimiento Revolucionario Tupac Katari; MRTK), which favored alliances with the left, and the Tupac Katari Indigenous Movement (Movimiento Indio Tupac Katari; MITKA), which advocated for the self-determination of indigenous peoples. The MRTK joined the electoral arena in the 1980s, and from it emerged Víctor Hugo Cárdenas, the Aymara vice president who accompanied the neoliberal Gonzalo Sánchez de Lozada in the 1990s, at the time of hegemonic multiculturalism. Later, the MITKA created an armed wing, in which the Aymara leader Felipe Quispe and the sociologists and mathematicians Álvaro García Linera and Raquel Gutiérrez participated.

Finally, there was an academic, historiographical, and sociological line illustrated by Silvia Rivera Cusicanqui and Xavier Albó. While Rivera directed the Workshop of Andean Oral History (Taller de Historia Oral Andina), promoting an alternative historiography that aimed at recovering the long-term memory of the struggles, connecting it with the short-term memory, Albó aimed at developing a history of Katarism "from below" (Nicolas and Quisbert 2014, 45). In short, Katarism proposed an alternative view that differed from Marxist revolutionary nationalism, in whose political and interpretive horizon there were no Indians or communities (García Linera 2007). Its political potency was expressed especially in CSUTCB, the trade union organization that was the protagonist of the great struggles of the previous decades, from which emerged, in addition to Felipe Quispe, Evo Morales himself (as representative of the six federations of coca growers of the Cochabamba tropic).

In addition, many people highlight Fausto Reinaga's influence on the Katarist discourse, even though he never participated in it. Beyond the obvious propagandist nature of his work, Reinaga promoted an *indianista* vision contrary to the idea of a *cholo* or mestizo Bolivia and to the workerist left, in texts such as *La revolución india* (The Indian revolution; 1970) and *Tesis india* (Indian thesis; 1971). Reinaga also founded the Indian Party (1970)—with no effect on national politics—and contributed to the discussion on *indianismo* and decolonization (his references to Frantz Fanon are constant), stressing the idea of the Indian not as an "ethnic minority" but as an "oppressed nation."

In short, although to different extents and in different ways, critical anthropology and Katarism contributed to the process of indigenous emergence and to the development of new models of indigenous militancy critical of the dominant paradigms (*indigenista*/nationalist, socioeconomic or classic Marxist, or exclusively *campesinista*), supporting the new organizational framework that vindicated autonomy and regard for Indianness as central topics.

The "indigenous awakening" cannot be understood without relating it to the growing relevance of international law in the context of the decolonization process that began after the end of World War II. Until the 1960s collective rights were not explicitly recognized by the United Nations (UN), since the exclusive subject of international law was the nation-state.[44] The 1948 Universal Declaration of Human Rights established equal rights and the principle of nondiscrimination, questioning the colonial paradigm. Thus began a process of decolonization, especially in Africa and Asia, where European powers had implemented an imperial policy. In this context, the UN took up the challenge of contributing to decolonization processes around the world, creating a number of institutions (special committees and human rights covenants) to ratify its commitment to peoples' right to self-determination.

However, the process whereby indigenous peoples in the Americas went from being considered "ethnic minorities" to "indigenous peoples and nations" was neither easy nor linear. While the decolonization doctrine was a watershed, the extensive legislation did not take into account those indigenous peoples who lived under conditions of discrimination and internal colonialism in republics that had been independent since the nineteenth century, as was the case in Latin American countries.

Thus, the process required the participation of indigenous organizations and leaders, as well as scholars and international NGOs, which, especially from the 1980s onward, engaged in intense discussions to introduce the issue of collective rights in the global agenda, in order for the indigenous peoples of the Americas (north and south) to be considered "colonized peoples." The UN in turn created a special committee (Committee of 24) on the granting of independence to colonial countries and peoples, endorsing the independence of dozens of countries from 1961 to the mid-1970s. It was in this context that indigenous peoples of the Americas began making demands in their struggle to be considered colonized peoples. In 1971 the UN Economic and Social Council authorized the Sub-Commission on Prevention of Discrimination and Protection of Minorities to elaborate a "study of the problem of discrimination against indigenous populations." The study was directed by rapporteur José Martínez Cobo, who compiled information on indigenous peoples around the world. Although indigenous peoples refused to be treated as "minorities" in their own territories, Martínez Cobo's report concluded with a series of recommendations that supported the demands of those peoples. Finally, in 1989 these recommendations were embodied in the modification of Convention 105 on Indigenous and Tribal Populations of 1957, which was replaced by International Labour Organization (ILO) Convention 169, which constituted an important innovation in the field of international law and opened the doors to a new paradigm, recognizing the collective rights of indigenous people as such, instead of the rights of individual people who are indigenous (Anaya 2006, 33). One of the main points of the convention was indigenous peoples' property rights over traditional lands, their right to be consulted as social groups through their representative institutions, and their collective right to maintain their own institutions and cultures. This convention was incorporated into most Latin American constitutions reformed between the late 1980s and the mid-1990s. It establishes free, prior, and informed consultation and determines that states shall hold consultations, including when modifying legal provisions on land and territory.

This process of broader rights was crowned by the Declaration on the Rights of Indigenous Peoples in 2007, adopted by the UN General Assembly. The text recognizes self-determination for all indigenous peoples. On the other hand, unlike Convention 169, the declaration fully incorporates the principle of free, prior, and informed consent for the removal of indigenous groups from their lands and for the adoption and implementation of legal and administrative measures that affect them, among other situations. In addition, it orders states to make reparations for all intellectual, cultural, or spiritual property that the indigenous groups have lost without their free, prior, and informed consent. On the other hand, it should be noted that these conventions are nonbinding, but by incorporating them in their constitutions, national states commit themselves to apply them, thus making them tools for indigenous organizations and human rights NGOs to exert pressure on those states.

In regional terms, in addition to these international norms, the Inter-American Court of Human Rights, which is part of the Organization of American States and whose pronouncements and sentences, unlike those of the aforementioned bodies, are binding, is also important. Other international instruments for the recognition of indigenous peoples were also established over time, such as those adopted by the 1992 UN Conference on Environment and Development, the Rio Declaration, and the more detailed "Agenda 21," which include topics related to environmental rights and so-called sustainable development.

In sum, in spite of the obvious gap between international norms and their application in the various Latin American countries, the notion of indigenous autonomy is at the basis of the new paradigm of collective rights. The appropriation of these legal tools accompanies the processes of empowerment of indigenous movements and organizations, in a context of increased ethnic conflicts and territorial disputes with transnational corporations and national states, especially since 2000, with the rise of extractivism.[45]

The Multicultural Paradigm Versus the Paradigm of Autonomy

GLOBALIZATION AND MULTICULTURALISM

Asymmetrical globalization implied dismantling the collective regulation frameworks developed in the Fordist era (in Latin American terms, the populist/developmentalist model), sustained on a state-centric approach, and entailed the establishment of the market as the primary mechanism for inclusion in accordance with the new demands of global capitalism. This resulted in a significant change in the patterns of social inclusion and exclusion, reflected in growing inequalities and an aggravation of the processes of dualization and social fragmentation. At the same time, these processes weakened national states as regulators of economic relations and led to the emergence of new frontiers and new forms of sovereignty beyond the nation-state.

The debates on the consequences and scope of globalization in relation to the nation-state are multiple and complex.[46] From a critical perspective, the analyses highlight the important transformations brought about by the globalization process at the level of the nation-states—which lost part of their sovereignty over economic processes and act as "moderators of national competitiveness in global competition, rather than as competitive national states" (Hirsch 2001) or as metaregulatory agents. In any case, globalization can be understood as a process whereby the political, social, and economic frontiers are surpassed, transforming the nation-state and giving rise to new forms of sovereignty and a new organization in the relationship between the economy and politics (Altvater 2000).

The transformations in the 1990s led to a change in the significance of the state and to a phenomenon of fragmentation of sovereignty. The formation of new frontiers (new economic blocks and political units) that concentrate the activity of developed nations resulted in processes of regionalization and fragmentation of the world economy, while illustrating the growing asymmetries between the nations of the North and the South. In peripheral countries, globalization deepened the processes of transnationalization of economic power, while dismantling the social state in its "populist/developmentalist" version. The background for this process was the "lost decade" (the 1980s, with the debt crisis, episodes of hyperinflation, and processes of pauperization). Consequently, the arrival of a new socioeconomic order implied a conjunction of both processes, including both opening and deregulation of the economy as a profound reform of the state apparatus, together with a "modernizing" discourse. Latin America entered the era of the Washington Consensus, which placed financial growth at the center and implied a policy of adjustments and privatization. The process of adjusting the state was crucial, but rather than being "extinguished" or appearing as a "residual" phenomenon, the state was reformulated, not only "toward the outside," but also "toward the inside," in terms of its interventions with respect to the most vulnerable sectors affected by neoliberal policies.

The dissolution of the regulatory model associated with the Fordist regime (whose impact in Latin America was always relative) also led to a reformulation of the role of the individual and of intermediate organizations in society. It is not by chance that a part of social theory focused on analyzing those processes in terms of new dynamics of individualization, believed to be the other side of the globalization process. In other words, in times of globalization, society requires individuals to take care of themselves and, regardless of their material and symbolic resources, to develop the necessary support networks and abilities to guarantee their access to social goods. However, the other side of deregulation is both individuation and the emergence and reinforcement of community ties and intermediate institutions (civil society organizations), which acquired a new key role in the very processes of subjectivation.

In short, globalization has two major dimensions: On one hand, understood as vertical globalization, it brings about new forms of domination, arising from both the transnationalization of capital and economic interdependence. On the other hand, understood as horizontal globalization, it has a double and contradictory scope: It entails a process of commodification of social affairs and strong individualization but also leads to the affirmation and defense of cultural diversity and local identities. The latter reading also entails a flourishing of identities, "related to the resistance of identity groups, but also to the globalizing logic of capital itself" (Díaz Polanco 2006b, 142). Thus, neoliberalism was accompanied by a new paradigm, multiculturalism, conceived as an ideology of diversity and the glorification of difference, with important consequences for Latin American countries with a significant indigenous population.

NEOLIBERAL MULTICULTURALISM AND ITS FACETS

Being different in order to be (because we are) modern.—CHRISTIAN GROS, speaking of multiculturalism, 2006

Multiculturalism is often criticized for its depoliticizing effects, in its search for an identity politics that disregards all issues related to inequalities or restructuring the economy (the tension between equality and difference). In this regard, it has been defined as "a method to manage diversity" (Bennett 1998), "the hybrid coexistence of diverse cultural life-worlds" (Žižek 1997, 176) in conjunction with global capitalism, or a politics dedicated to "administer[ing] differences" (Díaz Polanco, 2006b).

The multicultural paradigm, which had a significant impact in the countries of the North as a result of the massive migrations that took place beginning in the 1960s, is based on the concept of ethnic minorities. Toward the late 1980s, many analysts reflected on the new tensions that arose from immigration and the resulting cultural diversity, and called attention to the need to understand and accept cultural pluralism and implement policies that recognized such diversity. There were, however, great discrepancies between the theoretical positions of internationally renowned authors, who either invoked a multicultural citizenship based on minority rights (Kymlicka 1996) or alluded to the construction of a regime of recognition among equals (Taylor 1992).[47]

Conceived as "identity-based mediation with the political sphere" derived from multiple transformations, the multicultural paradigm was applied differently depending on the political contexts (Martuccelli 2008, 41). Of course, the political context of the expansion of multiculturalism in Latin America was very different from that in the North. This new paradigm was introduced in Latin America in a context of neoliberal reconfiguration of the state and intense indigenous mobilizations (Gros 2006). Neoliberalism, which became a sort of "single worldview" after the fall of the Berlin Wall and the collapse of Soviet communism, guided that dizzying process of reformulation of the state's role, activating new forms of intervention toward subaltern sectors. In this context, paraphrasing Nancy Grey Postero and León Zamosc (2005), multiculturalism was equated to the efforts of neoliberal and democratic governments to administer and organize ethnic differences through changes in their laws and constitutions (what Dona Lee Van Cott called "multicultural constitutionalism"). Regardless of regional differences, in Latin America multiculturalism was fostered by multilateral lending agencies (World Bank) and was implemented by the state, which promoted—in accordance with neoliberal logic—a policy of decentralization, seeking to create a sort of "multicultural governance," through both cultural management policies and poverty management.

Multicultural policies seduced Latin American intellectuals and scholars, especially in Andean countries such as Bolivia, Peru, and Ecuador, where the state has historically been weak and the role of community-based social organizations, as well as NGOs and foreign cooperation agencies, has been most important. In Bolivia, for example, the emphasis on ethnicity enabled an unprecedented agreement between a sector of Katarism and neoliberals. World Bank loans and programs were mainly destined for projects aimed at a chain of intermediaries who in turn reached out to the indigenous sectors, reformulating their role with the state.

In this context, we can identify two types of criticism of multiculturalism in Latin America. On one hand, there is a reading of the new theory in terms of the practice of domination, based not only on the importance acquired by external players but also on the role of the state as a player that organizes, manages, mediates, and seeks to control difference, constituting itself as a source of (new) dominated identities. On the other hand, a second line of interpretation points to the ambivalence of culturalism or, rather, proposes to insert multicultural policies in a recursive dynamic between the state and its apparatuses—through which the (potentially disruptive) action of social movements can emerge.

In the first line of thought is the work of the prominent Mexican anthropologist Héctor Díaz Polanco, who argues that multiculturalism considers differences to be nonconflictive, for they are cultural rather than political. This positive view of difference leads to the "praise of diversity" and the celebration of tolerance under the umbrella of "universal inclusion" (Díaz Polanco 2006b, 50–51). Multiculturalism thus signaled a (new) passage from ethnocide to ethnophagy, the latter understood as a process at the level of the Latin American nation-state, which included an "appetite for diversity," "for digesting or assimilating the communal," "for engulfing the other," rather than the brutal actions of the past (genocide/ethnocide) (50–51). Ethnophagy expressed itself as a set of "subtle forces that dissolve" the system by abandoning programs and actions aimed at destroying the culture of ethnic groups. In this regard, something similar to what happened with *indigenismo* as a dominant narrative occurred with multiculturalism. "Experience has shown that a 'good' *indigenismo* that serves the emancipation of peoples is impossible" (51). Multiculturalism operated as a sort of fifth column, just as *indigenismo* did in relation to indigenous peoples, whom it prepared to be *indigenista* ideologues instead of indigenous intellectuals (29). We thus found ourselves before a new deception of reason, another form of ethnophagy, in this case in accordance with the neoliberal cultural project operated from the top down.

Likewise, Argentine-Brazilian anthropologist Rita Segato distinguishes between what appears associated with the new identity politics (which operate as regimes of classification of customs, of culture, through the concept of "ethnicities") and the politics developed from below, identified with the return of the indigenous. Revisiting Indian essayist Partha Chatterjee, Segato contrasts "the homogeneous time of the nation" with the "heterogeneous time" manifested in the multiplicity of collective subjects that struggle to produce, return to, or give continuity to their own collectively developed historical narratives, giving rise to different historical "times" (2007, 21).

Finally, according to French anthropologist Guillaume Boccara, multicultural policies, seen as ethno-development, had a triple effect: territorialization, standardization of cultures, and professionalization of their bearers, introducing heteronomous logics where there had been relatively autonomous dynamics. "Indians are encouraged to become the ethnographers of their own community, and the new devices to manage difference and poverty contribute to insert them in a new field of generally dominated positions" (2011, 196).

In short, these three cursorily outlined critical perspectives contrast heteronomous multiculturalism with processes arising from an autonomous dynamic from below by social movements and organizations aimed at reinventing Indianness. In other words, from this perspective, it is impossible to conceive a critical or counterhegemonic multiculturalism.

There is a second type of position also derived from critical diagnoses that focus on the ambivalent nature of multiculturalism in Latin America, related to the social dialectics or recursive dynamics that these processes trigger from below, while highlighting the specificities of Latin American processes from a comparative standpoint. Thus, for example, according to the French specialist Cristian Gros, we should not forget that as a new definition of the nation, multiculturalism is accompanied by the recognition of new rights and intervenes after twenty years of indigenous mobilization, which cannot be interpreted solely as the result of manipulation by a Machiavellian state or the product of *indianista* NGOs (2006, 267). From his standpoint, the process of indigenous mobilization led to a politicization of cultural identities that was far from rejecting their belonging to the nation. Thus, while ethnic mobilizations appealed to a new imaginary that differed from mestizo nationalism, it was not conceived outside the nation; on the contrary, the multicultural or multiethnic nation aimed at overcoming that horizon, "perpetuating itself through mutation" (267). The emergence of an ethnic citizenship came hand in hand with the demand to "ethnicize the nation," which distinguishes Latin America from the segregationist and communitarian trends in other latitudes, as demonstrated by the Zapatista slogan "Never again a Mexico without us" (quoted in Gros 2006, 266–67) or the indigenous slogan in Ecuador, "Nothing only for Indians" (see Ospina 2022).

An even more suggestive interpretation is that of the US anthropologist Charles Hale (2002), a researcher of Central American indigenous communities, who argued for the need to assess whether the multicultural policies applied in Latin America resulted in a redistribution of resources to indigenous people through social movements, or whether they reinforced essentialist expressions of the groups. The author identifies two different types of multiculturalism: a "managed multiculturalism" with conventional liberal characteristics (also called "corporate" or "difference" multiculturalism), which celebrates cultural pluralism but implements few lasting changes for the members of the culturally oppressed group, and a "transformative" multiculturalism, mainly concerned with "redistributing power or resources" (Hale 2002, 494). Accordingly, it is important to distinguish between "top-down" and "bottom-up" multiculturalism, respectively. A second axis to consider is that if, contrary to its classical precursor, neoliberalism's cultural project contributes to revaluing and strengthening civil society and its "intermediate groups," then "neoliberal doctrine is predicated not on destroying the indigenous community in order to remake the Indian as citizen, but rather, re-activating the community as effective agent in the reconstitution of the Indian citizen-subject" (496).

It is true that the state not only "recognizes" the indigenous community, civil society, culture, and so on but also reconstitutes them in its own image, diverting them from their "radical excesses" and encouraging them to construct subjects (especially through NGOs), a task that would otherwise fall on the state itself. However, in Latin America the neoliberal project faced a complex network of heterogeneous social organizations that sought to open spaces to maneuver where counterhegemonies could be created. Thus, without overestimating the struggles "from within," it is certain that "the general analysis of what neoliberal multiculturalism is also points to the most effective means to confront its menace: social movements that simultaneously contest the relations of representation and the distribution of resources on which the neoliberal establishment rests" (Hale 2002, 498). It should be added, however, that in isolation from each other, these challenges tend to lose their transformative potential.

In sum, the issue of the dynamics established between identity politics and social organizations/movements remains an open discussion not devoid of complexities. It is true that multilateral agencies and official bodies invoked these forms of participation based on the recognition of difference in order to develop a "low-intensity" ethnic citizenship whose benefits to the new scheme of neoliberal domination cannot be ignored. However, there are nuances to the purely functional nature of the recognition of cultural rights. In this regard, it is worth recalling that reality is never lineal, for while the demand for identity/communitarian self-organization is, on one hand, a mandate promoted "from above" for the obvious purpose of social control and management of identity/otherness, it is also true that in certain cases, in the context of the struggles "from below," it has paved the way to new political opportunities. The most emblematic case, which demonstrates the double nature of multiculturalism, is Bolivia. In the 1990s, under neoliberal governments, indigenous rights were incorporated into the Constitution, and an educational reform was implemented that introduced bilingual education. Gonzalo Sánchez de Lozada, the president who consolidated the neoliberal turn, had as vice president Víctor Hugo Cárdenas, an indigenous politician and renowned member of the moderate wing of the Katarist movement. According to Nancy Grey Postero and León Zamosc (2005, 277), three laws directly related to multiculturalism were enacted: the Law of Popular Participation (Ley de Participación Popular; LPP), which decentralized the state by dividing the national territory into municipalities; the agrarian reform law, which created the Communal Lands of Origin (Tierras Comunitarias de Origen; TCO), defined as geographic spaces that constitute indigenous peoples' habitat; and the creation of specific institutions such as the Undersecretary's Office for Ethnic Affairs. As Postero notes, it was "a symbolic integration" that did not bring about material changes. For example, the impacts of both the agrarian reform and the actions of the Undersecretary's Office were limited. This was not the case, however, with the LPP, which effectively created new spaces for local participation. Xavier Albó, a strong advocate of the law, said that "with it, a key instrument to build local power was set in motion" (2008, 50). Not all was a matter of folklorizing identities in institutional spaces and taming social actors—by creating autonomous municipalities and indigenous districts, the LPP created new political opportunities for rural unions to advance toward institutional politics (Stefanoni 2010b, 118). The history of the Movement for Socialism–Political Instrument for the Sovereignty of the Peoples (Movimiento al Socialismo–Instrumento Político por la Soberanía de los Pueblos; MAS-IPSP), today the governing party, and of Evo Morales's dizzying rise in national politics is proof of the new structure of political opportunities created by the LPP, together with the institution of uninominal seats in Congress. It was in this context that the thesis of the "political instrument" of peasant/indigenous organizations emerged.[48] Officially, the MAS-IPSP was born in 1999, with a number of local electoral victories and the winning of several mayorships. In a repressive context, MAS-IPSP grew at a very fast rate, especially in rural districts. In 2002 Evo Morales was less than two points behind Gonzalo Sánchez de Lozada in the presidential elections.

In short, in spite of the new attempts at integration, in Bolivia the passage from the "allowed Indian" to the "rebellious Indian" was quick and vertiginous and had unforeseeable consequences for the political and economic elite.[49] Beginning in 2000, rural and urban social movements and organizations once again occupied the public space and the streets, with collective demands for national control of natural resources and deprivatization of basic services, which would lead to a reconfiguration of the political space. By 2005 one of the great achievements of Bolivian rural and urban social organizations was the convergence on a common program (the "October agenda"), which inscribed the collective struggles in a broader political horizon and enabled the rise to government of the Evo Morales/Álvaro García Linera pair.

AUTONOMY AS A NEW PARADIGM

For many people, the dominant multiculturalism deployed policies aimed at recognizing cultural diversity and folklorizing the local (on a global scale) for the purpose of blocking demands by integrating and demobilizing indigenous organizations.[50] However, the results varied widely depending on the case and context, because, in general, demands for autonomy and resistance to the model were strengthened by the struggles against neoliberal adjustment. In this context, the notion of autonomy gradually emerged as the great utopia that mobilized indigenous organizations and *indianista* thought.

Generally speaking, *autonomy* refers to the right of indigenous people to control their territories, to make sustainable use of their natural resources, and to create their own forms of self-government (Bengoa 2009). As a new paradigm in dispute, it has a double origin at the intersection of the local, the regional, and the global, for it refers to *indianista* struggles and ideas developed between the 1970s and the 1990s in different Latin American countries, as well as the recognition of collective rights based on the debates—and achievements—carried out in the international arena in the context of the new human rights paradigm. Let us recall that the debates at the UN resulted in the 1989 ILO Convention 169, and later in the UN Declaration on the Rights of Indigenous Peoples, which finally settled the internal discussions on self-determination as a key element in the process of recognizing collective rights.

At the regional level, it is worth highlighting the pioneering nature of the resolution of the conflict between Miskito Indians and the Nicaraguan government in the midst of the Sandinista revolution, which in 1987 led to the establishment of an "autonomy statute" encompassing about 50 percent of the national territory and 12 percent of the country's population (González 2010, 51). The Nicaraguan experience was a watershed for some Latin American anthropologists, allowing them to reflect on autonomy from a new theoretical/political perspective. Likewise, as Díaz Polanco (1991, 118–19) clarifies, the emergence of the debate on autonomy is related to the process of nationalization of struggles, which, in addition to Nicaragua, developed in countries such as Colombia,

Ecuador, and Chile, where organizations struggled for the recognition of regional autonomy.

In this sense, we witnessed a qualitative change from previous periods: From the 1980s onward, indigenous peoples burst into the political scene and became political forces on a national scale. This process of "nationalization" favored a broader political perspective that in many cases resulted in broader discursive platforms and programmatic horizons. "It is in this context that the autonomy regime, as a proposed solution to national ethnic conflicts and a legal/political framework whereby answers can be found to sociocultural demands, has become the subject of debate and analysis in recent years, as never before" (Díaz Polanco 1991, 118).

A symbolic turning point on this path toward autonomy as a myth and horizon was the counterfestivities on the fifth centennial of the "discovery" of America, for which there were several preparatory encounters and reflections that united organizations from the Andes and the Amazon with the rest of the continent. But even before that, there were a series of milestones that clearly demonstrated a change in the direction of indigenous protagonism. Thus, 1990 seems to signal an organizational turning point, with the first encounter of indigenous peoples held that year in Quito, where the participants arrived at the conclusion that "without an Indian government and territorial control, there is no autonomy" (quoted in Burguete Cal y Mayor 2010, 78). That same year, the Confederation of Indigenous Nationalities of Ecuador (CONAIE) carried out a series of blockades throughout the country, forcing then President Rodrigo Borja to negotiate. Never before had indigenous people appeared as "influential actors in Ecuadorian politics" (Pajuelo Teves 2007, 133). Also in 1990, the Confederation of Indigenous Peoples of the Bolivian East (CIDOB), one of the most important organizations in the Bolivian lowlands, which until then had had little visibility, organized a thirty-four-day march to La Paz called the March for the Territory and Dignity, which was a turning point for the demands of indigenous organizations in Bolivia. The marchers met with indigenous organizations from the highlands and were received by then President Jaime Paz Zamora, resulting in the creation of five indigenous or interethnic territories by presidential decree. From that point on, the concept of territory continued on its extraordinary rise, adopted by the organizations in the highlands as well.

Speaking of autonomy implies speaking of *the territory*, which refers to a set of spatial, economic, symbolic, and cultural dimensions. Even though until recently the concept of territory seemed to have an exclusively technical character, reserved for discussions among geographers, urban planners, and architects, in recent decades it became a sort of fetish notion and disputed concept for both indigenous/peasant organizations and other urban and rural movements. As Bernardo Mançano Fernandes (2009) says, "We coexist with different types of territories that produce and are produced by different, constantly disputed social relations." On the other hand, territoriality is related to the territory's uses and forms of appropriation. This takes place in a relational and complex space in which logics of action and rationalities that entail different assessments intersect, which can lead to a "tension of territorialities" (Porto Gonçalves 2001).[51]

The notion of territory has become emblematic today, a sort of "total social concept" that is key to read the position of the various players in conflict and, even more, the operation of society in general, in the current phase of capital accumulation. Thus, for indigenous communities, the territory comprises a set of dimensions related to the control of space and natural resources and the affirmation of a certain culture and historicity and a particular relationship with nature. Conceived from a multidimensional perspective, the territory is at the origin—or configuration—of a certain identity and gradually institutes a "territorial/identity question," with its particularities according to region and country, which "involves frameworks for confrontation and strategies of domination and resistance, of sovereignty and emancipation" (Rojas Piérola 2009, 157).

To conclude this section, I would like to mention some of the challenges posed by the notion of autonomy in terms of ethnic struggles and theoretical/political changes. One of the great challenges was how to conceive the transformations of the state in the context of the incorporation/acceptance of autonomy, whether as a political regime or incorporated under other modalities that imply secondary recognition (autonomous regimes). The struggles' demand for autonomy led to the establishment of certain regimes of territorial autonomy recognized by the state. There are at least six Latin American countries whose constitutions recognize some sort of regime of indigenous or multiethnic autonomy: Panama (1972), Nicaragua (1987), Colombia (1991), Venezuela (1999), Ecuador (1998), and Bolivia (2009). In addition, there are the de facto autonomies emerging in Mexico (González 2010, 36).

The communities are undoubtedly the instrument or point of departure for the construction of autonomies. However, it is important to distinguish between communitarian autonomy and regional autonomy, as Francisco López Bárcenas (2011, 87–91) and Héctor Díaz Polanco (2008, 251) do. Communitarian autonomies emerge as a concrete expression of indigenous peoples' resistance to colonialism. In the dynamics of the struggle, the communities sought to have their rights recognized, to transform/validate through the law what already existed in practice (recognition of their land and territory and their right to elect their own authorities, to exercise community justice, to establish a community police force, etc.). International legislation recognizes such rights; however, since they are recognized as "communities" and not as "peoples," they are subordinated to the local government, thus limiting the viability of those rights. Regional autonomies in turn emerged as a means to go beyond the communities (López Bárcenas 2011, 89), based on the model of Nicaraguan regional autonomies and Spain's autonomy regime. According to López Bárcenas, even though some social movements advocated for regional autonomy in opposition to communitarian autonomy, their actions demonstrated the viability of their articulation (as exemplified by Zapatismo, as we shall see below). Furthermore, in addition to these communitarian and regional tendencies, "there are those who demand the foundation of national states based on indigenous cultures" (90). This process of refounding the state was finally denominated the *plurinational state*, a concept that initially emerged in Ecuador in the late 1980s and was one of the main objectives of the constituent assembly in the context of the new Bolivian government, with the rise of Evo Morales.

For Díaz Polanco (1991, 2008), true, complete autonomy implies not only the recognition of cultural rights but also self-determination of indigenous peoples, that is, a legal political regime that recognizes their right to elect their authorities (self-government), to control their territories (and their natural resources), to exercise justice (indigenous justice), to legislate their internal life, and to manage their own affairs. As a new political paradigm, it poses new challenges regarding the transformation of the state, for it implies breaking with its centralist logic. It implies conceiving a new concept/challenge, paving the way to imagine "a pluralist transformation of the state" (García Linera et al. 2007).

Finally, among the many studies on the topic, it is worth examining the distinction proposed by Araceli Burguete Cal y Mayor (2010), who argues that autonomy has been understood in basically two ways by indigenous struggles. On one hand, there is autonomy as an end, with various (regional) expressions, such as in Nicaragua, or as a fundamental part of the organization of a plurinational state (the Bolivian challenge). On the other hand, autonomy as a process is related to the new political grammar of indigenous struggles, through which peoples and organizations deploy strategies, proposing spaces of freedom, territorial control, and self-government. "Both strategies account for the progressive construction of a theoretical/political, conceptual, and programmatic field that has made the right to self-determination its inspirational axis" (65).

In sum, autonomy has become one of the most employed and debated concepts today to understand the processes of indigenous mobilization in Latin America, but it also refers to an indigenous political project that proposes a crucial reform of the national state. For this reason, we will return to the subject when discussing some of the current debates. Before doing so, however, it is important to examine the specificities of the Peruvian case, which we have not included in the examples examined so far.

THE DILEMMAS OF THE PERUVIAN CASE

Many authors have written about the exceptionality of the Peruvian case in the current context of emergence and reinvention of Indianness, wondering why there is no Indian movement in Peru, as is the case in Bolivia and Ecuador. Considering that the latest CEPAL data (2014) estimate that the indigenous population represents 24 percent of the total population, the lack of a clearly representative national indigenous federation might seem to be not just an exception but a failure.

As Xavier Albó (2008, 171) observes, it is paradoxical that Peru, a pioneering country in conveying indigenous peoples' political potential, did not participate in the rise of the struggles and the intellectual elaboration of Indianness that characterized Latin America from 1970 onward. It suffices to recall the work of the precursor Manuel González Prada, as well as the interesting debates carried out in Mariátegui's time, to perceive the importance of this political tradition.

A number of factors explain this process of "de-Indianization."[52] On one hand, after Mariátegui's death, *indigenista* positions were condemned by the Third International and the Communist Party in favor of a more uniformly class-based strategy. In later years, the deployment of a peasant identity, the preeminence of a class-based language in the two agrarian confederations, the persistence of derogatory content associated with the term *Indian*, its association with the rural context and illiteracy... in short, the lack of a (true) state *indigenismo*—to confront and question—beyond the late military populism experienced with Velasco Alvarado, reinforced the process of de-Indianization by gradually absorbing indigenous people as peasants. It is also important to recall that as Degregori (1995) and de la Cadena (2000) analyzed, the Inca past was reappropriated early on by the Cuzco elite as part of its strategy to differentiate itself from the Hispanicizing coastal elite, which made it difficult for the Andean peasants to (re)appropriate it as well.

The de-Indianization process is also related to the increased complexity of ethnic categories, visible in the emergence of new social groups among subaltern sectors (the *cholo* or indigenous mestizo, the *serrano* or highlander, the *plebe urbana* or urban populace). Some authors argue that there was also no group of indigenous intellectuals who spoke their languages and elaborated a critical view of reality, as was the case with the Katarists in Bolivia (Montoya

Rojas 2006, 238). De la Cadena goes even further, stating that "most intellectuals believed that Indians were incapable of creating their own leadership. Only those who had overcome their Indianness and had become *cholos* were peasant leaders" (2000; 2004, 329).[53]

The decline of the *indigenista* current is also related to the "Shining Path effect," which obliterated any chance of recovering the Andean utopia. All authors underline the disastrous effects of the civil war in the 1980s and 1990s, in particular the Shining Path's strategy toward peasant sectors, who were the main victims of the dirty war, which claimed the lives of more than seventy thousand people—three-fourths of the total population of Quechua and Aymara origin, according to Rodrigo Montoya Rojas (2006, 239). As a result, unlike Bolivia and Ecuador, Peru was not exactly a hospitable context for NGOs, missions, or even trade unions, due to the levels of repression and persecution by both the Peruvian army and the Shining Path (Lucero and García 2006).

Although multiculturalism did not have the same state presence as it did in Bolivia, it was partially adopted by the government of President Alejandro Toledo (2001–6), a *cholo* who promoted Inca symbolism and sought to build ties between the state and indigenous confederations (with the COPPIP, Conference of Indigenous Peoples of Peru), even though his government soon excluded them and deployed an anti-indigenous policy.[54] A second line of interpretation, which complements and also qualifies the de-Indianization thesis, is proposed by Marisol de la Cadena (2000; 2004, 322), who raises the cultural force of miscegenation and deploys as one of her central hypotheses the emergence of an indigenous culture that goes beyond Indianness and includes subordinated definitions of the mestizo. In other words, rather than concealing the Indian, there was a different definition of "indigenous culture" that included the mestizo or defined itself as such, shaking off the negative or stigmatizing elements of Indianness that allude to poverty, illiteracy, and rurality (322–33). It is not by chance that her book is entitled *Indigenous Mestizos: The Politics of Race and Culture in Cuzco*.

Finally, there is a third line of reading opposed to the "teleological discourse" of some observers who seek to incorporate Peru into the general Indian recovery movement (Lucero and García 2006). In addition to considering that historically Amazonian organizations have a longer tradition in Peru than in many places in Ecuador and Bolivia, they conclude that in contemporary Peru, as in other countries, there is a broad spectrum of indigenous identities and movements. Nor is it possible to ignore that new organizations have emerged in recent decades, even outside the large peasant confederations—among them, the National Confederation of Peruvian Communities Affected by Mining

(Confederación Nacional de Comunidades del Perú Afectadas por la Minería; CONACAMI), which successfully placed the discussion about megamining on the national agenda, while going beyond an environmentalist language critical of the development model to the reaffirmation of an indigenous identity and the defense of cultural and territorial rights. Along this line of radicalization, the Andean Coordinator of Indigenous Organizations (Coordinadora Andina de Organizaciones Indígenas; CAOI) was created in 2006, bringing together organizations from Peru, Bolivia, Colombia, Chile, and Argentina. However, it is important to recognize that CONACAMI's process of "Indianization" is more discursive than practical, deployed by its leaders rather than at the grassroots level, related to the "Bolivian effect" as a result of contact with different Bolivian organizations, and strengthened by Evo Morales's rise to the presidency.

On the other hand, we must include in the Peruvian organizational map the Interethnic Association for the Development of the Peruvian Rainforest (AIDESEP), the main organization that brings together the Amazonian populations, vindicating their indigenous identity, thus complicating not only the traditional binary established between the sierra and the coast but also the assertion that there is no elaboration of Indianness in Peru. It is important to emphasize that CONACAMI's and AIDESEP's actions in recent years are related to the struggles against transnational corporations and the state, in the face of the expansion of the extractive frontier (megamining, oil, megadams, agribusiness). Thus, even though AIDESEP operates at a regional scale, its presence in the current universe of indigenous struggles questions the notions of "absence" or "failure" regarding the "return of the Indian" in Peru—or at least it indicates that such statements must be nuanced.

In short, in Peru the tension field between the indigenous, the peasant, and the mestizo, and between the rural and the urban, developed in a particular manner, gradually distancing itself from the type of *indianista* demands that are dominant today in Latin America, which does not mean, however, that there are no social movements and organizations that claim an indigenous identity. They are peoples struggling for the observance of collective rights, especially ILO Convention 169, which establishes the right to prior consultation.

TOWARD A MULTICULTURAL PARADIGM IN ARGENTINA

For paradoxical reasons, Argentina entered the multiculturalist paradigm almost without having gone through the integrationist *indigenista* paradigm. Thanks to the contribution of indigenous organizations, NGOs, and specialists on the subject, the reform of the 1994 Constitution definitively swept away

Article 67, Section 15, replacing it with Article 75, Section 17, which states, "To recognize the ethnic and cultural preexistence of Argentine indigenous peoples. To guarantee respect for their identity and their right to a bilingual and intercultural education; to recognize the legal status of communities and the communal possession and ownership of the lands traditionally occupied by them; and to regulate the acquisition of other lands suitable and sufficient for human development; none of them shall be alienable, transferable, or subject to encumbrances and embargos. To guarantee their participation in the management of their natural resources and other interests that affect them. The provinces may exercise these powers concurrently."

Argentina has legislation in line with the new times, incorporating the most advanced international regulations on the subject. For example, ILO Convention 169—one of the fundamental tools for the defense of land and territory, which establishes free, prior, and informed consultation—adopted by all Latin American constitutions, was incorporated in 1994, even though it only became effective in 2001. Likewise, in 2007 Argentina accepted the UN Declaration on the Rights of Indigenous Peoples.

Thus, far from being exclusive to countries with a strong communal tradition, the process of political empowerment—and the new threats to indigenous communities—includes nations such as Argentina, where, since the 1970s, through the 1990s, and to the present day, there has been an important and persistent process of identity reconstruction. This process has been further driven by the struggles of different indigenous communities and organizations against the various forms of extractivism, especially the expansion of the soybean and mining frontier, land grabbing and real estate speculation—through tourism and residential developments—and the exploitation of conventional and unconventional hydrocarbons. In addition, in 2006, at the organizations' request and in an increasingly conflictive context, Law 26.160 was passed, prohibiting evictions of indigenous communities and ordering the implementation of a territorial survey. Finally, at the provincial level, there is important legislation on indigenous peoples that reflects national and international regulations. Some of this legislation, such as the new provincial constitution of Neuquén, reformed in 2006, declares the "ethnic and cultural preexistence of indigenous people as 'an inseparable part of the provincial identity and idiosyncrasy.'"

However, this legal framework deployed at various levels (provincial and national, following international regulations) differs from reality. To get an idea of this, it suffices to examine the final report of the UN Rapporteur on Indigenous

Peoples, James Anaya (2012), who visited Argentina in 2011 to gather testimonies and complaints from the communities. The report paints quite a troublesome landscape, highlighting environmental and cultural impacts, fragmentation of the social fabric, lack of prior consultation (ILO Convention 169), violent evictions, criminalization, and repression, among other issues. This report demonstrates not only that the current legislation is not applied but also that, despite the existence of "emergency" regulations such as the aforementioned Law 26.160, very few provinces have initiated land surveys, while violent evictions continue (in Formosa, Neuquén, Salta, and Jujuy, among other provinces). Nor should we forget that the great crisis of 2002 led to an important inflection in the relationship between the state and indigenous peoples, to the extent that it once again encapsulated the indigenous issue in poverty assistance programs (Lenton and Lorenzetti 2005). Their definition as "vulnerable subjects," as poor people, tends to naturalize the problem and to minimize indigenous peoples' claims as political subjects.

On the other hand, in those years, groups considered extinct, such as the Selk'nam (Ona) community in Tierra del Fuego, the Huarpes in San Juan and Mendoza, and the Rankulches, as well as indigenous collectives in exclusively urban contexts, began making identity-based demands. The emergence of these demands has led to debates on the issue of authenticity, highlighting the importance of markers such as language or even "rurality," sustained in an essentialist and not constructivist or dynamic understanding of ethnicity. In addition to this debate, there is another one on the "Chilean" origin of Mapuche peoples, a recurrent accusation by economic elites and conservative political sectors against one of the most active and mobilized peoples in the country, especially in the province of Neuquén (Impemba 2013).

On the other hand, at the beginning of this chapter, we referred to the Museum of Natural Science in La Plata, inextricably linked to the so-called Conquest of the Desert and racialist positivism, where indigenous remains were exhibited for more than a century. In 1991 the descendants began demanding the restitution of the remains of Cacique Inacayal to his community of origin in Teca, in Chubut province. This first restitution finally took place in 1994 after the respective law was approved (1991). As Liliana Tamagno, professor of anthropology at the National University of La Plata (Universidad Nacional de La Plata), observes, this initiated a path of no return.[55] In 2001 the restitution of Cacique Rankulche Panguitruz Guor—also known as Mariano Rosas—had greater institutional support and public presence (Tamagno 2009, 108). That same year, National Law 25.517 was approved, defining and regulating a policy of restitution of remains. In one of its articles, the law establishes that "the mortal remains of aboriginal people, whatever their ethnic characteristics, which are part of museums and/or public and private collections, must be restituted to the indigenous peoples and/or communities of origin that claim them." The norm was enacted in 2010 and established that the National Institute for Indigenous Affairs (Instituto Nacional de Asuntos Indígenas; INAI) would be in charge of coordinating and carrying out the restitutions.

Special attention must be paid to the enormous work carried out by Colectivo Guías, University Research Group on Social Anthropology, created in 2006 to "respond to the demands made by indigenous peoples to the Faculty of Natural Sciences and the Museum of the National University of La Plata, to stop exhibiting all human collections that are part of that museum and to restitute them to their communities." Since 2006 the collective has promoted four restitutions (Pepe et al. 2014).

On the other hand, although there are appeals to the plurinational state and autonomy, the dominant paradigm is multiculturalism, in the context of a national government that has engaged with indigenous communities and organizations from a national-popular standpoint. In other works, I have analyzed how Kirchnerism updates the populist narrative and its various phases (Svampa 2011). Briones, who specifically addresses how the national-popular approach toward indigenous organizations has operated, follows a similar line: "As a synthesis of this new reading, INAI's president Daniel Fernández explains that, with the Kirchner administrations, the country resumed the lost 'national and Latin American course,' which implies recognizing that we are 'a nation consolidated in its mestizo roots and its pluricultural nature, with a multiethnic population that is the historical subject of sovereignty'" (2014, 27).

As a result, as was the case in other areas (human rights organizations, organizations of the unemployed, cultural sectors, and trade unions), the populist narrative reconfigured the public space, creating a severe division in the militant field between those who support the government and those who do not. While the upsurge of a historical indigenous adherence to Peronism can be explained by a number of factors, many leaders acknowledge that Kirchnerist governments "created unprecedented spaces for dialogue between the state and indigenous people" (Briones 2014, 28), although of course there are many organizations that maintain an independent and critical stance.[56] However, this articulation between a populist and an indigenous/communal matrix is symptomatic of a weakness rather than a strength, since it has by no means translated into an integral *indigenista* policy that encompasses both their right over land and territory in the face of the advancement of the extractive frontier, and a policy of reparation in the face of indigenous genocide.

As Walter Delrio and colleagues (2010) argue:

The current Argentine government, which has made progress in making visible and vindicating the memory of the victims of the last dictatorship, has not similarly recognized the genocide and crimes against humanity committed against indigenous peoples. In the specific case of the trial regarding the events in Napalpí in 1924, the state refuses to recognize the Qom or Tobas as a specific ethnic group, arguing that, in that case, a crime against humanity possibly does expire. At the same time, it fosters educational plans with the specific purpose of promoting interculturality, bilingual education, and tolerance. The case of Rincón Bomba, which took place in Formosa in 1947, is in a similar situation.

Finally, even in a highly dramatic and barely visible context, indigenous people have helped place the issue of the territory and territorial and socioenvironmental problems on the public agenda. There are a number of common threads and elements present in eco-territorial disputes, from the long conflict in the Loma de la Lata oil field (Neuquén) beginning in the mid-1990s, to the persistent persecution of the Qom of the Primavera Community (Formosa), all the way to the recent conflicts due to the exploitation of conventional and nonconventional hydrocarbons: ethnic discrimination, environmental racism, nonrecognition of indigenous rights over the territory, lack of prior consultation as established in ILO Convention 169, violent evictions, sustained criminalization based on criminal offenses such as "usurpation," and murders and dubious deaths in the areas around the agricultural frontier (Chaco, Tucumán, Formosa, Salta, Santiago del Estero).

In short, the weight of the original genocide, the onerous debts accumulated by the Argentine state toward indigenous peoples, and most especially the expansion of the extractive frontier in the context of the current accumulation model once again raise the question of the place of native peoples in Argentina today. It is no doubt a disturbing question that coincides with the revival of long-term memory, since once again indigenous peoples seem to occupy territories coveted by capital—whether because of megamining, dams, or tourist and residential megaprojects, indigenous people seem to have once again become an obstacle to "development."

———

In recent decades, we have witnessed a rise of indigenous people and an opening of political opportunities, evident in the conjunction of the international agenda (the discussions at the UN, in the context of the decolonization process, of the collective rights of indigenous peoples, which resulted in ILO Convention 169 and the UN Declaration of the Rights of Indigenous Peoples), regional and national agendas (crisis of the modernizing, developmentalist state; the failure of integration according to a mestizo/peasant identity; the increasingly massive presence of indigenous people in the cities), and political/ideological issues (the crisis of Marxism and the revaluation of an identity construction anchored in culture).

In a tension field between the competing paradigms of multiculturalism and autonomy, what some have called *ethnic citizenship* was gradually consolidated, first based on the demand for cultural rights, followed by—or in parallel with, depending on the case—indigenous peoples' demand for self-determination and self-government. As in other latitudes, the very process of mobilization implies different ways of understanding identity: from primordialism, which asserts that there is an identity prior to the Spanish conquest and the constitution of the national state, to those who understand identity as a cultural construct, a positive identity reformulation that resignifies the colonial past in both rural and urban contexts; in both cases, the appeal to ethnicity results from historical forces, making it both structural and cultural (Jean and John Comaroff, cited in Bartolomé 2006). Likewise, the appeal to ethnic citizenship becomes an essential political tool in the dynamics of empowerment of indigenous peoples, especially in the process of the defense of land and territory, in a context of expansion of the extractive frontier.

By positively reappropriating certain concepts in a context of struggle, indigenous peoples aim to invert the hegemonic common sense (the stigmatization of the Indian), to disrupt or modify the frameworks of colonial domination (the monocultural state), and to reformulate them in a new language whereby Indians are conceived as subjects and political actors, based on the exercise of collective rights and their demand for autonomy. As Díaz Polanco (2008) says, when we say *autonomy* when speaking of the processes of indigenous struggle, we are alluding both to the recognition of collective (cultural and territorial) rights and to self-determination, a concept with a decidedly political content. On the other hand, in the context of struggles for territorial recognition and control and for autonomy, and with the contacts with other insurgent collective subjects—urban and rural, cultural and social, youth and women—new frameworks for collective action gradually emerged: a new nonconformist narrative constituted in Latin America at the crossroads of indigenous discourse and environmentalist language, where different horizon-concepts converge: the rights of nature, common goods, environmental justice, food sovereignty, Good Living or Living Well.

In short, the challenges are as enormous as the paradoxes. On one hand, the expansion of collective rights goes hand in hand with the expansion of the frontiers of capital—in its new phase of accumulation, linked to extractivism and dispossession. On the other hand, once the Washington Consensus was questioned and the limits and distortions of the multicultural rhetoric were recognized, even in the context of new governments considered progressive or leftist, the *indianista* narrative collided with the national state narrative, linked to the Latin American populist tradition.

2

Between the Obsession with Development and Its Critique

In the eighteenth and nineteenth centuries, in the context of various political and economic revolutions, the notions of progress and civilization became powerful core ideas that gradually shaped a certain worldview or grand narrative about modernity. These core ideas had a significant impact on the social thought and the politics of the various Latin American countries in the nineteenth century, where the obsession to enter "progress" and modernity was inextricably linked to the desire to eradicate "barbarism" in the Americas and its "endemic evils," associated with the indigenous population and the Spanish Catholic legacy.

In the twentieth century, after the end of World War II, the notions of progress and civilization were replaced by the category of development, which, like its predecessors, became one of the core ideas of the modern hegemonic discourse. However, the various discourses and narratives define development differently depending on the factors and ideas with which it is associated. Over time, these various incarnations of the concept led to different problematics, among which are those related to the relationship between development and progress, development and nature, or development and freedom (Unceta Satrústegui 2009). The field of development and its various problematics thus became a rather complex subject involving a myriad of economic, political, and social institutions and actors, which must be understood in the context of different national, regional, and global scales and agendas. As a result, we find a multiplicity of intervening actors: governments, multinational corporations, national and international bodies, social organizations and movements, nongovernmental organizations (NGOs), technicians, scholars, and intellectuals, among others.

In this chapter, I examine two problematic fields: the relationship between development and progress and that between development and nature. On the one hand, the first problematic field—the relationship between development and progress—led to the emergence of the productivist paradigm, whose axes are economism and the idea of indefinite or unlimited growth. This paradigm was hegemonic and mostly unchallenged until 1940, and even today—in spite of the various philosophical, economic, and ecological critiques that have undermined its bases and legitimacy—it has an extraordinary ability to adapt itself and incorporate new languages, occupying a prominent position in the dominant discourse. On the other hand, the second problematic field has to do with the tense relationship between development and nature, historically based on a dualist ontology and a hierarchical view (of subordination of nature to the notion of development). This field is increasingly linked to environmental issues, which have been incorporated into the international agenda since the 1970s, together with new social movements and reflections by thinkers and intellectuals concerned with environmental degradation and the future of civilization. The emergence of the concept of sustainable development, its various incarnations, and its later failure illustrate the political and intellectual challenge of filling the increasingly visible gap between development and environmental protection.

Given the above, I present some of the lines of the productivist paradigm and the environmental paradigm as they have been formulated in Latin America. First, I examine the Economic Commission for Latin America and the Caribbean (Comisión Económica para América Latina y el Caribe; CEPAL) in terms of the topics addressed by it and some of its authors, who introduce the concept of center/periphery to read asymmetries and obstacles to development. Second, I propose an examination of the notion of sustainable development and the alternative perspectives that have emerged in Latin America, regarding both the productivist paradigm and the sustainable development paradigm. Here I approach the second problematic field by briefly examining the representation of nature in Latin America, as well as the emergence of new disciplines and social movements that problematize environmental issues.

The Development Paradigm

The legacy of classical thinking was the consolidation of a productivist conception of progress based on material achievements and the rise of economics as a paradigmatic "science" to explain such processes. As José Manuel Naredo (2006) explains, the idea of an economic system, with its merry-go-round of production, consumption, and growth, and the mutation of the latter into development, was imposed. As a result, production was no longer considered a means, becoming an end in itself, emphasizing and recording in monetary terms only the positive part of the economic process (overshadowing the degradation that the process inflicts on its physical and social surroundings). Thus, growth of the national income was perceived as universally desirable regardless of its content, external factors, or unintended consequences. Likewise, economic growth was considered more important than distribution, thus becoming a goal in itself, so that the degree of a country's development was measured by its production capacity, that is, the set of goods and services produced by a country (gross domestic product [GDP]). Thus emerged "the mythology of economic growth," one of whose consequences was economistic reductionism.

The mythology of economic growth found a new and decisive impulse at the end of World War II, which signaled the recognition of US hegemony and the beginning of the decolonization process in Africa and Asia. Thus, beginning in 1944, a series of economic institutions and international bodies centered on the issue of development were created, among them, the United Nations (UN; formerly the League of Nations), the Food and Agriculture Organization of the United Nations (FAO), and a number of regional economic commissions: the Economic Commission for Asia and the Far East (ECAFE) in 1947; the Economic Commission for Latin America and the Caribbean (CEPAL) in 1948; and the International Bank for Reconstruction and Development (IBRD) in 1944, among others. The International Monetary Fund (IMF) was also created in 1944. In this context, in his inauguration speech, US President Harry Truman announced, "The old imperialism—exploitation for foreign profit—has no place in our plans. What we envisage is a program of development based on the concepts of democratic fair-dealing . . . that contributes to the improvement and growth of underdeveloped areas" (quoted in Naredo 2006, 178). Truman's speech thus positioned the nascent international institutional framework around the issue of development, while introducing the notion of underdevelopment to refer to "backward" countries, which was relatively new in the economic and political language. It is commonly said that this speech was a watershed in political and symbolic terms, because from then on the development/underdevelopment duality would be employed to explain economic, social, and political inequalities between countries. Thus, while underdevelopment—in which almost one billion people lived—became a contemptible condition from which it was imperative to escape, development became a universal, homogeneous value, the supreme object of desire and the new Western mythology (Esteva [1992] 2002).

It was in this context that development economics emerged, becoming an important subdiscipline of economics that dealt with the obstacles to sustained economic growth that emerged in certain contexts—basically in the countries that became independent after World War II—and sought ways to overcome them. The subdiscipline was articulated with the Keynesian ideas dominant at the time. Its better-known representatives were Ragnar Nurkse, Paul Rosenstein-Rodan, Walt Rostow, William A. Lewis, and Gunnar Myrdal, among others, considered "the pioneers of development" (Unceta Satrústegui 2009, 7).

In the early 1960s, the UN proclaimed the "Development Decade," motivated by the belief that the solution to all problems was the effective transfer of technology from rich countries to poor ones. Economic growth was to follow a series of stages, outlined by Rostow (1960) in his renowned book *The Stages of Economic Growth: A Non-Communist Manifesto*, which argued that the backwardness of the less developed nations was transitory and a necessary stage in the historical process of societies. From this evolutionary standpoint, development was only a matter of time. Hence, backward countries should derive inspiration from the more advanced economies and follow their example. By following guidelines and acting judiciously, they could enter the takeoff phase and launch themselves into growth, shortening the distance between them and the rich or developed countries.

In Latin America a growing concern with the issue of underdevelopment led to a new economic and social approach that questioned the evolutionary and normative viewpoint of the hegemonic discourse. Thus, a new, original, and heterodox theory of development emerged, not only offering a different explanation but also proposing public policies to overcome the obstacles to development present in underdeveloped countries. This theory was elaborated within CEPAL, and its main intellectual representatives were Raúl Prebisch, Celso Furtado, Aníbal Pinto, and Juan F. Noyola, among others. I shall present the main axes of CEPAL's perspective on development below.

CEPAL ... our only prestigious cultural institution at an international level, and justly so. Only taking into account the effects of the scale and type of recruiting can one explain the apparent miracle achieved by CEPAL: an organization financed by the United Nations (and therefore indirectly by the United States) becomes a center for Latin American identity and a new, autonomous, and creative thought. We need ten or twelve CEPALs in Latin America. Let us be clear: ten or twelve, not four hundred.—TORCUATO DI TELLA, "La formación de una conciencia nacional en América Latina" (The formation of national consciousness in Latin America), 1966

In 1948 Argentine economist Raúl Prebisch published his work "El desarrollo de la América Latina y algunos de sus principales problemas" (The development of Latin America and some of its main problems) (republished in 2013), a sort of political theoretical manifesto that set the bases for a new paradigm, the structuralist paradigm, calling for people to adhere to it not only throughout the continent but also in other parts of the planet. In his presentation Prebisch explained the differences between the economies of the center and those of the periphery through a comparative analysis centered on Latin America's commercial evolution and history. This was the decisive step toward the construction of a theory of international economics based on the distinction between two poles, the center and the periphery, whose fundamental core was the deteriorating terms of interchange for Latin America.

Prebisch's first main argument was that the problematic of development in Latin America was by no means a matter of time but rather illustrated a problem of the economic structure, directly related to the international division of labor.[1] That was the origin of our peripheral condition. The central thesis is that while the center has a diversified structure, generates technical progress, and increases its productivity, the periphery has a simple structure and benefits from technological advances only when the center allows it. Thus, categories such as center, periphery, and structural heterogeneity became central to understanding underdevelopment as a historically determined cultural form, whose consequence is that most of the effects of capital accumulation and technological incorporation go to developed countries and not to peripheral ones.

Likewise, the periphery's limited productivity generates a labor surplus that tends to push wages down and hinders the domestic market's expansion. One of the main problems is therefore the deteriorating terms of exchange, which explains why the prices of raw materials grow more slowly than those of manufactured products. An economy based on the specialization of primary products can certainly grow at certain moments (when an economic cycle is on the rise). This happened, for example, with Argentina's agro-export model, but a change in international conditions (lower raw material prices) revealed a very weak and vulnerable economic structure.

The proposal created by CEPAL under Prebisch's leadership had heterodox consequences, since, according to it, Latin America should reject the formulas associated with classical economics, which sentenced the subcontinent to economic specialization by country (the "comparative advantages" of primary-export production), in order to forge its own path. On the other hand, the stages of development were far from uniform. Tardy development in peripheral countries exhibited different dynamics from those of the nations that had developed early on, such as European countries or the United States. In proactive terms, there were two basic ways to overcome a country's peripheral condition in the international division of labor: On one hand, a series of structural and institutional reforms to foster industrialization, substituting a model of "outward growth," centered on the production and export of raw materials, with a model of "inward growth," driven by import substitution industrialization (ISI). On the other hand, CEPAL understood the state as a "core idea."[2] In view of structural failures and weak economic actors, a key concept was state planning, which implied asserting that it was the state that should lead the development process. As a result, development was understood as a process of global structural change that implied profound reforms in terms of public policies. Thus, state intervention implied, among other things, planning development, designing a national accounting system, increasing public investment, protecting strategic areas, and creating state corporations, especially in industrial areas (Nahón et al. 2006). With this objective in mind, the Latin American Institute for Economic and Social Planning (Instituto Latinoamericano de Planificación Económica y Social; ILPES) was created in 1962, with headquarters in Chile, in order to train technicians and develop projects and public policy recommendations.

In short, industrialization in Latin America should encompass three articulated axes: "equilibrium in the balance of payments as a macroeconomic objective; recognition that the primary sector of Latin America's economy was produced and manufactured by the central countries, especially the United States; and capital formation as a result of domestic savings" (Gutiérrez Garza 1994, 122–23). However, this model of ISI was a long-term strategy, since, in the short term, Latin American economies faced deficits in the balance of payments. There were also internal obstacles to development, such as the structure of agrarian property (the excessive concentration of land property) and the low levels of agricultural productivity. Hence, industrialization had to be undertaken in conjunction with an agrarian reform that ensured a more equitable distribution of land. Also, the technology employed in the industrial sector was at the root of the meager job creation, which further aggravated the tendency toward structural unemployment (the floating population). Both elements—agrarian property and industrial technology—contributed to a greater concentration of income (Mathias and Salama 1983, 140).

Finally, it is important to note that in analytic terms, one of CEPAL's central approaches was the historical-structural perspective, attributed to Prebisch. For Osvaldo Sunkel and Pedro Paz, unlike the classical method—which is abstract and historical, that is, both deductive and inductive, and disregards the fact that any elaboration of data requires a prior hypothesis—the historical-structural method posits that that prior hypothesis is all-encompassing. Therefore, one part can never be explained in isolation but only in its relationship to the whole. "For example, one cannot explain the specialization of Latin American economies without taking into account a center that, through its own industrialization, conditions the way the periphery operates." It is a matter of establishing the relationships among structure, system, and process (Sunkel and Paz 1970, 94).

Under Prebisch's direction and with Celso Furtado's initial participation, CEPAL exerted a significant political and intellectual influence between the 1950s and the mid-1970s, after which it began a strong process of political and intellectual mutation. In that early phase, it developed very significant political autonomy, becoming a center for the production of reflections and public policy proposals, in spite of opposition from the United States, which even attempted to close is offices in 1951. The support of Brazil's then President Getúlio Vargas was essential for the victory in this early battle for the autonomy of ideas (Furtado 1985). Adopted by economists, sociologists, technicians, and politicians, the CEPAL current advocated for an integral public policy program that would contribute to consolidating the state's role as a planning entity. This policy, which aimed at industrialization in the periphery of capitalism, was known as *developmentalism*. However, even though CEPAL's proposal is evidently related to developmentalism as an economic ideology, it is important to note that such a relationship does not mean that they are the same. In other words, CEPAL's proposal is an important component of the so-called developmentalist model but cannot be reduced to the latter, which had different versions or variants in practice. Developmentalism as an economic ideology accompanied the actions of different political regimes in Latin America, from populist ones (Juan Perón in Argentina, Getúlio Vargas in Brazil), which stimulated demand and consumption by expanding the domestic market, to those specifically denominated "developmentalist" (Juscelino Kubitschek in Brazil and Arturo Frondizi in Argentina), which focused more on investment and conferred an important role on foreign capital. Developmentalist models were also implemented in countries such as Venezuela (1958), Peru (1962), and Chile (1964). US researcher Kathryn Sikkink (2009) examines the differences between the developmentalist project in Brazil and Argentina and explains its success in Brazil as a result of the consensus it enjoyed among the elites, while in Argentina the dichotomy of Peronism/anti-Peronism hindered such a consensus, thus preventing the consolidation of a developmentalist model. Later, its successful adoption by authoritarian governments, analyzed by Guillermo O'Donnell (1973) as authoritarian modernization, demonstrated the versatility of the developmentalist model, reduced in this case to an industrialization program.

Another essential player was the aforementioned Celso Furtado, a Brazilian economist who joined CEPAL in its first years (1949–57) and played an important role in the construction of a Latin American network for dissemination, debate, and even recruiting. In spite of his youth, Prebisch named him director of the Division of Economic Development of the young institution. Furtado also translated Prebisch's writings into Portuguese and published many articles in the *Revista Brasileira de Economia* (Brazilian journal of economy), debating CEPAL's standpoints with other colleagues. In those early years, Furtado engaged in important debates with representatives of the orthodox economic thought and was in charge of creating and strengthening ties between CEPAL and various institutions (such as the National Economic Development Bank) and corporate players in Brazil (businesspeople and the military). This explains the significant spread of CEPAL's perspective in Brazil, where developmentalism was much more entrenched than elsewhere and where the Getúlio Vargas administration promoted frequent debates on the subject of industrialization.

Furtado left CEPAL in 1958 and then, until 1964, served in different positions in Brazil's political structure, as director of the National Economic Development Bank in charge of the Northeast, and later as superintendent at the same institution. In the meantime, he distanced himself from conventional economics, incorporating sociological elements when describing the specificity of development in Brazil (Mallorquín 1994, 68). From a structuralist socioeconomic perspective, he established a distinction between modernization and development (Furtado 1981) and reflected that the problem in Brazil was that import substitution had been at the service of modernization. The heterogeneity of the Brazilian economy was a result of the fact that modernization had come first, and only later did the economy prepare itself to respond to the demands of that modernization. The other sectors that did not present that demand were left behind or were incorporated into a backward economy (4).

In 1964, after the military coup in Brazil, Celso Furtado went into exile and, like many other Brazilian intellectuals, ended up in Chile, where he gave a series of lectures at ILPES; those ideas were gathered in the book *Subdesarrollo y estancamiento en América Latina* (Underdevelopment and stagnation in Latin America; 1966), where he coherently argued that the efforts toward ISI had been an alternative for some time but that the technology that Latin America had to assimilate in the mid-twentieth century required little labor force and was extremely demanding relative to the size of the market. Under such conditions, there was a tendency toward monopoly or oligopoly and a concentration of income, which, by conditioning demand, directed investments to certain industries. "The experience in Latin America has demonstrated that this type of import substitution industrialization tends to lose momentum when the phase of 'easy' substitutions ends, eventually resulting in stagnation." For that reason, development cannot derive from free markets. Since the leading classes do not understand the problem and insist on maintaining the status quo, "those who truly struggle for development in Latin America perform a revolutionary role, whether consciously or not" (48–49).[3] Furtado also argued that ISI aggravated the dualism of the labor market, widening the gap between the modern sector and the precapitalist economy, without a reduction in sight for the latter. The phenomenon of marginality in urban spaces also worsened (98). In short, what was later called the "theory of structural blockage," related to the exhaustion of the import substitution model, highlighted the limits of not only the developmentalist experience but CEPAL itself.

Within CEPAL, the modernizing sociological wing was represented by José Medina Echavarría. The Spanish sociologist, a translator of Max Weber, was incorporated in order to overcome the economistic approach and was in charge of introducing a sociological perspective to the issue of development. Medina Echavarría worked at CEPAL for twenty-five years, from 1952 to 1977; he was director of the Division of Social Affairs at ILPES and the first director of the School of Sociology of the Latin American Faculty of Social Sciences (Facultad Latinoamericana de Ciencias Sociales; FLACSO) as a UNESCO officer, among other positions, and published several works where he laid down his view of development, among them *Social Development of Latin America in the Post-War Period* (1963). Medina Echavarría did not share the Germanian diagnostics in vogue regarding structural duality and sought to replace this thesis through the sociological concept of "structural porosity," which argued that traditional aspects coexisted with modern aspects in Latin American societies, which in the long term represented an obstacle to development (Morales Martín 2013).

Finally, CEPAL decided to unite economic and social aspects through an interdisciplinary project, which resulted in the creation of a new concept in 1971—that of *development styles* (Gutiérrez Garza 1994). The commission's journal, *CEPAL Review*, devoted a special issue to this discussion, where the contributions of Aníbal Pinto, whose text had a predominantly economic focus, and those of Jorge Graciarena, who emphasized the need to include the dimension of state power, stood in opposition.[4] Pinto ([1976] 2008) examined the various typologies as development styles, defining them as "the way in which human and material resources are organized and assigned within a particular system with the object of solving such questions as what goods and services to produce; how; and for whom," and characterized the dominant development style as centralizing and exclusionary, given the unequal distribution of income and an alarming presence of critical poverty. Graciarena (1976) in turn proposed an unorthodox perspective and criticized the vagueness of the very notion of development styles and the general level of which it is a part—the development system or strategy. He also proposed going beyond fragmentary approaches and wondered what type of synthesis to produce. Beyond the difficulties in elaborating a single definition, he underscored the need to move toward a development strategy that incorporates social elements—education, health, housing, and social security, among others—and a reading that includes sociological and political elements.

In short, the mid-1960s saw what Waldo Ansaldi calls "the turn from CEPAL thought to social structures (without abandoning the analysis of economic structures)" (1991, 33). The limits of ISI became evident, and the question emerged of where "the flaws" were. And although CEPAL's approach continued to be structuralist, "the question of social actors arose" (33). It is in this context that the various critiques must be understood, among them those of M. Conceição Tavares, who early on, in 1964, observed that there were clear limits to the ISI model and that it had reached its final stage, since it did not extend to other sectors, especially agriculture and cattle ranching, nor did it establish the bases for an autonomous development of Latin American economies, which was evident in the phenomenon of economic strangling by foreign forces and the resulting problems in terms of deficits in the balance of payments (Gutiérrez Garza and González Gaudiano 2010, 45; Pécaut 1989, 205). This thesis anticipated the theory of *structural blockage* developed by Celso Furtado and revisited by the advocates of dependency theory. The Brazilian author underscored the model's internal limitations and the weakness of the agricultural and cattle ranching sector and referred to the specter of economic stagnation, to which he attributed structural characteristics. Another analytic element added to the list of obstacles to development had to do with the structural imbalance of Latin American economies, in which two sectors with different productivity and prices existed: the primary sector, whose costs and prices were lower than international ones, therefore favoring exports; and the secondary sector, whose costs and prices were higher than international ones, because it employed large amounts of imported raw materials and was therefore unable to produce exports. Failing to acknowledge and correct this structural imbalance resulted in recurrent crises due to a shortage of currency, generating a specific dynamic— stop-and-go cycles—that required a special currency exchange policy that differed from that of the developed countries (Brieva et al. 2002).

As a result of those obstacles and limitations, in the mid-1960s, the illusion of development came to an end, giving rise to a new era of Latin American thought and social sciences, no longer centered on development but on dependency. Gradually, CEPAL lost what had been its main characteristic, that is, "the tendency toward globalizing (interdisciplinary) analyses with a strong historical content" (Ansaldi 1991, 37). Its later evolution and its growing engagement with the issues proposed by the global or international agenda, in the context of Latin American dictatorships and, later, with the arrival of neoliberalism together with the Washington Consensus, increasingly distanced CEPAL from the critical thought that had characterized it at least during the first stage of its existence (1950–70).

Nature, the Developmentalist Illusion, and Rent Seeking

Humboldt and Bonpland were dazzled by America, and by tropical America in particular, with the splendor of its exuberant vegetation, its geography, which contrasted sharply with the Mediterranean human scale, and its animals, which never stopped seeming "new" to the members of expeditions from the old world who saw them for the first time. Humboldt and Bonpland fell in visual love with that America, a love recoded and transmitted according to categories of European thought.—MIGUEL DE ASÚA, in a book coedited with Pablo Penchaszadeh, *El deslumbramiento: Aimé Bonpland y Alexander von Humboldt en Sudamérica* (Dazzlement: Aimé Bonpland and Alexander von Humboldt in South America), 2010

Various authors have underscored the anthropocentric character of the dominant view of nature, based on the Western idea that the latter is a "basket of resources" and "natural capital" (Gudynas 2004). In Latin America this idea was further promoted by the belief that the continent was the location par excellence of great natural resources. In other words, historically, the region's "comparative advantage" consisted of its capacity to export nature.

Since they were first colonized, the Americas were characterized by their "geographic obstacles" and "dangerous landscapes," understood as pure geography: The extension of their surfaces, the immense distances, the difficult access, and natural obstacles conditioned the advancement of colonization and favored the isolation of inland areas (Cunill Grau 1999, 13). The emptiness of the seas that separate Europe from America was followed by the immense spaces of the new continent, characterized by their magnificence and heterogeneity— jungles, forests, savannas, plains, deltas, wetlands, mountains, highlands, deserts (Cunill Grau 1999, 43). As Angel Rosenblat argues, "The first view of America reveals the transformation of American nature in the eyes and language of the European conquerors" (quoted in Cunill Grau 1999, 79). Yet such metamorphoses were constant: America incarnated everything from a paradisiacal utopia or earthly Eden, to the new bestiary, a cartography populated by old and new monsters, hybrid infrahuman and subhuman beings, and other fabrications, to the myth of El Dorado that so profoundly obsessed European conquerors and that persists to this day with new names.

The views of American nature in the imaginary of the Spanish Conquest actually oscillate between two main ideas: astonishment, on one hand, and inferiority, on the other. The former derives from the foundational myth and is supported by the incarnation of the legend of El Dorado (Cerro Rico de Potosí). One variation of the myth of astonishment is the view of America as an extraordinary continent, marked by its exuberant and imposing landscapes (geography/ natural sciences), whose material equivalent was precious metals. America was thus born as a producer and exporter of raw materials, especially metals. In that context, Potosí signaled the beginning of large-scale industrial mining and therefore synthesized the principle of accumulation and America's birth certificate. This happened early on in Peru, Bolivia, Brazil, and Chile, as well as in North America, in California and Canada, toward the second half of the nineteenth century: "Those treasures express an old dream of humanity: the power to suddenly change a fate that until then had seemed determined by poverty and anonymity, gaining access to pleasures and a formerly inaccessible opulence, in a sort of 'inversion of the world' that is reminiscent of the profound aspirations that, in other ways and for a period of only a few days, are revealed in Carnival festivities" (Lavallé 2011, 8).

The material counterpart of El Dorado is the pillage of natural resources, in line with the different economic cycles. This perverse dialectic, as Horacio Machado Aráoz (2014) argues, confronts us with the two-faced character of colonialism: on one hand, developmentalist phantoms, incarnated in luxury, progress, ostentation, investment, and cost-benefit calculations; on the other hand, the phantoms of horror, visible in unprecedented poverty, hunger as punishment and deprivation, and the sacrifice of millions of lives. In this context, primary landscapes, baroque scenarios, and the endless extensions that obsessed travelers and scientists acquired a new meaning in the context of the various economic horizons. One clear example of that cyclic motion is Peru's history, which went from the silver cycle, to the booms in rubber, guano, and saltpeter, and back to the mining boom today.

The second idea is based on America's alleged inferiority as a young and immature continent—an idea presumably founded on scientific arguments (zoology/geography). Thus, in the eighteenth century, voyagers and naturalists traveled through the Americas with the aim of mapping the new world and elaborating a classification system. It was Carl Linnaeus who established the category of *Homo sapiens*, placing European man at the top (Pratt [1992] 2007; 2010, 73).[5] Likewise, in the second half of the eighteenth century, the idea of an immature continent was strongly advocated by Georges L. Buffon, a French scientist who elaborated a meticulous cartographic survey, naming, ordering, and labeling American geography. Starting from the hypothesis of the diversity of American and European species, he concluded that America was inferior. To him, "the New World was different, but on a different scale. When he describes the American lion, he perceives with a sudden flash of intuition that this so-called lion is not a lion at all, but some other beast peculiar to America. For a start, it has no mane, and then it is also much smaller, weaker, and more cowardly than the real lion. What is certain is that, in America, Buffon only found small animals. There were no rhinoceroses, nor hippopotamuses, nor camels, nor giraffes, nor elephants." The tapir of Brazil, despite being a large animal comparable to Africa's species, "is the size of a six-month-old calf, or a very small mule." The llama, a sort of American camel, was smaller than the tapir (Gerbi 2010; 1982, 3). In contrast, America had an overpopulation of reptiles and scavenger birds, the climate was hot and humid, the vapors were harmful, the insects were dangerous, the animals were degenerate, and native men were small and weak. Buffon also adhered to the monogenist view (i.e., contrary to the theory of evolution, which was already being discussed at the time and whose paradigmatic author was Charles Darwin), as illustrated by his concept of variation (miscegenation), which was seen as degeneracy.

However, the thinker who most influenced the view of America as an immature and inferior continent, defined as pure nature, was Georg Wilhelm Friedrich Hegel. The German philosopher revisited Buffon's theory and took it to the extreme, applying it not only to the animal kingdom but to the entire American reality. According to Hegel, America was a natural phenomenon, pure geography, and he therefore included it in a chapter of his book on the philosophy of nature. He based his arguments on three factors: The first was immaturity, since the fundamental distinction was between the New World and the Old World. "Everything [in America] is new, and by new here Hegel means immature and feeble; its fauna is weaker, but to make up for that it has a monstrous vegetation" (Gerbi 2010; 1982, 392–93). The fact that indigenous people were easy prey for Europeans and were in the process of extinction was also a sign of its weakness. The second reason was its immobility—the opposition between America and Europe is best illustrated by the dichotomy between "peoples without history" and "peoples with a history." America had no history; it was pure nature, which meant that it was immersed in endlessly repeating cyclic processes. According to Hegel, peoples without history were stationary and changeless peoples immersed in superstition, lack of culture, and barbarism. In contrast, the universal spirit expressed itself dialectically in different peoples, who became aware of themselves through history, creating institutions, memory, culture, the state, and writing—all of them fundamental elements for the development of the spirit as consciousness. The third cause was impotence—that is, America was a continent with no potency, "devoid of development and internal dialectics. . . . None of its parts, no moment in particular, is preferable to another. Richness and diversity are but arbitrariness and disorder" (2010; 1982, 389–90).

One thinker who rejected the dominant zoological perspective was the great German naturalist Alexander von Humboldt. Unlike Hegel, Humboldt knew America, having spent long periods there between 1799 and 1830, that is, between the end of the Spanish empire and the wars of independence, when he had the chance to interact with the political and intellectual elites of the time. His work was quite influential and exerted a long-term seduction not only on Europeans—such as Darwin—but also on many Americans, who saw American nature through Humboldt's eyes. Together with Frenchman Aimé Bonpland, Humboldt provided a different view full of amazement before America's inordinate and extraordinary nature. As Pratt analyzes, Humboldt "reinvented South America first and foremost as nature. Not the accessible, collectible, categorizable nature . . . , but a spectacle capable of overwhelming human knowledge and understanding, . . . [a fusion of] the specificity of science with the esthetics of the sublime" ([1992] 2007; 2010, 229). For Humboldt, the primeval, abundance, and innocence constitute a sort of conceptual triad exemplified by tropical jungles, high mountain ranges, and vast plains, which compose the image of inordinate nature "that speaks to man, to science, but that omits man from its narrative, a nature that needs no human being to exist" (229). In sum, scientism and romanticism converged in a reading that valued American nature and its primeval landscapes, viewing them in a new light.

However, the end of Spanish dominion over America also paved the way to new horizons, related again to the original idea of the Spanish conquest, which Pratt denominated "the capitalist vanguard," which saw America as a privileged continent-reservoir of great natural resources. Humboldt's fascination with a new and virgin world was put aside, and nature was increasingly reduced to raw materials—amazement was replaced by the rhetoric of the conquest, driven by a pragmatic and economistic perspective.

To conclude, it is important to emphasize that the idea of an abundant and extraordinary nature led to different views and narratives in Europe's eyes and language: on one hand, the myth of El Dorado, materialized in a double-headed landscape of great riches but also great dangers, of luxury and pillage but also poverty, hunger, and horror. On the other hand, the idea of the continent's inferiority related to the zoological and geographic thesis, supported by the representation of the continent as young and feeble, which also conveniently illustrated the opposition between nature and culture (America-Caliban as pure geography, as peoples without a history). Finally, the second view derived from amazement consolidated the idea of America as inordinate nature, an everlasting source of energy, sustained by the omnipresence of baroque natural scenarios, primeval landscapes, and endless extensions. This representation in fact contributed greatly to a positive reassessment by Americans themselves of the extraordinary character of the continent's natural reality, and fostered the myth of El Dorado in its most secular version, that is, one focused on economic cycles and the international division of labor.

National Variations of the Curse of Abundance

A resignified nature allows us to include in our historical accounts not just a more diversified set of historical actors, but a more complex historical dynamic. It enables us to replace what Lefebvre calls the "ossified" dialectic of capital and labor by a dialectic of capital, labor, and land (by land, following Marx, he means not only the powers of nature but also the agents associated with it, including the state as sovereign over a national territory). The dialectic of these three elements helps us see the landlord state as an independent economic agent rather than as an exclusively political actor structurally dependent on capital, and to conceptualize capitalism as a global process that forms intimately related centers and peripheries rather than as a self-generated system that expands from active modern regions and engulfs traditional and passive societies.—FERNANDO CORONIL, *The Magical State*, 1997

Heterogeneity and immensity gradually shaped an ambivalent image of nature in the Americas. That two-sided image, for example, is present in Domingo Faustino Sarmiento's *Facundo* ([1845] 1988): On one hand, American nature is portrayed as an enormous and threatening monster associated with inferiority and backwardness, that is, with barbarism; on the other hand, it is praised for its abundance and potential. That being so, once the social and political forces of barbarism were defeated, it would be possible to domesticate nature in order to bring the required progress to our lands. This double face of Janus is evoked in a renowned essay on the Spanish-American novel by Mexican writer Carlos Fuentes (1969), where he asserted that there were four great recurrent themes in our narrative: the dictator, the exploited masses, the writer (who inevitably takes the side of civilization against barbarism), and, last but not least, nature. Even though the greatest conflict was between civilization and barbarism, for Fuentes, the greatest literary character was without a doubt the continent's immense and untamable nature, which represented a great challenge for American humankind.

This notion of an overwhelming nature and of Latin America as the place of vast natural resources par excellence fostered an El Doradian view that was greatly influential in Latin America's social and political imaginary. The topic has been developed by several authors, especially by historians and economists, and through it, that of the curse or paradox of abundance. Generally speaking, the thesis is based on three axes: the consolidation of the primary-export model based on raw materials; the capture of extraordinary income and its derivative, rentierism; and parasitic oligarchies. The thesis seems simple in its logic: America's prodigal nature, that is, the abundant wealth of natural resources and the enormous profits derived from exports in the context of the international division of labor, led to a rentier and parasitic mentality in the dominant social classes, which translates into a distorted productive structure that largely explains both social inequalities and impoverishment in societies. In its minimal expression, the thesis represents a strong criticism of the primary-export model, which expanded unequally throughout the subcontinent from colonial times onward, in tune with the various economic cycles and the booms in raw materials.

There are so many incarnations and formulations of that thesis in Latin America that it is impossible to systematize or summarize them. I will therefore present four such readings related to three countries: those of René Zavaleta Mercado for Bolivia, Milcíades Peña for Argentina, and Rodolfo Quintero and Fernando Coronil for Venezuela. It is also worth noting that the processes analyzed in each country, while they refer to the long-term memory of colonial pillage, involve different historical periods that entail processes related to middle-term memory. Zavaleta most clearly introduces us to long-term memory through the history of the "infertile surplus," linking it later to the War of the Pacific and the most recent cycles of exploitation of metals and minerals; Milcíades Peña demolishes the myth of great Argentine wealth, fin-de-siècle Argentina, and the agro-export model based on the extraordinary rent of the land; and, finally, the Venezuelan authors describe the different aspects of the oil culture from 1930 onward.

The Bolivian essayist René Zavaleta Mercado conducts a two-sided analysis. On one hand, he proposes that the background for the War of the Pacific (1879–83), in which Chile fought Bolivia and Peru, was the issue of the dispute over surplus. The conflict is a reflection of the *surplus myth* derived from the fantasy of abundance. This myth is a global allegory, which is not only a result of capitalism but also, in Latin America, "one of the most foundational and primeval" myths ([1986] 2009, 34). Through the dispute over surplus, the Bolivian author also refers to the El Dorado myth "that every Latin American hopes for in his soul"—a sudden material discovery (of a natural resource or good) that certainly generates a surplus, but a surplus understood as "magic," "which in most cases has not been employed in a sensible manner" (34). This gave rise to the elitist, vertical, conservative notion that wealth creates power, in opposition to the idea that the people create power through revolutionary action. "In this sense, America is a conservative continent because it believes more in transformation through surplus than through an intellectual reform" (36). On the other hand, Latin American history is full of very concrete examples of the "fruitlessness of surplus": "Potosí itself screamed that what matters is not the surplus, but who gets it and for what purpose" (38). In other words, the great problem is that surplus and its availability (the existence of extraordinary rent) did not contribute to building the nation. Thus, Zavaleta's obsession has to do with the issue of controlling the surplus (transforming it into "state matter," accumulating it rather than losing it) in order to keep from repeating the history of pillage and dispossession that has characterized Andean countries since the conquest.

Milcíades Peña, an Argentine Marxist historian, distinguished himself by demolishing myths, that is, the dominant interpretive theses on Argentine history. In his book *Historia del pueblo argentino* (History of the Argentine people), written between 1955 and 1957, he referred to what he explicitly titled in a separate section "the curse of easy abundance" (2012, 77), referring to the extraordinary profitability of the Argentine pampa, the heart of the agro-export model (meat and cereals). Peña differed from the leftist circles of the time, which argued that the type of economic and social organization present in Latin America in colonial times had been feudal. Revisiting the economist and historian Sergio Bagú, he argued that since the Spanish and Portuguese conquest, Latin America had entered the global capitalist system, incorporating a pattern of capitalist organization of a particular type—colonial capitalism. He also combated the myth of the superiority of English colonization over Spanish colonization, which in his opinion led to the racialist theses of nineteenth-century positivism. Peña focused on factors such as the social structure instead of race or social inheritance—that is, on objective elements—to explain social behavior. Those elements were land, availability of a labor force, and the nature of production, which explained the true bases for the two different fates. It was in this regard that he appealed to the thesis of "the curse of easy abundance," which in his opinion was key to explaining the decisive difference between the north of the United States and Río de la Plata. He writes, "In Río de la Plata there was the pampa, that immense grassland where cattle theology, if it existed, would have located Paradise. At first, the colonizers had to make efforts to survive, but only at first. Afterward, the pampa and cattle did their thing. Why till the land? Why go out and face the river and the ocean, if the pampa provided leather and meat that the world market demanded with the same eagerness as it did metals from Potosí or tobacco from Virginia?" (79). Like the planters in the South of the United States, the oligarchies lived off the export business, accumulating wealth that required neither bourgeois initiative nor farmers' personal labor. "The farming or commercial oligarchy appropriated the wealth of the pampa and built with it a civilization of leather and meat based much more on nature's generosity than on the productive work of men" (79).

Hence, the background for this characterization is the opposition between productive capitalism, which led to autonomous industrial development, and colonial capitalism, in which the dominant classes were parasitic and *capitalized on backwardness*, exporting natural riches barely processed by human labor (Peña 2012, 80). This, and only this, is the reason for the difference from the United States, where the colonizers' fortune was due to the fact that they did not find excessively abundant means for survival—there was no exploitable indigenous labor nor products worth exporting through the import of slaves—and where, on the other hand, there was great wealth in terms of the means for work, which the colonizers profited from through productive labor.

Finally, the Venezuelans' analyses have more to do with the various socioeconomic consequences of the oil economy, which range from foreign dependency to the emergence of a certain local/national cultural configuration. The issue was introduced early on by the great writer Arturo Uslar Pietri, who on July 14, 1936, published an article entitled "Sembrar el petróleo" (Planting oil) in the Caracas daily *Ahora*, where he argued for "the need to redirect the resources derived from oil profits to stimulate the nonoil sector of the national economy in order to ensure the country's integral development" ([1936] 2005, 232–33). This concern was also present in other analyses centered on the critique of oil rentierism and the need to make use of the wealth to diversify the economy. Rodolfo Quintero focused his analyses on the oil culture in his book *Antropología del petróleo* (Anthropology of oil; [1972] 2014), where he defines that culture as a lifestyle with its own structure and defense resources, with modalities and social and psychological effects that deteriorate the "criollo" cultures, resulting in very clear features related to monopolistic capital. The oil culture is understood in terms of "the culture of conquest," to the extent that it creates a philosophy of life to transform the population into a productive source of raw materials (45). Likewise, in his book *Venezuela violenta* (Violent Venezuela), Orlando Araujo ([1968] 2013, 129) analyzed, among other topics, the emergence of a sterile or parasitic bourgeoisie that benefited from the oil business. Oil is "like God, who is omnipresent even if sometimes we cannot see Him or, like Proteus, who assumes one thousand different forms to disconcert and exterminate those who dare stand in His way" (100).

But the thinker who took his reflections further was Fernando Coronil, who in his book *The Magical State: Nature, Money, and Modernity in Venezuela* (1997, 2) speaks of the relationship between oil and the idea of a "magical state." Oil appears as something fantastic and fosters fabulous fictions that substitute for reality. Its capacity to awaken fantasies "allows state leaders to turn political life into a blinding spotlight of national progress" (2). Coronil maintains that the deification of a historically weak state is directly related to Venezuela's transformation into an oil nation—that is, a petrostate. Everything belongs to the domain of amazement, of collective fantasy with its images of progress and development, while the state boasts of its magnanimity, transforming subjects into recipients of its magic tricks.

In short, Peña and Zavaleta agree in their concern over national development (an autonomous national capitalism) by analyzing the role of extraordinary gains resulting from the massive export of primary products. However, while Peña believed that the abundance of land and means contributed to the consolidation of a parasitic and rent-seeking oligarchy (Argentina), Zavaleta argued that the problem was not the surplus itself but the fact that it was obtained by other countries through the international market. Both Argentina and Bolivia faced the failure of accumulation, whether through a deficient or dependent capitalism (Peña) or through the consolidation of an apparent or failed state (Zavaleta). The Venezuelan authors also insist on this double figure—parasitic oligarchy and a failed state. The latter also illustrate the critique of the rent-seeking character of Venezuela's economy and society. In this respect, Coronil, a partisan of the decolonial turn, adds a critique of the Eurocentric perspective, recognizing the historical significance of nature, which allows rethinking the dominant narratives regarding the historical development of the West and questioning the idea that modernity was the result of a self-propelled West.

The Emergence of the Environmental Question

The changes observed in the past five decades have been immense. Generally speaking, we have seen the crisis of the notion of modernization and the emergence of the environmental question. The critique of development and of the myth of economic growth as the great homogenizing narrative paved the way to a new space for the expression of various political and philosophical perspectives on the relationship between human and nonhuman nature. On one hand, a number of international conferences gave rise to the paradigm of sustainable development. Likewise, the incipient ecological thought was associated with a critique and revision of the paradigm of progress and modernization, questioning the anthropocentric view of the relationship between humans and nature. On the other hand, in Latin America we witnessed the crisis and failure of the developmentalist project and the later incursion into a monetarist phase characterized by the Washington Consensus and asymmetrical globalization. The critiques encompassed, first of all, the developmentalist project and its real-life expressions; second, the realization of its limitations and social shortcomings resulting from widening social gaps between the center and the periphery, in addition to racial and gender gaps; and, finally, what Koldo Unceta Satrústegui (2009) called the "social turn," which paves the way to a critical field regarding the increase in poverty and inequality. In this section, I examine these alternative perspectives, in tune with the proposals emerging from the global agenda: first, the vicissitudes and discussions that led to the elaboration of the concept of sustainable development; and, second, the responses elaborated from the South.

Toward the Paradigm of Sustainable Development

Since René Descartes and Francis Bacon, ontological dualism has been at the heart of modern Western science, emphasizing human control and dominion over nature, an anthropocentrism that extended to many other areas. One of the consequences of that paradigm is the depreciation of all things different: of women relative to men, of nature relative to humans.

The many environmental disasters experienced in the first half of the twentieth century revealed the relationship between industry and the environment and gradually led to the emergence of an incipient environmental consciousness. The first denunciations thus emerged, such as Rachel Carson's book *Silent Spring* ([1962] 2022), which denounced the effects of agrochemicals on birds; in 1966 scientists such as Barry Commoner highlighted the risks of the techno-industrial complex, and the economist Kenneth Boulding proposed replacing the current "cowboy" economy with a closed-quarters economy adequate to

"Spaceship Earth," which has limited resources and finite spaces for pollution and waste disposal (Pierri 2005). Ecology as a critical approach and the first environmentalist movements emerged in response to the various denunciations of the growing environmental degradation and the awareness of the limited availability of natural resources on the planet, in the context of the expansion of industrial dynamics and the consolidation of the myth of economic growth.

On a global level, the first important contribution to environmental issues was the Meadows Report, *The Limits to Growth* (Meadows et al. 1972), elaborated by the Club of Rome, which recounts the limits to the exploitation of nature and the latter's incompatibility with an economic system founded on infinite growth. The report emphasized the serious dangers of pollution and the future availability of raw materials, which would affect the entire planet if the style and pace of economic growth were to continue. The result was the emergence of a space to question the industrialist view centered on infinite growth, while clear signals were sent to the countries of the South, warning that the industrial development model of northern countries was far from universally applicable. As we shall see later in this book, the report elicited different responses from the South.

Also in 1972, the First United Nations Conference on the Human Environment was held in Stockholm, which resulted in a declaration adopted by national states, where a closer relationship between the impacts of economic development and the "human environment" started to become evident. The idea of "progress" as unlimited growth persisted, but the declaration warned that humans' current power to transform nature could harm the "human environment." Although the declaration does not fully propose the paradigm of "sustainable development," the main features of that paradigm begin to emerge. Thus, Principle 1 states that humankind "bears a solemn responsibility to protect and improve the environment for present and future generations" (United Nations 1972, 4). In this context, the United Nations Environment Programme was created, with headquarters in Nairobi, and a recommendation was made to establish June 5 as World Environment Day.

Ecological thinking further developed in the 1980s after the serious accident at the Chernobyl nuclear plant in Ukraine (1986), as well as several oil spills or "black tides," such as the case of the supertanker *Exxon Valdez* (Alaska, 1989). These events had very significant international repercussions and ended up establishing the environmental question in social consciousness. In 1987 the United Nations World Commission on Environment and Development presented the study *Our Common Future* (also known as the Brundtland Report), which popularized the idea of sustainable development (United Nations 1987). Five years later, in 1992, the United Nations Conference on Environment and

Development was held in Rio de Janeiro (Brazil). These international conferences served to unify the various perspectives in vogue in the face of the growing interest in the environmental question. Beyond its obvious complexity, related to the political and ideological dispute surrounding its definition and scope, the concept of sustainable development clearly differed depending on the different understandings of the relationship between humans and nature and between growth and the environment. In this regard, there are two opposite views: on one hand, an ecocentric or biocentric approach regarding the relationship between humans and nature, stressing environmental degradation and the limited natural resources available; and, on the other hand, a view that, in spite of the reformulations and the critiques of the myth of growth, continues with an anthropocentric perspective that prioritizes development over the environment.

The various incarnations of the paradigm of sustainable development signaled the victory of the anthropocentric conception, which posited that growth, development, and the environment could coexist. Thus, the point of departure for the Brundtland Report was that development and the environment were inseparable, but it inverted the classical formulation of the problem, moving away from ecocentrism, which viewed development as the cause of environmental degradation, and adopting an anthropocentric perspective, asserting that it was essential to keep environmental degradation from limiting development (Pierri 2005). The paradigm of sustainable development in turn required the creation of a new legal framework. While priorities were established, reflected in the order of the words that named the model (i.e., promoting economic growth first and later, once such growth was ensured, beginning to address environmental issues and the rights of future generations), it was imperative to develop new principles and legal tools capable of responding to the new reality, which was not foreseen in the Napoleonic Code (Svampa and Viale 2014). That new legal framework was consolidated in the Rio Declaration, whose Principles 15 and 17 establish the new environmental legal principles—the precautionary principle and the preventive principle. This is why a distinction is usually made between weak and strong sustainability. In this regard, I would like to quote Eduardo Gudynas at length:

> Wherever the environmental dimension is assumed, a first set of stances is adopted, currently known as weak sustainable development. The current environmental crisis is acknowledged and a form of development that does not destroy its ecological base is proposed. But this stance considers that development responds directly to economic growth, and that changes are processed especially within the market, accepting the

various forms of the commodification of nature and applying scientific and technical innovations. It is a position in tune with the Brundtland Report, since it accepts economic growth as the main engine for development (the problem is therefore how to grow). A second set of stances, which we shall call strong sustainable development, argues that Nature's entrance into the market is not enough, and proposes a stronger critique of the orthodox stances regarding progress. It is a position that somewhat deepens its critique of conventional development, and while it continues to consider Nature as a form of Capital, it advocates for the need to safeguard the critical components of ecosystems. The difference between a weak and a strong stance was pointed out early on by Daly and Cobb (1989) among others. (Gudynas 2011a, 80)

The notion of human development also emerges, linked to the United Nations Development Programme (UNDP) and inspired by philosophical writings such as those of Amartya Sen (2000), who associates human development with the notions of equity, freedom, and competencies. While it does not constitute an alternative to the economistic perspective maintained by dominant neoliberalism, the notion of human development has served to complicate the category by incorporating other indicators in addition to economic ones, related to education, health, and gender, among others.

In short, the Brundtland Report consolidated the victory of a weak view of sustainability. Other, more radical proposals in tune with deep ecology that advocated strong sustainability, such as those of Norwegian thinker Arne Naess, were put aside. Likewise, as we shall see in the next section, other critical proposals elaborated early on in the countries of the South, or through a dialogue between the latter and the countries of the North, were also left out.

Alternative Concepts and Perspectives from the South

Since the beginning of the discussions on development and its limits, alternative approaches were proposed in the South, as well as various responses to the report *The Limits to Growth*. I would like to examine some of the contributions elaborated between the 1970s and 1980s, since, in spite of the biases they might present, they were important elaborations by Latin American intellectuals. They were basically critical positions, several of which have been forgotten today, that disagreed with the views emerging in developed countries regarding the responsibilities and tasks to be accomplished in the face of environmental degradation and pollution. As a result, they clashed with a hegemonic episteme, that is, with a deliberate effort by representatives of the most powerful countries to obstruct, neutralize, or ignore those contributions, to the extent that they differed from or openly disagreed with the notions and paradigms deployed from the North regarding the environmental question.

The first such approach refers to the concept of *ecodevelopment*, resulting from a dialogue between the North and the South that, as many specialists have observed, enjoyed a fleeting success. It was elaborated in a number of meetings, among them, the Founex Seminar (Switzerland, 1971), the Cocoyoc Conference (Morelos, Mexico, 1974), and the seminar organized by the Dag Hammarskjöld Foundation in Stockholm, Sweden, in 1975. But it was at the conference in Mexico that a declaration was issued where the concept of ecodevelopment appears, highlighting the structural nature of environmental problems and the global crisis, insisting that socioeconomic inequalities and environmental degradation are a consequence of the current development models and lifestyles, and stressing the need for alternative development models and a new international order (Martins 1995, 46, cited in Pierri 2005).

The Cocoyoc Declaration set a precedent by establishing that the problem was not population but the unequal distribution of wealth and that inequalities are not the result of certain geographic conditions but of neocolonial forms of exploitation. Influenced by dependency theory, it also argued that it was developed countries, with their high levels of consumption, that had caused the underdevelopment of peripheral countries and that therefore should reduce their participation in pollution. After the Stockholm conference, the concept of ecodevelopment was revisited by Ignacy Sachs, a UN consultant on environmental issues, who defined it as "socially desirable, economically sustainable, and ecologically prudent development" (1980, 109). For the author, ecodevelopment offered planners a different rational criterion from the economic or monetary criterion, based on complementary ethical postulates: intragenerational (between present generations) and intergenerational (with future generations) solidarity. Furthermore, it led planners to cultural anthropology and ecology, since the concept responded to the cultural contributions of populations in terms of their relationship with the environment. In sum, ecodevelopment was understood as endogenous, participatory, based on the local reality, responding to its needs, promoting a symbiosis between human society and nature, and open to institutional changes (I. Sachs 1981). The Mexican president, Luis Echeverría, who participated in the last day of the discussions of the Cocoyoc Congress, supported its resolutions (Gutiérrez Garza and González Gaudiano 2010, 83). However, the term *ecodevelopment* was short-lived and was abandoned even by its promoters. It was Henry Kissinger, the head of US diplomacy, who took the necessary measures to veto the use of the term in international forums (I. Sachs 1994), promoting the adoption of the sustainable development paradigm instead.

On the other hand, we must not forget that, perhaps more than in other latitudes, in Latin America the left—whether in its anticapitalist or its populist incarnation—was quite opposed to the environmental currents that emerged in the context of the critiques of the productivist paradigm. Not only did those critiques question some of the pillars of Marxist thought—a clear heir of modernity—but, with few exceptions, most of the Latin American left viewed the ecological problematic as a concern imported from rich countries, which aimed at reaffirming the inequalities between industrialized nations and those in the process of industrial development or aiming for it. This issue reemerged in 2000 in the rhetoric of Latin American progressive governments.

As mentioned above, the 1972 Meadows Report, *The Limits to Growth*, elicited many reactions by Latin American intellectuals. The influential economist Celso Furtado elaborated a response in his brief book *The Myth of Economic Development* ([1974] 2020), where he questioned whether the structure of the global economic system was sufficiently well known to project long-term trends, since the assertions made in the report elaborated by MIT technicians ignored the specificity of the phenomenon of underdevelopment, which, far from constituting a phase of development, as Rostow would have it, was a distortion caused by the relationship established between dominant and dependent countries since the Industrial Revolution (Furtado 2020; 1974, 23). Furthermore, the industrialization of the capitalist center was founded on the creation of massive markets, while in the periphery, only the dominant minorities reproduce that lifestyle, and the vast majority is excluded from consumption. Hence, the hypothesis of collapse would be well founded only if the system tended to generalize the current lifestyle of the capitalist center. For Furtado, one of the indirect conclusions of the report was that the lifestyle fostered by current capitalism could be preserved only for a minority (industrialized countries and the dominant minorities of underdeveloped countries), since any attempt to generalize it would lead to the system's collapse. This conclusion was important for Third World countries, since it demonstrated that the economic development proposed as a model by international bodies and developed countries was a myth: "We now know that Third World countries can never develop" (2020; 1974, 28).

Another conclusion was that this dilemma (which Furtado did not consider a dilemma but a "fantasy worthy of an electronic brain," since it only took into account the reality of rich countries) could be solved only by implementing structural transformations that associated the primacy of social interest with regard to the use of scarce resources with the creation of more egalitarian societies. Therefore, in the Third World, rethinking the limits of natural resources implied rethinking consumption, with the interest of society and the creation of more egalitarian societies in mind, developing other patterns of consumption—that is, developing a longer-term productive system. This did not guarantee that no pressure would be exerted on natural resources, but at least the pressure would be much smaller than it would if the prevalent lifestyles in the dominant system were expanded (Furtado 2020; 1974, 32).

In the same line of thought as Furtado's was the Latin American World Model, elaborated by a group of mostly Argentine intellectuals who questioned the Meadows Report, considering that it was imbued with a neo-Malthusian logic typical of the hegemonic discourse, which linked environmental degradation and the future scarcity of natural resources to population growth. In effect, the proposal of the Meadows Report recommended zero population growth for rich countries and population control for poor ones. In response, an interdisciplinary group of specialists elaborated an alternative model in 1975, "Catastrophe or New Society? A Latin American World Model," under the institutional umbrella of Fundación Bariloche and coordinated by geologist Amílcar Herrera (2004), who had previously written about the relationship between science and politics. The report explicitly affirms the normative character of the so-called Latin American World Model (i.e., its goal was not to study current trends but to point to desirable goals, to a world free of backwardness and misery), even though in actual fact there were clearly prospective lines in its presentation (Fundación Bariloche 1976a, 1976b). The report argued that the devastating use of natural resources and environmental degradation were not related to population growth but to the high levels of consumption by the richest countries, which imposed a priori a division between developed and underdeveloped countries. The planet's privileged sectors should therefore reduce their excessive consumption and their growth rate in order to lower the pressure on natural resources and the environment. According to Enrique Oteiza (2004, 10), "After a period of intense exploratory work and internal debate, we decided to build such a model employing the most advanced methods of systems theory available at the time, establishing a dynamic function focused on satisfying a series of basic, fundamental needs on which there was already an important consensus in 1970 among those who worked on problems of this sort. . . . It is important to note that, based on the work of Fundación Bariloche, a number of theoretical/methodological approaches adopted the notion of basic needs developed in the Latin American World Model."

On the other hand, the Latin American World Model considered that the obstacles were not physical but political and social, so that preserving the environment had more to do with the type of society built than with insurmountable physical limits. It also deployed a strong criticism of consumer society.[6] The society proposed by the Latin American World Model is therefore non-consumerist, with production determined by social needs instead of profit. In spite of this, the model proposed had faith in technology and argued that there were no scientific reasons to believe that an ecological catastrophe or scarcity of natural resources would occur in the foreseeable future. It was therefore a wager on political and social change from a different perspective than the hegemonic discourse, which it questioned because it did not foresee the construction of a model based on the transformation of power structures (Oteiza 2004).

In sum, Fundación Bariloche's proposal, like Celso Furtado's, reflected an autonomous and counterhegemonic thought process elaborated in the periphery, which, in spite of its developmentalist limits, questioned the coloniality of knowledge and pointed to structural reforms that included conceiving not only a more egalitarian society but also other patterns of consumption adequate to social needs. At the same time, both proposals declared their faith in progress and technology. They emphasized the political, paying less attention to environmental dimensions, which would become increasingly relevant in the political scenario and the global agenda. Finally, it is worth noting that even though the Latin American World Model was translated into English and French, the perspective elaborated by Fundación Bariloche did not have the expected international impact. There is no doubt that, beginning in 1976, with the arrival of the worst civic-military dictatorship in Argentine history, endogenous factors conspired against the continuity and evolution of this critical perspective.

In the late 1960s and early 1970s, a number of reflections concurred on the need to debate the very nature of development processes and programs and their capacity to satisfy various necessities related to human well-being. In this regard, Unceta Satrústegui (2009) detected a first field of criticism or anomalies relative to poverty and inequality, in what some thinkers called the *social turn*. In spite of the positive results in terms of an increase in GDP per capita, it was difficult to conclude that there had been an increase in development, since poverty, unemployment, underemployment, and inequality had not diminished. The second field of anomalies at that early stage had to do with the progressive degradation of the environment and of natural resources, and the third was related to gender inequality. One final field was the discrepancy between economic growth and respect for freedom and human rights. It was in this context that the concept of *maldesarrollo* (maldevelopment) emerged in an attempt to explain the global and systematic failure of development programs, both in so-called underdeveloped countries and in "developed" countries in the global system.

The term *mal desarrollo*—spelled as two separate words—was employed by several authors. One of the first ones was Celso Furtado, who, in his critical distance from CEPAL's ideas, increasingly emphasized the difference between industrialization and modernization, and between growth and development, to the point of maintaining that ISI had brought about industrialization without development. For Furtado, underdevelopment and maldevelopment were the same side of the coin and were therefore nearly synonymous. But he also referred to the dislocation (regional and structural heterogeneity) and increase in inequalities (not only social inequalities but also inequalities between the countries of the North and the South)—a notion further explored by the advocates of dependency theory, albeit without employing the term *maldesarrollo*.[7] That term was revisited by René Dumont and M. F. Mottin (1982) in a book that examines three Latin American countries—Brazil, Mexico, and Peru—and points out a paradox: a subcontinent with considerable growth in terms of productive forces and wealth produced, with a strong industry, with enormous (even delirious) cities with more pollution and traffic jams than those of industrialized countries, and extravagantly wasteful of natural resources and their labor force. Hence, inequality, wastefulness, and pillage were the dimensions that characterized maldevelopment, without, however, understanding it as the opposite of the presumably "good development" of Europe and the United States.

In other places of peripheral capitalism, the notion of maldevelopment gradually acquired more conceptual density. It was the title of a 1990 book by Samir Amin: *Maldevelopment: Anatomy of a Global Failure*. But in the South, it was the Indian physicist and environmentalist Vandana Shiva who revisited the concept of maldevelopment to read it from a geopolitical and gender perspective. Development, which should have been a postcolonial project, together with progress and material well-being for all, implied a Westernization of economic categories. In order for it to be viable, it was necessary for the global powers to occupy the colonies and destroy the natural local economy. Development, the production of commercial surplus, thus became a source of poverty for the colonies and even led to the creation of internal colonies:

> Development was thus reduced to a continuation of the process of colonisation; [a model] based on the exploitation or exclusion of women (of the West and non-West), on the exploitation and degradation of nature, and on the exploitation and erosion of other cultures. Economic growth

was a new colonialism, draining resources away from those who needed them most. The discontinuity lay in the fact that it was now new national elites, not colonial powers, that masterminded the exploitation. . . . As a culturally biased project it destroys wholesome and sustainable lifestyles and creates real material poverty, or misery, by the denial of survival needs themselves, through the diversion of resources to resource intensive commodity production. (Shiva [1988] 1995, 30–31, 41)

Thus, the poverty created by development is no longer cultural and relative: "It is absolute, threatening the very survival of millions on this planet" (Shiva [1988] 1995, 42). "Maldevelopment is the violation of the integrity of organic, interconnected and interdependent systems, that sets in motion a process of exploitation, inequality, injustice and violence" (34). Although Shiva's contribution was published at a much later date—the 1990s—it is important to highlight the close association that characterizes maldevelopment as an anti-neocolonial critique not only of development but also of the patriarchal model, which gave rise to one of the most prolific lines of ecofeminism.

FROM DEVELOPMENT ON A HUMAN SCALE
TO POSTDEVELOPMENT

On a global scale, the 1980s signaled the end of a cycle, characterized by a crisis of emancipatory languages, the collapse of "real socialisms," and the beginning of a new cycle, the neoliberal consensus, whose triple axes were the proclaimed end of ideologies, the demonization of state intervention, and the liberation of forces "favorable" to the market. In Latin America the 1980s, the so-called lost decade, was characterized by democratic transitions (the end of military dictatorships), an increase in poverty (in just the last four years of the decade, the number of poor people in the subcontinent increased by 25 percent), and, toward the end of the decade, episodes of hyperinflation (Venezuela, Argentina, Bolivia, Nicaragua). This context of economic and social decomposition was accompanied by a discourse of economic opening together with what would later be known as the Washington Consensus. In different Latin American countries, with nuances and specificities, the new accumulation regime dismantled the already eroded bases of the national-developmentalist model and set a different model in motion, based on structural reforms to the state, that is, an adjustment in state spending, a policy of rapid privatization, the import of goods and capital, and financial opening.

In this context, development as the great homogenizing narrative temporarily disappeared from the political and academic agenda, not only in Latin

America, but in other latitudes as well. This decline was not unrelated to the fact that in the context of a crisis of the left, Latin American social sciences, especially political economy and political sociology, which had led critical thinking for decades, underwent a profound political and epistemological transformation. While, on one hand, the economy in its neoclassical and orthodox version focused on productivity and the recovery of macroeconomic indicators in the context of the various adjustment and stabilization models, sociology, on the other hand, gradually shifted to a more modest understanding of social knowledge, in conjunction with the expansion of anthropology and other more ethnographic epistemological perspectives, or tended to develop a strong institutionalist bias that prioritized the study of the transformations of post-dictatorship democracies and distanced itself from the radical/revolutionary ethos of the 1960s and 1970s.

In this context, many Latin American authors critical of macrosocial, planning-oriented, and centralizing development argued for the need to elaborate an inclusive and participatory understanding of development, defined at a different scale and respectful of peasant and native cultures, that contributed to strengthening local and regional economies. The "development on a human scale" approach, whose main author was Chilean economist Mandref Max-Neef, together with Antonio Elizalde and Martín Hopenhayn, thus emerged in the late 1980s. This approach proposes a reading or a redefinition of the economic system based on the satisfaction of basic human needs within a social and ecological framework. The theory of development on a human scale questions the economistic approach, which is based on the notion that individual well-being depends on the global wealth of the nations and can be measured through the GDP—that is, the set of goods and services produced by the country, later enhanced by its relation to the size of the population: GDP per capita. Although it questions both developmentalism and neoliberalism, it makes a distinction between them. The failure of developmentalism cannot be attributed to its shortcomings or lack of creativity; its errors are related to both economic and financial imbalances, to its highly concentrated economic structure, and to its approach to development, which is predominantly economic and disregards emerging social and political processes, especially after the Cuban Revolution. In contrast, while "developmentalism has generated reflections, monetarism generates recipes" (Max-Neef et al. 1986, 11). Those recipes failed dramatically in Latin America, leaving behind a profound void, further increasing social costs.

In contrast, development on a human scale proposes elaborating a qualitative growth indicator for people. Its point of departure is that human needs have traditionally been considered infinite and constantly changing depending on the period and the culture. However, basic human needs are the same in all cultures and all historical periods. What changes through time and between cultures are the ways or the means employed to satisfy those needs (Max-Neef et al. 1986, 22). Each economic, social, and political system adopts different styles to satisfy the same basic human needs. One of the aspects that defines a culture is its choice of means for satisfaction, which are culturally constructed. Goods are a mechanism that allows subjects to improve their means to satisfy their needs. When goods become an end in themselves, life is put at the service of artifacts, and not the other way around. As a result, in the context of the current civilizational crisis, "the construction of a humanist economy requires reflecting on the dialectic between needs, means for satisfaction, and goods." Hence, development on a human scale "focuses on satisfying basic human needs, on generating ever-increasing levels of self-dependency, and on the organic articulation of human beings with nature and technology, of global processes with local behaviors, of the personal with the social, of planning with autonomy, and of civil society with the state" (28).

In short, the perspective summarized here proposes a critical/humanist approach: It is based on a critique of productivism while questioning the consolidation of a consumerist society, which places excessive emphasis on goods and not enough on needs and means to satisfy them, thus leading to an unsustainable society. It understands poverty from various angles, based on the idea that any unsatisfied human need results in poverty. Likewise, the magnitude of unemployment and its persistence, as well as hyperinflation in Latin America, generate pathologies that are not only individual but also collective and that hinder finding solutions to the problems. However, the counterproposal is not the creation of an ascetic society—one that places excessive emphasis on needs and means for satisfaction and negates desire—but an ecological and sustainable society bent on satisfying needs in qualitative terms, attempting to improve the means for satisfaction and vindicating subjectivity.

However, the most radical criticism of the hegemonic view of development came from poststructuralism. In 1992 Wolfgang Sachs coordinated *The Development Dictionary*. Mexican thinker Gustavo Esteva, who was in charge of the chapter "Development," launched a devastating critique that emphasized the invention of development and its counterpart, underdevelopment, by the United States and the other Western powers at the end of World War II—a dichotomy that, from Esteva's viewpoint, was aggressively colonialist. His critique highlighted the monocultural nature of the development metaphor, since the peoples from non-Western cultures were not allowed to define the forms of their own social life ([1992] 2002; 1996, 56). Likewise, it examined the various adjectives applied to the concept, from endogenous development to sustainable development to human development, as means to attenuate the colonialist model.

This critical reading was further explored by Colombian anthropologist Arturo Escobar, who, in tune with the interrogations derived from *indigenista* currents, proposed dismantling the modern notion of development as a discourse of power, in order to reveal the main mechanisms of domination (the distinction between development and underdevelopment; the professionalization of the problem—the experts—and its institutionalization in a network of national, regional, and international organizations), as well as the concealment or belittlement of other experiences and local knowledges and vernacular practices. It is important to emphasize that the point of poststructuralist critique was not to propose a different view of development but to question the ways in which Third World countries were defined as underdeveloped and therefore needful of development. As the Colombian author explicitly states, the question was not "How can we improve the development process?" but "Why, through which historical process, and with which consequences were Asia, Africa, and Latin America conceived as the 'Third World' through the discourses and practices of development?" ([1990] 2005, 18).[8] Hence, one of the axes of the notion of postdevelopment was the critique and deconstruction of development, so that it would no longer be the organizing principle of social life. Other axes proposed by that notion are reappraising vernacular cultures, reducing the dependency on expert knowledge, and creating a sustainable social, cultural, and ecological world.

The idea of postdevelopment was criticized by both neoliberalism and Marxism because of its discursive approach, which disregarded the fact that the true problems of development were poverty and capitalism. In addition, it was criticized for presenting a view of development that was too general and too essentialist and a romanticized understanding of local traditions and social movements, failing to consider that the local is also configured by power relations. Escobar acknowledged the relevance of some of the critiques (Unceta Satrústegui 2009) but stressed that the idea differed from dominant approaches in that the latter saw knowledge as a representation of reality, arguing that there was an ontological truth, while poststructuralism is based on a constructivist epistemological position always founded on history.

There is no doubt that Arturo Escobar's writings have been highly influential in Latin America's environmental thinking and political ecology and their search for an alternative proposal through a different type of rationality and relationality from dominant thinking, founded on collective construction, the principle of reciprocity, and local knowledges, whose protagonists or bearers par excellence are social movements, among them indigenous and Afro-descendant movements. It is not by chance that his reading points to the way in which vernacular epistemes upset modern knowledge, proposing other relational worldviews that break away from or question Western dualism. This radical perspective, which proposes reflecting on the relations between human and nonhuman nature with a relational worldview, is one of the various approaches that Gudynas (2012) has denominated "alternatives to development," in opposition to "development alternatives," among which the Uruguayan author also includes superstrong sustainability, biocentrism, and deep ecology.

SOCIAL MOVEMENTS, ENVIRONMENTALISM, AND POLITICAL ECOLOGY

For a long time, in the West, the history of collective struggles and forms of resistance was associated with the organizational structures of the working class, believed to be the privileged actor of historical change. The organized action of the working class was understood as "social movement," since that class seemed to be the main actor, and potentially as the privileged expression of a new alternative for society, different from the capitalist model in place. However, beginning in 1960, the multiplication of the spheres of conflict and changes in the popular classes revealed the need to broaden definitions and analytic categories. To that end, the category—both empirical and theoretical—of "new social movements" was created to characterize the action of the various social movements that expressed a new politicization of society, by taking to the public arena topics and conflicts that had traditionally been considered private or had been naturalized, associated with industrial development.

It is in this context that we must understand ecologist or environmental movements, which together with feminist, pacifist, and student movements illustrated the emergence of new cultural and political trends. There is no doubt that both ecology and ecologist movements were an offspring of 1968, which signaled a political/cultural turn marked by libertarian student uprisings in the countries of both the North and the South, from Paris and US campuses to Prague and Mexico City, where the movements were violently repressed. The incipient ecologist movement focused its criticisms on productivism, a feature of both capitalism and Soviet socialism, and united in its critique of nuclear energy.[9] As mentioned above, the 1970s signaled the incorporation of environmental issues into the global agenda. International institutions and new platforms for intervention (such as UNDP), various ecologist organizations, the first green parties (with the German party as the model), and many NGOs emerged, with very different standpoints and ideological origins, from the most conservative to the most radical. In Latin America, although there were conservationist organizations in several countries as early as the 1950s, they had little effect. In works written in the 1990s, Enrique Leff and Eduardo Gudynas, two key authors on the topic, noted the heterogeneity of the incipient environmental movement and its multiclass character, albeit with a strong presence of the middle classes (Gudynas 1992), and emphasized its weak identity, cohesion, and continuity (Leff 1993). This weakness was no doubt related to the central idea held by Latin American political elites, whether of the right or the left, that the environmental concern was an issue relevant to industrialized countries, since the main problem related to pollution in Latin America was poverty. On the other hand, an incipient environmental perspective was promoted by the pioneers of environmentalism, that is, those who participated in the debates held in the various international conferences on sustainable development, who began generating an expert knowledge independent of the large transnational conservationist organizations. Each country has its own cohort of environmentalist pioneers. For example, in Argentina one of the most outstanding pioneers was Miguel Grinberg, creator of the mythical journal *Mutantia*, which introduced many topics related to ecology, while always remaining quite critical of the process of expropriation of the "green" discourse by transnational power.

In the 1970s and 1980s, the number of environmentalist groups grew, but a strong trend toward institutionalization also emerged. In Brazil the first dissenting environmentalist movement was undoubtedly that of the *seringueiros* (rubber tappers) in the state of Acre, who introduced a specific form of territoriality by engaging in the dispute over the meaning of *sustainable development*. This territoriality considered the population as an "environmental conservation unit" and initiated an interesting dialogue between tradition and modernity (Porto Gonçalves 2001, 83). The rubber-tapper movement became internationally renowned after the murder of activist Chico Mendes (1988). On the other hand, at the time, as Eduardo Viola (1992) argues for the Brazilian case, rather than actual ecologist movements, there were social movements with a socioenvironmental dimension derived from their interaction with environmentalist groups. Among them, Viola mentioned the following: flood victims; rubber tappers, whose interaction with environmentalist groups allowed them to elaborate the extractive reserve program; indigenous movements, whose interaction with environmentalist groups, especially international ones, allowed them to provide a better explanation of the environmental protection dimension of their struggle for land and the demarcation of reserves; some sectors of the landless rural worker movements, especially in the South, which introduced an environmentalist dimension into their struggle for agrarian reform; sectors of the women's movement willing to articulate feminist and environmentalist issues, even though at the time there was no ecofeminist group like those of the First World; sectors of neighborhood movements (in response to the evident violence against the environment committed by industry); consumer defense movements, many of whose members had prior experience in environmentalism; occupational health movements, which brought together trade union activists and public health physicians; and a small sector of the student movement; among others.

CRITICAL PERSPECTIVES: FROM ECOLOGICAL ECONOMICS TO POLITICAL ECOLOGY

Environmentalism is thus inscribed in the transition from a modernity characterized by cultural homogenization, the unity of science, technological efficiency, and the market logic, to a new civilizational project oriented toward alternative development styles based on the sustainability of the various ecosystems on the planet and the cultural heterogeneity of the human race. Environmentalism is thus part of an alternative modernity that seeks to deconstruct the logic of capital and decentralize power in order to build a different social rationality.—ENRIQUE LEFF, "Cultura democrática, gestión ambiental y desarrollo sustentable en América Latina" (Democratic culture, environmental management and sustainable development in Latin America), 1993

The emergence of the environmental question paved the way for the consolidation of new branches of knowledge or disciplines, among them, political ecology, ecological economics, and environmental history, which have greatly expanded in recent decades, in both the countries of the North and Latin America, among whose many authors Enrique Leff, Eduardo Gudynas, Arturo Escobar, and Guillermo Castro Herrera stand out. Alongside these debates, different disciplines have developed, such as environmental economics, which aims at overcoming a monetary definition derived from conventional economics, defining itself as "a science for the management of sustainability" (Pengue 2009, 56).

One pioneer in problematizing these issues was CLACSO's Political Ecology Work Group, coordinated by the sociologist Héctor Alimonda, which brought together several of the most renowned representatives of the broad field of ecology in the continent. In addition to those named above, it included authors such as Henri Acselrad, Roberto Guimarães, Marcos Gandasegui, Walter Pengue, Roberto Moreira, and Pedro Jacoby.[10] There were other contributions, such as those of Héctor Sejenovich from ecological economics and those of Germán Palacio from environmental history.

From political ecology and environmental philosophy, one of the richest and most complex approaches is that of Mexican thinker Enrique Leff, creator of various core concepts: "environmental rationality," "environmental knowledge," "dialogue of knowledges." Leff underscores the social sciences' neglect of nature and epistemic blindness. According to Leff, considering environmental issues has been unthinkable for the social sciences. Revisiting Weberian sociology's notion of rationality, Leff undertook the task of defining the concept of environmental rationality from a critical/comprehensive perspective. The thesis, of an epistemological nature, addresses the forms of knowing, conceiving, transforming, and dominating the world. It is therefore not only a matter of the passage from the time of progress to the time of risks but a civilizational crisis that implies a crisis of knowledge. The environmental question is not circumscribed to a matter of ecological sensibility related to cultural change; it is a reflection of the modes of thinking that have made the world unsustainable.

In this regard, in an article published in 2006, Leff proposed reconceiving political ecology as a "field under construction," based on the articulation of critical thought and political action. According to him, political ecology poses a question regarding the most recent processes of transformation of humans' existential condition, in terms of not only the conflicts of ecological distribution but also the relationships between people's lifestyle and the globalized world. Several critical disciplines converged in the paradigm of political ecology—among them, ecological economics, environmental history, environmental law, political sociology, anthropology of the relationship between culture and nature, and political ethics. Likewise, Leff argues that ecology's fundamental contribution is political and not merely epistemological, since, on one hand, it points to the denaturalization of nature, of the "natural" conditions of existence, of "natural" disasters; and, on the other hand, the ecologization of social relations (Leff 2006). In sum, political ecology is a territory in dispute where new cultural identities are being built around the defense of nature, culturally resignified, through the resistance struggles in existence today. These struggles, as we shall see in the second part of this book, stand against the various forms of extractivism throughout the continent and defend other languages that revalue the territory. Finally, political ecology is also a new political epistemology, whose search for integration and complementarity of knowledges goes beyond interdisciplinary approaches, recognizing the strategies at play in the field of power and focusing on the notion of dialogue and knowledge exchange.

On the other hand, many specialists have been studying these new conflicts characterized by an unequal distribution of risks, including Joan Martínez Alier (2004) and Henri Acselrad (2004a, 2004b). These authors argue that it is environmental justice movements that have pointed to the unequal conditions of access to environmental protection. Martínez Alier baptized these movements emerging in the Southern or peripheral countries as "popular ecology" or "ecology of the poor." The Catalonian economist referred to a current that focuses on environmental conflicts at the local, national, and global levels, which it argues are caused by the globalized reproduction of capital, the new international and territorial division of labor, and social inequality. This critical perspective also underscores the geographic displacement of the sources of resources and waste matter. These movements, even if they did not recognize themselves as environmentalist at first, have undertaken a struggle for environmental defense and protection, acquiring a growing importance in recent years. This is due to the growing demand for raw materials and consumer goods from developed countries, which threatens the social and ecological sustainability of territories and ecosystems in the medium term. The accumulation of environmental damages thus inevitably refers to issues related to the ecological debt, as well as the state's social and political responsibility—indolence, complicity and abandonment, exclusion and racism, to which the state subjects urban or rural populations with less economic and political power.

Finally, for Acselrad, the distribution of environmental costs tends to highlight historical patterns of environmental injustice, which reflect profound inequalities not only between the countries of the North and the South but also within our societies, in terms of social class, age, ethnicity, and gender. Thus, the notion of environmental justice "implies the right to a safe, healthy, and productive environment for all, where the environment is understood as a whole, including its ecological, physical, built, social, political, aesthetic, and economic dimensions. It therefore refers to the conditions that permit the free exercise of that right, preserving, respecting, and fully developing individual and group identities and the communities' dignity and autonomy" (2004b, 16). This approach, which emphasizes the inequality of environmental costs, a lack of participation and democracy, environmental racism toward native peoples deprived of their territories in the name of unsustainable projects, gender injustice, and ecological debt, has given rise to various environmental justice networks in Latin America since the 1990s, in countries such as Chile (Latin American Observatory of Environmental Conflicts [Observatorio Latinoamericano de Conflictos Ambientales]) and Brazil (Environmental Justice Network [Rede de Justiça Ambiental]).[11]

———

Unlike in earlier times, when environmental matters constituted one of the various dimensions of struggles, rarely explicitly assumed, those matters are currently being resignified in territorial and political terms. We are undergoing what Enrique Leff calls "the environmentalization of indigenous and peasant struggles and the emergence of a Latin American environmental thought" (2006, 37–38). On the one hand, this environmentalization dynamic translates into the emergence of different *socio-territorial movements* (not exclusively indigenous/peasant) that struggle against private sectors (mostly transnational corporations) and the state (at its various scales and levels), tending to broaden and radicalize their representation and discursive platform by incorporating other topics such as the critique of development models, understood as monocultural and increasingly destructive. On the other hand, we also observe the emergence of a Latin American environmental thought, evident in the creation of critical and core concepts that point to a new environmental rationality.

3

Dependency as an
Organizing Axis

Dependency theory is an achievement of Latin American social thought. It is a great breakthrough for knowledge in general, but its point of departure was Latin America's specificities.—THEOTÔNIO DOS SANTOS, "'Argentina puede negociar hoy mejor que Brasil'" (Argentina can negotiate today better than Brasil), 2003

In an assessment of dependency theory elaborated in 2002 by one of its most important living representatives, the Brazilian Theotônio dos Santos, he provided a list of prominent names and currents in Latin American social sciences, which included Gilberto Freire, José de Castro, Raúl Prebisch, Caio Prado Junior, José Medina Echavarría, Gino Germani, and Florestan Fernandes, and concluded that "the accumulation of these and other methodological proposals in the region reflected the growing density of social thought, which went beyond the simple application of reflections, methodologies, or scientific proposals imported from the central countries, paving the way to a Latin American theoretical field with its own methodology and thematic identity and to a more realistic praxis. Dependency theory attempted to be a synthesis of this intellectual and historical movement" (2002, 7).

However, dependency theory has been highly questioned. Many critics believe that its approach is simplistic, reductionist, and hardly conducive to a rigorous and complex socioeconomic and political analysis. Its critics range from those who argue that it has more to do with a self-evident commonsense notion that contributes little to analysis to those who see it as a "magical" concept that anticipates too many conclusions even before conducting any study. There are also those who dismiss it for having a purely ideological connotation derived from earlier times—an "evil of the times" or a sort of "youthful sin" of Latin American thought.

From my perspective, it would be of little use to view dependency theory through a traditional lens, although viewing it through a postmodern one would not be much of an improvement. Rather, a comprehensive historical analysis of that theory is necessary in order to grasp the contextual wealth of its debates, as well as its theoretical shortcomings, without giving in to either a temptation to idealize or a swift dismissal, to which the post–Berlin Wall ideological climate has led us.

During the long and intense years between 1950 and 1975, which was one of the richest and most fertile periods for theoretical production and political/ideological debates in Latin America, new descriptive and analytic categories were generated and discussed, such as dependency, asynchrony, structural heterogeneity, marginality, internal colonialism, disarticulation, and variegation (*abigarramiento*), among others. Although all of them illustrate the extraordinary creativity of Latin American thought at the time, the category that stands out for its capacity to radiate and reorder the critical field is that of dependency. The notion of dependency permeates all economic, social, political, and even cultural analyses; it illuminates with a certain color each of the debates of the time, placing them in a common horizon of discussion, generating a shared perspective in the intellectual field and, at times, a cognitive closure.

In short, beyond the uses and abuses derived from its enormous resonance and its overpoliticization as a general reading matrix, the category of dependency contributed to establishing a broad theoretical field with common concerns, integrating and fostering other analytic categories of Latin American critical thought, while inspiring a large number of research studies on the history and conflictive dynamics of the various national societies. For that reason, the purposes of this chapter are both to expound on the central contributions of dependency theorists and their debates and to show how this theory-concept became a sort of *common interpretative frame* for a significant part of Latin America's critical intellectuality of the time. Generally speaking, frames organize experience and orient both individual and collective action; they serve to construct a certain interpretation of reality. In this respect, I argue that between 1965 and 1979, dependency theory became a sort of *structure* or *master frame* in Latin America's academic/intellectual field. This explains its ability to relate to other categories of the intellectual field in order to broaden the topics of analysis and debate, thus extending the theoretical field of dependency and even transforming or overdetermining other issues and reading frames. Certain social conditions, a structure of political opportunities, and an updated critical tradition in the social sciences led to an alignment of the frames, through the connection, thematic expansion, and extension of the field around dependency theory.[1] In other words, the emergence of dependency as a master frame favored the creation of a space for Latin American debate and circulation of original ideas, which enabled us to speak of Latin America as a historical/political unit, beyond the obvious regional differences.

This extraordinarily fruitful period in theoretical and intellectual terms began during the second postwar period, at the time of import substitution; grew with the crisis and exhaustion of developmentalist populisms, especially after the military coup in Brazil (1964); and started declining, taking a more dramatic turn, with the various dictatorships in the Southern Cone (Bolivia, 1971; Uruguay, 1973; Chile, 1973; Argentina, 1976).

As Nildo Domingo Ouriques (1994, 180) argues, there are three geographic axes of dependency theory: Brazil, Chile, and Mexico. Brazil comes first, since it was there that the main intellectual representatives of dependency emerged: Fernando H. Cardoso, Theotônio dos Santos, Ruy Mauro Marini, and Vânia Bambirra, several of whom went into exile in Chile after the 1964 coup. Even the German economist Andre Gunder Frank went through several universities in Brazil before arriving at the phenomenal political laboratory that Chile became at the time. A number of events related to the political climate at the time contributed to the emergence of this perspective—among them, the discussion seminars on Karl Marx's *Capital* organized at the University of São Paulo by the foundation of the Workers' Politics Marxist Revolutionary Organization (Organização Revolucionária Marxista Política Operária; POLOP), which brought together several of the intellectuals who would later become key thinkers of dependency theory, and the forced exile resulting from Humberto de Alencar Castelo Branco's dictatorship (1964) and the novel character that Brazilian intellectuals attributed to that dictatorship.

The second geographic axis was Chile and the beacon experience of the time: the failed "Chilean path to socialism." The specific foundational location of dependency theory was the Center for Socioeconomic Studies (Centro de Estudios Socioeconómicos; CESO) of the Faculty of Economics of the University of Chile, which brought together many intellectuals of the region in an atmosphere of lively theoretical and political discussions. Finally, the third geographic axis was Mexico, a country of refuge where many intellectuals—Brazilian, Chilean, Argentinean, and Uruguayan, among many others—persecuted or expelled by the different military dictatorships of the Southern Cone went into exile. It was also in Mexico that this cycle of political radicalization came to an end, giving way to a new cycle marked by reflections on political defeat, ideological ebbing, and aperture to new topics, which included abandoning revolutionary ideals and positively reassessing the institutional democratic system.

The mood at the time bore the imprint of two disciplines, political sociology and political economics, whose concepts and categories of analysis were elaborated in conjunction with critical social thought, closely linked to the different variants of Marxism, in a sociopolitical climate influenced by the Cuban Revolution, Maoism, and decolonization currents. In this context, dependency theory paved new avenues to critical thought, establishing a general common framework of understanding and explanation, whose point of departure was none other than the will to reflect on the specificity of Latin American societies, at a time of significant political and economic changes (the advance of monopoly capital), breaking to a significant extent with the normative schemes provided by the dominant epistemological and political matrices. At the same time, as a general reading matrix, dependency theory broadened the problematic theoretical field, illuminating other categories of the time, such as marginality and internal colonialism, which gained greater visibility thanks to their employment of dependency theory as a general frame of reference.

Considering this complexity, this chapter is divided into two parts. In the first part, I present the main lines of dependency theory, focusing on the contributions of the "founding" generation, which includes Fernando H. Cardoso, Andre Gunder Frank, Theotônio dos Santos, Vânia Bambirra, and Ruy Mauro Marini. I also propose a journey through what I call the broader field of dependency. I thus examine the debate on marginality, a category whose *origins* can be understood only in the context of the discussions on dependency theory, even though it stands on its own and has an independent trajectory. In the second part, I present the main topics of some of the controversies that shook the field of dependency: first, the *mode of production* in Latin America (feudalism or capitalism); second, the role of the *national bourgeoisie* and the new reflections on the *role of the state*; and, finally, toward the end of the cycle, the disagreements and controversies within the dependency field itself.

Part 1: The Categories Involved

Dependency as a "Beacon" Category

It is not by chance that, in this phase, specialists in the social sciences, whether economists, sociologists, or political scientists, are the intellectuals par excellence, replacing ideologues, the nation's architects, and even party intellectuals. This shift in prestige takes place as theorizing on stagnation and dependency becomes imperative. For it is the specialist who now has the power to interpret the whole of "reality."—DANIEL PÉCAUT, *Entre le peuple et la nation: Les intellectuels et la politique au Brésil* (Between the people and the nation: Intellectuals and politics in Brazil), 1989

Many authors argue that there is not only one dependency theory but several of them, or even a "current of ideas" (dos Santos) sustained by a series of common elements. Others claim that it is actually not a theory at all but rather an "approach," a "perspective," or "innumerable contributions" (Beigel 2006; Sotelo Valencia 2005; Roitman 2008a) that do not constitute a theoretical paradigm. There is no doubt that, as a critical category, dependency made a dazzling entry into the history of Latin American social sciences, a success that later extended to other fields and institutions, such as political parties, social movements, journalism, and even cultural magazines (Beigel 2006). It was productive both analytically and politically; that is, not only did it describe and explain the national and regional situation from a historical/structural perspective, linking it to global processes common to all Latin American nations as peripheral countries, but it also had a very significant political impact.

But while the impact of dependency theory in Latin America and globally was enormous, it also quickly fell prey to its own success, as its dizzying dissemination in the academic and extra-academic fields led to many misunderstandings and simplifications, caricatured appropriations, and fierce criticisms from across the political/ideological spectrum. In a 1974 text on the sociology of the time, Pablo González Casanova argued that "the so-called dependency theory was—seen in retrospect—the academic version of a new political line of the forces of the Latin American left; but precisely because of its ambiguity, the term became the verbal domain even of the spokespersons of antipopulist dictatorships" (201). This trivialization required what could be described as demonstrations and counterdemonstrations by its most emblematic representatives in response to the criticisms, while internal quarrels multiplied.

From my perspective, dependency became a theory that aimed at a totalizing understanding of social matters, or, more precisely, a general reading matrix that proposed a structural articulation between the economic and the political realms. On the basis of this general postulate, dependency theory constructs its margins and limits with respect to other theories (functionalism, the developmentalism of the Economic Commission for Latin America and the Caribbean [CEPAL], orthodox Marxism), allowing different variations and transformations around a common corpus and language (center/periphery, development/underdevelopment, circulation/production, and imperialism/nation, among others). In addition, dependency fostered an enormous production of theory and research. In a well-publicized 1974 text, Fernando H. Cardoso rightly wrote, "A review of the literature on Latin America produced in the past five years demonstrates that there is almost a break between past and present topics. This break brought to the forefront, in international bodies, universities, and institutions usually cautious in this respect, a new way of conceiving the relationship between imperialist and dominated countries. More important, there was a surge of analyses on the state, local bourgeoisies, trade unions, workers and social movements, and ideologies (not to mention studies on marginality and urbanization), in one way or another inspired by the frame of reference of dependency studies" (109).

We therefore witnessed a very prolific period in which national research studies on the social and economic evolution of the various countries multiplied, creating new avenues to approach the already complex problem of the relations between social classes and the dynamics of capital accumulation and between the national and global scales.

Generally speaking, the category of dependency emerged as something more than a common diagnosis or a sort of critical concept regarding the impossibility of autonomous development in the capitalist periphery—something that ran counter to the proposals of CEPAL economists and planners. For its most representative authors, the notion of dependency actually connected a critical diagnosis of Latin American societies in the context of the global society to a commitment to political change through revolutionary means. The fundamental thesis of the advocates of dependency is that underdevelopment is not merely another phase of capitalist development but a product of the expansion of central capitalism. On the other hand, the notion of dependency emerged from a diagnosis regarding the new forms of penetration of concentrated international capital into peripheral economies, a situation that put an end to the populist/developmentalist experiments and entailed repositioning the local bourgeoisie in its relation to monopoly capital.

For many, dependency was an obligatory complement to the theory of imperialism, an expression of the new phase of internationalization of capital. The concept of dependency implied recognizing relations of domination between central and peripheral countries, and, within these, between social classes; structural dependency therefore referred not only to external forces (external dependency) but also to the relationships between the external and the internal and their forms of articulation (political, social, economic). Therefore, external domination is impracticable if the dominant interests of the hegemonic centers are not articulated with the dominant interests within the dependent societies themselves. It is not by chance that there was an effort to establish typologies and to account for the new forms of dependency as they were enacted in the various national scenarios.

The epistemological break undertaken by the dependency field was therefore twofold, for it encompassed both CEPAL's positions and structural functionalism. On the other hand, in political terms, it also proposed a more radical view of national and social liberation, in opposition to the orthodox Marxist strategy associated with the Communist Party. First, the category of dependency was founded on the critique of CEPAL's theory of development, although it also drew on the latter by revisiting an important organizing axis: the distinction between center and periphery, which had such outstanding descriptive power and was so long-lasting that it transcended a wide variety of theoretical models. The influence of Paul Baran and his works on the topic of underdevelopment, published in the 1950s, and that of Celso Furtado, whose 1966 thesis on structural stagnation implied a break with CEPAL's proposals, is often acknowledged.[2] From the standpoint of dependency, the relationship between center and periphery should be read in hierarchical terms, since relations of power and domination not only hinder or prevent the periphery's development but also produce underdevelopment, consolidating—at one end of the equation—the "development of underdevelopment" of the periphery (Frank 1967a). From this perspective, without abandoning a binary scheme, the advocates of dependency resignified the development/underdevelopment duality, questioning the very possibility of autonomous development in peripheral nations.

Second, the category of dependency spread throughout Latin America until it incorporated in its master frame the so-called critical sociology (Franco 1979; Beigel 2006), which emerged in opposition to "scientific sociology," incarnated by two of the founding fathers of the discipline in Latin America: José Medina Echavarría in Mexico and Gino Germani in Argentina. In epistemological terms, the so-called scientific sociology was based on the structural-functionalist paradigm, whose main academic proponent was Talcott Parsons. That current's expansion entailed an immense advancement of sociology throughout the continent, evident in the number and quality of publications, the consolidation of the professional field, and the connections with international centers of production. By the mid-1960s, however, all critical currents pointed against it, on the grounds that it was a theoretical perspective that lacked the necessary conditions to interpret Latin America's reality correctly. When explaining the persistence of underdevelopment in Latin America, for example, functionalism referred to "internal obstacles" and "deviations," thus reducing transitional problems to the traditional values and attitudes of the social players (I. Sotelo 1972, 139). On the other hand, functionalism could say or explain little about the Cuban Revolution and the new militant ethos established after 1959, all of which had a significant impact on the shift in positions—both political and epistemological—held by a large part of Latin America's intelligentsia.

Brazil had its own particular expression of critical sociology, reflected in the emergence of a new university Marxism, which represented a strong theoretical and generational shift. As various specialists on Brazilian sociology (Martins 1998; Pécaut 1989), as well as the protagonists themselves (dos Santos, Cardoso, Marini, Bambirra), argue, the seminars on Marx organized beginning in 1958 at the University of São Paulo under the aegis of Cardoso and Arthur Giannoti, in which a whole generation of Brazilian scholars participated, including the most emblematic representatives of dependency, played an important role. The seminars' objective was theoretical, since the point was to read *Capital* in epistemological terms, in search of new groundings for the social sciences (Pécaut 1989, 201) and hence a new research methodology. The first result was a series of studies on Black populations in Brazil, conducted by Cardoso and Octavio Ianni and published in 1962, in which both referred to the dialectical method to describe and explain the society and period examined. It is worth adding that these seminars on the study of *Capital* were also replicated in Santiago de Chile in the context of CESO, as Theotônio dos Santos reminds us (interviewed in Vidal Molina 2013, 191).

In sum, in tune with the new critical sociology, the advocates of dependency questioned the classical functionalist view, which operated under an evolutionist and normative paradigm, emphasizing other approaches to Latin America's reality. This new approach proposed undertaking a more integrated analysis (instead of a partial or specialized analysis, as scientific sociology proposed); abandoning the neopositivist method and replacing it with a different, historical/structural methodological perspective; considering the object's historicity, which therefore entailed a dialectical analysis based on a periodization with well-defined historical cycles; and emphasizing complex international phenomena related to the new dynamics of capital expansion. The result was a revival of Marxism in the region as an epistemological and political matrix, with a tendency to develop a totalizing view of political, economic, and social processes in Latin America (Franco 1979, 275).

As a result, dependency as a category was consolidated in the theoretical field of the new Latin American Marxism. For that reason, it was strongly attacked and criticized, especially by orthodox Marxism, represented by the Communist Party, which argued that capitalism's objective conditions in Latin America were not sufficiently mature; the party therefore pointed to a democratic/bourgeois revolution. Advocates of dependency theory (and of the new Latin American Marxism in general), on the other hand, rejected the stage logic, believing that the new forms of penetration of concentrated international capital into the economies of the periphery had signaled the end of the populist experiences and a repositioning of the local bourgeoisie, which, far from being an ally, was now associated with monopoly capital. At the same time, the failure of populist/developmentalist experiences as a means for change in the face of the new dependency paved the way to explore other paths and forms of revolutionary commitment, exemplified at the international level by nationalist and decolonial movements, and at the continental level by the Cuban Revolution, the Chilean path to socialism, and the various guerrilla movements in other countries of the region.

In spite of the obvious differences between its most emblematic representatives, there are a number of elements common to dependency theory. First is the notion that the obstacles to development do not stem from backwardness (whether viewed through an CEPAL or a functionalist lens) but from the way in which the economies of peripheral countries articulate with/within the international system. This is what is meant by *dependency*, doubly understood in terms of both external and internal factors and the internal structure of peripheral societies, as Vânia Bambirra argued: "The most relevant common aspect of dependency theory is undoubtedly its questioning of the possibility of an *autonomous* national development (note well: *autonomous*)" (1978, 13). Some thinkers spoke of a "situation of dependency" (Cardoso and Faletto 1979a); others of "conditioning" (dos Santos [1978] 2011) or "concrete conditioning" (Bambirra 1978). A second common element is the belief that dependency must be understood within the general framework of the theory of imperialism (Cardoso, Marini, dos Santos), which is strongly linked to the notion of the *unity of the capitalist system*, a topic elaborated by various authors, among them Frank and dos Santos. The third element is the characterization of the *current phase* at the time (the late 1960s) as different from the previous ones, due to the growing presence of monopoly capital in dependent societies.

This was understood as "a new form of dependency" (dos Santos [1978] 2011), although the reading of the economic, political, and social consequences of the hegemony of monopoly capital led to a split within the dependency field (regarding the role of the state and the national bourgeoisies). Furthermore, this diagnosis was the basis for different political positions: those who argued for the coexistence of *dependency and development* (Cardoso and Faletto) and those who stressed the dilemma of the *development of underdevelopment or revolution* (Frank), or *socialism or fascism* (dos Santos), among others. There were also those who aimed at establishing a social typology and different forms of dependency, especially Cardoso and Faletto, dos Santos, and Bambirra.

Finally, dependency theorists were concerned with the issue of methodology, which Cardoso and Faletto put on the agenda, advocating a historical/structural or dialectical method, which not only addresses the relationship between structure and action at the international and national levels in processual and dynamic terms but also inscribes the analyses in a more global and long-term historical perspective. This demand had to do with the conviction that many of the errors in the interpretation of Latin American development were not a matter of data but of deficiencies in the methodological conception, since the theories had been conceived to justify a certain type of development rather than to explain it (Bambirra 1978, 7).

THE FOUNDATIONAL CORPUS OF DEPENDENCY THEORY

As is well known, the classical founding text is *Dependencia y desarrollo en América Latina* (Dependency and development in Latin America; [1969] 2003; 1979a), coauthored by Fernando H. Cardoso and Enzo Faletto and published in 1969, which circulated as a draft or preliminary text in 1967 in the context of the Latin American and Caribbean Institute for Economic and Social Planning (Instituto Latinoamericano de Planificación Económica y Social; ILPES) in Chile. It was, however, from 1965 onward that a broad and heterogeneous group of authors started to publish in a different theoretical line, including, in addition to those already cited, Andre Gunder Frank, Theotônio dos Santos, Ruy Mauro Marini, Edelberto Torres Rivas, Orlando Caputo, Vânia Bambirra, Aníbal Quijano, and Franz Hinkelammert, among many others. Pablo González Casanova (1974, 196) also established 1965 as a key date, with the publication of Octavio Ianni's "Sociología de la sociología en América Latina" (Sociology of sociology in Latin America) and Rodolfo Stavenhagen's famous and brilliant essay *Seven Erroneous Theses About Latin America* (1967), which attacked the fundamental premises of functionalism (dual societies, diffusionism), Marxism (the worker-peasant alliance), the theses of the ideologues of imperialism, and the national bourgeoisie. It was also in 1965 that the controversy between Andre Gunder Frank and Rodolfo Puiggrós regarding the modes of production in Latin America began.

Cardoso and Faletto's much-published and often-cited 1969 book, *Dependencia y desarrollo en América Latina* ([1969] 2003; 1979a), implied a significant change in the theoretical and methodological perspective applied to the study of Latin America's reality. Avoiding any form of mechanicism, the work emphasized the historical-structural or dialectical method and the need to develop an integral perspective in order to explain the transformations that occurred in Latin American countries beginning with the 1930 crisis. On one hand, it highlighted the "situation of dependency," which expressed itself in the form of structural domination and entailed a connection to outside forces; on the other hand, dependency was not understood only as an external structural variable but had to be analyzed also in terms of class relations within the dependent society itself. Latin America therefore did not present "deviations" from the European and US standard that had to be corrected but a different condition derived from its peripheral situation. In this sense, the situation of colonial dependency experienced at the time reflected a double linkage or ambiguity, visible in external dependency and at the same time in the actions of the social forces that attempted to gain a certain autonomy and overcome that dependency. For Cardoso and Faletto, this was "the core of the sociological problem of the national development process in Latin America" (1979a; [1969] 2003, 29).

Another fundamental hypothesis of the book was that in the phase of outward growth, peripheral societies related to the international market in basically two antipodal manners: through national control of the export production system, on one hand, and through the consolidation of an enclave economy (mining, plantations), on the other. Each of these types of relationship had subtypes and nuances, but the difference between them was of great importance when analyzing the transition period (i.e., the opening to political and economic participation by other social sectors, including the middle classes), since both the patterns of social integration and social movements, through which the political life and the profile of Latin American societies were defined, assumed different connotations in countries that managed to maintain national control over the export system compared to countries where an enclave economy typical of the outward development phase prevailed.

On this line of analysis, Cardoso and Faletto posited that "the transition" would lead to a new social situation, characterized by the development of policies that tended to consolidate the internal market and industrialization, that is, import substitution industrialization (ISI). As a result, between 1950 and 1960, internal development associated with ISI was characterized by two tendencies or orientations: satisfying the domestic market, or the orientation toward participation, with its dose of social and economic distributionism; and promoting the growth of new dominant sectors of the economy linked to the domestic market, which attempted to preserve the system of internal domination. That was the meaning of "developmentalist populism": a system of domination in which contradictory interests and objectives were expressed and articulated.

However, beginning in the 1960s, a crisis of the previous system of domination and the emergence of a new situation of dependency were observed, forcing various countries (especially Brazil, Argentina, and Mexico) to open their domestic markets to external control (direct foreign investments in the peripheral industrial economies). This important change resignified dependency, reformulating it and inscribing it in a new framework—a new "situation" characterized by both transformations in the productive structure, with increasing levels of complexity, and economic and social situations of exclusion for the working classes. Cardoso and Faletto thus explained the passage from representative democratic regimes (developmentalist populism) to authoritarian-corporate regimes, which reorganized the army and the public bureaucracy, rather than the internationalized national bourgeoisies.

In their conclusions, the authors attempted to go beyond the opposition between development and dependency, underscoring the viability of an increase in development and its coexistence with a new—stronger—reformulation of the ties of dependency, in the context of the new phase of global capitalism. Thus, contrary to the optimistic view of developmentalist theories and the pessimism upheld by those who denied the possibility of development, the book posited development with dependency, or, rather, associated dependent development. Along the same lines, in a 1979 postscript published after the failure of the Chilean path to socialism and in a Latin American context characterized by military regimes, the authors once again underscored their rejection of interpretations of dependency that portrayed multinational corporations as the demiurges of history, overvaluing external factors and overlooking the importance of global and national political factors (Cardoso and Faletto [1969] 2003, 176–77). Furthermore, they argued that ten years of economic growth (1969–79) had demonstrated the ability of several Latin American states to "act," which meant that there was now "less dependency" (193).[3] In the context of associated dependent capitalism or, more generically, "dependent industrialization," "the state becomes a strategic element that operates as a floodgate that allows the passage of the history of capitalism in industrializing peripheral economies" (195). Consequently, it was the political struggles surrounding the state that would redefine the new forms of dependency.

Cardoso returned again and again to the possibilities of dependent industrialization—that is, that there was "a possibility of dynamism in dependent capitalist economies" undergoing a process of industrialization under the control of international monopoly capital. This, however, required understanding that this form of industrialization did not involve the actions of a "European-like" bourgeoisie, but neither did it involve those economies' own Narodnik-style development model, which according to Cardoso was assumed by CEPAL and quite a few populisms. Rather, the formula implied affirming the expansion of capitalism and, simultaneously, the aggravation of (new) contradictions ([1973] 1977, 402–3).

Another founder of dependency theory was Andre Gunder Frank. One of his best-known essays is "The Development of Underdevelopment" (1966). According to Frank, the key to understanding resided in analyzing the way in which Latin America was subordinated or subjected to the central countries. His interpretation emphasized socioeconomic relations and questioned both the thesis of diffusionism and that of dual societies, so widely assumed in Latin America, in order to explain social and economic heterogeneity or the abyss between traditional and modern societies. In this respect, Frank argued that "underdevelopment in Latin America is the result of its secular participation in the process of international capitalist development" (1966; 1967b, 163). Underdevelopment is therefore not the result of the survival of archaic institutions or the lack of capital in regions that have remained isolated from world history. On the contrary, underdevelopment has been and continues to be generated by the development of capitalism itself.

According to Frank, "the class structure in Latin America was formed by the development of the colonial structure of capitalism, from mercantilism to imperialism" (1968, 3). This relationship of domination took place in the form of concentric circles: The successive metropolises (Spain, England, the United States) have subjected this colonial structure to economic and political exploitation. That same colonial structure is reproduced within Latin America, where the national metropolises subjected their provincial centers, and the latter subjected the local population, through internal colonialism. One of the conclusions of this reading was that the class struggle and the anti-imperialist struggle were intertwined. The immediate enemy was the national and local bourgeoisie, and the main enemy was imperialism, but the anti-imperialist struggle should take place through the class struggle against the immediate (national, local) enemy, which led to a confrontation with the imperialist enemy. The model for this struggle was guerrilla warfare, illustrated by revolutionary Cuba and exemplified by Che Guevara's ideas.

Another outstanding representative of dependency theory is the Brazilian thinker Theotônio dos Santos, who made important contributions to positioning it in the global framework of the theory of imperialism. His many works include *Socialismo o fascismo: El nuevo carácter de la dependencia y el dilema latinoamericano* (Socialism or fascism: The new character of dependency and the Latin American dilemma; 1972), a compilation of essays written during his exile in Chile, but his best-known text is *Imperialismo y dependencia* (Imperialism and dependency; [1978] 2011). He is probably also the thinker who has reflected most in terms of an overall assessment of dependency theory (dos Santos 2002) and who, together with Vânia Bambirra, has made the greatest headway toward an integrating synthesis.

From his perspective, neither Vladimir Lenin nor other Marxist theoreticians examined imperialism from the standpoint of peripheral countries; while the specificity of the development of capitalism in the center gave rise to the theory of colonialism and imperialism, in the periphery it gave rise to dependency theory. For that reason, dependency must be understood in the global context of the theory of imperialism, but taking into account its specificity, without automatisms; conceptualizing it; understanding it; studying its mechanisms and historical legacy. Dos Santos's point of departure is that it is difficult to explain what is meant by *dependency*, given the sheer amount and diversity of works that have placed it at the center of discussions on development. It is important to note, however, that from his perspective, dependency is not an external factor—rather, it is a "condition." He also revisits Cardoso and Faletto's use of "a situation of dependency" to refer to "a certain group of countries whose economy is conditioned by the development and expansion of another economy to which it is subjected" (dos Santos [1978] 2011, 361). Interdependence, an unequal division of labor, a high concentration of capital and domination by the international market, the monopolization of the possibility of saving and investing by a small group of central countries . . . these are all elements that condition and limit the possibilities of development in peripheral countries.

The Brazilian author makes a distinction between the *basic forms of dependency* in the context of the development of capitalism, their relationship with the hegemonic center and their links to the international system, on one hand, and *dependent national economies*, which must be studied in terms of how they are structured within the international system and as a result of it, as well as their role in its development, on the other hand (dos Santos [1978]

2011, 364). He thus proposes three types of basic forms of dependency: a commercial-export *colonial dependency*; *financial-industrial dependency*, consolidated in the late nineteenth century and characterized by the domination of large capital in hegemonic centers and its outward expansion to invest in the production of raw materials and agricultural products consumed in the hegemonic centers; and, finally, *technological-industrial dependency*, consolidated in the postwar period and characterized by technological-industrial domination. While the first and second forms of dependency configured export economies, the third form gave rise to what dos Santos denominated "new dependency."

In this new form of dependency, industrial production is variously conditioned by the demands of the commodities and capital markets. The productive system that developed in dependent countries became highly conditioned: On one hand, the preservation of the agrarian and mining structures led to a combination of more advanced economic sectors, which obtained surplus value from the more backward ones, and external and internal dependent "metropolitan" and "colonial" centers. The unequal and combined nature of capitalist development at the international level is thus reproduced internally. Another conditioning factor is the need to create an industrial and technological structure driven by the interests of multinational corporations rather than by internal development needs (dos Santos [1978] 2011, 377). Finally, another conditioning factor is technological transfer from the hegemonic centers to very different societies, which has unequal impacts and exacerbates social and technological problems.

Two general conclusions can be derived from this. The first is that the obstacles to development are not the result of backwardness but of the way in which these economies articulate with/within the international system. The second is that, in agreement with Frank and contrary to Cardoso, the new dependency precludes autonomous national development. Developmentalist populism demonstrated the limits of autonomous development and therefore led to significant frustration in various social sectors. In this context, there are only two possibilities: choosing among existing alternatives or undertaking a qualitative change—either *socialism* or *fascism*. In tune with this second alternative, dos Santos believes that furthering the political and social struggle entails political opportunities. The new forms of dependency imply a greater protagonism of monopoly capital and a strong presence of accumulative mechanisms of dependency (debt and international aid, among others) and demand a redefinition of relations, at both the international and national levels. In this dynamic context, the system is unable to resolve the contradictions it generates within dependent economies, both in the advanced sectors and in the elimination of the most backward ones. As a result of the system's need to increase regional dependency, with the emergence of subimperialism or dominant subcenters, conflicts deepen at the continental level and pave the way to a socialist alternative.

Vânia Bambirra, also a Brazilian thinker, is the only woman cited in this stellar list of authors of dependency theory. Her reading agrees with the general positions of dos Santos and Marini, defending a radical and Marxist perspective. Her contribution to dependency theory comprises two fundamental axes. On one hand, she conducted a study on the internal state of the art based on the critique (or anticritique) of both the developmentalist branch of dependency theory (Osvaldo Sunkel, Aníbal Pinto, and others) and the orthodox Marxist perspective (paradigmatically incarnated by Agustín Cueva), as well as the ultra-left-wing *foquista* avenue (a revolutionary theory proposed by Ernesto "Che" Guevarra), which she considered unviable. On the other hand, she developed a typology of dependency for the purpose of generating intermediate categories of analysis that articulated the more general frameworks with empirical analysis. In this line of thought, Bambirra defended the status of dependency as a theory, insofar as the authors—with the exception of Cardoso—shared a common approach that posited the impossibility of autonomous national development. This denial was in part related to her analysis of the role of the bourgeoisie in the context of the new dependency: "What we propose, on the basis of a description of the real situation in Latin America, based on evident data and a vast empirical observation undertaken in a very large number of research studies, is that, as the bourgeoisies in our continent associated as a class with foreign capital, they had to renounce to their own autonomous national development projects. In this respect, and only in this respect, they cannot hold a national project, they cannot defend the interests of the nation independently of the interests of foreign capital, because they are associated with it as minor partners" (1978, 65).

Also, for Bambirra (1978, 8), dependency studies do not refer to a dependent capitalist mode of production (which does not exist as such) but to the study of *dependent capitalist economic and social formations*, which accounts for the coexistence and combination of different modes of production under the hegemony of capitalism. The work in which she developed these topics is *El capitalismo dependiente latinoamericano* (Latin American dependent capitalism; [1974] 1999), where she established a typology of dependency. In that work she revisited the theoretical framework developed by dos Santos, defining dependency as a "conditioning situation." On the other hand, Bambirra believed that the analysis of post-1945 processes was insufficient, a fact that inspired her work on the typologies in order to provide intermediate categories of analysis, taking the second postwar period as her point of departure—that is, the new objective conditions imposed by the advancement of monopoly capitalism in the dependent periphery. The result was an interesting set of typologies: The first one includes those countries with an incipient form of old industrialization, that is, prior to the postwar period (Argentina, Brazil, Chile, Mexico, Uruguay, and Colombia); the second one refers to those that began their industrialization after the war, some of them with foreign capital (Peru, Venezuela, Ecuador, Costa Rica, Guatemala, Bolivia, El Salvador, Panama, Nicaragua, Honduras, the Dominican Republic, and Cuba); and, finally, the last includes those countries that had not yet begun industrializing (Panama, Haiti, and Paraguay). Bambirra thus sought to establish a dialogue between different variants of dependency, developing a critique within the field of dependency from a Marxist perspective. She also skillfully attempted to respond to the various critiques from outside the field, especially in her text *Teoría de la dependencia: Una anticrítica* (Dependency theory: An anti-critique; 1978), written during her exile in Mexico.

To conclude, I would like to mention one of the most important and ambitious foundational theoreticians of dependency, Ruy Mauro Marini. Marini's wager was to establish the Marxist bases of dependency theory, whose point of departure was the recognition of the insufficiency of the existing intellectual categories to explain the situation of peripheral societies/economies. According to him, when referring to the Latin American case, we should speak of a *sui generis form of capitalism* (2008, 100). In the mid-nineteenth century, when Latin American countries consolidated as independent republics, a group of countries started to gravitate toward England; ignoring each other, they established ties with the imperial center as countries that were providers of raw materials and importers of manufactured products. This unequal international division of labor determined the region's future development. From then on, a situation of dependency was established, which—in terms of recursive dynamics—could only lead to increasing dependency. In this regard, Marini concluded that Frank's formula regarding the "development of underdevelopment" was "impeccable," even though he was wrong in conceiving colonial dependency and the current dependency as homogeneous. Simply stated, continuity does not necessarily imply homogeneity.

Like other dependency theorists, Marini argued that the character of capitalist accumulation and its penetration of and interchange with the dependent countries experienced new inflections, which reinforced its unequal and combined nature. His contribution in this respect is two highly controversial concepts: The first has to do with the superexploitation of the labor force in dependent societies; the second is the notion of subimperialism, applied specifically to Brazil.

In his development of the thesis of the superexploitation of the labor force, Marini explained that it is due to the fact that, since in Latin America circulation is separate from production, basically located in the foreign market, workers' individual consumption does not interfere in the product's creation, although it does determine the share of surplus value. As a result, there is a tendency to exploit the labor force as much as possible, without concern for the necessary conditions for the workers' recovery as long as they can be replaced by new arms. The replaceability of the proletariat is therefore much more extreme than in countries with advanced capitalism, where the surplus value, in the current development phase, is more related to an increase in the productive capacity (relative surplus value) than to an increase in labor force exploitation (absolute surplus value). This tendency to rely on a type of absolute surplus value is also congruent with the meager development of productive forces in Latin America's economy and with the type of activities carried out, which are more extractive and agrarian than industrial. Furthermore, foreign capital and technologies are imported in response to the consumption patterns of the upper classes, thus maintaining the tendency to compress popular consumption (Marini [1969] 1974, xvii). The incorporation of techniques and technologies by production economies based on the superexploitation of labor aggravates unemployment and underemployment, as demonstrated by the literature on marginality. Following the dialectical process, the accumulation dynamics under conditions of superexploitation intensify the concentration and centralization of capital (monopolization), benefiting those branches of industry that disregard popular consumption. Thus, capital realization tends to shrink the domestic market. In short, dependency occurs not only at the level of the circulation of commodities between the center and the periphery but also at the level of production.

Regarding the second concept, that of subimperialism, we begin by asserting that, like for other authors, Marini's point of departure was the theory of imperialism, and in this line he argued that the world market had been reorganized under the hegemony of the United States and that the superabundance of resources in the hands of international corporations required new markets. The extraordinary development of capital goods, together with accelerated technological progress, led to the export of obsolete machinery and equipment from the central countries to the dependent ones. Every advancement in Latin America's industry thus consolidated its economic and technological dependence on the imperial centers. As a result, levels or hierarchies between countries were established, according to the branches of production that had developed or could develop, and other countries were denied access to this type of production, turning them into mere consumer markets. This process of rationalization of the division of labor resulted in a subimperialism associated with the metropolis, aimed at exploiting its neighboring countries. Such was the policy of Castelo Branco's military government, which Argentina in turn tried to emulate (Marini [1969] 1974, 19). Following the model of "antagonistic cooperation" (60) with the United States, Brazil intended to become "a center of irradiation of imperialist expansion in Latin America, even creating the bases for its own military power" (75). Finally, subimperialism is not a strictly Brazilian phenomenon; it is a particular form of industrial economy that develops in the context of dependent capitalism (Marini 2008, 136).

In sum, Marini's contribution was of significant importance not only because of its originality, as it fully incorporated the issue of capitalist production through the superexploitation of the labor force into the field of dependency, but also because of its visionary nature regarding the category of subimperialism, whose potential was greater than expected, as I discuss in the second part of this book, which focuses on current debates.

Dependency as a Broader Field: Approaches to Marginality

It makes no sense to pose the question of the meaning of marginality in functionalist terms. Marginality today, like the industrial reserve army yesterday, is a product of the system. Their common function is to capture the rate of surplus value. Social disharmony is necessary for the system to function.—SAMIR AMIN, *Unequal Development* (referring to the theses by Jóse Nun and Fernando H. Cardoso), (1973) 1976

With a penchant for totality, a clear antipositivist character, and a passion for the concrete (understood in Marxist terms as "the set of many determinations"), the new Latin American sociology or critical sociology defined its own nature in terms of its desire for change, its projection toward a utopian horizon. In this context, among the various categories present in the intellectual field, those of marginality and internal colonialism stand out. Both inscribe their reflections in the broader field of dependency, since their proposals strongly question dualist theses and seek to explain the situation of underdevelopment from a relational perspective. In this section I focus exclusively on presenting the bases and debates surrounding the notion of marginality.

The concept of marginal population started to be used in Latin America after World War II to designate the "inhabitants" who settled in the peripheries of large cities under miserable conditions. The term's sociological origin was an article by Robert Park of the Chicago school, entitled "Human Migration and the Marginal Man," published in 1928. It became known in Latin America thanks to the French Jesuit Roger Vekemans, who directed the Center for Economic and Social Development of Latin America (Centro para el Desarrollo

Económico y Social de América Latina; DESAL), an international body based in Santiago de Chile. It was there that the first theoretical developments were elaborated on the subject of marginal groups, defined as "not incorporated," in reference to the integrated social system. Their lack of participation was explained at the time by cultural disintegration and social atomization.

It was in the context of DESAL that three Argentine sociologists, José Nun, Miguel Murmis, and J. Carlos Marín, returned to the concept and resignified it in a preliminary report entitled *La marginalidad en América Latina* (Marginality in Latin America), published in 1968 by the Instituto Torcuato Di Tella. A year later, Nun and Murmis each published an article in a special issue of *Revista Latinoamericana de Sociología* (Latin American journal of sociology) dedicated to the topic, where they expanded on concepts such as marginal mass and types of marginality, respectively (Nun 1969b; Murmis 1969). Although Aníbal Quijano had elaborated *Notas sobre el concepto de marginalidad social* (Notes on the concept of social marginality) for CEPAL in 1966, it was not until February 1970 that he published an article on the concept of marginal pole in Lima. Thus begins a rich and long collective reflection on marginality, which clearly draws on Latin American Marxism, employs concepts from dependency theory, and also refers to the theory of unequal and combined development and the theory of imperialism.[4]

Before we review the central ideas and their most representative authors, it should be noted that marginality has a twofold dimension, relational and territorial, while also referring to different epistemological matrices. Thus, in the first place, the notion of marginality in Latin America encompassed two dimensions: "a territorial imprint and a relational perspective" (Delfino 2012, 20). The first is associated with a new type of urban marginality that emerged around the 1930s, evident in the expansion of precarious settlements (slums, *villas miserias*, favelas, *cantegriles, barriadas*), which multiplied in the peripheries of large cities between the 1950s and 1960s as a result of urbanization processes or migration from rural areas to the cities. The second—the concept's relational dimension—indicated that the marginal, the peripheral, was always defined in opposition to an urban center that enjoyed certain housing and living conditions, which were employed as the basis to judge deficiencies or the level of negativity. Migration, urbanization, territoriality, and marginality are therefore closely related concepts.

Second, there are at least four aspects of marginality. The first refers to economic marginality (whether under the concept of marginal mass or marginal pole). In this framework, marginality is understood as a social relation related to the labor market and production relations, as Nun, Murmis, and Quijano propose. The second aspect refers to the theory of modernization, which connects the causes of marginality (especially urban marginality) to the problems of transitioning from a traditional to a modern society. This line of interpretation is developed by Gino Germani. The third aspect analyzes marginality from a socio-spatial perspective, based on the expansion of settlements in poorly equipped peripheral areas. One of the most important authors of urban studies is Brazilian thinker Lúcio Kowarick, who in the late 1970s introduced the concept of urban despoilment, although several prior works by Quijano on urbanization, dependency, and imperialism are also part of this line. A fourth aspect, very widespread and much criticized at the time, has to do with the cultural dimension of marginality, illustrated by the work of anthropologist Oscar Lewis (*Five Families*, [1959] 1975; *The Children of Sánchez*, [1961] 2011), who proposes the notion of the culture of poverty to reflect on marginality as a place of specific behaviors, segregated or dissociated from the rest of the socioeconomic system.

Considering especially the first two aspects, the concept of marginality suggests a dispute between two epistemological matrices: the structural-functionalist matrix, led by Gino Germani, and the Marxist matrix in its Latin American conceptualization, developed mainly by José Nun, Aníbal Quijano, and Miguel Murmis between 1968 and 1969. While, from the theory of modernization, marginality highlighted a structural duality—the split between a traditional and a modern sector—for the advocates of the Marxist perspective, marginality was the product of a relationship of interdependence related to the exclusionary dynamics of capital, intensified in the context of the new dependency. In addition, there were also interpretative differences within the dissenting field, as is evident in the debate between José Nun and Fernando H. Cardoso or in Aníbal Quijano's critical reading.

In the following pages, I provide an overview of the debate on marginality within the dependency field, before summarizing the ideas associated with Gino Germani and concluding with a brief presentation of some of the dilemmas related to the issue.

BETWEEN THE *MARGINAL MASS* AND THE *MARGINAL POLE*

José Nun's 1969 article published in *Revista Latinoamericana de Sociología* devoted to the topic was entitled "Superpoblación relativa, ejército industrial de reserva y masa marginal" (Relative overpopulation, industrial reserve army and marginal mass).[5] Nun was also in charge of presenting the dossier, where he announced that the subject of marginality seemed to him imbued with good intentions and poor conceptualizations. "Its use is tempting due to its apparent simplicity, when in fact its meaning is always complex, since it refers to something else that endows it with meaning—one can only be *marginal* relative to something else" ([1969] 2001, 19).

In order to clarify a series of theoretical points, Nun ([1969] 2001, 40) examined the renowned chapter 23 of volume 1 of Marx's *Capital* ([1867] 2024), which deals with the concepts of "relative overpopulation" and "industrial reserve army," which according to him were located at different levels of generality. The concept of marginality was thus the pivot of that difference. According to Marx, the relative overpopulation is that part of the population that is shut off from both the means of reproduction and its products. But this surplus population is relative not to the means of subsistence but to the current mode of production. However, its effects on the system are of different types—they can be functional, nonfunctional, and afunctional. The industrial reserve army—that is, the unoccupied labor force—is conceived as a functional effect (since it allows increasing the capitalist's rate of profit, lowering the costs of the labor force). By contrast, what he calls "marginal mass" refers to a low level of integration in the system caused by unequal and dependent capitalist development, which, combined with various processes of accumulation in the context of chronic stagnation, produces a *nonfunctional* relative overpopulation, related to the hegemonic forms of production.

It is important to note that Nun's objective was to analyze the marginal mass, which he conceived as a relationship and not as an attribute. He therefore did not intend to engage in a reflection on social subjects or certain activities (understood as marginal) per se. The result was a very broad concept that included a wide variety of different descriptive situations. In this line, he argued that in the Marxist tradition there was a tendency to identify the "relative overpopulation" with the "industrial reserve army," blending two different analytic levels and thus overlooking the analysis of other nonfunctional modalities or effects. This analytic hurdle derived from Marx's work itself, elaborated in a prior phase of capitalist development (competitive capitalism), and was also marked by capitalist development in England. But in the phase of monopoly capitalism, the increase in corporate rationality came together with a growing irrationality of the system, which turned a part of the relative overpopulation into a marginal mass, whose nonfunctionality was an undesired effect of the behavior of economic players but one derived from objective contradictions: agrarian backwardness, a labor force strongly conditioned by the availability of capital, technological restrictions, neocolonial dependency; all of this aggravated the problem of the absorption of the labor force, resulting in the transformation of that which in other contexts would have been conceived as an industrial reserve army into a marginal mass in Latin America. Differently from the industrial reserve army, the latter was not so much a transitional form but rather a constitutive feature of dependent capitalist economies, in the context of the consolidation of concentrated international capitalism. In this context, Nun adhered to the thesis of stagnation and crisis, in a scenario that foresaw a deepening of transnational monopoly capital.

Nun's article elicited a fierce response by Brazilian sociologist Fernando H. Cardoso. In a text full of erudite references to *Capital*, Cardoso characterized the Argentinean's thesis, based on the distinction between floating overpopulation and industrial reserve army, as "unspecific," "superfluous," and hardly applicable. Beyond his methodological objections, Cardoso ([1971] 2001, 181) believed that the concept was not applicable because it did not describe a situation of deprivation, nor did it foresee a type of behavior (more or less social and political integration), since both the employed and the unemployed were considered marginal, as was evident in the monopoly sector. He also criticized Nun's thesis of the stagnation of industrial employment, since, in his opinion, the facts contradicted it, reflecting instead a nostalgia toward "lost developmentalism," which translated into a catastrophic view of reality.

Nun (2001, 187) responded to Cardoso's criticisms by arguing again that *marginality* was one of those commonsense signifiers that could mean whatever one wanted but that his analysis had focused on elaborating not an empirical concept or a hypothetical construction but rather a *theoretical concept* that reflected on issues such as unemployment, underemployment, underconsumption, and social decomposition from a Marxist perspective. He argued that examining the issue of marginality in terms of productive relations justified introducing a new concept that was not sufficiently specified in the studies on capitalism and especially in Marx. At the same time, he understood that the concept was unable to found an autonomous horizon, that is, a "theory of marginality"; however, what Cardoso interpreted as lack of rigor or precision—in other words, the breadth of the concept of marginal mass—was for Nun absolutely necessary in order to account for the heterogeneity of socio-professional categories (from employed to unemployed) included in the concept. The increase in labor precariousness in the 1980s and the increase in unemployment in the 1990s proved Nun right. In 2001 Nun published a new book on the subject, republishing his earlier articles (including those related to his controversy with Cardoso) and revisiting the notion of marginal mass. In addition, the book sought to build bridges to, but also make clear distinctions from, the sociology of the social question proposed by several French authors (Robert Castel, Pierre Rosanvallon, and Jacques Donzelot, among others).

Miguel Murmis in turn laid down his ideas in the article "Tipos de marginalidad y posición en el proceso productivo" (Types of marginality and position in the productive process"), also published in 1969. According to Carlos Belvedere (1997), it was Murmis who gave most "substance to marginality," by elaborating a typology of relations of marginal insertion in the labor market. Murmis analyzed the marginal forms of insertion of the labor force related to superexploitation, where "the typical relationship of capitalist exploitation resulting from a stage of dependent capitalist development is not established" (1969, 415). Based on his own survey, he established a different typology: On one hand, there were those forms of marginality that imply fixation, that is, the persistence of certain forms that limit the condition as a free worker, such as the semiservile employment of indigenous people or the use of the labor force in factories and plantations, as well as the subsistence of activities of direct producers, but in conditions that preclude accumulation. On the other hand, there are those situations where the laborers have already become "free workers" but do not find the conditions that enable them to establish a stable relationship with employment, whether because they cannot sell their labor force full-time or because of the instability of their employment.

Finally, in a line more closely related to Nun's proposal, there are Aníbal Quijano's analyses and his notion of the marginal pole. According to the author, there are two interdependent systems: a central or hegemonic nucleus and a marginal pole. The latter was constituted by a set of activities and economic relations that perpetuated, in a fragmentary manner, those that characterized the dominated groups in the "hegemonic nucleus." From his perspective, two decisive phenomena affected the transformation of Latin American economies: the generalization of the industrial production of goods and services as a hegemonic sector, and its emergence in its monopolist modality. Grafted into Latin America, these elements produced abrupt changes in Latin American economies, since they neither modified nor replaced by eradication the previous sectors but combined with them, giving rise to a new articulation of economic matters. But as they became hegemonic, they ended up modifying the relative position of the preceding elements, their functions, their concrete characteristics, which therefore became a product of those changes instead of a mere remainder of prior conditions or surviving elements of the past. They therefore occupied a lower level due to the loss of resources, products, and markets, as a result of their inability to gain access to the new means of production that presumably accompany technological development. An undervalued level of the economy was thus created, comprising a set of activities derived from the labor relations, which employed residual resources of production, with a precarious and unstable structure and limited income, generating a subsistence economy for their own consumption, without creating surplus ([1970] 2014, 136 et seq.). The marginal pole was therefore related to a consistent lack of the essential production resources present in the dominant levels of the economy.

Like Nun, Quijano also examined chapter 23 of volume 1 of *Capital* to argue that the development of the leading sectors turned that floating or excluded population into a permanent tendency rather than a secular or transitory one (2014a, 158). This situation was worse in underdeveloped countries because of the phenomenon of economic dependency, which also led to the hypertrophy of large cities at the expense of the countryside. Thus, the emergence of such a depressed marginal pole generated a more heterogeneous, more unequal, and more contradictory dependent economic structure, which should be understood in relation to monopolistic hegemony. Regarding the marginal labor force, it led to a process of social differentiation within the working class itself—a sort of subclass that added a (new) burden to the active proletariat (163).

In short, beyond the differences, the thesis on marginality successfully anticipated several structural problems of Latin American societies, among them the state's management of the surplus population. According to Nun ([1969] 2001, 28), the phenomenon of marginality unveiled a serious structural problem that sooner or later the state would have to respond to, given the risk of the afunctional population becoming dysfunctional due to its exclusion from hegemonic forms of production. Likewise, in other articles on the subject written between 1968 and 1970, and in agreement with other authors of the dependency field, Quijano warned about the new tendencies of the state regarding these groups, evident in the alternating use of repression and the implementation of paternalistic welfare policies. On the other hand, Quijano introduced the novel idea that even under precarious conditions and a shortage of goods and services, a network of relations of mutual aid gradually emerged, which he tentatively denominated "a survival structure" ([1970] 2014, 94) and which pointed to the growing importance of family networks.

MARGINALITY AND THE FUNCTIONALIST MATRIX

From the functionalist field, the main contribution was made by sociologist Gino Germani, who headed DESAL together with Vekemans. Germani proposed a distinction between the descriptive and the causal levels; recognizing the existence of multiple dimensions and even different intensities within the same form thus allowed one to solve the dilemma posed by the concept. An important element was the relative nature of marginality, since the common assumption was the lack of participation in those spheres to which it was believed the individual or group should have access. In other words, marginality was judged based on the comparison between an actual situation and what it should be.

Rather than an exhaustive approach (description and causes; a detailed analysis of factors, typologies, and profiles), Germani posited the relationship between marginality and a liberal conception of human rights: He therefore argued that the perception of the phenomenon in terms of deprivation or scarcity and its denaturalization was related to the expansion of the principles of equality and freedom, as well as a growing awareness of the violations of those principles. In this evolutionary line, "the notion of marginality is only the last or most recent expression of the process initiated in the modern world by the Enlightenment . . . to conquer the rights of man or achieve their progressive extension to all sectors of society" (1973, 35–36).

This evolutionary process explains its denaturalization but not its persistence in a context of increasing modernization. For that reason, Germani was forced to (re)introduce concepts associated with the structural-functionalist matrix. The analysis of marginality was definitively tightly linked to the modernization process conceived in a broader sense—its promises, frustrations, maladjustments, and deviations, attributed to both personal and collective characteristics. It was basically the asynchronies or maladjustments in the process of transitioning from a traditional to a modern society that generated institutions, values, attitudes, modes of behavior, partial structures, social categories, and regions in the country's interior that, in the same time period, attained different degrees of modernization and development (Germani 1973, 52).

On the other hand, when assessing Nun's hypotheses on the structural character of the "marginal mass," Germani proposed a different reading of its functionality in the current society. From his perspective, if marginal people can live and reproduce, it is because they produce goods and services in low-productivity sectors—something that Quijano had insisted on—whose market was composed of employed worker sectors but with lower income, such as midlevel industries that did not belong to the monopoly sector. Hence, far from being "afunctional," the marginal sector allowed the survival, under conditions and levels of traditional life, of a sector excluded from the modern market, thus indirectly ensuring the system's survival (Germani 1973, 49).

Another important point was the peculiarity of marginality in Latin America. It is true that Germani warned of the problems (or pockets) of marginality that persisted in advanced countries, as well as the marginality present in the precapitalist period, characterized by general insecurity. However, he highlighted three factors that explained Latin America's specificity. First, there is the enormous size of the marginal sector in the region, which is much greater than what was seen in the industrial revolution in the nineteenth century. The second is European immigration, since from the late nineteenth century to 1930, sixty million Europeans settled in the Americas, thus displacing marginality to the new countries, which managed to partially absorb it. Latin America therefore functioned as an "escape valve," and now this emigration was replaced by rural-to-urban internal migration. The third is the type of predominant industrial technology, which was imported from the more advanced countries and was not intended to absorb labor force but to reduce its employment in production. Therefore, "the situation of dependent development could operate either directly or through a delay in development as a result of dependency" (Germani 1973, 49).

Finally, in an attempt to integrate views associated with other paradigms, Germani argued that marginality also referred to configurations or constellations simultaneously composed of various different forms. There were therefore partial marginalities (in terms of opportunities for education, social mobility, political participation, prestige), as well as a generalized marginality (characterized by nonparticipation). But this sector was not external to society—Germani did not discuss whether or not it was a social class—but existed within it or was eventually exploited by one of the participating sectors, thus being excluded from the enjoyment of rights.

MARGINALITY AND THE TWO FACES OF JANUS

The lumpenproletariat, once it is constituted, brings all its forces to endanger the "security" of the town, and is the sign of the irrevocable decay, the gangrene ever present at the heart of colonial domination. So the pimps, the hooligans, the unemployed, and the petty criminals, urged on from behind, throw themselves into the struggle for liberation like stout working men. These classless idlers will by militant and decisive action discover the path that leads to nationhood.—FRANTZ FANON, *The Wretched of the Earth*, (1961) 1963

In a compilation published in Mexico in 1975, which included works by Fernando H. Cardoso, Theotônio dos Santos, Sergio Bagú, and Héctor Silva Michelena, among others, the Venezuelan Armando Córdova identified some of the problems related to "employment, unemployment, and marginality." Córdova (1975, 59) questioned the numbers of the marginal population in Latin America, which, according to data from CEPAL, was estimated at 30 percent of the labor force, that is, about eighty-five million inhabitants, including the dependents of the unemployed. But the author argued that the number could be underestimated, since, according to DESAL, cited in the report by Murmis, Nun, and Marín, "In Latin America, even in the most integrated countries, marginality affects 50% of the population, reaching 70% or 80% in some countries" (Córdova 1975, 59).

Given the growing dimensions of the phenomenon of marginality in Latin America, a disquieting question arose in the dependency field regarding the political potential of the marginal population, which many thinkers considered a "subclass" (Quijano) and others simply included in the category of *lumpenproletariat* (Frank). Marx, who is profusely cited on the subject, had been quite clear, especially in *The Eighteenth Brumaire of Louis Bonaparte* ([1852] 1994), where he considered the *lumpenproletariat* as declassed, "the scum of society," a political instrument of the dominant classes. But many things had changed since Marx's time, especially in the former colonies or peripheral countries. Thus, Frantz Fanon, in his symbol-book on decolonization, *The Wretched of the Earth* ([1961] 1963), highlighted the political potential of the marginal or declassed sectors, although he also pointed, not without concern, to the ambiguities of spontaneous behaviors, which were easily manipulable by the dominant sectors. In a chapter suggestively entitled "Spontaneity: Its Strength and Weakness," after ranting against the conservative tendencies of the peasant masses in industrialized countries, Fanon speaks of the "embryonic proletariat," referring to the landless peasants, *lumpenproletariat* who migrated to the city and settled in overcrowded and miserable peripheral neighborhoods. The *lumpenproletariat*, however, was characterized as declassed people who found the path to nationhood through militant action. Hence, a few pages later, Fanon warned of the need to pay attention to the marginal masses, since the revolution was unfeasible without them: "Colonialism will also find in the *lumpenproletariat* a considerable space for maneuvering. For this reason any movement for freedom ought to give its fullest attention to this *lumpenproletariat*. The peasant masses will always answer the call to rebellion, but if the rebellion's leaders think it will be able to develop without taking the masses into consideration, the *lumpenproletariat* will throw itself into the battle and will take part in the conflict—but this time on the side of the oppressor" (136–37).

Even though the narrative of decolonization and the new revolutionary nationalism had a very significant influence on the radical left at the time, not all advocates of dependency theory agreed with Fanon's reading, despite the fact that, in the Latin American scenario, where the alternatives seemed to come down to economic stagnation or revolution, the issue of the subject of change was more crucial than ever. Behind the profuse explanations of the new phenomenon of marginality, there was also a deep mistrust of the political potential of the marginal population. Not only was it far from clear that it was a sort of "embryonic proletariat," but there was also the—already mentioned—issue of the political and social management of the surplus population through welfare policies, which was already becoming relevant. On the other hand, if the marginal sectors were assimilated to the *lumpenproletariat*, they had no place in the social structure, and if they did, it was as underemployed—a transitory or incomplete condition that turned them only into a sort of "subclass."

There was another issue at play, since, unlike orthodox standpoints (associated with the Communist Party), the radical left rejected the possibility of building a class front with the national bourgeoisie, which therefore required exploring new alliances in the heterogeneous world of the popular classes. The marginal sectors were certainly capable of organizing (the emergent urban social movements demonstrated it), but they could also be manipulated by the dominant sectors. Thus, Andre Gunder Frank wondered, "Is the 'floating' or 'marginal population,' which might comprise half of the urban population in Latin America, a *lumpenproletariat*? Are these people in fact ideologically untouchable and politically incapable of organizing? Imperialism and the bourgeoisie do not believe so, and until now have been extremely successful in using them for their own political ends" (1969, 20).

Also in a pessimist line of thought, Nun (1969a) argued that the notion of marginal mass pointed to the problems of integration in the system, which imposed specific means for social integration. In this regard, it was worth insisting on the difference between "industrial reserve army" and "marginal mass," since, while the former implied a constant absorption/expulsion by the market and had therefore something in common with active workers (in fact, the distinction between active army and reserve army was aleatory), the same was not the case for those who constituted the marginal mass as a result of unequal, combined, and dependent development, since there was no common, homogeneous basis for political solidarity or for an effective "cooperation plan." According to Nun, this implied both "a hope and a risk" (1969a). The hope was related to the nature of potential contradictions; the risk was derived from the fact that, in the mediation of conflicts and contradictions, other forms of deviant, desperate struggles could emerge, represented by populism and other forms of manipulation. It should be noted that Nun was not assessing the possibility of other solidarity networks (as other authors suggested) generated outside the realm of labor, capable of giving rise to a process of emergence of solidarities and collective consciousness.

Dos Santos in turn believed that the quintessential revolutionary category was exploitation (urban and rural workers) and not misery (the marginal population). The marginal sectors, like the petite bourgeoisie, were a breeding ground for the anarchic left instead. Nonetheless, dos Santos (1972, 212) believed that the great revolutionary potential of the subproletariat comprised by the marginal sectors should not be overlooked, even though those sectors could not become the revolutionary vanguard.

Finally, one of the closest positions to Fanon, that is, to the thesis of an "embryonic proletariat," was that of Ruy Mauro Marini, who, reflecting on the failure of the left in the context of the Brazilian coup d'état in 1964, and more specifically on the experience of the Workers' Politics Marxist Revolutionary Organization (Organização Revolucionária Marxista Política Operária; POLOP), argued that underestimating the underemployed and unemployed population had been an unforgivable mistake. The mistake consisted in accepting the way in which bourgeois ideology represented that "marginal mass," which was presumably surrounding the city in order to be "integrated" into the system. According to Marini, empirical observation demonstrated that "a significant part of those masses is composed of unqualified workers who work in construction or in small businesses or constitute a reserve army for them, and another important part provides poorly paid services, especially domestic services. It is true that the degree of material and moral misery that prevails among them makes them more prone than any other layer of the population to become part of the *lumpenproletariat*; but it is also true that what appears as crime or vice is the expression of violence and despair, and therefore places it on the threshold of revolution" ([1969] 1974, 160–61).

In sum, given the political diagnosis (stagnation, impossibility of a class alliance), the issue of the political potential of the motley world of the subaltern classes became crucial; however, Fanon's position was adopted by only a few authors. In any case, the diagnosis was ambivalent: On one hand, the theses of deviationism and diffusionism were questioned, underscoring the peculiarity of the periphery (structural dependency) and the worsening situation (new forms of dependency; consolidation and expansion of marginality). On the other hand, since the left at the time was set on a worker's outlook, it found it difficult to conceive that ties of solidarity and organization could develop in places other than the factory or the context of wage labor.

Part 2: Debates in the Field of Dependency

The main debates that took place in the field of dependency at the time had to do with the issue of the singularity of Latin American societies. Therefore, in this section I first examine the debate on the mode of production of Latin American societies in colonial times. Far from being a Byzantine debate, the issue of the feudal or pan-capitalist character of Latin America was directly related to a series of definitions and political strategies regarding the possibilities for political and social change. Second, I examine the issue of the role of the national bourgeoisie in the context of the new dependency. This second debate revisits one of the recurring topics in Latin American thought and social sciences: the hunch that social subjects are always unfinished or incomplete as collective players.

The Debate on the Mode of Production and Its Various Moments

What type of economy was it that the Spanish and the Portuguese organized here, in the midst of the enormous native populations of America and Africa? Was it feudalism, which was decadent at the time in the old continent? Was it capitalism, whose glitter and potency was documented at the time by the Italian heyday and Iberian seafarers? Was it something different from both, albeit incorporating some of their basic characteristics?—SERGIO BAGÚ, "Índole de la economía colonial y la economía como capitalismo colonial" (Nature of the colonial economy and economics as colonial capitalism"), (1949) 2007

The debate on the modes of production present in Latin American history experienced various phases or moments and began even before the spread of dependency theory. For some, it was a sort of new version of the discussion regarding the transition from feudalism to capitalism undertaken in Europe by the economists Maurice Dobb and Paul Sweezy from a Marxist perspective, which proposed two opposing views of the origin of capitalism (S. Rodríguez 2007). While Dobb argued that capitalism could only be understood by studying the transformations that took place in the sphere of production (productivist thesis), Sweezy, inspired by historians such as the Frenchman Henri Pirenne, maintained that it was necessary to take into account the rise of mercantile capitalism in modern Europe based on the accumulation of commercial capital in medieval cities, which led to the generalization of large-scale capitalist circulation (circulationist thesis).

Among the authors who first questioned the thesis of feudalism and the dual society was the Argentine historian and economist Sergio Bagú, who examined the topic in two pioneering works, *Economía de la sociedad colonial: Ensayo de historia comparada de América Latina* (The economy of colonial society: Essay on comparative history of Latin America; [1949] 1992) and *Estructura social de la colonia: Ensayo de historia comparada de América Latina* (Colonial social structure: Essay on comparative history of Latin America; 1952). Bagú intended to reflect on the modalities of Latin American capitalism since colonial times. According to him, Latin America had been part of the colonial capitalist system since the conquest, adopting a capitalist form of social organization but with its own particular style—what the author denominates "colonial capitalism."

Among the elements of capitalist organization in Latin American colonies, the demand for capital, the existence of financial capitalism, the organization of production for the world market, the configuration of a commercial market, the existence of wages, and, finally, the difference between the city and the countryside stand out. However, the predominance of a pattern of capitalist relations did not prevent the existence of other forms of social relations and productive organization, of a feudal and slaveholding nature, among which the author underscores the existence of latifundia or large land properties, the presence of forms of servitude (encomienda), the configuration of closed economic units, and the existence of unproductive social classes linked to various levels of imperial and ecclesiastical power. Finally, regarding slavery in the Americas, it was the most extraordinary engine of European commercial capital accumulation. According to Bagú, indigenous and Black slavery, which was not feudal but capitalist, was essential for a process of capitalist accumulation that allowed Europe to develop modern industries and the United States to achieve an extraordinary economic development in the nineteenth century.

In a sort of dependentism avant la lettre, Marxist historian Milcíades Peña also shared the same perspective in his work *Historia del pueblo argentino* (2012). The book examines Argentine history from colonial times to the first Peronism. Far from crude Marxism, Peña applied a dialectic that privileged structures, social conditionings, and power relations between different social classes. In this context, he argued against the myth of the superiority of English over Spanish colonization in the Americas and emphasized the nature of production to explain the real bases of the two different paths. He thus underscored the relationship between geography and social structure, referring to "the curse of easy abundance" to explain the parasitism of the dominant classes in Río de la Plata, as well as the consolidation of a "colonial capitalism." Hence, questioning the hypothesis of the feudal nature of Spanish colonization, Peña argued that the content, motives, and objectives of Spanish colonization had been decisively capitalist. From his perspective, the theory of the feudal character had served the "*criollo* Muscovites" to promote the idea of the need for an antifeudal revolution that would pave the way for the capitalist stage. Against them, Peña revisited Bagú's theses, arguing that the production system structured by the Spanish in the Americas was opposed to the basic structure of feudalism. In this respect, Peña maintained, "Of course, it is not industrial capitalism. It is trading-post capitalism, 'colonial capitalism,' which, unlike feudalism, does not produce on a small scale for local consumption but on a large scale, employing large masses of workers, aiming at the local market structured around the establishments that produce for export. These are capitalist characteristics, but not of industrial development, which is characterized by free wages" (2012, 67).

The second phase of the controversy took place in 1965, involving the German thinker Andre Gunder Frank, on one hand, and the Argentine Rodolfo Puiggrós, then exiled in Mexico, on the other.[6] As mentioned above, far from being merely theoretical, the debate had political implications, since, if the origin and current nature of Latin American societies is feudal, what is needed is a democratic bourgeois and anti-imperialist revolution. But if Latin America has been capitalist since the conquest, its backwardness is the result of the dependent nature of its incorporation. If it was fully capitalist, the path to the future resides in the struggle for a socialist revolution.

Frank's main thesis was that the conquest had placed Latin America in a situation of increasing subordination and colonial and neocolonial dependency relative to the single world system of expanding commercial capitalism. This colonial relationship to the capitalist metropolis formed and transformed the class structure and even the culture of Latin American societies, thus conditioning its present changes (Frank [1969] 1973, 23). This perspective left no room for the thesis of the dual society: Ever since the conquest, all regions, from the most dynamic or modern to the most backward or traditional, had been tied to the world market and were exploited in the context of the capitalist system. Hence, promoting an alliance with the national or anti-imperialist bourgeoisie, as Puiggrós suggested, was not only pointless but an interpretative mistake with very high potential political costs, since industrialization and foreign capital were two sides of the same coin. Differently stated, development and underdevelopment were part of the same capitalist dynamic.

In his response to Frank, the historian Rodolfo Puiggrós (Puiggrós and Frank 1966) argued that America had saved Spain's feudalism from death and that that country transferred the elements of its decomposing feudal regime to the transatlantic territories. In spite of its singularities, the colonial mode of production did not have the characteristics of the capitalist mode of production. Puiggrós pointed to the absence of the following capitalist elements: capital accumulation and reinvestment, developed mercantile production, the existence of capitalists and workers, land rent and commercialization of agrarian property, wide circulation of commodities in internal markets, manufacturing independent of the agrarian economy, and institutions, an ideology and a state that represented the nascent bourgeoisie. The most serious error, concluded Puiggrós, "is to mistake mercantile economy for capitalism." In addition, according to Puiggrós, neither trade nor investments in mines, manufacturing, and colonizing enterprises (all of them elements of commercial capitalism underscored by Frank) changed the colony's peculiar mode of production, which adopted forms characteristic of feudalism.

Frank responded by emphasizing that his statements and studies were based on "facts," not on "arguments," once again rejecting the hypothesis of the absence of capitalist elements in Latin American colonial economies, such as capital accumulation and investment, large-scale exploitation, or the importance of the export of precious metals. The current "capitalist decrepitude" and under-development could not be explained by the persistence of feudal characteristics to be overcome by capitalism but was a historical and continuing result of capitalist development itself in a single world system. Hence, the path to follow was neither national capitalism nor a return to the old Marxist typology of the Asiatic mode of production.

A second stage of the debate took place in the 1970s, more closely related to the academic field, as Sebastián Rodríguez (2007) argues. On one hand, Ernesto Laclau (1973) added arguments in the line developed by Puiggrós, underscoring the theoretical and analytic weaknesses of the scheme presented by Frank; on the other hand, Brazilian historian Ciro Cardoso characterized the specificities of the colonial mode of production. Generally speaking, Laclau shared Dobb's theses, since he considered it necessary to go from the analysis of the circulation of capital to that of the mode of production. Likewise, Laclau believed that Frank provided such a broad definition of capitalism that it was impossible to derive concrete conclusions from it, such as the expiration of the democratic/bourgeois stage in Latin America. Laclau also attempted to specify what was understood by a feudal mode of production, arguing that Frank confused different analytic levels between mode of production and social formation. This explained his view of feudalism as a closed system, impervious to market forces. According to Laclau, "the precapitalist character of the dominant relations of production in Latin America not only was not incompatible with production for the world market but, on the contrary, was strengthened by it. The feudal regime of the haciendas tended to increase the servile exactions imposed on peasants as the growing demands of the world market drove them to maximize the surplus. Hence, the foreign market, far from constituting a force that disintegrated feudalism, tended to accentuate and consolidate it" (1973, 35–36).

Nor could it be said that there was a single way of relating to the metropolis, since the available empirical evidence derived from vast regions of the continent, in countries such as Peru, Mexico, Bolivia, or Guatemala, made the thesis of capitalism untenable. The nineteenth century aggravated the process, resulting in a peasantry subjected to servile obligations, which today lives in a situation of "second servitude," with variations throughout the continent, rather than as agricultural wage laborers. Finally, asserting the feudal nature of relations of production in the agrarian sector did not imply maintaining the thesis of the dual society, which opposed a dynamic and modern sector to a backward and stagnated one.

On the other hand, the Brazilian Ciro Cardoso intervened in the debate, broadening the characterization in terms of mode of production. According to him, wages, personal subjection, and slavery had existed in all periods and in the context of different modes of production. That being so, servitude could not be equated to feudalism, nor could wages be equated to capitalism. His approach was innovative in its development of the particularities of a specifically American mode of production. He therefore proposed a different category, that of a *dependent or colonial mode of production*, which included several types: the mode of production based on indigenous exploitation, established in the regions of the great pre-Columbian cultures; the colonial slaveholding mode of production, established by Europeans in regions with small indigenous populations and with favorable conditions for export activities; and, finally, the mode of production based on the diversified and autonomous economy of small landowners in North America (C. Cardoso 1973, 153–54). All of these contributions were later collected in a book entitled *Modos de producción en América Latina* (Modes of production in Latin America), first published in 1973 by *Cuadernos de Pasado y Presente* (Notebooks of the past and present), when he was already in exile in Mexico (Sempat Assadourian et al. [1973] 1979). In only six years, six editions of the book were published.

Finally, the Ecuadorian Agustín Cueva also participated in the long debate over the feudal or capitalist character of Latin America, pointing out some of its contradictions or paradoxes. One of them was related to the aforementioned "political effects" of the thesis, in terms of the association between the circulation hypothesis/pan-capitalism/revolutionary view and the productivist hypothesis/feudalism/reformism or class front. Cueva underscored the paradox in the fact that the armed groups struggling to establish socialism in Latin America at the time (the 1970s) were convinced that there was a feudal sector in the subcontinent. Hence, the theoretical review undertaken by some intellectuals had little relevance for the revolutionary practice underway (Cueva [1975] 2010, 236). Another paradox was the fact that the thesis that was apparently the most revolutionary and authentically Marxist (Frank's) was based on the theoretical bases provided "by bourgeois social science, which defined capitalism as an open economy or in terms of the mere existence of currency and trade; that is, contradicting Marx's entire work and other classical works of Marxism" (237). Finally, Cueva made a critical assessment of this discussion that went beyond it, attacking the "neo-Marxist" (dependentist) intellectuality above all, accusing it of being distant from the workers' movement and imbued with a strong nationalist and populist tradition—in short, intellectuals with a grassroots background that was far from Marxist and Leninist and that, in his opinion, tended to read Marx through Weberian, structuralist, or CEPAL lenses (240). He also questioned the myth of Latin America's "indomitable originality" that pervaded Ciro Cardoso's theses.

Although few thinkers adhered to the pan-capitalist thesis maintained by an increasingly criticized Andre Gunder Frank, the true "closure" of the debate was accomplished by the renowned historian and sociologist Immanuel Wallerstein, who in 1974 published the first volume of *The Modern World-System*, titled *Capitalist Agriculture and the Origins of the European World-Economy in the Sixteenth Century*, which backed most of Frank's theses (Wallerstein [1974] 2011). Wallerstein's book developed a theoretical framework to understand the historical changes involved in the emergence of the modern world. His study of two key cases—the production and commercialization of silver in Spanish America and of sugar in Portuguese America in the sixteenth and seventeenth centuries—reinforced Frank's theses and limited the thesis of Latin American feudalism (S. Rodríguez 2007). Thus, paradoxically, it was the contributions from the center that validated the victory of dependentism, beyond the fact that those theses demonstrated the connections between dependency theory and the world-systems theory, as Wallerstein and other authors acknowledged.

The Role of the National Bourgeoisie in the Context of Dependency

Latin American social thought suffers from a curse: its late arrival in history. States without a nation, people without history, states without legitimacy, citizens without rights, social classes without projects, and modernizations without modernity. These are some of the paradoxes surrounding sociological work in our region. Theoretical debate has therefore focused on deciphering the characteristics that have led our realities to be unfinished realities.—MARCOS ROITMAN, *Pensamiento sociológico y realidad nacional en América Latina* (Sociological thought and national reality in Latin America), 2008

The field of dependency focused especially on understanding the changes in the national bourgeoisie in the context of dependent capitalism in its monopolistic phase. These changes reflected an important inflection, evident in its abandonment of its role as a "national" bourgeoisie in a context of class alliances (typical of the populist phase) and its passage to a different situation, characterized by its prompt subordination to international capital as a minor or local partner, together with conservative or reactionary positions.

In the context of the new dependency, the debates regarding the dominant classes revolved around three axes. The first referred to the emphasis on the players' internal composition. There was an interest in analyzing the relationship between the different segments of the bourgeoisie (unity or fragmentation) and between these and the other social players (relationships of cooperation [alliances] and conflict [opposition, contradiction]). The second axis was the need, given the conditions of Latin America's economic insertion, to analyze the levels of dependency or subordination of the local bourgeoisie to international capital. Finally, another axis, directly related to the previous one, inquired into the existence, or not, of a leading class, which at the time was reflected in the need to distinguish between national and local bourgeoisies.[7]

Regarding the first axis, Fernando H. Cardoso and Enzo Faletto's book (1979a) established differences according to stages and countries, through a historical/structural analysis. The national process approach focused on the role of the bourgeoisie and its unity or fragmentation as a social class. This reading emphasized that in the Latin American case, the bourgeoisie was understood as "capitalist producers or entrepreneurs," in contrast with the landowning oligarchy or the "agrarian lords," which differed from the European bourgeoisie. The book also established a typology of national cases. Thus, for example, in the case of societies organized on the basis of the national control of the export productive system (Argentina and Brazil), the authors recognized the existence of an important bourgeois sector, but the crisis and transition toward a new phase of capitalism led to at least two concrete situations in terms of processes of domination, depending on whether there was "class unity" in the dominant social classes.[8] The first case occurred when the dominant sector of the export system became the hegemonic bourgeoisie and imposed a particular order on the other class fractions, thus exhibiting class unity—a situation illustrated by Argentina's Buenos Aires bourgeoisie. A second case, which implied greater instability, was when class unity was attained through a "confederation of oligarchies," whereby the various agro-export sectors reached a tacit agreement among them (the case of Brazil prior to 1930).

On the other hand, the degree of diversification of the national productive system also conditioned the forms of transition in terms of schemes of bourgeois domination. Thus, diversified export economies facilitated the development of productive sectors that focused on the domestic market, giving rise to the first industrial centers and leading to the emergence of an urban bourgeoisie and popular/worker sectors. In the case of enclave economies, the weakness of national economic groups forced the latter to maintain a more exclusionary form of domination, since their ties to the enclave sector depended on their capacity to guarantee an internal order that provided that sector with cheap labor.

Even though this general scheme offered new typologies, it was strongly criticized because the transition stage—toward competitive capitalism—seemed to be conditioned from the beginning by the way the national economy had been incorporated into the process of the international division of labor at the time of the development and consolidation of the nation-state. There was therefore a sort of nearly unavoidable "fate" related to the foundational moment (as Bambirra argued), even though the analyses and the typology focused on studying the contradictory value orientations within the dominant sectors (the relationship between agro-export sectors and traditional sectors) and the ambiguities of underdevelopment.

The second and third axes were more strongly intertwined, since, given the changes produced in the context of the new dependency, there was an interest in characterizing the bourgeoisie's ties to the outside and the modalities of internal domination. In this respect, a first response came from Frank, in a rather eloquently entitled book: *Lumpenburguesía, lumpendesarrollo* (*Lumpenbourgeoisie: Lumpendevelopment*; [1969] 1973; 1972b). By *lumpenbourgeoisie*, Frank understood the social class that was employed as a minor partner by international capital. In this context, an anti-imperialist alliance with the bourgeoisie, as the Communist Party proposed, was impossible, since the "imperialist clutch" or the "neo-imperialist encroachment" forced Latin America's bourgeoisie to further exploit its presumed worker and peasant allies, thus depriving them of its political support. The path to national or state capitalism was sealed by neo-imperialism (Frank 1968, 27). Theotônio dos Santos reflected in a similar manner. In his opinion, the bourgeoisie of backward countries was essentially "capitulating" and was willing to sacrifice national development and the country's economic and political freedom for the sake of economic support and internal security, both of which imperialism promised (dos Santos 1972, 122).

In *Subdesarrollo y revolución* (Underdevelopment and revolution; [1969] 1974), Ruy Mauro Marini argued that Latin America's industrial bourgeoisie had evolved from the idea of autonomous development—together with a Bonapartist policy (populism)—to an effective integration with imperialist capital, which led to a new, more radical form of dependency. It was developmentalism, in fact, that consolidated the myth of the national bourgeoisie opposed to imperialism, but this assertion developed in a different historical context. On the contrary, the scenario at the time manifested a process of denationalization of the local bourgeoisie; a new form of dependency thus consolidated the estrangement between the bourgeoisie and the popular masses, increasing exploitation and denying labor rights.

In the fourth of his famous *Seven Erroneous Theses About Latin America*, Stavenhagen forcefully criticized the idea that "the national bourgeoisie is interested in breaking the power and domination of the landowning oligarchy" (1967; [1965] 1981). In his opinion, the interests of the new elite (modern industrialists and entrepreneurs) and the traditional upper class (large landowners) were not opposed; on the contrary, there were ties between agrarian and industrial capital and between these and foreign capital. The bourgeoisie and the oligarchy complemented each other—both were interested in maintaining the domination regime based on internal colonialism, which benefited both social classes. Hence, along the same lines as Frank, Stavenhagen questioned the thesis of the class alliance proposed by the Communist Party and added a critical assessment of the failure of agrarian reforms in the populist period.

One of the strongest opponents of this reading, which proposed a limited understanding of the local bourgeoisies, seen as "paper tigers," was Fernando H. Cardoso. Already in his postscript to *Dependency and Development in Latin America* (Cardoso and Faletto 1979b), the author made it clear that an *associated dependent development* was possible, which implied asserting that the bourgeoisie played an active role. In 1973, in a lecture suggestively entitled "Eppur si muove" (republished in 1977), Cardoso insisted on the dual character of the bourgeoisie: In colonial times, it was neither precapitalist nor feudal, nor did it constitute an agrarian bourgeoisie *stricto sensu*. It was a bourgeoisie with elements from mercantile capitalism, and others derived from the slaveholding or encomendero character of the social relations of production. In the present, the failure of national populism, Castrism, and the economic practice expressed in the penetration of foreign capital had put an end to the concept of the "national bourgeoisie" ([1973] 1977, 216–30). According to Cardoso, this was contradictory because, in countries with a strong non-enclave type of capitalist development—such as Brazil—it could not be said that the bourgeoisie would disappear as if by magic or that it was solely determined by foreign factors. The process was undoubtedly more complex, since "local bourgeoisies redefine themselves" (216–30). It was impossible to speak of stable attributes of the bourgeoisie—class relations are dynamic and recursive, and it is therefore necessary to examine how the bourgeoisie relates to the other social classes. Thus, for example, while the Mexican bourgeoisie associated with monopoly capital but controlled the state through a civilian government, Brazil's bourgeoisie had been unable to do so (coup d'état); and both of them differed from Argentina's bourgeoisie, which had to deal with the Peronist working class, which meant that the end of populism was an unreasonable abstraction (230).

In Cardoso's opinion, what had ended was the national-developmentalist model, that is, a certain bourgeois ideology, which should not be understood as the end of the national bourgeoisie. In his critiques of other dependency theorists and even advocates of the theory of marginality, Cardoso criticized this "confusion." The crisis should be attributed to the developmentalist model and to the illusion—of alliance, development, and redistribution—that it had implied. The problem of other dependency theorists was therefore that the limits of a particular model had been mistaken for the limits of a system under constant transformation.

The debate on the character of the bourgeoisie entered a new phase after the intervention of Guillermo O'Donnell, who shed light on the topic from a novel standpoint in his 1978 article "Notas para el estudio de la burguesía local, con especial referencia a sus vinculaciones con el capital transnacional y el aparato estatal" (Notes for the study of the local bourgeoisie, with special reference to its connections with transnational capital and the state apparatus; O'Donnell 1978b). O'Donnell's contribution was twofold: On one hand, he developed certain theoretical and methodological criteria to study the local industrial bourgeoisie; on the other hand, he analyzed the role of the state regarding both transnational capital and the local bourgeoisies, which he had previously presented in "Apuntes para una teoría del Estado" (Notes toward a theory of the state; 1978a).

O'Donnell explained that he preferred to speak of a local bourgeoisie and not of a national bourgeoisie, since in his opinion the issue of whether the bourgeoisie could be considered "national" should be the corollary, rather than the premise, of the analysis. He also expressed his surprise at the lack of studies on the subject. Taking the analysis of the urban and industrial sector of the local bourgeoisie (excluding other sectors such as the rural, financial, and commercial bourgeoisies) as his point of departure, O'Donnell attempted to understand the role of the local industrial bourgeoisie in a context of transnationalization of capital. In agreement with Cardoso's analyses, he believed that dependency had become fertile soil for many oversimplifications, one of which was to conceive international capital and imperialism as almighty demiurges, which implied, among other things, a lack of autonomy of the local bourgeoisie. In his opinion, this did not imply denying the high degree of subordination of the local bourgeoisie to transnational corporations, but neither did it imply asserting that, in the subordination phenomena he intended to analyze, the local bourgeoisie was not sufficiently autonomous to become a social subject of its own or to have conflicts with transnational capital.

His main argument was that the topic of the local bourgeoisie should be approached from the broader perspective of the dynamics of the transnationalization of capital. To that end, he underscored the notion of "development style," which is determined by the center through the growth pattern of its most dynamic units and the supply of goods from the latter. In order for national businesses to succeed, they had to incorporate that growth pattern, participating as fully and mimetically as possible in those dynamics, for example, as providers of production equipment for transnational corporations, thus further expanding the process of transnationalization of capital. The result is therefore a growth pattern that, on one hand, implies industrialization (whose most dynamic component is the set of goods destined for high-income sectors) and, on the other hand, "consolidates a headless productive structure devoid of autonomous driving forces resulting from the production of production goods and its concomitant generation of technology to create new products" (O'Donnell 1978b, 19). This is what is meant by *associated dependent development*, as Cardoso and Faletto called it, which demonstrated the structural ambiguity of the local bourgeoisie: On one hand, the layers of the local bourgeoisie that participated became the most dynamic and privileged elements; on the other hand, that same participation helped reproduce a growth pattern and a process of transnationalization of capital that placed those layers in a condition of organic weakness and subordination to transnational capital, thus reproducing themselves worldwide as the dynamic vanguard of that process. Hence, the result of this particular style of development was a skewed form of development and a headless productive structure.

O'Donnell elaborated a similar reflection regarding the state: On one hand, the state apparatus tends to build a national society; on the other hand, it becomes a co-promoter of transnational capital. This constituted the "dependent capitalist state." Furthermore, the local bourgeoisie had to reproduce itself as a national social class, thus requiring a national state for tutelage. The need to be part of the state apparatus was especially urgent for a bourgeoisie that was aware of its own frailty, which in turn became one of the main driving forces of its corporate organization: "This implies that it has to present itself as a national social class even though the reproduction of a transnationalizing growth pattern subordinates it to transnational capital and establishes the whole of society as a headless and therefore economically dependent productive structure" (1978b, 31).

In sum, O'Donnell's reading put an end to a cycle of debates on the role of the local bourgeoisie and opened research to new concerns. His meticulous arguments and the analytic density of his proposal restored the complexity of analyses of social classes—especially regarding the local bourgeoisie—keeping them from getting lost or being effaced behind social structures. At the same time, the state also exhibited that twofold, contradictory dimension.

Dependency: Internal Disputes and Hegemonic Discourses

Based on this observation, everything becomes coherent: the omnipresent predominance of the category of dependency over the category of exploitation, of the nation over social class, and the dazzling success of dependency theory in all intellectual milieus. Even the illusion that, with this, the "narrowness and limitations" of classical Marxism had been overcome.

And how could this theoretical "overcoming" be otherwise, if in the same political practice the intellectual vanguards believed they could replace the proletariat in its revolutionary tasks?—AGUSTÍN CUEVA, "Problemas y perspectivas de la teoría de la dependencia" (Problems and perspectives of dependency theory), 1979

Between July 8 and 12, 1974, the Ninth Latin American Congress on Sociology was held in San José de Costa Rica, devoted to reflecting on Latin American sociology in the past twenty-five years. The works were published five years later in a two-volume work entitled *Debates sobre la teoría de la dependencia y la sociología latinoamericana* (Debates on dependency theory and Latin American sociology; Camacho 1979), which for many thinkers represented a sort of "first trial against dependency theory," due to the critical voices present in the text: from the left, Agustín Cueva and other Marxist intellectuals, who questioned the ambiguities and failures of dependency theory from a Marxist perspective; and from the right, Argentine sociologist José Luis de Imaz, who suggestively entitled his 1979 article "¿Adiós a la teoría de la dependencia?" (Farewell to dependency theory?). The book also included Cardoso and Faletto's postscript to *Dependency and Development in Latin America*, published in 1979 (see Cardoso and Faletto 1979a, 1979b), in response to the critiques from the field of dependency that asserted that associated dependent development was unviable.

It was the beginning of the decline of dependency theory, due not only to the trivialization of the concept and the growing oversimplification of some of its contributions, which became the target of myriads of criticisms and disqualifications, but also to the new political conditions experienced in Latin America in the context of the military dictatorships. While there were growing criticisms that claimed that dependency did not qualify as a theory, often reiterated with little grounding, there was also a sort of homogenization of the criticisms.

The fiercest critic was the Ecuadorian Agustín Cueva, who questioned the eclectic matrix of dependency theory, which he considered a sort of "neo-Marxism without Marx" (1979, 66). He also argued that dependency theorists continued to operate in the problematic field imposed by developmentalism and that they were trapped in an economistic perspective, which explained a certain "nostalgia for lost national capitalism" (73). He questioned the unimodal character of the notion of dependency, "whose limits of theoretical relevance have never been defined and whose insufficiency is evident when elaborating vast schemes of interpretation of Latin America's historical development" (73). Finally, like Francisco Weffort, Cueva believed that dependency theory tended to substitute the analysis of social classes with a national approach, which in political terms implied adherence to—or "deviation" from—different forms of "revolutionary nationalism." This did not mean that the contradictions between independent imperialist countries and dependent ones did not exist; their existence was evident, but the empire/nation pair derived from a greater dichotomy, that is, class contradictions. In sum, in Cueva's opinion, "class analysis and class struggle were the Achilles heel of dependency theory" (1979, 75).

Several authors with links to the dependency field—Aníbal Quijano (Quijano [1970] 2014, 127) among them—had already decried the fact that the term *dependency* had become a magical and omniscient instrument. In 1974, in an often-cited and much-disseminated text entitled "Notas sobre el estado actual de los estudios sobre dependencia" (Notes on the current states of studies on dependency), Fernando H. Cardoso revisited the concept in order to revise its theoretical status and define the problematic field. He discussed its impure origins, denying that the concept was separate from history and that theory was distant from politics (93). Regarding its theoretical status, he wondered, "Notion, concept, 'theory,' 'concrete' characterization, or what else?... As 'dependency' becomes a 'confusing amalgam' of undetermined relations and articulations (as it has done in some texts), and as there are efforts to develop a theory based on the 'opacity' of a hazy concept, my immediate reaction is to refuse the status of science to this sort of ideology" (107).

Cardoso later asserted that dependency did not have the same theoretical status as other categories of the theory of capitalism, such as surplus value, exploitation, expropriation, and accumulation, because it was actually "defined in the theoretical field of the Marxist theory of capitalism" (1974, 107). In Cardoso's opinion, once the confines of dependency were established, there was no reason to deny it as a theoretical field on its own, albeit inscribed within the framework of the Marxist theory of capitalism, and also as a complement to the theory of imperialism.

In another important text, eloquently entitled "Eppur si muove," already cited, Cardoso insisted on the idea that, internally, this new form of dependent relation allowed a certain social dynamism, and provocatively spoke of "attempts at social aperture" ([1973] 1977, 233), which, because he did this at a time of military dictatorships, cost him quite a few criticisms. More than anything, his position regarding the coexistence of development and dependency through dependent associated capitalism is far from Frank's and Marini's prognosis, with whom he debated the subject.

Previously, Frank, considered by many a sort of caricature of the positions of dependency theory, had also been compelled to respond to the many criticisms elicited by his proposals. He did so in the book *Lumpenburguesía: Lumpendesarrollo; Dependencia, clase y política en Latinoamérica* (*Lumpenbourgeoisie: Lumpendevelopment; Dependence, Class, and Politics in Latin America*), written in 1969 (see Frank 1972b). In the introduction, entitled "Mea culpa," he cites a review of his book *Capitalismo y subdesarrollo en América Latina* (Capitalism and underdevelopment in Latin America; 1965; 1967a) that stated, "It is an impressive and convincing presentation of the decisive manner in which, since the conquest, the fate of Latin Americans has always been affected by events taking place away from their continent and beyond their control" (1970; 1973, 13).[9] Frank explained that that was not his thesis, that, in his opinion, dependency was not merely external and independent of the class structure, something imposed on Latin Americans from outside and against their will; rather, "it is the infusion of the satellite's national economy with the same capitalist structure and its fundamental contradictions ... which organize and dominate the national life of the peoples, in economic, political, and social terms" (1970; 1973, 13).

Frank also discussed dos Santos's methodological criticism, which argued that Frank had failed to overcome a functionalist structural position—hence the static nature of his system, which reaffirmed "continuity in the midst of change." As a result, the changes that had taken place appeared to be "irrational" or the product of random factors. To confront this criticism, Frank was obliged to perform a number of acrobatic rhetorical leaps, referring especially to prior texts in which he delved into the historical dynamics. In "Mea culpa," he also criticized the word *dependency*, which he believed had become a fashion employed by reformist bourgeois and Marxist revolutionaries alike (1970; 1973, 18). But in the afterword, written in 1972, Frank went even further. The text bears the provocative title "La dependencia ha muerto, viva la dependencia y la lucha de clases" ("Dependence Is Dead, Long Live Dependence and the Class Struggle: An Answer to Critics"; 1972a), and in it he offers his own version of the origins and tensions of dependency theory, which in his opinion is related to a "critically alternative ... revolutionary strategy inspired both by the Cuban Revolution and the Sino-Soviet debate" (1974, 88).

Had dependency died, then? In his opinion, there was mounting evidence that dependency—both the old version (developmentalist dependency) and the new version (dependency in terms of revolutionary theory)—was in the process of concluding its natural life cycle. Frank argued that "the starting shot for this new aperture" was his book *Capitalism and Underdevelopment in Latin America* (1967a), written between 1963 and 1965, and some other texts of his authorship, while *Lumpenbourgeoisie: Lumpendevelopment*, written in 1969, was the swan song of this concert, even if other stars sang new variations of this melody (1972b; 1973, 166–67). An intense life for a brief cycle, which, in addition to being self-referencing, had led to the metropolitan revolts of 1968 and 1969 but also to the appropriation by the establishment's forces of notions such as dependency theory, development of underdevelopment, and even subimperialism.

In short, the trivialization of dependency theory had ended up caricaturing its arguments—and, in this respect, Frank was well ahead of its other representatives. It is not by chance that the criticisms also came from the dependency field itself, by authors such as Marini, Weffort, Fernando H. Cardoso, and dos Santos. His hyperradical and extremely schematic political views were its weakest link, which exacerbated criticisms from the outside and infuriated his fellow travelers. For example, in the aforementioned article on the current state of dependency studies, in a single, crystal-clear footnote, Fernando H. Cardoso (1974, 98) downplayed Frank's influence on dependency studies and limited his role to the critique of functionalism and the sociology of development, reaffirming that his characterization of the historical-structural process of evolution of capitalism was "orthodox." Theotônio dos Santos, in turn, even though he agreed with a number of assumptions related to the advancement of the internationalization of capital and its global expansion, criticized Frank's undialectical conception implicit in the idea of "continuity in change," which he derived from his successful formula "the development of underdevelopment." In 1978, as he elaborated a genealogy of dependency theory, dos Santos wrote, "A significant part of recent criticisms of the concept of dependency focused mainly on Gunder Frank's arguments, challenged by many of the thinkers who developed the concept. A later self-criticism by Gunder Frank himself confounded everyone who has been working with that concept in the same theoretical field. It is therefore necessary to delve deeper into the topic" ([1978] 2011, 423).

However, what announced the end of the cycle was the bitter debate between Fernando H. Cardoso and Marini in 1978. It was initiated by José Serra and Cardoso (1976), who wrote a fifty-page article entitled "As desventuras da dialética da dependência" (The misadventures of the dialectics of dependency, a title that evoked a famous book by Maurice Merleau-Ponty against Jean-Paul Sartre), which, in a most destructive manner and with copious adjectives, attacked Marini's theses developed in *Dialéctica de la dependencia* (The dialectics of dependency; Marini 1973; 2022). The latter responded with no fewer pages and certainties, in an article entitled "Las razones del neodesarrollismo" (The reasons for neodevelopmentalism; Marini 1978). Both works were published in a 1978 special issue of *Revista Mexicana de Sociología* (Mexican journal of sociology). I do not intend to examine the debate in detail but to explore its main lines of argument, given its importance. Generally speaking, Cardoso and Serra crudely criticized a large part of the dependency field, which they ascribed to the rupturist left. They emphasized that those critics who had argued that the only alternative to national developmentalism in the context of capitalism was economic stagnation were wrong, since they mistook the unfeasibility of the populist project for the failure of capitalist development. This fact, together with the "demonstrative effect" of the Cuban Revolution and an inadequate analysis of the consciousness and situation of the worker and peasant social classes, had led many thinkers to believe that once the democratic-bourgeois stage was discarded—since it did not exist—the alternative was for the urban and peasant proletariat to assume the task of promoting development, removing all obstacles and paving the way to socialism (Serra and Cardoso 1978, 14). Finally, they argued that the type of analysis undertaken by authors such as Frank and even dos Santos and Marini in the late 1960s and early 1970s had contributed to rationalizing the arguments that justified the armed struggle.

More specifically, Serra and Cardoso attempted to dismantle Marini's two main theses—that of the superexploitation of the labor force in dependent economies and that of subimperialism. One of their main arguments attempted to demonstrate that Marini had undertaken a sort of mistaken displacement of Prebisch's theory regarding the deterioration of the terms of interchange between central and peripheral countries, transforming it into a theory of unequal interchange, which became the point of departure to later locate inequalities in the realm of exchange and in the field of production. In this sense, they accused Marini not only of erring in terms of economic theory but also of committing an economistic reductionism that shunned a reading in terms of the class struggle. For Serra and Cardoso, on the contrary, only politics could displace the parameters of the class struggle in one direction or another. Hence, economistic reductionism "killed the nerve of political analysis" and was based on a sort of "catastrophism that does not come to fruition" (1978, 27).

Likewise, Marini's subimperialism was just another "reductionist" expression, a "theory" built "from deduction to deduction" that exhibited errors in terms of both theory and data (for example, regarding Brazil's increase in military spending). Finally, the authors explained that their efforts to demolish Marini's ideas had to do with the fact that "there is perhaps no one in Marini's line of thought who was more intellectually ambitious than him. That being so, he demonstrated better than anyone that his apparently dialectical analysis actually performs an ungodly economic reductionism that, by obscuring historical alternatives and political options at each juncture, establishes the primacy of economism and voluntarism" (Serra and Cardoso 1978, 51). They concluded that in his "voracious analysis," Marini's mistake was to attempt to uncover the "laws of dependency," without realizing that his theses went imperceptibly "from erroneous economism to suicidal political voluntarism" (52).

Marini responded to the criticism with fewer cheap shots but equal emphasis and hostility, making it clear that the authors' intention was to influence the young Brazilian generation, which was mostly unaware of his writings due to the dictatorship's censorship. He defended his two theses, providing data and responding from the standpoint of Marxist theory, and accused his critics in turn: In his opinion, Cardoso and Serra did nothing but confirm an idyllic and apologetic view of capitalism (Marini 1978; 2008, 168). On the other hand, he argued that their attack against the presumed "economic reductionism" in his work *The Dialectics of Dependency* bordered on caricature and had to do with the authors' sociological or politicized conception of the class struggle, conceiving the economy only as the general framework in which the political struggle takes place. Marini referred to Marx's texts to reaffirm his rejection of the presumed autonomy of politics vindicated by Cardoso and Serra, and finally attacked the "neo-developmentalism" of the "unfortunate critics," who assimilated capitalist processes in both advanced and dependent societies, instead of analyzing the latter's particularities. In this respect, he—prophetically—predicted that Cardoso and Serra's text announced a sort of return to CEPAL and its developmentalist illusions regarding the industrial bourgeoisie and its role in the context of national capitalism after World War II. Marini correctly accused them of professing a timid and shameful neo-developmentalism that would nonetheless soon cast aside its inhibitions . . .

Viewed from a distance, this end-of-cycle debate decisively illustrated the different positions regarding the connections between economics and politics. On one hand, Marini's—and Bambirra's—analyses focused on economic factors, a choice that both defended from a Marxist standpoint. Cardoso and Faletto's analyses, on the other hand, had a sociological bias; later, Cardoso emphasized the autonomy of politics, in tune with his ideological viewpoints. More than anything, however, the debate anticipated an epochal change that questioned the revolutionary ethos and revalued democracy in its formal and institutional dimension.

This end of the cycle also implied a thematic shift due to the arrival of highly repressive dictatorships. These dictatorships gave rise to a deeper reflection on the changes in the state's role in the context of the new dependency. As early as 1972, in his book *Modernización y autoritarismo* (Modernization and bureaucratic-authoritarianism; 1972; 1973), O'Donnell proposed the category of "bureaucratic authoritarianism"—later replaced by the "bureaucratic authoritarian state"—

questioning those views that associated development and democracy, as well as the characterizations of military regimes as "fascist," reformulating the relationship between "economic development" and "political pluralism," in order to demonstrate that political authoritarianism (and not democracy) was the most likely outcome of the highest levels of modernization in South America's context at the time (1972, 22). The distinctive features of bureaucratic authoritarian regimes were exemplified by Argentina and Brazil. On the other hand, O'Donnell's work analyzed how the bureaucratic authoritarian state could contribute to the development model without implying economic stagnation, as most advocates of dependency theory had maintained. In their postscript Cardoso and Faletto (1979b) had already formulated the need to reconceive the state's nature and its crucial place in contemporary history in the context of associated dependent development. Revisiting O'Donnell's (1972, 197) analyses, which concluded that authoritarian bureaucratic states and international capital were mutually indispensable, Cardoso and Faletto spoke of "elective affinities" in the alliance between international oligopolistic capital, state enterprise, and the local bourgeoisie.

In characterizing military regimes, both the Bolivian René Zavaleta Mercado and the Ecuadorian Agustín Cueva reintroduced the category of *fascism* from a Marxist standpoint, but it was dos Santos's consistent analysis that relaunched discussions on the subject. Dos Santos had characterized Brazil's military government as fascist in 1964, based on the emergence of new, highly repressive forms of political domination, even though—differently from European fascism—it did not have the support of mass movements and depended on the state, due to the disappearance of the petite bourgeoisie. An intense debate thus began regarding the new character of Latin American dictatorships, employing various categories of analysis: neo-fascism, dependent fascism, underdeveloped fascism, police state, Bonapartism. Between 1975 and 1977, several articles were published on the subject in *Revista Mexicana de Sociología*, as well as a compilation on "Fascism in America" published by *Revista Nueva Política* (New politics journal) in Mexico. Finally, dos Santos's arguments were questioned and refuted by Hugo Zemelman and Atilio Boron, who examined the use of the category of fascism in a historical and comparative context (Trindade 1982).

———

In recent decades, quite a few thinkers have kicked the dead horse, invoking other paradigms or epistemological matrices and other political contexts, accusing dependency theory of being simplistic or reductionist, by attributing the evils of Latin American underdevelopment to the transnationalization of capital and the decline of national bourgeoisies. However, as we have seen, the most outstanding representatives of dependency theory not only attempted to endow a broad and sometimes all-encompassing notion with conceptual contents, debating the meaning and scope of the situation or condition of dependence, but also, appealing to a historical structural analysis, made important contributions to an understanding of the different Latin American societies and their historical cycles.

On the other hand, dependency theory was characterized by a totalizing zeal that led to the prompt and effective establishment of a general interpretative framework to read Latin American processes, constituting not really a paradigm but, as I have argued, a sort of "master frame" that shed a new light on political, social, economic, and cultural processes—reconfiguring the intellectual field and its relationship to politics. Its impact was such that it fostered one of the most creative, but also tragic, moments of Latin America's political—and intellectual—life. Likewise, its connection to the revolutionary ethos, then characterized by a mistrust of reformism and a rejection of the democratic party system, was reflected in the assumption of a radical political outlook and commitment.

This tragic nature, which was increasingly evident with the various military dictatorships, was anticipated by Theotônio dos Santos (1972), who expressed it as a dilemma between socialism and fascism: "The option that has been developing in this process is therefore between, on one hand, a profound social revolution that allows establishing the bases for a new society on the ruins of the old, decadent order and that endows Latin America with a most important role in the foundation of the world of the future, and, on the other hand, the victory of the most retrograde and barbaric forces of our time, *which can only occur through the physical destruction of the popular and mass leaderships of its militants*" (61).[10]

Thus stated, the dilemma summarized the incompatibility between *dependency* and *democracy*, an argument reasonably questioned by Fernando H. Cardoso and José Serra, who believed that dependency and democracy were in fact compatible, especially in light of the emergent political processes in Brazil. But this implied that crisis and economic stagnation was not the only possible outcome, and neither was revolutionary rupture, as many advocates of dependency theory had envisaged. Most dependency theorists had failed to foresee that the military dictatorships of the 1960s and 1970s in the Southern Cone would make the necessary alliances—with the local bourgeoisie and international capital—to articulate repression and authoritarianism with economic growth, independently of the social costs, as Guillermo O'Donnell analyzed.

The other pole of the dilemma formulated by dos Santos relative to the physical destruction of militants and political and social leaders, however, became a reality. By 1978 the situation in the region was dramatic: In a sort of domino effect, institutional governments had been overthrown, grassroots forces had been defeated, and the Southern Cone went through a long night of military dictatorships that led to the death, forced disappearance, and exile of thousands of militants of the middle and lower classes. It was therefore not only theoretical issues that shattered dependency as a common frame but the political reality itself, which, in the urgency of defeat, required reflecting on the new nature of military dictatorships and, later, the emergent transition scenarios.

On the other hand, one of the greatest limitations of dependency theory was that it was stuck in developmentalist categories. As various authors observed, among them Ramón Grosfoguel, Gustavo Esteva, Arturo Escobar, and Koldo Unceta Satrústegui, the difference with CEPAL's current was that most of the advocates of dependency believed that autonomous development was only possible by breaking with the capitalist system and establishing socialism. There was therefore no critique of the underdevelopment/development duality; rather, a developmentalist narrative from a socialist or rupturist standpoint was assumed, placing the nation-state at the center and establishing autonomous development as the goal.

In the early 1980s, in a context that demonstrated the decline of the most radical political standpoints, a new debate began regarding the crisis and transformation of authoritarian regimes and the forms of transition toward democratic regimes. Beyond national specificities, the new cycle reflected a common positive reassessment of formal democracy as an institutional system and the denunciation of state terrorism on behalf of the defense of human rights (formerly considered liberal). This change also signaled a shift from sociology and political economics to political science, in order to address the problems implicit in the transition: the institutionalization of political pluralism, the challenges to understanding the forms of organization and expression of "civil society," respect for the democratic rules of the game, and the effects of an authoritarian political culture—and the need to dismantle it.

This democratic/reformist turn, with its various mea culpas and political/epistemological conversions, was read from the standpoint of the dilemma between authoritarianism and democracy, which proposed a search not for a new utopian horizon but for a principle of social cohesion, a new democratic pact, especially in those Latin American societies that struggled to emerge from a period of strong political repression and exclusion. Dependency, which until recently had been the driving category of an entire era and the master frame of a generation of intellectuals and scholars, linked to the revolutionary ethos, thus disappeared from the theoretical and political horizon of Latin Americans. In addition, the critiques against voluntarism and the rupturist discourse of the 1960s and 1970s seemed to agree with the demand for hyperprofessionalism that permeated Latin American social sciences beginning in the 1980s. The defeat was so great that, as Carlos Acuña (1994) points out, the discourse of the 1980s returned to many of the vices prior to dependency theory: "The bourgeoisie once again became one of the many 'interest groups'; capitalists became mere 'entrepreneurs' managing their businesses; and liberal pluralism, despite its apparent death, turned out to be in fine health."

In the 1990s a second wave affected emancipatory languages more directly on a global scale with the collapse of the so-called real socialisms and the end of the bipolar world, which paved the way to an era characterized by the hegemony of neoliberal thought. Did this mean that dependency had stopped being a valid category of analysis to study Latin America's new economic, social, and political processes?

4

Populisms, Politics, and Democracy

From the mid-twentieth century to the present, populism was for Latin American sciences what caudillismo was for essay writing in the nineteenth century—a recurring topic with continental ambitions and one of the founding subjects of Latin American political and social thought. However, so much has been written in both Latin America and elsewhere, and the concept has been so often invoked, often depriving it of its analytic potential, that quite a few authors, referring to its confusing or murky nature, have suggested abandoning it in order to avoid the risk of "trafficking with serious intellectual contraband" (Quijano 1998, 185), while others call for a sort of "moratorium" on the concept (populism) and its adjective (*populist*) (Saint-Upéry 2008a).

In my opinion, the debates regarding populisms continue to be relevant not only because of their ever-changing nature but also because of the phenomenon's ambivalence, which explains why its conceptualization is often trapped in a sort of entredeux, typical of Latin American thought. In this regard, populism's dual character must be understood in historical terms, in its ever-ambiguous relationship to democracy. In an archaeological exercise, the issue takes us back to the struggles for independence from Spain, at a time when democracy was associated with the inorganic and the plebeian. This characterization already revealed a situation of ambiguity and tension, visible in both the weakness of the new republic's institutions (the *kratos*) and suspicion of the masses (the tyranny of the *demos*). This twofold reality inspired contrasting and paradoxical views. First, in the nineteenth century, political readings appealed to the ancestor-category of caudillismo, which encompassed the times of anarchy and civil wars, the victory of localisms and inorganic federalisms, and the later personalist dictatorships (Juan Manuel de Rosas in Argentina, Porfirio Díaz in Mexico). These forms of leadership shared the plebeian and often plebiscitary character of their governments, a trait that gradually became a structuring dimension of American politics, a sort of political habitus reflected in the persistent ties between the masses (*nontoneros, plebe*) and their leaders (caudillos). Second, the caudillista leaderships and regimes of the nineteenth century in Latin America paved the way to certain modalities of participation of the masses, even though the forms of popular expression were considerably limited in political, social, and economic terms. However, far from illustrating a paradigm of participatory democracy, these regimes were full of conservative and authoritarian elements (personalism, discretionality, and traditionalism, among others).

As a result, democracy in Latin American countries became associated early on with excess (the tyranny of the majority) as well as deficit (institutional weakness). But the first democratic experiences in the continent were judged mainly in relation to excess. It is not by chance that it was against inorganic and plebeian democracy that the idea of a "possible" republic gradually developed, based on a distrust of the masses and the limitation of political rights, on which both conservatives and liberals converged, unequivocally embodied in the design of the constitutions of various countries in the region in the nineteenth century. In this context, participation was limited and distorted in a restrictive form of democracy, in which the fear of a plebeian uprising often went hand in hand with the recurrent manipulation of the popular vote by the elites.

In this chapter I discuss some lines of interpretation and debate among the many readings of Latin American populisms.[1] I do so in different stages. First, I discuss the reading of populism as a myth and as an imaginary, while presenting a synthesis of the historical/structural readings surrounding the first populist moment, usually dated between 1940 and 1970. Second, I examine at greater depth some of the debates surrounding populism, its various sociocultural dimensions, and its political/ideological scopes. To that end, I examine five fundamental debates: (1) the debate regarding its origins, taking the Argentine and Ecuadorian cases as a point of departure; (2) the debate on populism (read from a peasant and indigenist perspective) and the possibility of an autonomous (revolutionary) avenue; (3) the debate that problematizes the relationship among the national/popular, socialism, and democracy, highlighting the process of construction of hegemony and the discursive turn; (4) those interpretations that emphasize plebeian aspects of populism, that is, the construction of a cultural identity from below; and (5) the debate on the interconnection between (neo)populism and neoliberalism.

At this point, before delving into the various readings, I believe it is necessary to clarify a few basic aspects of what I understand by *populism*. My reading focuses on three fundamental definitions. The first one is general and refers to the unavoidably complex and even contradictory nature of populism. In effect, populism is a political regime that presents both democratic and authoritarian elements, and whose objective is to achieve the "organized" participation of the masses, controlled by the state. Populism is thus constituted by the twofold reference to equality and hierarchy. In spite of this twofold matrix, it is from the standpoint of democracy that populism is best understood, since to a significant extent it responds to the (historical) need to shorten the gap between representatives and represented, a gap consolidated during the long period of liberal/conservative domination under military dictatorships or, more recently, after the neoliberal reforms. The second idea has to do with the interpretative framework established by populism to read politics. As has been insistently observed by many analysts, populism understands politics in terms of polarization and binary schemes, which implies selecting certain antagonisms, seen as fundamental and exclusionary, and simultaneously concealing or blurring other important conflicts. The third idea has to do with the constant tension that establishes populism at the crossroads between political opening and closure. This constitutive tension makes populisms eventually bring to the forefront of the discussions a disturbing and incisive question—in fact the fundamental question of politics: What type of hegemony is being built in this inevitable tension between the plural and the organicist? Double matrix, polarization, interpretative framework, and construction of hegemony are the topics that, in my opinion, constitute the essential core of Latin American populisms. Finally, as I attempt to demonstrate in the second part of this book, beyond the common elements and specific temporalities of the various countries, it is necessary to revisit typologies that illustrate the existence of different types of populisms.

Part 1: Readings of Populism

Populism as a Myth and an Ideology

Rather than associating populism with its social roots, the reading that emphasizes its association with myth considers that the true nature of the populist phenomenon is ideological. In a book published in 1965, US historian Richard Hofstadter identified five fundamental elements of populism as a myth: first, the notion of a golden age, with its appeal to popular nostalgia; second, the concept of natural harmonies (once the exploiters are eliminated); third, the dual version of the social struggle (antagonism between the people and those in power); fourth, a conspiracy theory of history (which it presumably shares with Marxism); and, finally, the denunciation of the primacy of money and finances—that is, of speculators. The central idea—which the author extracts especially from his analysis of US populism—is that the people are considered as an innocent and homogeneous being, which expresses itself in the antagonism between productive interests and exploiters (Hofstadter, *The Age of Reform*, discussed in Martuccelli 1995, 208). This line of reading that associates populism with a mythical structure is also developed in the works of the Frenchman Pierre Birnbaum (1979), for whom the concept was rooted in the myth of the antagonism between the people and those in power (*le peuple et les gros*), shared by both the right and the left.

The myth's function was related to its capacity to restructure the actors' mental and social field. This perspective was further developed by French historian Alain Pessin (1992), who conducted a study of ideologies as substitutes for mythical thought. According to the author, populism performs a mental operation that does not consist in attaining intrinsic truth but in bearing witness to a truth that populism reveals and inaugurates, something that could be denominated "mythological truth" (19). Pessin believes that it was populist thought, together with socialist thought, that positioned the social question as a problem in the nineteenth century, but unlike socialism, it did not understand it as the interplay of forces or within a logic of the social. For populism, the people are summoned to solve the social question, but "the people" is not a social category. Populism is therefore not a program; in its minimal expression, it is the desire, without temporal considerations, for justice to spread throughout the world, to do its work, to cure the wretchedness of the humble, and to reorient people's lives. Hence its origins in mythical thought. On the other hand, Pessin sees in the myth—that is, in mythical images, symbols, and narratives—not marginal deviations from modern thought but a dynamic and permanent principle through which a significant relationship between humans and the world arises. This means that a sociology of the imaginary must be developed. Following Claude Lévi-Strauss, he argues that if the myth can be understood as "an answer for which there is no question" (1968, 40), then we should follow that path, since populism provides a multitude of answers regarding the social question, more than the question demands.

The French historian Pierre André Taguieff (1996) conducted several studies on the subject. Taguieff emphasized the all-encompassing and polymorphic nature of populism, which does not define a certain political regime or ideological content but rather "a political style applicable to different ideological frameworks" (27). While Taguieff underscores the ambiguity of Latin American populisms, he focuses especially on the European phenomenon, which in the French case was represented by Jean-Marie Le Pen. It was through Le Pen's populism that he derived a sort of *ideal type*, taking into account the leader's demagogic nature and the type of call made, which he summarizes according to five main features: the political call to the people, a call to the people as a whole, a direct call to the true people, a call for change within the status quo, and a call to discriminate individuals according to their ethnic or cultural origins (1996, 57–63).

The anthropologist Imelda Vega Centeno (1991) offered a Latin American reading of populism as a myth, applied to the Peruvian case. Vega Centeno argues that populism reactivates the mythical/symbolic capacity to mobilize the population in question massively and foster expectations and will to power with unforeseeable consequences. In the 1930s Víctor Haya de la Torre had successfully reactivated this mythical/symbolic capacity, bringing to the current reality the various forms of participation entrenched in the collective imaginary of the Andean myth of refuge or harm (Vega Centeno 1991). Faced by the "harm" caused by the conquest, a narrative of "refuge" is constructed: A politically and militarily defeated society develops a way of apprehending reality and history that serves to conceal itself in the presence of the invader. This narrative also provides an interpretation of life and history that allows it to continue living and waiting in spite of defeat. Haya de la Torre thus established a complex form of relationship with the people's socio-cognitive system: Thanks to his words, people could continue living, believing, and struggling, in spite of persecution and failure.

In short, these readings reduce populism to a myth, whose basic unit is nostalgia for the organic community or an imaginary somewhere between religion and politics that, in both cases, implies an antiliberal and hence antidemocratic view of politics. It is undoubtedly valid to inquire into the type of democracy brought about by populism—the tendency toward unanimism and the affirmation of substantive democracy; however, in my opinion, the readings summarized above do so at the cost of a significant conceptual and practical reduction, by denying the possibility of other forms of democracy (participatory or direct democracy) or demonizing the forms of plebeian democracy.

On the other hand, this sort of approach quickly tends to associate populism with fascism, which in Latin America's specific experience leads to an inappropriate and disqualifying interpretation. For some, populism shared three elements with fascism: addressing the social question outside of both unbridled capitalism and socialism; an emphasis on political style; and anti-intellectualism. The two first elements have been profusely analyzed and have been proven to be far from determining. On the other hand, anti-intellectualism in Latin America's populist experiences has little to do with the construction of a new political and cultural order as an expression of a civilizational crisis, and less with the glorification of an aesthetic of violence, as is the case with fascism and Nazism. Together with the social question and personalist leadership styles, the "populist mythology," if such a thing exists, is above all the expression of the entry of the world of the excluded into the new political and social order—an entry that allows solving the social question, symbolically bridging the gap between representatives and represented.

In short, this hetero-referential reading, which fosters a strongly disparaging and critical view of populism, derives, more than from the identification of populism as a myth, from the association between populism and fascism, as well as the reduction of democracy, identified exclusively as liberal and representative democracy. Hence, the critique tends to become a sort of atemporal and recurrent political reading to disqualify any type of populist political experience, associating it with all the evils of contemporary politics and the distortions of democracy.

Historical-Structural Perspectives

We will now synthesize some of the readings that underscore the historical-structural character of populism and that present it as a development model closely related to the stage of import substitution and domestic market strategies. In a significant part of Latin American sociological and political literature, there is a "consensus" regarding the "era" of national-popular regimes: the period from 1929 to 1959–64, marked by the impossibility of importing manufactured products and the development of a substitution industry focused mainly on the domestic market (inward growth, according to the Economic Commission for Latin America and the Caribbean [CEPAL]). The unity of the populist phenomenon was anchored on the "populist moment." This was the economic context (accumulation of idle reserves during World War II and the development of exports after it) in which oligarchic domination was questioned in various Latin American countries and in which populist regimes were later consolidated through broad social pacts (through which the traditional sectors lost power in favor of new, emergent groups), and redistributive policies conceived as veritable "consolidation strategies" of these social groups.[2] For an entire sector of Latin American social thought, the first populisms therefore expressed an interclass government pact that corresponded to the moment of the "displacement" of foreign capital by national capital (or, rather, the creation of new alliances) and the expansion of the domestic market. There was therefore a "privileged relationship" between populism and the import substitution phase.

In the context of this widespread interpretation, we can identify at least four different approaches, according to the emphases and topics with which populism is associated: those that associate populism with modernization (Gino Germani and Torcuato Di Tella), populism with the social pact (Francisco Weffort, Abelardo Ramos, and Julio Cotler, among others), populism with dependency (Octavio Ianni, Fernando H. Cardoso and Enzo Faletto), and populism with development (Alain Touraine). They are complementary readings that, beyond the limitations of the populist experiences and their assessments, exhibit a number of common features: the transition period to industrialization, the viability—and limitations—of inward growth (import substitution), the political incorporation of the popular masses, the leader's role, and the effort to mobilize the masses in an organized manner.

POPULISMS AND MODERNIZATION

One of the first general readings of populism was elaborated by the influential Italian sociologist based in Argentina Gino Germani, from a structural-functionalist perspective. Even though the study focuses on Peronism, Germani's reading aims at more general conclusions. His approach was elaborated in the book *Política y sociedad en una época de transición* (Politics and society in a time of transition; 1965), where he revisited Karl Deutsch's concept of social mobilization to analyze the changes occurring in countries that went from traditional to modern ways of life. In this transition, the traditional consensus was destroyed, which was evident in the deteriorating traditional social, economic, and psychological bonds and in the mobilized people's search for new communal ties capable of providing a sense of personal identity and a means to protect their interests. In this transition process, deviations from and asynchronies with the sequential and normative model could arise, as illustrated by European countries, where mobilization processes coincided with social integration processes through political parties and trade unions. In contrast, in Latin America, the mobilization process took place within archaic structures that questioned modern forms of political representation. The result was what Germani called "asynchronies," evident in a number of effects (the *fusion effect*, which reinforces traditional features at an ideological level, and the *demonstrative effect*, which increases the level of aspirations), thus precluding integration as a result of mobilization. In Germani's opinion, this fusion effect operated mainly in the realm of ideologies, which allowed endowing the lower classes with aspirations and social rights equal to those of developed countries, even if they preserved noneconomic attitudes typical of traditional societies. Hence, the growing distance between the various dimensions of social life presented a problem: Economic development was not accompanied by political democracy. This lag or asynchrony led to the emergence of national-popular movements in various Latin American countries once the masses exhausted the channels for expression and participation provided by the social structure. Thus, a dynamic of manipulation of the masses, a primarily authoritarian leadership, and a nationalist ideology were the expression of heteronomy and participation. Germani's proposal not only returns to a dualist view of the social, through the opposition between traditional and modern societies, but also constitutes one of the first general explanations of populism, albeit at the cost of its sociological demonization.

Torcuato Di Tella (1983) reflected in the same vein. In his analysis of the process of mass mobilization, he emphasized that both the existence of an elite committed to that political process and liberalism's decline as an engine for change enabled the emergence of the populist experience. In developed areas, the social form was a product of the Liberal Party, based on the middle classes and later on the workers' movement, adopting a gradualist view of social change. Hence, class divisions only fleetingly crystallized in the revolutionary hypothesis, due among other things to an improvement in the standard of living and social mobility. But in underdeveloped areas, the demonstrative effect led to a revolution of expectations, but economic expansion lagged behind as a result of demographic growth, dependence on the markets, and premature attempts at redistribution. This created a quagmire, by raising expectations well above the possibilities of satisfying them. The abyss between aspirations and their satisfaction led to an incongruence in terms of status. "They have reasons for revenge but are also motivated to foster modernization and development" (Di Tella 1983, 84). The incongruous groups and the available masses struggle against each other and share a common hatred of the status quo.

Finally, the transition process paved the way to a new constellation of spontaneous peasant leaders, characterized by their impermanence and their extreme emotivity, who led mass movements whenever the masses experienced those frustrating conditions. Their short-term perspective and their simplistic or conspiratorial outlook blamed the current evils on the action of concrete groups and implied a trust in direct action, as was the case with revolutionary trade unionism or anarchism in the early twentieth century. These spontaneous leaders were only able to lead broad movements for short periods of time, after which they gave way to more organic and bureaucratic leaderships. It was this worker "spontaneity" which was later co-opted by Peronism's authoritarian and demagogic structures, thus leading it away from its original intentions.

POPULISMS, THE STATE, AND THE SOCIAL PACT

For other authors, populism is understood from the perspective of the state's political role in Latin America, rather than from its social origins. Populism is thus explained according to the mode of intervention of state power. A number of analyses in this line explain the emergence of these regimes as a response to the inability of Latin American bourgeoisies' to guarantee social domination and to determine the direction of the modernization process.

There are at least four different approaches in this line of thought. The first one was elaborated by Brazilian thinker Francisco Weffort (1978, 1994) with his characterization of populism as a "state of compromise," resulting from the Latin American bourgeoisie's inability to ensure its class hegemony and hence the constitution of a state distanced from private interests in an attempt to dominate the entirety of the social body. Populism was therefore an ideology of substitution in a context of evident crisis of the hegemony of the dominant classes. From an ideological standpoint, it was merely a tactic to confront concrete situations, rather than a global and strategic conception of society. However, it was a complex political phenomenon related to two factors: on one hand, the crisis of the oligarchy and liberalism; on the other hand, the political weakness of the dominant urban groups as they attempted to replace the traditional oligarchy in traditionally agrarian and dependent countries. As the most complete expression of the irruption of the popular masses in the process of urban and industrial development, populism demanded a process to incorporate those masses into the political arena.

In more general terms, for Weffort, populism is more than a phenomenon of mass manipulation. That phenomenon existed, but it was never absolute. Accepting that theory meant endorsing the liberal view that understood populism as an emotional relationship between the masses and a leader characterized by his lack of principles. Populism is above all an extolment of the public realm of the state—a democratization by authoritarian means (Weffort 1978, 61). The difference from Western representative democracy is that the state appears directly before all citizens; all organizations become mediators between the state and individuals; that is, they become annexes of the state, rather than autonomous bodies.

Other authors also underscore the prevalence of political categories over social categories. Among them, the Frenchman Alain Touraine (1988) characterizes populism as a form of social intervention by the state. One of the issues that explains this phenomenon is the multidimensionality of action in Latin America, which traditionally has combined class struggle, national struggles, and anti-imperialist struggles. This segmentation of collective action is indicative of the disparity between the objective situation and the capacity for action, or what Touraine (1988), in accordance with a long tradition of Latin American concepts on the topic, denominates "disarticulation." No central principle orients collective actions, which reflects the weakness of class-based parties but also of social movements. This explains why collective action in Latin America is effective only when it combines all three dimensions, which is precisely what populism does. There is therefore no representativeness between social groups, political forces, and ideological expression. There is no clear separation between the state and civil society. The state intervenes as the main political actor, and the social actors respond to the state's intervention more than to the initiatives of other social actors. From this perspective, the state is not a mediator between already constituted social classes but the true "builder" of social classes, which do not exist independently of its intervention. This peculiar articulation also reflects the very limited autonomy of social actors (Touraine 1988). In short, this second approach proposes understanding populism as a Latin American mode of development oriented by a politics of redistribution. In economic terms, it is characterized by a limited and dependent capitalism together with a high rate of investment, and in social terms, by structural heterogeneity and a strong urban political/cultural participation.

In this line, there is a third approach that reads populism as a specific strategy of capital accumulation. Argentine sociologist Carlos Vilas argues that it is an accumulation strategy essentially founded on increasing personal consumption and eventually distributing income. It therefore corresponds to a strategy undertaken by a certain part of the bourgeoisie in a certain stage of capitalist accumulation (1994, 124). Like Russian populism, this reading underscores the importance of small property. In terms of the political/ideological dimension, populism is relatively autonomous and has its own specificity. More than a class alliance, the author sees an unstable system of a balance of compromises, imposed "from outside" the classes and fractions implicated by the state (133). The populist state was in charge of guaranteeing the relations of power and reproduction, which led to the belief in a separate state beyond the block of forces in power.

A final version entails a more radical view of this perspective, reading populism as a variant of "Bonapartism." This view was held by a wide variety of authors, from Marxist ones to others with a functionalist approach. For example, for Milcíades Peña, Peronism was a form of Bonapartism, which explained both the preservation of the bourgeois order and the estrangement of the working class from autonomous struggle, depriving it of class consciousness. Juan Perón had derailed the demands of a growing and combative workers' movement by channeling them through the state (Peña 2012, 484). Hence, as in other capitalist countries, state-driven unionism benefited the capitalist interests that drove the economy—interests that the state undoubtedly served (487).

From a different epistemological and ideological matrix, Torcuato Di Tella later revisited the hypothesis of Bonapartism and articulated it with that of worker spontaneity. He argues that Peronism's emergence as Bonapartism was enabled by the elites' disunity, since, while most industrial sectors opposed Perón, there were also those that did not support him but benefited from his politics and therefore did not comprise a solid opposition. This disunity favored the arrival of Peronism as a mass movement led by small elites. Hence, the thesis of Bonapartism explained, on one hand, the passivity of the masses and, on the other, the fact that the interests defended were those of the upper sectors and not the lower classes, which meant that power passed from the middle and upper elites to a different sector of the upper elites (Di Tella 1983).

POPULISM, DEVELOPMENT, AND DEPENDENCY

For a whole line of interpretation, populism was the main promoter of developmentalist policies in Latin America, albeit constrained by the new situation of dependency. Populism was therefore read as a "moment" that corresponded to a phase of the evolution of the contradictions between the national society and a dependent economy. Thus, for example, for Cardoso and Faletto, "developmentalist populism" is an ideology that corresponds to the expansion of import substitution industrialization (ISI), characterized by the development of policies that tended to consolidate the domestic market. As a result, from 1950 to 1960, inward development exhibited two tendencies or orientations: satisfying the domestic market, or an orientation toward participation, with its doses of social and economic distribution; and promoting the expansion of new dominant sectors in the economy that sought to consolidate the system of inward domination. "Developmentalist populism" (Cardoso and Faletto [1969] 2003) was precisely that, a system of domination in which contradictory interests and objectives coexisted and interacted. In this context, not only the role of the state was important but also the way in which it expressed itself as an instrument of domination relative to the groups that composed it.

However, starting in the 1960s, the exhaustion of the populist-developmentalist model became evident in a crisis of the previous system of domination and the emergence of a new situation of dependency, which forced the various countries (especially Brazil, Argentina, and Mexico) to open their domestic markets to external control (direct foreign investment in the peripheral industrial economies). As we said in the previous chapter, this important change resignified dependency, reformulating it and inscribing it in a new framework—a new "situation," in which transformations of the productive structure at increasing levels of complexity and economic and social situations of exclusion of the popular masses coexisted. This was Cardoso and Faletto's explanation for the passage from regimes of representative democracy (developmentalist populism) to corporate-authoritarian regimes.

This line of structural interpretation was corroborated by other intellectuals of dependency theory. Theotônio dos Santos, for example, argued that developmentalist populism had revealed the limits of autonomous development, thus generating significant frustration in various social sectors. The new forms of dependency implied an important protagonism of monopoly capital and the strong presence of cumulative mechanisms of dependency (debt and international aid, among others), which required a redefinition of relations, at both the international and the national levels. In this dynamic context, the system was incapable of resolving the contradictions it generated in dependent economies, both in the advanced sectors and in the elimination of the more backward ones.

Finally, Octavio Ianni (1975), from a perspective close to dependentism, argues that populisms in Latin America occurred at a time when the class society was being definitively consolidated. In this phase, the politics of the urban classes emerged and, in industrial centers, the struggle against oligarchies and archaic forms of imperialism. This stage corresponded to the final moment of the process of dissociation between workers and the means of production, due to the formalization of capitalist economic relations. Finally, in the cultural arena, populism expressed the process of secularization of culture. Ianni also noted that the class character of populism does not appear immediately and that it was important to distinguish two main levels: a populism of the upper levels (bourgeois elites and the middle classes), which left the masses to their own devices (Juan Perón, Jacobo Árbenz, João Goulart) and promoted class harmony; and a populism of the masses themselves—workers, migrants, the lower middle classes, radicalized students, and left-wing political parties. When political and economic contradictions worsen, a metamorphosis of mass movements into class struggle occurs or may occur. Of course, populism expressed a political alliance, but this did not mean that there was a break between populism and the political past of the working class; rather, the former constituted a phase or moment of the political labor movement. In reality, in its very process of evolution, populism revealed its own limits. The crisis of the "inward" developmentalist project also signaled a crisis of mass politics.

Part 2: The Debates over Populism

Functionalist Readings of Its Origins and Their Critiques

In Latin America the first interpretations of the emergence of populism and its social bases were located in a double matrix: On one hand, they underscored the (negative) presence of lumpen and plebeian elements related to the persistence of the caudillista heritage; on the other hand, and as a consequence of this fact, they denied the labor origins of the experience.[3] However, both readings were based on different epistemological matrices, since while the former was more related to the political party struggle, and its spokespersons were leaders and writers from the institutional left, the latter derived from the first academic interpretations, related to functionalism.

Of course, the emphasis on the lumpen and plebeian character of the social bases was related to the impact produced by the entry of the lower classes into the public space, and even more to their forms of participation. In political and cultural terms, lumpen are those sectors located outside the social structure as a result of being declassed or excluded. Karl Marx and his characterization of Bonapartism contribute to this type of reading, which, as we have mentioned, had innumerable followers in Latin America. However, the issue of the emergence of the plebeian has other connotations as well, since it refers to a process of self-affirmation of the popular as rejected and excluded beings, on one hand, and to an iconoclast and anti-elitist critique of the dominant culture. Thus, in general, when the plebeian in Latin America are spoken of, references are made to certain cultural traits of the excluded, but when the onslaught of the plebeian specifically is alluded to, this cultural and symbolic dimension is associated with processes of structural change.

It is well known that the emergence of Peronism in Argentina resulted in a schism in the left, which reacted negatively, questioning the labor origins of Peronism and associating it with Domingo Sarmiento's liberal motif of barbarism versus civilization and progress. Both the Socialist Party and the Communist Party deployed this type of reading. For example, socialists acknowledged that there were barbarous regions in society—otherwise stated, that, together with the "working classes," there were "dangerous classes" that, from their marginality, threatened to transform worker uprisings into acts of social delinquency. It is worth noting that according to this view, this was a prepolitical problem, that is, a cultural and educational problem.[4] In short, the first reading of populism elaborated from the standpoint of (leftist) politics inquired into its spurious class origins, relating the experience to the lumpen condition and native barbarism and nineteenth-century caudillismos.

As mentioned above, in the 1950s Gino Germani elaborated one of the first academic interpretations of populism, with continental aspirations. Germani's socio-structural interpretation of Peronism was founded on the normative and sequential reading that established a split between the traditional and the modern. The arrival of a new contingent of workers devoid of ideology and the inability of the existing political parties to provide it with an adequate means of expression led to a situation of "anomy" that was capitalized on by new political movements led by elites with the necessary flexibility to make use of these movements. The presumed "ideological availability" of the masses thus became the main explicatory factor: Peronism was the result of a partial political participation of the masses and a demagogic manipulation. On the other hand, this interpretation relied on a structural and psychosocial distinction between "new workers" (of a rural and traditional origin with little political culture) and "old workers" (of an urban tradition, many of them European immigrants, with a political culture). By extension, one could conclude that the first Peronist labor militants were workers without a political background, manipulated by a leader and subordinated to the state apparatus. There were other reasons as well—for example, for most Latin American countries, and especially for the recently mobilized layers, the symbols of democracy did not have a positive meaning.

Beyond the evident social, economic, and ethnic differences, there are important points of agreement between Germani's reading of the origins of Peronism in Argentina and the leftist intellectual Agustín Cueva's reading of the origins of Velasquismo, in reference to José María Velasco Ibarra, the Ecuadorian caudillo who came to power in 1934 and who, with a number of interruptions, dominated the country's politics for forty years. Cueva's foundational reading was inscribed in a matrix that combined the orthodox leftist perspective with a structural-functionalist approach. In a 1972 text, Cueva formulated an interpretation of the origins of Velasquismo, appealing to Germani's thesis of manipulation of the masses, whereby, while not speaking of "new workers," his main hypothesis was that the social bases were the "urban subproletariat," whose stronghold was the coastal city of Guayaquil. In this significantly influential article, Cueva argued that neither the economic crisis nor the crisis of hegemony was sufficient to explain the emergence of a populist solution such as Velasco's. If the latter was successful, it was thanks to the emergence of a new social and political context related to the transformation of Ecuador's cities in the 1930s, which the author denominated a "mass situation" ([1972] 2007, 51). Which masses was he talking about? According to Cueva, the collapse in the 1930s led to an important crisis in the peasant sector, forcing the latter to migrate to the city, to Quito and especially to Guayaquil, which created "tension areas in the cities due to the emergence of an urban marginal sector" (54). As a result, this capitalist crisis—and not a crisis of a traditional sector of the elites—gave rise to a "subproletariat" that was socially and politically available, waiting for a redeemer: "Dissatisfied with their new fate, poverty-stricken and psychologically forlorn, more rebellious than ever because the traditional controls no longer had a sufficient hold over them, yet also unable to find a revolutionary solution, this subproletariat could foster nothing but a populism such as was inaugurated by Velasco and that of course is not the only one in Ecuador" (Cueva [1972] 2007, 55).

Cueva's thesis implied a number of consequences and articulated aspects of Germani's and Di Tella's structural-functionalist reading with those of certain Marxist lefts. However, it differed from the functionalist perspective by disassociating the Ecuadorian process from a phenomenon of economic modernization. Rather, he argued that it was a matter of a crisis of capitalism (massive unemployment). Hence, even if Velasquismo had an element of preservation of the bourgeois order, Cueva rejected the notion that in its origins it synthesized a confrontation between the liberal bourgeoisie and the export-oriented oligarchy, mediated by the actions of an authoritarian leader. He also underscored Velasquismo's tense relationship with the middle classes and its anti-intellectual character, which was also related to its mestizo composition, which had constituted a symbolic challenge to the white elites, thus reinvesting the lower and marginal sectors, represented by the new government, with a certain dignity. However, the main aspect of Velasquismo was that it had resolved the impasse between the dominant classes and the control of the subordinate ones.

Finally, rurality and caudillismo, and an ideological amalgam that combined Catholic elements and charisma, rituals, and religious ceremonies that appeared as replacements for political transformation in the hands of a marginal population, and that transformed Velasco almost into a sort of priest of a popular religion, related Cueva's reading to that of Argentina's leftist political parties (communists and socialists). However, there was no disdain for the plebeian in Cueva, as was the case with the Argentine left. Rather, his reading aimed at demonstrating the phenomenon of "false consciousness."[5]

To return to Argentina, in the early 1970s, in a context of a revaluation of Peronism from the left together with a rejection of the functionalist paradigm, Germani's reading was strongly questioned. The most significant rebuttal came from the sociologists Miguel Murmis and Juan Carlos Portantiero (1971), who analyzed "the constellation of social forces" (175) that characterized the situation prior to the origin of Peronism. Their central thesis underscored the unity of the working class, thus rejecting the distinction in terms of work security and political orientations and participation between new and old workers. According to the authors, one of the main issues was that while the process of industrialization driven by traditional forces had signaled the beginning of state intervention in different spheres, it had not been accompanied by social legislation. As a result, political repression and restrictions on consumption accentuated "the workers' opposition to the system and the growth of union organizing" (174), which did not prevent, however, the establishment of an increasingly closer relationship between trade unionism and the state, which Peronism later consolidated. Hence, the labor sectors were subjected to a process of capitalist exploitation and accumulation without distribution of income and without social interventionism, which led to of a series of worker demands that encompassed the entire working class. In this context, new and old trade unions developed a policy of alliances with the state apparatus, without, however, renouncing their aspirations for autonomy through a nationalist-democratic and distributionist program, as the creation of the Labor Party demonstrates.

On the other hand, the authors underscored that the joint participation of new and old workers entailed a certain programmatic continuity with previous demands of worker organizations, in a multiclass alliance that was already a tendency in trade unionism prior to Peronism. The conclusion of Murmis and Portantiero's study was clear: The old trade union guard had a relevant participation in the political operation that consolidated Peronism. Later, and from different angles, other empirical elements were added that confirmed the revisionist hypothesis. In short, underscoring the ideological changes of the labor movement at the time, especially prior to 1943, several studies demonstrated the effective co-optation of the leaders of the old trade unions and the participation of the old and new working classes in the emergence of Peronism.

Regarding Ecuador, Cueva's reading was also strongly echoed in 1980, when the political scientist Rafael Quintero published *El mito del populismo en Ecuador: Análisis de los fundamentos del Estado ecuatoriano moderno (1895– 1934)*, derived from his doctoral dissertation. In it, he argued that Velasquismo was not a univocal or homogeneous phenomenon and that it was therefore worth theorizing the various Velasquismos from 1940, 1945, 1952, 1960, and

1968, as some historians had already observed. The difference between Quintero's and Cueva's approaches was the characterization of the social bases of the first Velasquismo. Quintero believed that the first analyses conducted by Ecuador's political sciences mistakenly associated populism with Velasquismo, contributing to establishing the "myth of populism" both in Ecuador and abroad. Cueva's arguments, focusing on the notion of the marginal subproletariat, followed this line of thought. Relying on the analysis of primary sources (an electoral analysis at the district level, conducted for the first time in Ecuador), Quintero demonstrated that Velasco's victory in 1933 was not due to the support of the urban subproletariat, since the decisive votes were more rural than urban. He also demonstrated that the votes that ensured Velasco's victory came from the central and northern Sierra and not from Guayaquil (Quintero 2009, 15). Hence, the main social bases of the first Velasquismo were the rural middle classes rather than the urban subproletariat, which was reflected in a rural clientelism that ended up shaping the new political coalition.

As the historians Juan Maiguashca and Lisa North (1991) observe, the authors in dispute conducted a class analysis and posited that Velasquismo was a means to control the dangerous masses, even though differences arose when identifying the bases to sustain their arguments. "Their disagreement in this regard appears to be a matter of emphasis, since both authors conceive Velasquismo as a political instrument through which the leading landowners of the 'traditional' Sierra and those of the 'capitalist' Coast joined forces in order to defend their common interests, in a context of mass protests and even rebellion. Based on this assessment, both of them see a 'Junker road' to capitalist development" (91). However, Quintero's text went further, questioning—through his critique of Cueva—speculative interpretations of populism. In his opinion, Cueva's reading merely reproduced the hypothesis that related voting in favor of Velasco with a social sector (the urban subproletariat) based on the historical experience of other Latin American countries (Quintero 2009, 27).

In the 1970s the debate in Argentina was both academic and political. The emerging "critical sociology" in the academic left not only questioned structural functionalism, considering that it was a theoretical orientation that lacked the necessary conditions to interpret Latin America's reality correctly (where, as we saw in the previous chapter, dependency as a common framework and the paradigm of revolution as a political framework enjoyed particular theoretical and epistemological relevance), but also implied a positive reassessment of Peronism from the left. In Ecuador in 1980, the controversy had other nuances: While two leftist intellectuals engaged in a confrontation, there was no positive reassessment of Velasquismo. At some point, Quintero shared with Cueva the

Marxist-functionalist perspective but not the class characterization of Velasco's social bases. This position gradually deepened: In the late 1990s, in a new edition of the book where the debate was reproduced, Quintero questioned not only Cueva's essay form but his broad employment of the category of populism as a general concept to account for the political participation of the worker and/or marginal sectors.

The Debate over Populism and the Autonomous Path

No misinterpretation of Marx is more grotesque than the one that suggests that he expected a revolution exclusively from the advanced industrial countries of the West.—ERIC HOBSBAWM, *Pre-Capitalist Economic Formations*, 1965

A second reading perspective goes back to the Russian origins of the term *populism* (*narodnichestvo*), considering it as the expression of another, noncapitalist ideology related to the peasant lifestyle and communal property. One author who analyzed the fundamental elements of Russian populism and derived more general conclusions was the historian Andrzej Walicki, in an essay published in the renowned 1969 compilation by Ghita Ionescu and Ernest Gellner, entitled *Populism: Its Meanings and National Characteristics*. In his classical article, Walicki cited Richard Pipes, who established that two meanings of the term *populism* were already in place in Vladimir Lenin's time: The first was related to a narrow historical use in reference to a certain moment of Russia's revolutionary struggle in the 1870s, consolidated in the movement "Going to the people," led by sectors of the Russian intelligentsia in their attempt to spread ideas of social reform among the peasantry. One branch of the movement later developed into revolutionary terrorism, culminating in the czar's murder in 1881, while the other branch adopted Marxist viewpoints. The second meaning is broader and refers to a thought current with internal differences that posited the notion that capitalism was not inevitable and advocated other, noncapitalist paths to development, related to the peasantry and its forms of organizing. The peasantry was portrayed as endowed with virtues, whose forms of organizing were necessary for a harmonious integral development of society, in contrast with the decadence experienced in the city.

In Walicki's opinion, this idealization of the rural commune and the rejection of capitalism coincided with the publication in 1867 of the first volume of Marx's *Capital*, which contained a grim description of the consequences of the primitive accumulation of capital (dispossession, uprooting, banishment from the city, exploitation, an increase in misery), compounded by Marx's critical view of formal democracy. The Italian historian Franco Venturi, author of one of the great books on Russian populism, also argued that this critique of capitalism could already be found in Alexander Herzen, who, after participating in the labor struggles in France and Italy in 1848 and 1849 and analyzing their defeats, concluded on the need to foster a new generation to develop revolutionary ideas in Russia—to create a sort of psychological ideal of the "complete revolutionary." From Venturi's (1981, 156–57) perspective, the essential ideas of Russian populism were distrust of democracy in general, belief in the autonomous development of socialism in Russia, the future role of Russia's communal structure, trust in the peasantry's strength, and the need to create a revolutionary type—all of them related to the idea of a complete revolutionary.

The populist critique of capitalism consolidated the idea that it was necessary to avoid the capitalist stage by all means, which implied separating the means of production from producers and a process of social differentiation that implied regression and disintegration. In this line, populisms vindicated the communal property of the land, which could be seen in an incomplete or deficient manner in Russian villages, and concluded that preserving it was the shortest path to socialism: "the development of relations between labor and existing property" (Walicki 1969, 92).

On the other hand, this interpretation underscores that the way that populism has been read owes much to Lenin and his critique (Díaz Polanco 1978). Lenin not only provided populism with a more concrete historical and sociological connotation but also perceived the double Janus face of populism, which had a reactionary side (populist socialism based on small producers) and a general democratic side with a progressive character (Walicki 1969, 94). More concretely, for Lenin, populism was an expression contrary to capitalism that adopted the standpoint of small producers, who—ruined by capitalist development—advocated for the abolition of both capitalist and feudal forms of exploitation. In Lenin's opinion, populists were romantics who expressed a petite bourgeois utopia that idealized precapitalist economic and social relations. It should be noted, however, that Lenin's critique was partial, since populism was a reaction against capitalist development not only in Russia but also in other latitudes; it was not only the ideology of small producers but also the first expression of the specific features of backward countries, whose economic structures reflected a conflictive coexistence between the traditional and the modern. In this line of thought, Russian populism constituted a response to not only Western capitalism but also Western socialism, the product of a reaction of a democratic intellectuality in a backward peasant country, in a primitive phase of capital (Walicki 1969, 117–20).

According to the line of interpretation developed above, the notion of populism ended up referring not only to the Russian experience but also to that of other backward countries with an important current or former peasant population. Thus, the idea that the peasantry held the noblest values of the people, and therefore could constitute a central political actor capable of leading the reform process, started to spread. As a result, populism was associated with the peasant parties that multiplied around 1920 in different countries in eastern Europe, before declining after the great 1930 crisis for various political and economic reasons.

Peasant populism had very significant repercussions in Latin America due to the important presence of peasant/indigenous sectors. I do not intend to examine the peasant question in Latin America at length, a subject that has its own specific importance in the history of the debates in the region. Rather, I would like to underscore that in our latitudes the discussion of the so-called peasant question only partially overlaps the debate on populism, especially with regard to the notion that the peasantry and its communal forms of organization are the bases for social transformation. Regarding populism, its relation to the peasantry thesis has to do with the affirmation of a sort of specific—some would say "autonomous"—political path beyond the perspective of classical capitalism and classical socialism, grounded on a positive assessment of the communal nature of peasant and indigenous agrarian structures.

In order to account for the richness of this reading, we must also consider the work of the "late Marx" (Teodor Shanin), who, questioned by the Russian populists, was obliged to reconsider rural communities. His letter to Vera Zasulich, where he insinuated the possibility of avoiding the evils of capitalism through a revolution based on the rural community (*obshchina*), *The Ecological Notebooks*, the *Grundrisse*, and the *Kovalevsky Notebooks*, where he speaks of the Russian rural commune and other possible forms of production, have been profusely cited after they were unearthed and disseminated in the 1970s. In Latin America authors such as José Aricó contributed decisively to their dissemination.

To illustrate this view, I discuss the reflections of five authors on the subject: José Carlos Mariátegui's vindication of the autonomous path to socialism, Aricó's reading of the subject, the Mexican anthropologist Díaz Polanco's Marxist critique of autonomous paths (critical anthropology and neo-*indigenismo*), the Bolivian Álvaro García Linera's neo-indigenist view, and, finally, the Argentine Carlos Vilas's reading, which elaborates connections between Russian populism and Latin American populism in its state-developmentalist version.

The first moment of peasant populism is examined in the work of the aforementioned Peruvian author José Carlos Mariátegui, who in his encounter with the Andean world was one of the first thinkers to underscore the importance of the survival of communities among indigenous/peasant populations, in the context of revolutionary struggle. These communities survived both colonial times and the liberal republic. According to Mariátegui, two phenomena stand out in Peru's reality: on one hand, the end of Inca communal socialism and the consolidation of a feudal order; on the other hand, the survival of communal property in spite of it all. The feudalism of which Mariátegui (1988, 51) speaks is not related to the communal agrarian structure but to another type of rural property founded on latifundia and indigenous servitude. On the other hand, the Peruvian author compared the survival of Peruvian communities with that of Russian communes. "Feudalism similarly let rural communes continue in Russia, a country that offers an interesting parallel because in its historical process it is much closer to these agricultural and semifeudal countries than are the capitalist countries of the West" (64).

As various authors point out (Alberto Flores Galindo, Aricó, Michael Lōwy), Mariátegui shared his faith in the community and the possibility of an autonomous path to socialism with the Russian populists—even if he did not read them. In Mariátegui's opinion, if capitalism in the Americas had been dynamic and vigorous, the communities would have been dissolved, and indigenous people would have gone from a mixed regime of community and servitude to a regime of free wageworkers, which would have led to a process of proletarianization. As we know, none of that happened. Mariátegui argues that latifundia gradually plunged the community into servitude but that elements survived that expressed "in part the spirit and substance of the ancient civilization" (1988, 77–78). These elements, related to practical socialism, have to do with the various forms of cooperation and association of indigenous people (the *minga* [collective work], for example) with collectivism (of the land, usufruct, the use of pastures and water). Hence, the defense of communism is far from founded on abstract values but instead based on collective practice. This implies recognizing that more than a hundred years of republicanism failed to instill individualism in indigenous people; instead, communism was their defense (83).

Therefore, the solution to the Indian problem—which for Mariátegui was the solution to the national question—consists of recovering elements of community or practical socialism, which are alive in Peru's society and contain possibilities for development and evolution. Hence, ethnic attributes should not necessarily be renounced. Rather, the community's survival, visible in elements of practical socialism, could spearhead social change, synthesized in the myth or the hope of a socialist revolution. As was observed in a previous chapter, this view differed from the one developed by Víctor Haya de la Torre in *El antiimperialismo y el Apra* (Anti-imperialism and Apra; 1936). Finally, in *Aniversario y balance* (Anniversary and balance sheet), Mariátegui (1972a, 248) argued that while socialism, like capitalism, is not an American doctrine, it has become a global movement. However, Mariátegui insisted, "Socialism is ultimately in the American tradition. Incan civilization was the most advanced primitive communist organization that history has known" (249), before concluding with the renowned phrase that socialism in America cannot be a copy but a heroic creation.

However, as the Peruvian essayist Alberto Flores Galindo argues in *La agonía de Mariátegui* (Mariátegui's agony), "None of that was enthusiastically received by the International: They disliked the emphasis on autonomy, but especially the defense of the peasantry and the resolute proclamation of socialism, all of which recalled the old controversy between Lenin and the populists in the mind of anyone knowledgeable of Bolshevik history" (1980, 48). The advocate of the community had to position himself close to Vera Zasulich or Herzen and in a different and perhaps even opposing perspective to the one elaborated in *The Development of Capitalism in Russia* (Lenin [1899] 2004), which Mariátegui never read. At the time—1929—Marx's writings on the "Asiatic mode of production" (unpublished until 1939) were unknown, and so was his correspondence with Vera Zasulich, where the issue of whether socialism required a prior capitalist stage or not was discussed in 1881 (Flores Galindo 1980, 49). Mariátegui's positions could certainly be associated with those of Vera Zasulich, to whom Marx responded in a renowned letter that same year.

Another phase began in the 1970s, when Latin America saw a return of *campesinista* positions. In his 1978 book *Mariátegui y los orígenes del marxismo latinoamericano* (Mariátegui and the origins of Latin American marxism), Aricó focused again on Mariátegui's reading of Marx, which also allowed him to reassess Mariátegui's "populism" and establish a few parallels with nineteenth-century Russian intellectuality, resorting to Franco Venturi's studies. For Aricó, condemning populism not only implied denying all ideological revolutionary movements "not directly led by the communists" but also highlighted the distance between the Marxist revolutionary movement and Latin American social movements (xxxviii–xxxix). This entailed three major consequences: first, the exclusion of all original search based on the study of the country's social reality instead of sectarian doctrines; second, a disdain for the revolutionary potential of the "degraded rural world," associated with backwardness; and, third, in the face of the rural world, which presumably lacked all historical potential, communists' conviction to struggle for the political and ideological destruction of all intellectual forms related to regionalism, *indigenismo*, and the peasantry (xxxviii–xxxix). Hence, the attacks against Mariátegui and the accusation of being a "populist" "has a defaming character and has a specific political purpose: to exclude an underlying topic in the strategic and tactical elaboration of the communist parties of non-European countries in the 1920s—a topic that associated them with Marx's inquiries in the 1880s, when, reflecting specifically on the Russian case, he glimpsed the possibility that in that country, precisely because of its backwardness and the still powerful presence of an institution that perished long before in western Europe, the rural commune, capitalism could be avoided altogether, moving directly to socialist ways of life and production" (xl).

In short, redeeming Mariátegui served to revalue a perspective whereby populism and *campesinismo*/neo-*indigenismo* are interconnected and shine a new light on the revolutionary hypothesis in the context of Latin American Marxism, based on the possibility of an autonomous path for non-European peoples, in an ever-conflicting relation between the various modes of production and historical periods. However, the main point was that these non-European peoples had other tools to carry out their own utopia or historical revolution.

Curiously, the same year that Aricó published in Mexico his compilation on Mariátegui and the origins of Latin American Marxism, Héctor Díaz Polanco, who years later became a key proponent of the paradigm of indigenous autonomy, published a critical article on *campesinista*/*indigenista* populism. In a long article entitled "Indigenismo, populismo y marxismo" (*Indigenismo*, populism, and marxism; 1978), the Mexican anthropologist discussed the tense relationship and the differences between these three poles. The article elaborated a Marxist/Leninist critique of the populism present in a certain *indigenista*/*campesinista* perspective. While acknowledging that populism represents a critical view of capitalism, Díaz Polanco, in tune with Leninism, considered it a romantic and petite bourgeois critique. This point is important because Díaz Polanco was in fact arguing with the populist currents in Mexico, illustrated in the intellectual field by the new *indigenismo* (*indianismo*) and critical anthropology. In Díaz Polanco's opinion, these culturalist readings had two problems: On one hand, they idealized the community, thus inverting ethnocentrism, positing the superiority of indigenous society. On the other hand, their advocates believed that they could accomplish that miracle within capitalist society.

Other approaches emerged in the 1990s, which, revisiting the perspective of the "late Marx," sought to examine the relationship between *indianismo* and Marxism. One such approach was that of the Bolivian sociologist Álvaro García Linera, who criticized the views of "primitive Marxism" (2007, 149) or orthodox Marxism regarding the agrarian world, revisiting Marx's texts on the

Russian rural commune. In this line, based on the reflections of critical Marxism, García Linera underscored the importance of a multilinear conception of history in Marx's later work. He argued that in the introduction to *Kovalevsky Notebooks*, Marx elaborated a complex view of historical development, quite different from the linear—and racist—schemes deployed by the Second International, later systematized by Joseph Stalin ([1938] 1985) in *Dialectical and Historical Materialism* and many manuals of orthodox Communist dissemination (García Linera 2008b, 27). Both Trotskyism and Stalinism in Latin America shared that linear and gradualist view, canonized by Stalinism. García Linera also observed that when analyzing the case of the Inca community, Marx had underscored the existence of other possible forms of production. In short, on this topic, García Linera rescued two central ideas from Marx that had the virtue of appealing to the Bolivian left: On one hand, Marx had observed the revolutionary character of the peasant community; on the other hand, he also noted the existence of external and internal forces that drove it to its dissolution (38).

To conclude this section, I would like to mention one approach that explores the relationships between Russian and Latin American populisms in a different manner. In an important compilation on populism published in 1994, the Argentinean Carlos Vilas argued that Russian populists did not question capitalism per se, nor did they propose abolishing private property; rather, they believed that, unlike in Europe, the particularities of capitalism in Russia—and by extension in backward countries—turned it into a transplanted, artificial, illegitimate, and hence impracticable phenomenon. Thus, Russian capitalism, which became monopolistic early on, became a mechanism to enrich a minority that, in addition, hindered the general development of the economy, did not contribute to expanding the market, and generated more misery. For that reason, what Russian populists proposed was "noncapitalist industrialization fostered by the state" (31), which could be achieved in two manners: on one hand, state control of large properties and large-scale production and, on the other hand, expansion and protection of small peasant and nonindustrial property. According to Vilas, a number of connections could be made between that line of thought and the populist experiences in the mid-twentieth century in Latin America, among them, the idea that populism enters peripheral societies in its monopolistic and industrial-financial concentration phase—hence the distrust in large property; the belief that consumption is one form of realization of surplus value and that, therefore, accumulation and distribution can be combined; the importance of the conspiracy hypothesis (the project's enemies are external); and the need for or emphasis on the active role of the state (36–37).

The National-Popular Debate

THE TWOFOLD NATURE OF THE NATIONAL-POPULAR

In the 1970s, in addition to the analyses of the socioeconomic conditions and the possible forms of political expression, another interpretative model emerged, based on the observation that none of the existing theories on populism specifically recognized the existence of a subject constituted in the national-popular experience. Both the hypothesis of manipulation of the masses and the employment of demagogy by the leader eluded this constitutive dimension (Valenzuela 1991). This reading also sought to set the analysis of the so-called populist moment apart, broadening it by resorting to Antonio Gramsci's perspective on the national-popular and his outline of the process of constructing a counterhegemonic collective national will.

In *La cola del diablo: Itinerario de Gramsci en América Latina* (The devil's tail: Gramsci's itinerary in Latin America), José Aricó (1988) recalled that the dissemination of the Italian author's ideas in the subcontinent had occurred in the context of two different historical moments: the period between 1960 and 1970, marked by the hopes awakened by Cuba and the shift toward dictatorships, and the 1980s, characterized by the decline of authoritarian regimes. It was clear that a key feature of Gramscian thought was the fact that it could not be reduced to the Leninist-vanguardist matrix. Revisiting Gramsci allowed articulating a new reading in conjunction with other concepts, among them, those of hegemony, the national-popular, passive revolution, and the broadened state. The possibility of reading these concepts in the mirror of Latin American reality had to do with the fact that the society about which Gramsci had reflected (Italy between the wars) was undoubtedly closer to Latin America than other European societies were.

But what is meant by *national-popular*, and how should it be conceived in the Latin American context? In an article entitled "Gramsci en clave latino-americana" (Gramsci through a Latin American lens), Juan Carlos Portantiero (1991) reflected on the *national-popular* category, a concept found in *Notes About Machiavelli, Politics and the Modern State* (1975), which alludes to popular tradition (especially literature) and the process of constructing a collective will. Portantiero argued that Gramsci did not have a "populist" view of the people, that he did not see it as the realm of the pure and unpolluted; rather, he believed that in it coexisted conservative forces that reflected the conditions of past ways of living and innovative, creative, and progressive strata. "What Gramsci proposed as a process of constructing a 'national-popular collective will'" was the need for this connection between a modern, secular, and scientific culture and the nuclei of 'good sense' in the contradictory popular culture. . . . His reflections on hegemony establish his discourse on the national-popular as a foundational category of the possibility of historical change" (Portantiero 1991). The central issue for Gramsci concerned the relationship between intellectuals and the people, through a "moral and intellectual reform," as well as the idea that the subaltern classes were not always able to overcome the corporate economic horizon, becoming counterhegemonic groups, assembling around them a national-popular collective will. For Gramsci, this collective construction entailed, as an alternative, the conjunction of democracy and socialism. However, given Latin America's political history, Portantiero reflected that what is related to the national-popular category is not necessarily the socialist alternative (the relationship between the national-popular and socialism has been rather troublesome) but the populist alternative. For that reason, Portantiero proposed reflecting on the basis of existing populisms, behind which he perceived the articulation of an anthropomorphic view of the state (paternalist caudillismo) as the central topic of political action.

In a similar vein, emphasizing the twofold nature of the national-popular, are the works of Bolivian thinker René Zavaleta Mercado (2006), who argued that every people has contradictory tendencies derived from its heritage. Thus, the Mexican tradition contained democratic rebellion but also the memory of servitude. The same was the case with the German tradition, in whose culture we find both a sense for political organization and anti-Semitism. For that reason, an intellectual and moral reform is necessary, that is, a selective recovery, since neither the proletariat nor the people in general inherently have a progressive program. The mass can also congregate around reactionary summons; it can also come apart, never constituting itself as a self-determined popular subject. It is not by chance that Zavaleta also took as his point of departure the fact that Latin American societies, and especially Bolivian society, were disarticulated, heterogeneous societies where different temporalities and forms of social, political, and cultural organization were hierarchically superimposed. In fact, the concepts of "multitude" and "mass" are broader than those of "class" and "proletariat" and are necessary to understand the structure of the national-popular. In short, Zavaleta's objective—which he intended to apply to the study of Bolivian political events, especially the 1952 revolution and the constitution of a "dual power"—was to analyze the structure of the national-popular in Bolivia in terms of self-determination and freedom.

In short, what this line of interpretation problematizes is the possibility of constructing a popular subject as a counterhegemonic power block, that is, one opposed to the general principle of domination. For that reason, populisms sooner or later bring to the forefront a disturbing and incisive question, in fact the fundamental question of politics: What type of hegemony is being built? Is it popular-democratic, or popular-organicistic or regional-state-driven? In my opinion, this is the key of the national-popular.

POPULISM, POLITICS, AND HEGEMONY

In this line, one of the most well-known readings in the academic world is that of the Argentinean Ernesto Laclau, who proposed a broader and more general interpretation of populism, associating it with the construction of a hegemonic popular-democratic project. From the beginning, Laclau developed a theory of non-class-based antagonism, founded on the idea that populism is a particular form of articulation.

It is important to note, however, that Laclau's work on populism, like that of other authors—among them Martín Retamozo (2006) and Gerardo Aboy Carlés (2010)—went through several stages. The first one, the Althusserian stage, took place in the 1960s and 1970s, when, in an attempt to avoid economistic reductionism, Laclau (1978) inquired into the problematic relationship between class and populism. To that end, he distinguished between the class struggle, which took place at the level of relations of production, and the popular-democratic struggle, which occurred at the level of political/ideological relations and could be articulated in one or several class discourses. Populism is a specific form of articulation of the demands for popular democracy. Otherwise stated, the populist discourse had the virtue of constituting the "people" in the form of "democratic-popular demands." But there were different types of populism: the populisms of the dominant classes (fascism, Peronism) and the populisms of the dominated classes (socialism). In this first stage, Laclau pointed to a possible continuity between populism and socialism, as well as the possibility of conceiving populism as fascism.

A second stage begins with the book *Hegemony and Socialist Strategy: Towards a Radical Democratic Politics* ([1985] 2014), coauthored with Chantal Mouffe, where the authors conduct an in-depth analysis of the difference between popular and democratic struggles from a post-Marxist and post-structuralist perspective. However, Laclau's focus at the time was not populisms but the new social movements, understood as a new attempt at a counterhegemonic formation. According to the new theoretical paradigm, there were no previously constituted identities nor a privileged political subject—all actors have to struggle within their own spheres in a plural political space and construct their collective identity gradually by articulating meanings.

Finally, a third stage was consolidated with the book *On Populist Reason* (2005), which, as we shall see later, takes part in the current debates on the subject. In it, Laclau returned to populisms, further refining his conception. The basis of populism is the division that organizes the social space into two opposing sides: people and the block in power. This is what Laclau denominates "the populist rupture," which articulates three dimensions: the equivalence of unsatisfied demands, their crystallization around certain common symbols, and the emergence of a leader whose words incarnate this process of popular identification. The development of a popular subject cannot be explained as the sum of preconstituted elements but as a process of articulation (a chain of equivalencies between subaltern demands) that reconfigures those elements.

In this latter work, Laclau does not simply identify populism as an inherent logic of the political; as Gerardo Aboy Carlés (2014) and the Uruguayan Francisco Panizza (2009) observe, there is a sort of shift of the political understood as hegemony to the political understood plainly as populism.[6]

BETWEEN HEGEMONIC TEMPTATION AND UNANIMITY

The works of Argentine thinkers Emilio de Ípola and Juan Carlos Portantiero contributed to problematizing the issue of the constitution of the popular subject from a Gramscian perspective, in open controversy with Laclau's pro-populist views. In a renowned article published in 1987, these two authors reflected on the "national-popular and the really existing populisms" from a perspective that privileged an analysis of social classes as subjects of historical action, that is, to account for (or not) the passage from corporatist action to the process of decorporatization of social classes (de Ípola and Portantiero [1987] 1994).[7] In Gramscian terms, the authors argued that the realm of the national-popular is common sense, which contains contradictory tendencies, that is, toward rupture as well as integration. Therefore, far from being a coherent system that resists oppression, the national-popular was "a field of struggle where all conceptions of the world and of life coexist" ([1987] 1994, 530).

The authors' objective was to discern the nature of populist ideology and of really existing movements. As an illustration of the national-popular, populism entailed a twofold process: the construction of the people as a political subject and the construction of a new state order. In the aforementioned article, de Ípola and Portantiero ([1987] 1994) distinguished between the national-popular and the national-statal; they also analyzed the way in which, in the passage from one to the other, the national-popular was "captured" by populisms. This "capture" was synthesized in the following steps: First, the antagonistic elements of popular demands were displaced, defining opposition only against a specific expression (oligarchic hegemony—the antipeople); second, these demands would be addressed with the same doctrinal matrix of the elite that led the movement; and, finally, the general principle of domination would be reconstituted, fetishizing the (now "popular") state and establishing an organicistic conception of hegemony.

The point of departure for the authors' undeniably sharp analysis was that there was a strongly organicistic conception in really existing populisms, and therefore the process of "capture" analyzed was far from constituting a "deviation." Thus, the main problem was that populism constitutes the people on the basis of organicistic premises that reify it in the state and deny its pluralist expressions, transforming differences into head-on opposition, articulating the popular field through the duality "friend versus foe." This process has a corollary in the mythologization of the leader who personifies the community. Concretely, Peronism illustrated perfectly this model of constitution of the political subject and its subjection to the state personified by the charismatic leader. As a result, Laclau's critique was founded on different aspects: On one hand, there was no continuity but rather rupture between populism and socialism; on the other hand, no really existing populism was antistate.[8] Thus, the state played not a provisory but a central role.

Of course, this did not imply that populism did not contain progressive elements. In an earlier text, de Ípola (1983) had undertaken a (discursive) analysis of progressive articulations, insisting on the idea that vindicating the national-popular was not "episodic" or a secondary dimension of Peronism's discourse and politics. We are therefore far from Germani's readings of the masses' irrational adherence to the leader. However, acknowledging these positive elements cannot lead us to disregard something constitutive of the Peronist phenomenon: the subordination of the national-popular to the national-statal and, therefore, to the general principle of domination (De Ípola 1983, 163).

In another text Portantiero also underscored the tension between the two principles—the popular and the state—associated with the Latin Americanist view that places the state at the center and that, through paternalist caudillismo, crowns the connection between the masses and the state with an anthropomorphic identification with the leader. In contrast with this state-centered standpoint, European socialists had a societal perspective that assumed that "in the face of a state closed to participation, the presence of the masses in it can only be guaranteed by an onslaught, whether molecular or violent, by society" (Portantiero 1991, 156).

In other words, the centrality of the state matrix generated from above positioned the leader as the keystone of the national-popular and explained its aversion to any attempt at constructing a self-determined popular subject. In other texts, we denominate this constitutive feature of populism "unanimism" (Martuccelli and Svampa 1997). By that we mean a political conception that always finds it difficult to conceptualize conflict and even to leave political room for other political parties. On the contrary, unanimism aims at imposing, mostly in a symbolic manner given its practical limitations, a unitary conception of society, whose major theoretical formulation never presents itself as opposed to democracy. On the other hand, unanimism does not reject electoral arithmetic and the individualist principle on which it is founded; on the contrary, in its Latin American versions, the ballot box is the basis for the "organic" representation of society. Finally, unanimism is not exclusively founded on a stratified conception of society, organized as a set of hierarchically structured units, where the upper levels incorporate the lower ones; on the contrary, if the hierarchies are respected, they are at the heart of an egalitarian and sometimes plebeian matrix. Hence the many analyses that focus on the hybrid character of national-popular movements—democratization processes articulated with antiliberal principles, which combine broader bases for social inclusion with the denial of a space for political deliberation.

In Argentina in the 1980s, the issue of the relationship between existing populisms and democracy became more pressing. In a postdictatorship historical context, the readings not only reinforced the explanation of the working class's rational choice of Peronism but also inquired into the relationship between Peronism and democracy. Thus, one of Juan Carlos Torre's inquiries was how to combine a movement for political and social reform commanded by a plebiscitary leadership with the preservation of a pluralist and democratic space. Reflecting with a historical perspective, Torre (1991) added that the mass support enjoyed by Perón was a political phenomenon that did violence to the conscience of a generation of intellectuals who believed that there was a continuity between the world of labor, social progress, and democratic values. Confronted with a movement that questioned the consistency of this conviction, the natural reaction was to seek a shelter-interpretation. The notion of "deviation" thus served to safeguard their threatened beliefs.

Questions of that sort are also present in the most recent reading by Gerardo Aboy Carlés, who analyzes the emergence and consolidation of a populist matrix in Argentina, illustrated by both Yrigoyenism and Peronism, characterized by significant ambiguity. Both movements aspired at representing the nation in its entirety and to that end assumed the form of a radical rupture with the prior political and social order. "Nation and rupture, to be more precise, national-state and national-popular references, had at first a conflictive coexistence that characterized Argentina's political trajectory" (Aboy Carles 2001, 312). Hegemonism was therefore linked to the very process of constitution of political identities and the expansion of citizenship. However, the most common readings underscored one or another element. Either they saw the populist phenomenon merely as transformism based on the leader's ability to manipulate and the idea of a United People as an "organic community," or they tended to emphasize the revolutionary dimension of the rupture (311–12). Both emphases obscured the richness of the concept of populism. However, what is certain is that neither Yrigoyenism nor Peronism was conceived as part of a pluralist political system. According to Aboy Carlés, the survival of these hegemonistic conceptions and the struggle to appropriate common elements was one of the main factors leading to the chronic instability of Argentine politics (313).

In short, these reflections on the limits of populism, on the twofold nature of the national-popular and its articulation with the populist hypothesis, and on the hegemonistic or unanimistic temptation inherent in really existing populisms concerned a sector of the Latin American left, especially between the 1980s and the 1990s, which sought not only to advance in the construction of an autonomous popular subject but also to read politics through the lens of democracy. This unanimistic conception and its effects on political life and the future of democracy were therefore one of the central topics of political studies conducted in recent decades. In many ways, and from various perspectives, it was a matter of demonstrating its permanence and its limits, as well as its successive transformations.

In the context of the crisis of Marxism, post-structuralist critique, and the linguistic turn, many studies based on discourse analysis were conducted in the 1980s and 1990s. Ernesto Laclau's first essay (1978), while presenting a more general view of the populist phenomenon, based its analysis on discursive operations, although not necessarily removed from the social structure. However, his later works, coauthored with Chantal Mouffe, on the new social movements (1985) proposed a rupture with the idea of a socially preconstituted political subject. Two of the most influential interpretations of Peronism from the standpoint of discourse analysis were the aforementioned work by Emilio de Ípola (1983) and *Perón o muerte: Los fundamentos discursivos del fenómeno peronista* (Perón or death: The discursive foundations of the Peronist phenomenon; 1986), by Silvia Sigal and Eliseo Verón. In the latter, the authors studied the discursive production associated with a field of social relations, which ranged from Perón's discourse in its various stages to that of the Montoneros guerrilla organization. Based on a "theory of the observer"—instead of the actor—the authors analyzed how Peronism had signaled the emergence of a new political style, a novelty confirmed by Perón's own discursive style, reappropriating democratic elements of the opposition's discourse and inserting them in a dichotomous realm that emphasized the opposition between the "fraudulent and exploiting" oligarchy and the exploited and working people. Different from Laclau, however, de Ípola and Sigal and Verón pointed to the organicistic aspects of Peronist discourse and the leader's intention of portraying himself as the incarnation of the totality of the social body. This movementist conception of politics and society implied rejecting a conflictive view of the social and constantly affirming the friend/foe opposition, in order to counteract the presumed dangers and dissociative effects produced by the enemy in the political arena.

The Arrival of the Plebeian Perspective

In recent decades, a new type of approach emerged that proposes examining history "from below" and emphasizes the plebeian as an essential component of the forms of participation of the popular in the context of populisms. The analysis of these elements—observed by various Latin American historians—in the configuration of a popular identity gave rise to what could be denominated a *plebeian perspective*, which became a basis for interpretation by employing concepts from English Marxism derived from the work of E. P. Thompson and Raymond Williams.[9]

This dimension of the plebeian once again leads us to Latin American history, to the time of postindependence political struggles, when democracy was associated with the inorganic and the plebeian onslaught. In the twentieth century, the different national-popular experiences once again placed the plebeian at the center of the political scene. In this respect, populism was marked by the notion of "excess," which encompassed, on one hand, the people's irruption into the public space and, on the other hand, the leader's unanimistic "One People" temptation (Martuccelli and Svampa 1997). This association between the plebeian and the forms of participation of the popular spread through most Latin American countries in the form of the "invasion" of the poor and excluded, who came down from the hills, the sierra, and the provinces to "surround" or "lay siege" to urban political and economic centers (Saint-Upéry 2008a).

The plebeian perspective found various national expressions, among them the Argentine and the Ecuadorian cases. In the Argentine case, one of the most significant contributions is the study on Peronism conducted by the English historian Daniel James, who, in his classical 1988 book *Resistance and Integration: Peronism and the Argentine Working Class, 1946–1976*, analyzed the way Peronism forged a cultural identity that signaled a rupture with other labor cultures at the time—a formula that owed its success to Peronism's capacity to provide the working classes with a feeling of social and political protagonism, by associating them with the representation of an industrial Argentina (James [1988] 1994). But, above all, this phase of Peronism permitted the contradictory expression of two types of reality in a single class consciousness: on one hand, the loyalty to a movement that proclaimed harmony between the social classes, the need to subordinate the interests of workers to those of the nation, and the importance of disciplined obedience to a paternalist state, and on the other hand, the emergence of forms of worker resistance and the consolidation of a counterculture. Finally, the working class demonstrated that it was capable of defending its interests, while challenging the established forms of social hierarchies and the symbols of authority.

James's interpretation underscored that the debates on the new and old working classes and on the formal organization of the working class had overlooked the concrete forms of mobilization and social protest that took place. From his perspective, the movement also served as a vehicle for a dissenting political culture that rejected everything that had previously existed in the political, social, and economic realms, and even established a sense of "blasphemy" against the norms of the traditional elite. In a previous article published in 1987, based on interviews, James analyzed the events of October 17 and 18, 1945, and through a Thompsonian lens deployed a reading that portrayed a situation of popular outbursts in the various urban centers during the marches, in a carnivalesque climate of breaking traditional norms and attacking various representative institutions. This festive and carnivalesque behavior, which could lead to violence, corresponds to what Thompson denominated as "counter-theater," that is, questioning symbolic authority. These attacks, which evidenced the unequal distribution of cultural power, also illustrated the way social hierarchies were spatially expressed, through an asymmetrical relation between the center and the periphery. Says James, "The October events violated such established conventions: the suburbs invaded the center" (James 1988, 456).

Those plebeian behaviors differed significantly from the official canonical version of the Plaza de Mayo march (an image of social and individual harmony of the working-class family) but also from the "other official version," which linked October 17 to lumpen elements. It is worth noting that James's explanation did not intend to replace a structural reading with a culturalist one but to illuminate other aspects of a phenomenon as complex and ambivalent as Peronism, demonstrating the heretical character of the October demonstrations, which revealed a symbolic struggle in the form of attacks against institutions considered "legitimate," with which subaltern sectors sought recognition of their worth and experience.

Likewise, in the aforementioned study we conducted with Danilo Martuccelli, published in 1997, we revisited the concept of a "structure of feeling" and applied it to the study of the transformations of Peronism.[10] The presence of a set of opposing processes and elements allowed us to speak, in the Argentine case, in terms of a structure of feeling and experience more than ideology and "social class," that is, representations elaborated on the basis of primary social experiences, interpreted through accumulated practices and translated into symbolic experiences. In that study, given the rise of neoliberalism in the Carlos Menem administration, we also asked what remained of the twofold reality that constituted this structure of feeling when the already traditionally feeble class consciousness was further weakened when the heretical counterculture of Peronism seemed to be dissolving. At the time, what we observed was a gradual erosion of the "workerist" values of Peronism and a reduction of Peronism to certain references to social welfare in the past. And yet this double weakening did not imply Peronism's definitive end as a primordial framework to perceive the social. Peronism remained the matrix from which a significant part of the popular sector experienced politics, even if such experience was increasingly destined to oblivion, abandonment, and humiliation.

Finally, in Ecuador the plebeian perspective or the perspective "from below" is illustrated by the study conducted by Maiguashca and North, who participated in the Cueva-Quintero controversy to analyze—once more—the origins and meanings of Velasquismo. In a long article published in 1991, the authors criticized the class approach developed by both Cueva and Quintero— one of them for its ambiguity and the other for its ahistorical character, since in their opinion Ecuador's society in 1930 was not an entirely consolidated class-based society. For that reason, they proposed a socio-regional analysis of the "class struggle" in Thompsonian terms, where concepts such as the "moral economy of the crowd" were central. On the other hand, the authors agreed with Cueva's analysis regarding the absence of an industrial proletariat but emphasized the changes in the class structure in the coastal region, where the old and the new coexisted in popular protests, as well as in the sierra region, where artisans, small merchants, and peasants stood out. The authors argued that it was in this context of generalized crisis that Velasco appeared as the "formula for mediation" (Cueva [1972] 2007, 81) employing Cueva's expression, for both conservatives and liberals, both parties being subjected in a clientelistic relation to the dominant groups that united in this circumstance. Velasco, who was known as a great mediator, emerged in this context of crisis and social displacement with a straightforward discourse that articulated the idea of hierarchy with the demand for rights for subaltern sectors, without questioning the system of domination or the traditional order. In this respect, Maiguashca and North agreed with Cueva and criticized Quintero, who did not acknowledge or accept Velasco's "mediating" function. There was nothing to mediate: He was an extension of the Conservative Party and the Catholic Church's clientelistic structures.

> We are before a discourse that, by insisting on the duties of the rich and the rights of the poor, is typical of the transition as characterized by E. P. Thompson. There is no perception of a system of domination beyond individual will in Velasco's thought. Due to the prevailing fragmentation and social mobility, the popular sectors could not have perceived that system either. To them, abuse, corruption, price manipulation, etc., were a matter of individuals, or at the most certain cliques: "the argollas." This is the fundamental correspondence between Velasco's message and the contradictory experiences lived by all subaltern sectors. (Maiguashca and North 1991, 111)

The historians concluded that Velasco's discourse and politics expressed wrongs and protests in traditional terms, not in those of a modern class-based society. Above all, however, this discourse was far from being conceived purely as an effort to manipulate or as "false consciousness," as the current readings of Velasquismo denounced, but rather as the consciousness typical of artisans.

The Debate on Neoliberalism and Populism

The 1990s saw a somewhat paradoxical return of the concept of populism—a return because quite a few authors attempted to read several of the regimes that turned to neoliberalism at the time of the Washington Consensus through the concept of neopopulism. This was especially the case with the Carlos Menem administration in Argentina (1989–99) and fleetingly the Abdalá Bucaram administration in Ecuador (1995–96), as well as that of Fernando Collor de Mello in Brazil (1990–92). It was paradoxical because this turn to neoliberalism took place in the context of the dismantlement of the so-called national-popular state and the crisis of traditional identities.

One of the first authors that paved the way to a reflection in terms of a "return to populism" was Mexican thinker Sergio Zermeño, who in a well-known article published in 1989, suggestively entitled "El regreso del líder: Crisis, neoliberalismo y desorden" (The return of the leader: Crisis, neoliberalism, and disorder), spoke of the twofold chaos experienced in Latin America: that produced by the end of the traditional order and accelerated development and that produced by the "wall of stagnation." In this swift passage to stagnation, there was a return to the leader-masses relationship but not in terms of classical populism (mediated by institutions created by the state) but of a more direct relationship that was indicative of the crisis of traditional identities and the arrival at a new stage characterized by atomization, individualism, anomy, and spontaneous outbursts. According to Zermeño, there was therefore a sort of emergence of the popular without a popular subject, that is, an apathetic and depoliticized mass whose counterpart was an order built on the basis of manipulation by the leaders or by a highly centralized bureaucracy.

On the other hand, while not speaking directly of neopopulism, Guillermo O'Donnell (1992) coined the concept of "delegative democracy" to refer to the traditional problem of recently established democracies. O'Donnell argued that the problems related to consolidation or institutionalization were aggravated by the repercussions of the economic crisis on social integration. The inherited situation of socioeconomic crisis and emergency, as well as the weakness of the social actors, led the president to adopt a decisionist style, assuming himself as the absolute authority while rejecting any form of accountability, whether horizontal or vertical. Everything pointed to a political concern with liberal democracy. While O'Donnell began by asserting that he intended to describe a "new creature," that is, "a type of existing democracy that has not yet been theorized" (1992, 5), he elsewhere related delegative democracies to the plebiscitary tradition, analyzed in terms of "Caesarism, caudillismo, populism, and so on" (15). At the same time, he argued that this was a new, peculiar type of democracy and that even if its characteristics overlapped with authoritarian elements, it remained a polyarchy.

In the same line, the ten years of Peronist Carlos Menem's administration tended to be interpreted in terms of neopopulism and delegative democracy in Argentina. The term *neopopulism* sought to explain the convergence between an exclusionary economic program and a certain political leadership style. A number of studies with different analytic perspectives contributed to this conceptualization.[11] Closer to home, the Argentinean Carlos Vilas (2003) underscored the conceptual oversimplification of the readings that attempted to transplant a historically situated concept (populism), relating it to neoliberalism through the hypothesis of neopopulism. For these theses emerging especially from US social sciences, populism was a permanent option in Latin American politics and ended up reduced to new forms of clientelism or caudillismo. From their perspective, populism was not so much a form of political articulation (or of the constitution of identities) as a political practice, a regime associated with a particular stage of peripheral capitalism.

In Ecuador, in 1998, almost twenty years after the debate with Cueva, Rodolfo Quintero reiterated that given the heterogeneity of populism and the tendency to associate it with phenomena that differed greatly from historical populism, such as the Menem government in Argentina and Alberto Fujimori's in Peru, the concept should no longer be used. In this line, following an academic congress in Quito, the book *El fantasma del populismo* (The phantom of populism; 1998) was published, compiled by Felipe Burbano de Lara, reflecting on the theoretical status of the concept of populism, examining its "scarce scientific grounding" and the "stigma" it entailed due to its assimilation of the "leader's return," "with no institutional or constitutional restraints in most cases, because he has the unconditional support of some sectors that follow him, which he is able to control in different manners from the moment he takes power" (quoted in I. Rodríguez and Pinto 1999, 409). The book attempted to break with "the oversimplifications of those who believe that, because of their recurrent use of rhetoric and the mobilizations fostered by their appeal to the popular, emerging leaders must be understood as populist or neopopulist" (I. Rodríguez and Pinto 1999, 410).

The concept's appeal, establishing continuities and ruptures between the old and the new populisms, as well as the recurrent stigmatization—since those who employed the concept of neopopulism did so in a critical and disqualifying manner—implied a greater danger: falling into nominalism or depriving of meaning a concept that was by nature broad and imprecise but rich in analytic inflections. The Argentine sociologist Aníbal Viguera (1993) expressed this in an interesting article, where he sagaciously criticized such uses and abuses and proposed recovering the concept's heuristic capacity by distinguishing two dimensions of analysis: one that defends populism as a "political style" and one that associates it with a "model of accumulation." Considering these two different levels, neopopulism clearly referred to those definitions that emphasized the political style, without linking it to any particular project. According to Viguera, developing an "ideal type" that combined both dimensions of analysis would allow one to overcome the difficulties resulting from the use of the term *populism*, providing criteria for observation and research. From this standpoint, it could be said that unlike classical populism, the neopopulisms of the 1990s articulated only one dimension, that is, political and leadership style, independently of the mode of accumulation.

———

Far from being a phantom in Latin American history, populism is a living and multifarious presence, a complex and ambivalent political phenomenon, whose *corsi e ricorsi,* interpretations, variants, and assessments are present in the various discursive territories—from sociology, history, and political philosophy to economics, anthropology, and political sciences. Its appeal is such that it forces us to question and debate once and again the fundamental political/ social agreements of our societies, our understandings of really existing democracy, the persistence of charismatic leaders, and the past and present variants in the processes of building hegemony.

PART II

Scenarios, Contemporary Debates, and Disputed Categories

Introduction to Part II

More than fifteen years have passed since Latin America, or some Latin American countries in particular, signaled an epochal change. Let us recall that since 2000 the struggles of the various social movements and indigenous organizations against neoliberal adjustments, questioning the Washington Consensus and denaturalizing the relationship between globalization and neoliberalism, and the later emergence of various governments generically characterized as progressive, left-wing, or center-left, positioned the subcontinent in a new transitional scenario.

These governments have been most commonly characterized as *progressive*, a very broad term, since its origins go back to the French Revolution and it refers to those ideological currents that advocated for individual liberties and social change ("progress" understood as a horizon for change). Thus, this generic denomination as progressive encompassed various ideological currents and political perspectives, from the most institutional to classical developmentalism to more radical political experiences: in Chile with Ricardo Lagos and Michelle Bachelet; in Brazil with Luiz Inácio Lula da Silva and Dilma Rousseff; in Uruguay with the Frente Amplio (Broad Front); in Argentina with Nestor Kirchner and Cristina Fernández de Kirchner; in Ecuador with Rafael Correa; in Bolivia with Evo Morales; and in Venezuela with Hugo Chávez and Nicolás Maduro, among others. Going somewhat further, some authors spoke of the "turn to the left" and "post-neoliberalism," and for the purpose of fine-tuning the diagnoses, they proposed differentiating between two lefts: the most radical and innovative governments (Venezuela, Bolivia, and Ecuador, with their constitutional reform projects) and more conservative progressive governments (Argentina, Brazil, Uruguay, and Chile).

However, this epochal change, which was accompanied by an important Latin Americanist narrative and produced significant expectations regarding broadened rights and forms of participation for the lower classes (constituent assemblies and new constitutions in countries such as Bolivia, Venezuela, and Ecuador), was met with serious limitations and increasing conflicts. On one hand, thanks to the boom in the world prices of raw materials, the various governments found themselves in a very favorable or even exceptional economic situation—a new cycle based on the mass export of raw materials, which combined high profitability and comparative economic advantages. On the other hand, beyond the nationalist rhetoric in vogue, in the context of the new economic cycle, the state's new role acquired various tonalities, one of its key elements being the association with private multinational capital, whose impact on the national economies, rather than diminishing, increased as primary/extractive activities grew and multiplied.

In this book we define the current phase of accumulation experienced in Latin America through the concept of "Commodities Consensus" (Svampa 2013). This characterization is based on the recognition that unlike in the 1990s, Latin American economies benefited greatly from the high commodity prices in the world market, which had an effect on the trade balance until 2011–13, when the so-called end of the commodity supercycle began. In this context, all Latin American governments, regardless of their ideology, returned to a productivist view of development, thus denying or avoiding the debates on the implications (impacts, consequences, harms) of the various development models, downplaying the collective and environmental rights of the populations and socio-territorial questionings and protests.

Thus, with time, the epochal change developed into a conflictive scenario, one of whose main characteristics seemed to be a (re)articulation between the populist tradition and the extractivist paradigm. Critical categories such as (neo-)extractivism, maldevelopment, new dependency, twenty-first-century populisms, and other more propositional categories such as autonomy, the plurinational state, Good Living, the commons, the rights of nature, ethics of care, and postextractivism permeated intellectual and political debates as well as social struggles at the time, proposing different—and sometimes opposing—ways of conceiving the relationship among the economy, society, nature, and politics.

These debates and new positions regarding the relationship among extractivism, the return of populism, the emergence of a new dependency, and the commodities boom divided critical thinking in Latin America. Unlike the 1990s, when the continent seemed to be equally reformatted by the neoliberal model, the new century saw a series of tensions and contradictions that were difficult to process. The passage from the Washington Consensus to the Commodities Consensus gave rise to a number of issues and paradoxes that tended to reconfigure the horizon of critical thought, presenting new theoretical and political conflicts.

In order to account for these conflicting scenarios, in the following four chapters I will examine the debates in Latin America surrounding the new and reworked topics studied in this book: the place of the indigenous, development, dependency, and populism.

5

The Ways of *Indianismo*

THE DEBATE ON THE RIGHTS

OF INDIGENOUS PEOPLES

Indigenous peoples' new political protagonism is related to both the long-term and short-term memory of their struggles: On one hand, the renewed legitimacy of the communal matrix derives from the successful struggles for recognition of collective rights in recent decades. On the other hand, this process of expansion of rights was accompanied by an encroachment of capital on indigenous territories. This antagonism has elicited different responses that, in spite of the existing tensions, all place autonomy and the defense of indigenous people's right of prior consultation at the center.

For this reason, in this chapter I examine three debates on the indigenous question in the continent: (1) the issue of autonomy, (2) the wager for the creation of a plurinational state, and (3) the disputes regarding the right to prior consultation. While the first two constitute an "offensive" response or proposal by indigenous people—whether in terms of de facto autonomy or plurinational constitutional proposals—the third debate has to do with a more "defensive" response by indigenous people, as they attempt to defend their lands and territories from the advancement of the extractive frontier associated with the new forms of capital accumulation.

Debate 1: Indigenous Autonomy: The Ways of Zapatismo

Autonomy comes from auto-nomos: (to give to) oneself one's laws. After what has been said about heteronomy, it is hardly necessary to add: to make one's own laws, knowing that one is doing so. This is a new eidos within the overall history of being: a type of being that reflectively gives to itself the laws of its being.—CORNELIUS CASTORIADIS, *Un mundo fragmentado* (A fragmented world), 1997

Our Zapatista word is small, but its step is large and walks afar and enters many hearts. The hearts that listened to us are those of men, women, children, and elders who want a democratic, free, and just country. These hearts helped us reach the Zócalo in Mexico City. These hearts want the same thing that we Zapatistas want and that everyone wants. We want a Mexico that sees us as human beings, that respects us and recognizes our dignity. For that reason, we want to join our small Zapatista voice to the large voice of all who struggle for a new Mexico. We came here to shout, together with everyone else: Never again a Mexico without us. That's what we want, a Mexico where everyone has a place with dignity.—COMANDANTA RAMONA at the Zócalo, Mexico City, October 12, 1996

There is a vast literature in Latin America with different approaches regarding the issue of autonomy, its possibilities, and its limits. The issue of autonomy paved the way for important political debates regarding the subjects/agents of social change; the conception of power and organizational models; the relationships between dissenting social organizations and movements and the national state; the latter's position regarding large transnational actors (corporations, cooperation agencies, and multilateral bodies); other (social, political, and trade union) organizations; and the scales of collective action (local, regional, national, global).

Some of these approaches are more general, theoretical, and political; others propose a more specific organizational discussion. Generally speaking, autonomy is related to a long and lively political discussion regarding strategies and emancipatory political horizons; specifically, autonomy is also related to an epochal dimension, a sort of militant ethos present in contemporary social movements, and a part of the new political grammar, which encompasses from urban cultural collectives to large social and territorial structures.

From a theoretical/political perspective, although the notion of autonomy related to the working class is present in some of Karl Marx's writings (see Modonesi 2010, 2011), it was examined at greater depth by the philosophers

Cornelius Castoriadis and Claude Lefort, promoters of the Socialism or Barbarism group in France in the 1950s; later, from a neo-Marxist perspective, it applied to the Italian autonomist experience (Potere Operaio [Workers' Power]) of the 1970s, illustrated by the reflections of Italian philosopher Antonio Negri, and currently involves an important sector of that country's critical philosophy (Paolo Virno, Sandro Mezzadra, and Maurizio Lazzarato, among others). As Massimo Modonesi (2011) proposes, autonomy not only refers to an organizational and decisional matter—"class independence"—but also to a strategic position regarding what is understood by a revolutionary project. Castoriadis summarizes it clearly:

> The revolutionary project is the historical goal of achieving a society that has overcome alienation. By alienation I mean a social-historical fact (institutional heteronomy), not a metaphysical given. In other words, it is the goal of an autonomous society that is not enslaved by its past or its own creations. I really mean "enslaved." ... What is an autonomous society? I first used the concept of autonomy, extended to society, in the sense of "collective management." I have now been led to give it a more radical content: no longer simply collective management (self-management) but the ongoing, explicit self-institution of society, meaning a state in which the community knows that its institutions are its own creation and is able to regard them as such, to reexamine them and transform them. If you accept that idea, it defines a unified revolutionary project. (2005, 60)

There is no doubt that it was the most recent writings by Antonio Negri, coauthored with US philosopher Michael Hardt, that, after a period characterized by a crisis of revolutionary languages and the consolidation of neoliberalism as the single discourse, reintroduced the topic of emancipation and autonomy in the global agenda, with the successful and controversial book *Empire* (Hardt and Negri 2000), which proposes a new reading of the confrontational dynamics between globalized capital and emerging social struggles. In tune with the writings of French philosopher Gilles Deleuze and Italian workers' autonomism of the 1970s, the work proposes conceiving revolutionary power as a counterpower, under the banner of dispersion, the rhizome, decentralization, the multitude, exodus—forms of popular power that are closer to the notion of the commune or workers' councils (constituent power) than to that of the centralist state (constituted power) established by the successful revolutions of the twentieth century. One of the book's virtues was that it deployed a specific narrative that reflected the emerging forms of political subjectivation in various parts of the planet, which questioned not only neoliberal globalization but also the organizational and revolutionary conceptions held by social-democratic and Leninist lefts. As a result, their proposal openly challenged the most traditional leftist thought based on classical understandings of power and of the modes of construction of hegemony.

This digression allows us to introduce the idea that autonomy is also a common collective framework present in various forms of resistance, from the smallest (cultural collectives focused on alternative communication, documentary film, popular education, and political art, among others) to small and large urban or rural social organizations that vindicate horizontality and direct democracy as central elements. Otherwise stated, in conjunction with this narrative of autonomy, we observe the emergence of a *new militant ethos* (Svampa 2005, 2010a) that considers it imperative to debureaucratize and democratize organizations and that radically distrusts political party and trade union organizations and all high-level instances for articulation. As an epochal phenomenon, the demand for autonomy illustrates an important transformation in the dynamics of construction of political subjectivities as a result of the changes in contemporary society in recent decades, a situation that a large part of contemporary social theory has conceptualized in terms of processes of individualization. It is for that reason that we speak of a narrative, since it is constructed as an identity-based story of production of subjects, where the actors' personal experience is more important than the subject's insertion in the community, the people, or the social class. Furthermore, it should be noted that as the historian Martín Bergel (2009, 288) proposes, autonomic social movements are fueled by practice rather than by a theoretical discourse; they assert "the epistemological and political superiority of the practical moment and the zeal for the irreducible singularity of each experience." Or as the analyst George Katsiaficas (2009, 151–67) emphasizes, they are characterized by a sort of "conscious spontaneity" that points toward changes in power and in everyday relations; that is, they fight against two forms of oppression: capitalism and patriarchy.

In Latin America the demand for autonomy is present in two of the main sociopolitical matrices that permeate social struggles and conflicts: the peasant/indigenous communal matrix and, more specifically, the autonomic matrix. While the former alludes to a political project that proposes the autonomy of indigenous peoples, the latter emerges as a demand of multiple social and collective organizations that focus on creating flexible and horizontal forms of organization, generally founded on democracy by consensus.

On the other hand, autonomy as a mobilizing myth has seen three successive moments—three different scenarios—in Latin America: First, it burst into the political arena as a democratic demand with the neo-Zapatista uprising in Chiapas in 1994 (*foundational moment*), which also constitutes the first movement against neoliberal globalization; second, autonomy had its *destituent moment* with the urban mobilizations and uprisings in Argentina (through assemblies, movements of the unemployed, recovered factories, cultural collectives) that questioned neoliberalism and rejected institutional forms of political representation (2002–3); and, third, in 2006 the axis shifted to Bolivia, where the demand for autonomy was associated with the project of creating a plurinational state (*constituent moment*), in the context of the Evo Morales administration.

Neo-Zapatismo constitutes the foundational moment of the demand for autonomy in the context of neoliberal globalization. Neo-Zapatismo burst into the political arena on January 1, 1994, dismantling the invisibility of the traditionally excluded indigenous communities of Chiapas through armed struggle and a radical political discourse that demanded democracy and autonomy from the Mexican state. No other revolutionary movement in Latin America elicited such continental and global solidarity or had such an impact on the emerging antiestablishment subjectivity. For while the Zapatista uprising entailed a powerful specific perspective (from and for indigenous peoples), it was far from ethnic fundamentalism or an identity-based closure. The defense of politics conceived from below, with its call for autonomy and dignity as fundamental mottos and for democracy by consensus, positioned neo-Zapatismo in tune with the emerging epochal ethos, which would make its public appearance five years later in Seattle (1999), in the mobilizations against the World Trade Organization, which marked the birth of the movement against neoliberal globalization. At the same time, its conception of power—neither hegemonic nor state centered—fueled innumerable debates within the lefts that disputed the antiestablishment field.

Neo-Zapatismo therefore has dimensions that have made it unique, both for its capacity to build "interclass, intergenerational, and international bridges" (Ceceña 2003) and for its persistence and dynamism in a conflictive context from 1994 to the present, in which the Zapatistas have uniquely alternated from guerrilla actions to negotiation, from silence to the word, from opening to civil society to closure in the indigenous communities in order to build their own institutions (Good Government Councils, *caracoles* [autonomous government centers]). This process of dissemination was also accomplished through the meaningful, or perhaps enchanted, words from Marcos, the movement's main spokesperson, with his particular way of mixing indigenous narrative with literary metaphor in the extensive communiqués addressed to public opinion. As Álvaro García Linera (2004) argues, neo-Zapatismo did not inaugurate the era of indigenous rebellions in the continent (there were prior ones in

Guatemala, Bolivia, and Ecuador), but it contributed to revaluing indigenous culture, communal democracy, and discussions on the modes of emancipation and to spreading these in dialogue with other nonindigenous and subaltern sectors of society.

Regarding the debate on Zapatista autonomy, two different moments can be clearly identified: The first was the demand for recognition of the collective rights of indigenous people though the San Andrés Accords, established through negotiations between the Mexican federal government and the Zapatista Army of National Liberation (Ejército Zapatista de Liberación Nacional; EZLN) in 1995 and 1996; the second moment corresponds to the Zapatistas' decision to build their own institutions through the Good Government Councils (Juntas de Buen Gobierno; JBGs) and the autonomous municipalities. In the first stage, the San Andrés Accords were part of the Cocopa initiative, which in no way threatened national unity, since it recognized indigenous rights within the framework of the Mexican state; it was supported by representatives from the main indigenous organizations, grouped in the National Indigenous Congress; and in previous years it was analyzed and discussed in many indigenous communities in the country.[1]

The initiative also guaranteed women's participation under equitable conditions. However, as is well known, the constitutional reform implemented in 2001 approved a law on indigenous people that distorted the San Andrés Accords, which led the EZLN to cut off all negotiations with the federal government.

After the institutional failure and a period of withdrawal and silence, Zapatismo entered a new phase in 2003, with the decision to develop its own institutions through the JBGs and the autonomous municipalities, independent of the state, which marked the beginning of a new chapter in the debate on autonomies. The bases for such autonomies were the territories under their control and the autonomous municipalities. The creation of the JBGs also responded to the need to organize and coordinate external support. The autonomous structures were meant to generate alternative education, health, and justice systems; different gender relations; alternative agroecological, production, and commercialization projects; and communication media, among others.

To what extent has this autonomy been consolidated in terms of political and socioeconomic self-government, especially in a context of military siege and attacks on the Zapatista bases experienced since 2007? There are several contradictory readings in this regard. According to Héctor Díaz Polanco (2006a, 45), the process announced with the creation of the JBGs implied an important step from the local to the regional, by addressing the need for coordination between the municipalities and the JBGs, since these cannot be conceived as small, disconnected units but rather as an archipelago.[2] According to one of its critics, the true strength of Zapatismo does not reside in autonomy (which is impossible, given its dependence on the nonagricultural market and its condition as a poor and backward zone) but in the assembly-based decision-making process regarding common affairs in each municipality, where administrators and leaders are elected and removed from office democratically and where the participation of women and youth in education and care for the elders contributes to democratizing gender and intergenerational relations (Almeyra 2008).

More than ten years after the beginning of the experience of de facto autonomy, the two aspects mentioned above are no minor matters. It is important to remember that Zapatismo has faced difficulties that are both internal (confrontations with communities that are not Zapatista and do not want to be) and external, especially after 2008, with Felipe Calderón's rise to power. In this context of unresolved war, "one of the most important characteristics of autonomy is the defense of the territory, since without it there is nothing" (Muñoz Ramírez 2009). The advancements in terms of depatriarchalization of gender relations are also an important achievement, especially considering that indigenous communities tend to be quite conservative and hierarchical.

On the other hand, the Zapatistas had to build their de facto autonomy with few economic resources and of course with no state support. Autonomy thus becomes a fragile matter that depends both "on the uninterrupted flow of material solidarity to the communities" and on Zapatismo's influence on power relations at the national level (Lang 2015, 251). In a Latin American context, where vulnerable populations and an important part of social organizations and movements are the object of social politics, this fact must be emphasized. In this regard, Uruguayan essayist Raúl Zibechi (2013) argues that Zapatistas have achieved not only political but also economic autonomy, reflected even in their rejection of the social programs received by communities surrounding the Zapatista territory.[3] Another interesting issue is the advancement of de facto indigenous autonomies in other parts of Mexico. The San Andrés Accords created a space of political opportunities for a discussion on autonomy for all indigenous people, in which many indigenous organizations and specialists on the topic participated. In 2001 these discussions were reignited in response to the constitutional reform that the government promised to implement but once again failed to carry out. This failure of the institutional avenue led to the construction of de facto autonomies in several Mexican states such as Guerrero and Oaxaca. With less political impact, this advancement in local autonomies (studied today by many specialists) implies the exercise of self-government (election of revolving authorities according to indigenous customs and traditions, the creation in some states of a community police force, the exercise of community justice, community administration of education).[4]

The advancement of local autonomies progressively reveals a model of construction of power in opposition to state power and the "bad government" represented by the Institutional Revolutionary Party (Partido Revolucionario Institucional; PRI) and the National Action Party (Partido Acción Nacional; PAN). Hence, Francisco López Bárcenas underscores that "with the decision to build autonomy, indigenous peoples seek to *disperse power*, to enable its direct exercise by indigenous communities" (2011, 97)—a different decentralization from that proposed by the World Bank since the 1980s. Autonomy is therefore a process under construction, whose reach cannot yet be assessed in terms of its impact and magnitude, although some authors see it as an irreversible process of struggle (López y Rivas 2011): local struggles that progressively address national problems in the context of globalization—the struggle for land and territory (food sovereignty; the struggle against the privatization of electric energy, oil, and natural resources).

On the other hand, it is interesting to note that unlike in Bolivia, where the meanings of autonomy were disputed with the regional opposition, in Mexico it emerges as an absolute prerogative of indigenous peoples in their resistance to the neoliberal expropriation policies carried out by the government. Also, differently from what occurred in Bolivia, where the fragility of the national state is a matter of historical origin and trajectory (an apparent state), in Mexico the process of construction of the national state conducted by the PRI throughout the twentieth century has been considered particularly "successful" (corporate state), even though today this statement must be nuanced given the expansion of drug trafficking networks. However, the opening to asymmetrical globalization and the commercial agreements established with the United States destabilized social relations and reoriented the PRI's state structure (Gilly 1997). It is therefore not by chance that one of the most outstanding aspects of the discourse of the various actors, as neo-Zapatismo has underscored, is the critique of the political class, seen as incapable of rebuilding the national state. As Raquel Gutiérrez Aguilar (2006) argues, it is in this specific context that indigenous peoples' demands are made under the banner of dignity and autonomy.

In short, to return to neo-Zapatismo: the construction of autonomy takes place in a context of war or unresolved military conflict, which has tended to worsen since 2008 with the federal governments of Felipe Calderón (2006–12) and Enrique Peña Nieto (2012–18), resulting in a military siege of autonomous territories. However, in spite of the immense difficulties, the Zapatista project remains alive—the *caracoles* have been in existence for more than twelve years.

Even after the significant misstep of "The Other Campaign," Zapatismo continues to surprise the world thanks to its capacity to modify its repertoires of action depending on the changing contexts and to its renewed creativity when rethinking its social and political alliances, both internally and externally. Recently, in an unprecedented process of opening more than twenty years after the uprising, Zapatismo decided to open the *caracoles* with the "Little School of Freedom," where people from all five continents spend time in the communities, allowing them to acquire a better understanding of Zapatismo though everyday living experience and collective work.

Debate 2: Bolivia: The Challenge of Founding a Plurinational State

In Bolivia the demand to refound the state as a plurinational state emerged from two main sources. The first was the indigenous organizations in the lowlands, assembled in the Confederation of Indigenous Peoples of the Bolivian East (Confederación de Pueblos Indígenas del Oriente Boliviano; CIDOB), which organized the March for the Territory and Dignity in 1990, resulting in their recognition as "autonomous territories." Five years later, in 1995, from CIDOB, the Assembly of Guarani Peoples (Asamblea del Pueblo Guaraní; APG) proposed holding a constituent assembly. The second source of the "demand and imagination of a Plurinational State" (Tapia 2011, 138–39) is the Katarist political and cultural current that since the 1970s has assumed the task of reinventing Indianness, articulating trade union identity with social class elements. Katarism vindicated the Aymara in terms of "the Aymara nation," reformulating—or intending to reformulate—"the symbolic frontiers in the collective imaginary" regarding the nation (García Linera 2004, 223).

In terms of the recent memory of the struggles, the so-called Water War (Cochabamba, 2000) inaugurated a new cycle of struggles by successfully expelling the transnational corporation Aguas del Tunari (Bechtel). In this context, the Coalition for the Defense of Water and Life, which brought together several social, urban, and rural organizations, put forth a political program that focused on the reinstatement of public service, the nationalization of natural resources, and the Constituent Assembly. In 2003, during the Gas War that resulted in the resignation of President Gonzalo Sánchez de Lozada, the various social, peasant, indigenous, urban, and rural forces and organizations converged in the so-called October agenda, synthesized in two demands: nationalization of natural resources and the Constituent Assembly. A new political context was finally inaugurated in December 2005 with the electoral victory of Evo Morales, an

Aymara peasant leader, with the middle-class criollo intellectual Álvaro García Linera as running mate, with 53.7 percent of the votes.

Bolivia thus became an extremely interesting and nearly unique political laboratory in Latin America, in which indigenous and plebeian elements, and the demand for democratization promoted by a heterogeneous set of both rural and "urban" social organizations and movements, seemed to come together in an unprecedented manner with the constituent proposals for a new state, the plurinational state, for which, though there were precedents (in other latitudes), no scripts or magical recipes were available.

Boaventura de Sousa Santos, who participated early on in a number of exchanges and debates in both Ecuador and Bolivia, argues that one of the fundamental paradoxes of refounding the state was the urgency to change reality in the short term, as well as the demand to reflect on civilizational transformations. This difficult combination of urgency and long-term goals leads us to think of a transformational but also experimental constitutionalism (2009a; 2010). Experimentalism allows "de-dramatizing the conflicts" and sketching a different temporal horizon, conceived in terms of successive revisions (trial and error). Furthermore, it enables something that constitutes one of the crucial demands of social movements: that the people continue to hold the constituent power, since once the constitution is elaborated, the people tend to disappear behind the constituted power (Santos 2009a, 53).

Was this enormous collective social energy unleashed between 2000 and 2006 maintained as an instituent power, or did it share the fate of so many other revolutionary processes, whereby the institutionalizing dynamics ended up freezing and expropriating the instituent power for the sake of the constituted power? Were the Movement for Socialism (Movimiento al Socialismo; MAS) as the governing party and Evo Morales as the top leader able to become the political mediators of a set of heterogeneous social organizations that expressed different lines of historical accumulation, or, as has so often been the case, did they end up transferring power—gradually or rapidly, depending on the case—to the executive and the MAS, in accordance with a centralist logic and the inertia of populist and/or presidentialist political traditions?

Although I do not intend to answer these dilemmas in this brief presentation, I will begin by saying that the conflicts and tensions present in Bolivia during Evo Morales's first mandate (2006–10) can be understood from two different perspectives. The first one has to do with the coexistence of two dimensions of the project for change: on one hand, the Indianist and plurinational narrative centered on the creation of the plurinational state and the recognition of indigenous autonomies (administrative and territorial); on the other hand, the populist narrative, marked by a state-centered, regulatory, and centralist dimension, as well as a certain way of conceiving participation and politics.[5] The second perspective has to do with the confrontation between the popular political project embodied by the new government and the one defended by the regional oligarchies. In the government's first years, the second scenario gradually configured an increasing polarization in terms of power relations and political logics, exacerbating the division into two opposing blocks: on one hand, social movements and organizations assembled around the leader; on the other hand, the regional oligarchies, entrenched in the Bolivian Media Luna, with its mayors and institutional elements.

In the context of these conflicts, from 2006 to 2010, the twofold dynamics of the decolonizing project became better defined. The implementation of the Constituent Assembly and, through it, the process of constitutional recognition of collective rights and the plurinational state led to an effective empowerment of social organizations but also to a transfer of the process's management to Evo Morales's charismatic leadership.[6] Furthermore, in a context of social and regional polarization, the demand for autonomy was subordinated to the need to consolidate a central and regulating state. It was in this context, characterized by this twofold tension, that certain debates on the plurinational state took place.

Between the Pact of Unity and the Redefinition of the State

The most complete expression of the indigenous political project is illustrated by the Pact of Unity ("Pacto de Unidad" [2006] 2007) signed by eight indigenous and peasant organizations that, in 2006, elaborated and published for the Constituent Assembly a document that proposed the creation of a communal and plurinational state, constituting eloquent evidence of the political outlook of important indigenous and rural social organizations regarding the Constituent Assembly's objective to refound the state. For the first time, the project synthesized a series of proposals aimed at the recognition and implementation of the pluricultural at several levels: a new territorial/state configuration based on the recognition of different types of autonomy—at the department, regional, and municipal levels and indigenous autonomy; the election of representatives according to traditional customs; constitutional recognition of community justice, communal property, and control of natural resources; and the recognition of interculturality. It also proposed a new land and territorial regime based on "native dominion" over nonrenewable resources held by native, indigenous, and peasant peoples. The proposed regime included not only participation in decision-making through enforceable popular consultations but also other demands by indigenous organizations and peoples, such as comanagement of natural resources with the plurinational state.

As mentioned above, differently from Mexico, in Bolivia the call for autonomy occurs in a space that is disputed with the regional oligarchies, to assert a segregationist political strategy with "a virtual sense of extraterritoriality" (Chávez León 2008).

The Pact of Unity defined native, indigenous, and peasant autonomy as "the condition and principle of freedom of our peoples and nations as a fundamental category for decolonization and self-determination; it is based on fundamental and generative principles that are the engines of unity and social, economic, and political articulation among our peoples and nations and with the whole of society. Its framework is the unceasing effort to construct a full life with our own forms of representation, management, and ownership of our territories" ("Pacto de Unidad" [2006] 2007, 200).[7] Regarding the land regime, the Pact of Unity proposed prohibiting latifundia and established as a mission of the plurinational state "the equitable distribution of land, observing the present and future needs of native, indigenous, and peasant peoples and the well-being of the whole population" (207). Another important innovation was the demand for recognition of legal pluralism (the coexistence, within the plurinational state, of native, indigenous, and peasant legal systems with the Western legal system on equal terms, with respect and coordination). Finally, the proposal also included creating a fourth power (social power) and implied an alternative recognition and institutionalization of the instituent power held by social organizations and movements. Although the developments were quite incipient, this social power was considered independent and autonomous from the state, formed by "representatives of civil society" (indigenous, native, and peasant nations and peoples; representatives from social organizations; and others), and with transversal social control functions (rather than self-government).

However, the later agreements in the hectic Constituent Assembly went in the direction of recognizing shared property among indigenous, native, and peasant nations and peoples and the plurinational unitary state. Likewise, the Constitution that was negotiated and finally approved in 2009 did not include enforceable consultations for exploration and exploitation of natural resources, only "informed consultations."

Part of this complex process is reflected in the theoretical proposals and political discussions that took place between 2007 and 2010 regarding the characterization and implementation of the plurinational state, promoted by different social organizations and nongovernmental organizations, as well as by institutional spaces such as the Vice-Presidency of the Nation. Historically, this debate also referred to René Zavaleta Mercado's diagnosis of Bolivia as a "variegated social formation," which indicates the overlap of several types of society and different historical times and views of the world, which coexist in an unarticulated manner, establishing relations of domination and distortion among themselves (Zavaleta Mercado 2006; Tapia 2013). For this reason, the recognition of autonomies and the challenge to create a plurinational state aimed at connecting the state and society, establishing a "non-dominating coexistence of the variegated" (Soruco Sologuren 2011, 87). Some of the most important contributions in this respect were provided by members of the Comuna group, that is, Luis Tapia, Raúl Prada, and Álvaro García Linera, vice president of Bolivia since 2006.

In 2004 García Linera published an important text on the topic, "Autonomías indígenas y Estado multinacional" (Indigenous autonomies and multinational state), where, in addition to reviewing the vast international bibliography on the issue of multiculturalism and the state, he proposed a new scheme for autonomous reconfiguration that recognized different levels of political self-government depending on the "political density and extension of the demanding cultural identities" (2008a, 249–54).

However, once in the government, García Linera gradually modified his view of the state. On one hand, his later reflections focused on characterizing the "state of transition" in the new field of struggle, in the context of an escalation of political and social confrontations with the regional oligarchies. While the concept of a plurinational state was increasingly naturalized in the political discourse, other concepts gained importance: crisis of the state, transitional state, catastrophic standoff, and branching-off point, thus signaling an increasingly state-centered reflection. As we argue with Pablo Stefanoni, "Perhaps García Linera's most significant political/ideological evolution was his passage—with few mediations—from his 'autonomist' positions to an almost Hegelian defense of the state as the synthesis of the 'general will'" (Svampa and Stefanoni 2007, 24).

One of the most original and creative perspectives on the Bolivian process was that proposed by Luis Tapia, who wrote several texts on the subject, among which *Una reflexión sobre la idea de Estado plurinacional* (A reflection on the idea of plurinational state; 2008) stands out. In that book Tapia reflects on the diversity of nations and community structures and on the tensions between recognition of diversity and the centrifugal tendency of statism, and inquires into how to conceive representation in a plurinational context where majorities coexist with ethnic minorities. In this line of thought, he warns of the dangers of the presidentialist regime to the effective implementation of a plurinational representative regime and proposes a collective power regime instead. In a later text (2011) derived from a meeting convened by the Vice-Presidency ("Debate sobre el cambio"; Vicepresidencia del Estado Plurinacional de Bolivia, 2010), Tapia argues that the plurinational state was reduced to a liberal format, resulting in the emergence of a weak plurinational state, organized in a hierarchical and not an egalitarian manner (2011, 161). Finally, he repeatedly argues that the notion of autonomy proposed by the Pact of Unity implied significant levels of co-decision-making with the plurinational state, especially regarding the exploration and exploitation of natural resources, and that the government party was instead bent on subordinating autonomy regarding this issue (150).

As vice minister of strategic planning, Raúl Prada Alcoreza focused on broadening the bases for administration through a new model of plurinational and community public administration. Thus, the programmatic proposal derived from the New Political Constitution of the State issued a "decolonization decree" (Supreme Decree no. 212) in 2009, which stipulated the creation of a school of administration—which did not come to fruition—to train the future administrators of the plurinational state in order to contribute "to the construction and consolidation of the new state administration by training public officials."[8] Prada Alcoreza (2010) promoted a decentralized view of the state, regarding "social participation" and "social control" as new linchpins, in order to advance toward a new conception of public administration, which should be plurinational, communal, and intercultural.

In late 2009 Bolivia saw the end of the regional resistance that characterized a significant part of the first presidential mandate, and the country entered a new era, marked by MAS's growing political hegemony. Thus, the conflict during the second government mandate (2010–15) was no longer external but internal to the change project itself. This became more visible after the confrontation between, on one hand, the MAS government, which increasingly affirmed its state-centered and populist logic, and, on the other hand, the actions of some organizations representing indigenous peoples (CIDOB and the National Council of Ayllus and Markas of Qullasuyu [Consejo Nacional de Ayllus y Markas del Qullasuyo; CONAMAQ), which, after the experience with the Pact of Unity, wavered between a plurinational logic and corporate demands centered on the defense of autonomies and the territorial rights established in the Plurinational Constitution.

In order to consolidate the new statehood, the government enacted a number of strategic laws that restricted the right to consultation and the autonomy of indigenous territories and facilitated the development of extractive projects. This critical trend in the project for change was openly expressed during the countersummit in Tiquipaya on climate change (April 2010), which brought to-gether in roundtable 18 (unauthorized by the government) those organizations that sought to debate the environmental question in Bolivia. In a context that, at the national scale, combined conflicts of interest with the MAS government (its failure to fulfill its promises) with the beginning of hydrocarbon exploration, en-ergy projects, highway construction, and mining concessions in indigenous terri-tories, without prior consultations or with deceptive ones, organizations such as CIDOB and CONAMAQ turned to an environmentalist language. In a context of confrontation and mobilization, they demanded compliance with the right to prior consultation, as established by International Labour Organization (ILO) Convention 169, enshrined in the Bolivian Constitution, and respect for organic structures (and rejection of voting and the pronouncement of parallel native authorities). This change in position also included a constant interaction with kindred social organizations in a Latin American militant space character-ized by an *eco-territorial turn* (Svampa 2010a), which the Bolivian experience contributed to forging and strengthening. But the turning point was undoubt-edly the Isiboro Sécure National Park and Indigenous Territory (Territorio In-dígena y Parque Nacional Isiboro Secure; TIPNIS) conflict, resulting from the construction of the second leg of the Villa Tunari–San Ignacio highway.[9]

On the other hand, there are few works that examine the process of estab-lishing Indigenous Native Peasant Autonomy (Autonomía Indígena Origina-rio Campesina; AIOC). Among the pioneering works is that by José Luis Exeni Rodríguez (2015), who analyzed the process of autonomies from three axes: government system, indigenous jurisdiction, and alternatives to development. After analyzing three case studies, Exeni Rodríguez concluded that autonomies were not a priority in the government's agenda. One of the problems highlighted was the difficulties in constructing them, given the obstacles and requirements imposed by public authorities and the centrality of municipal governments. An-other fundamental problem was the tension between autonomy as "essential to the plurinational state" and the extractive and neo-developmentalist bases of the latter. As a result, the AIOC's sovereignty over ancestral territories clashed with the state's resolution to control "its" territory, especially its dominion over non-renewable natural resources (Exeni Rodríguez 2015, 185).

As a result, the MAS government increasingly shifted toward defining the decolonization project in classical terms, understood as the need to democra-tize the state by controlling the surplus, modernizing the economy, developing efficient bureaucrats, and distributing land gradually. Thus, in spite of all the in-novations enacted by the New Political Constitution, it reaffirmed the central role of the nation-state and the executive branch. As Prada Alcoreza argues, "The fourth part of the Constitution, devoted to economic organization, implies serious tensions. It speaks of a plural economy but strengthens the state; it is the state that articulates the various forms of economic organization; the state is in charge of the entire productive chain, the industrialization of natural resources, and the support of small and micro business. The state becomes the promoter of the plural economy, which implies a tension between economic pluralism and a state-centered view" (2010).

Ten years have passed, and everything seems to indicate that, beyond the democratizing effects at the social level (which is no minor matter), the plurinational state faced serious obstacles in its implementation of the postconstituent process, among them the reorganization of power according to a centralist logic ("a state-centered model," according to Fernando Mayorga [2011, 85]), related to the consolidation of an extractive dynamic in consonance with a neo-developmentalist project. Furthermore, specialists on the topic warn of the risk of the "deconstitutionalization effect" (Exeni Rodríguez 2015) or counterreform, as could happen in the realm of the judiciary, which would threaten the transformational and experimental constitutionalism and would further hinder the construction of a plurinational state.

Debate 3: The Right to Prior Consultation

Another fundamental question is the right to prior, free, and informed consultation (PFIC) of indigenous peoples, since in the 1990s all Latin American constitutions incorporated ILO Convention 169 (1989) and later the United Nations (UN) Declaration on the Rights of Indigenous Peoples (2007). The issue is crucial because, in the past two decades, there has been a significant increase in extractive megaprojects related to the expansion of the oil, mining, energy, and agribusiness frontiers, among others, which directly threaten indigenous territories, multiply existing asymmetries, and imply an exponential increase in violations of fundamental rights.

Writing on the topic, the Colombian constitutionalist César Rodríguez Garavito speaks of "rights in the minefield of global capitalism" (2012, 9–14). The well-chosen metaphor "minefield" applies not only to the legal field but also to the economic (large interests related to extractivism at play, especially megamining, oil, and megadams) and social fields (territories where violent and distrustful sociability prevails and where any misstep can be fatal). Although Rodríguez Garavito has Colombian violence in mind, the metaphor "social minefields" can be applied today to all Latin American countries, given the highly conflictive socio-territorial situation.

A report by the Economic Commission for Latin America and the Caribbean (CEPAL 2014) on the situation of indigenous people, based on the reports by the UN Special Rapporteur on the Rights of Indigenous People (2009–13), underscores that one of the most serious dimensions of the conflicts created by the expansion of extractivism in indigenous territories is "the state's non-compliance with its obligation to carry out prior consultations of indigenous people and to adopt measures to protect their rights before granting concessions or authorizing extractive projects" (58). The CEPAL report also reproduces a map of extractivist industries, developed by the University of Arizona Project to Support the UN Special Rapporteur on the Rights of Indigenous Peoples, which reveals that all Latin American countries with indigenous territories experience socioenvironmental conflicts. The map identified at least 226 socioenvironmental conflicts in indigenous territories in Latin America from 2010 to 2013, associated with mining and hydrocarbon extractivist projects (CEPAL 2014, 139).

The issue, however, is far from simple. Should PFIC be interpreted in terms of consultation or of consent? Should it be nonbinding, or should indigenous people have the right of veto? The ILO establishes that consultations must be carried out in good faith and that their purpose should be to obtain the community's consent or at least to reach an agreement. Also, the Declaration on the Rights of Indigenous Peoples, adopted by the UN in 2007, went a step further by adopting the principle of free, prior, and informed consent before indigenous people are relocated from their lands and before legal and administrative measures that affect them are adopted and applied, among other situations. In addition, it determines that states must provide reparations for all intellectual, cultural, or spiritual goods that indigenous groups lost without their free, prior, and informed consent. Although these resolutions are nonbinding, they establish a strong commitment by the state and exert pressure on it to comply.

In this respect, Rodríguez Garavito (2010) distinguishes between a strong and a weak interpretation of the right to consultation. In his opinion, "international bodies such as the UN Rapporteurship on the Rights of Indigenous Peoples and the Inter-American Court of Human Rights (2007) have established more stringent interpretations of international law, especially regarding large development plans or investments with significant impact on indigenous peoples." The opposite end is a weak procedural conception such as the one expressed by Ecuador's Constitutional Court (48).

There are also other legal tools on the regional scale, such as the Organization of American States' Inter-American Commission on Human Rights (IACHR), based in Costa Rica, which is binding for American states. The reports by the

UN Special Rapporteur on the Situation of Human Rights and Fundamental Freedoms of Indigenous Peoples are also quite important, since they tend to lend visibility and political force to indigenous demands, investigating forms to overcome the existing obstacles to protect the rights of indigenous peoples, gathering information on violations of those rights, organizing missions to the conflictive regions, and elaborating reports.

In this regard, the IACHR has a tradition of guaranteeing rights. For example, in 2007, after analyzing five contentious cases, it elaborated an international legal framework to solve problems between states and indigenous communities. First, it established that the states have the duty to guarantee indigenous people's effective participation by carrying out consultations according to the communities' customs and traditions, accepting their decisions and providing information, and promoting communication between both parts; the consultations must be carried out in good faith through culturally adequate procedures from the first stages of the development projects, ensuring that the communities are aware of all possible risks. Second, it provided recommendations regarding the matters on which indigenous peoples must be consulted, among which are the extraction of natural resources in indigenous territories. Furthermore, it is the indigenous people, and not the state, who must decide who is to represent the indigenous people in each consultation. Finally, if it is a large-scale development plan or has a significant impact, the states cannot proceed without prior, free, and informed consent (Antkowiak and Gonza 2010).

One important advancement in terms of a strong interpretation was the sentence of the Inter-American Court of Human Rights (IACtHR) on July 30, 2012, regarding the Kichwa Sarayaku people in the Ecuadorian Amazon. The case is as follows: More than a decade ago, a denunciation was made against the Ecuadorian state for granting an oil extraction concession and allowing an Argentine corporation to perform seismic prospecting in the territory of the Sarayaku people without prior consultation. The IACtHR determined that Ecuador had violated the rights to prior and informed consultation, indigenous communal property, and cultural identity. The state was also held responsible for seriously endangering the rights to life and personal integrity, as well as for violating legal rights and guarantees and the legal protection of the Sarayaku people. As a result, the IACtHR determined that Ecuador must "remove the pentolite from the territory of the Sarayaku People." Furthermore, "the state must carry out an adequate, effective, and full consultation before initiating natural resource extraction projects. It must also provide 'compulsory courses' on the rights of indigenous people for government officials involved with indigenous people, and must organize 'a public act of acknowledgment of responsibility' for the violations. Finally, the Court determined that the state must pay US$90,000 for material harms and US$1,250,000 for nonmaterial harms to the Sarayaku People."[10]

In short, this sentence by the IACtHR was a milestone on the topic and is expected to have an impact on pending lawsuits regarding indigenous rights and the advancement of the extractive frontier. It is not by chance that since 2012–13 the IACtHR has been scrutinized by Latin American states—the Venezuelan government decided to withdraw from it, claiming that it is partial and morally decadent, and Brazil threatened to do the same after it received precautionary measures from the IACtHR that implied the suspension of construction of the Belo Monte megadam, undertaken without due consultation of the indigenous populations.

The Minefields of Latin American Capitalism

If we add prior consultation—which has not yet been done for mining activities—to communities that do not have the adequate profile for being consulted . . . anyone who wears a feather has the right to be consulted . . . well, things will be more difficult.—Manager of the Yanacocha mining company, Peru, May 2014

Previous, free, and informed consent (PFIC) is an increasingly complex and dynamic disputed social and legal field. For Latin American governments in times of neo-developmentalist extractivism, PFIC is more than a thorn in their side. In spite of their grandiloquent declarations in favor of the rights of indigenous people and in defense of Pachamama, all Latin American governments attempt to minimize PFIC and limit it to its weak versions, through laws and regulations aimed at establishing it as nonbinding consultations and at facilitating its tutelage or manipulation in a context of highly asymmetrical power relations.

This is true of democratizing governments such as the Evo Morales administration, which clearly manipulated the PFIC in the TIPNIS conflict. It is also true of Rafael Correa's government in Ecuador, which strongly criminalizes social struggles and which, in spite of having ratified PFIC, has not implemented it in practice and threatens to limit it and reformulate it under other forms such as prelegislative consultation. It is also true of Peru, where the successive neoliberal governments, from Alan García to Ollanta Humala, have sought to (violently) put an end to demands for the right to consultation and to circumscribe it to Amazonian peoples. It is also the case in Argentina, where legislative strategies regarding natural resources (such as the one regarding hydrocarbons in 2014, which includes fracking) have been approved without consultation of indigenous peoples. And it is also true of developmentalist Brazil under Dilma Rousseff's administration, which disregarded the IACtHR's precautionary measures that halted the construction of the controversial Belo Monte megadam in the state of Pará.

The issue of PFIC is therefore one of the most difficult and controversial topics of international, regional, and national legislation regarding the rights of indigenous peoples. Although it appears to be a "specialized instrument," in only two decades it has been the object of legal conflicts where large economic interests are at play, as well as the survival of indigenous peoples and other ethnic groups. For that reason, PFIC has become a fundamental strategy—albeit not the only one—in the dynamics of the struggles of indigenous organizations.

There were two turning points in Bolivia on the topic: The first was the end of the political expectations that indigenous organizations such as CIDOB and CONAMAQ had of the Evo Morales government; the second one was the TIPNIS conflict. In 2009 CIDOB and CONAMAQ authorities in La Paz still believed that their organizations' most important tool was the control and management of the natural resources in their territories, and not specifically the exercise of the right to prior consultation.[11] Three years after the beginning of the change process in Bolivia and shortly after the approval of the New Political Constitution that established the plurinational state and recognized autonomies, both organizations' main expectation was their participation in decision-making in indigenous territories. However, starting in 2010, this expectation gradually faded, and the organizations shifted from an offensive to a defensive posture, without, of course, abandoning the demand for autonomy, but strongly demanding the right to prior consultation. As mentioned in the previous section, this was accompanied by the issuance of a number of strategic laws by the government, among them the law that restricted the autonomy of indigenous territories. Hence, in a context of confrontation and mobilization, CIDOB and CONAMAQ started demanding respect for the right to PFIC from the Morales administration, as established in the Bolivian Constitution, and respect for organic structures (and the rejection of voting and the pronouncement of parallel native authorities), as well as "coherence between the discourse in defense of Mother Earth and the government's extractivist practice."[12] In June 2013 these organizations published a pronouncement where they reaffirmed "their struggle for the recovery and reconstitution of their ancestral territories and their real liberation in the context of a true Plurinational State" and demanded that the proposed Law on the Consultation Framework be subjected to prior consultation in order to obtain "explicit consent" before its approval and enactment (SERVINDI 2013).

The second turning point was the TIPNIS conflict resulting from the construction of the second leg of the Villa Tunari–San Ignacio de Moxos highway.

It is worth recalling that since 1965 TIPNIS has been a natural reserve, and since 1990 an indigenous territory, a habitat of Amazonian peoples such as the Yuracarés, the Chimanes, and the Mojeños. It was a multidimensional conflict, since, while it is clear that one of the project's objectives was to interconnect the country (a real and historical demand of many populations), the main issue was that the indigenous people involved were not consulted. In this context, it was not farfetched to believe that the highway would become the doorway to extractive projects with negative social, cultural, and environmental consequences (whether Brazil or any other country was the Bolivian government's partner).

At first, the MAS government escalated the conflict, thus demonstrating a not-very-pluralist tendency in the construction of hegemony. However, after several marches from TIPNIS to La Paz and an episode of repression in 2011, the Evo Morales government was forced to back down, suspending construction of that stretch of the highway. Ignoring the organizations' opposition (which considered that there was consensus in rejecting the construction without the need for a consultation), the government called for a consultation and clearly attempted to manipulate it in its favor. However, a report from the Catholic Church, elaborated together with the Permanent Human Rights Assembly of Bolivia in April 2013, stated that thirty-six communities rejected the highway construction; that the consultation "was neither free nor in good faith, nor did it comply with the standards for prior consultation, and [it] was conducted with kickbacks" (Asamblea Permanente de Derechos Humanos and FIDH 2013); that the communities' own norms and procedures were not respected; that information was not appropriately shared; and that no environmental, social, cultural, and economic impact studies were presented, among other problems.

It is therefore necessary to read the teachings derived from the TIPNIS conflict in a more general and regional manner, with regard to other processes of prior consultation in Latin America: In a context of escalating, virulent, and politicized conflict—where the various actors seem to participate in a zero-sum game—the process of conducting PFIC of indigenous people (as established by ILO Convention 169) is inevitably diluted, and the definition of its procedures, mechanisms, and topics becomes extremely complicated and controversial.

Other measures regarding the right to prior consultation are quite worrisome. Replacing all established norms, in March 2005 the government of Bolivia modified the regulations for participation and consultation for hydrocarbon-related activities (Gandarillas 2015). Another decree in May that same year allows hydrocarbon exploration in protected zones. Also, according to the Bolivian Documentation and Information Center (Centro de Documentación e Información Bolivia; CEDIB), in seven years there were at least forty-nine prior consultations without an environmental assessment, which means that the populations involved were unaware of the impacts of such activities.

In Peru the way that PFIC entered the political agenda reveals its conflictive and dramatic nature. On June 5, 2009, on Environment Day, indigenous communities of the Peruvian Amazon that had been protesting for almost two months against a series of decrees that threatened the Amazon were repressed by the Alan García administration in the Bagua province, about a thousand kilometers away from Lima, on the border with Ecuador. The repression took the life of about thirty Amazonian residents and ten police officers and resulted in an undetermined number of people missing.

However, the repression at Bagua and urban national and international solidarity with the Amazonian populations forced the Alan García government to revoke the decrees that directly affected the right to consultation and made the country discover the historically excluded Amazonian peoples. With 11 percent of the Peruvian population, the Amazon is home to sixty-six different peoples, fourteen of which have no contact with Western culture.

As a result, in May 2010 the Peruvian Parliament voted in favor of a consultation law for indigenous organizations in accordance with international legislation. However, the law was vetoed by President García, who made "observations" and sent it back to the Parliament. The points questioned had to do with the binding nature of the consultations and their scope, since the president was opposed to the inclusion of peasant peoples from the Andes. In May 2011, shortly after Ollanta Humala's electoral victory, the Law of Prior Consultation of indigenous people was finally approved. One year later, it was put into effect, but it was enmeshed in new controversies regarding the collective subjects to which it applied. The executive branch believed that only "native" communities could be considered indigenous, which included Amazonian peoples, but not "peasant" Andean communities or the *rondas campesinas* (autonomous peasant patrols), whose status is recognized by various national laws and which play an increasingly important role in the struggle against megamining.[13] As a result of the disagreements on the topic, two vice-ministers of interculturality resigned from office. The government was also late in publicizing a database on indigenous people, which was finally published in late 2013 and included fifty-two indigenous peoples: forty-eight Amazonian and four Andean (speakers of Quechua, Aymara, Uro, and Jacaru).

After the Law of Prior Consultation was approved in 2011, ten consultation processes were concluded, and fifteen were in progress by 2015 (Hiruelas

2015). However, Andean peoples have not been included in prior consultations regarding mining projects in their territories, which are the most conflictive, since, according to the Peruvian government, those communities are not native peoples but peasants, and as such, they have no right to be consulted. In this regard, the IACHR urged the Peruvian government to comply with the Law of Prior Consultation before implementing megaprojects in Andean indigenous communities (Jiménez 2015).

These are paradoxes of the de-Indianization process specific to the Peruvian case, as mentioned above. In Peru it is the state that decides who belongs to an "indigenous people" and who does not. Thus, PFIC excludes a broad spectrum of peasant populations (from Andean communities to *ronderos campesinos*), who have been opposing the advancement of megamining in their territories for years, which is the greatest source of social conflicts in Peru today and makes the mobilized populations more vulnerable, in a context of criminalization and repression of social protest.

Finally, the Argentine case is not very promising either. On May 20, 2010, the year of the republic's bicentennial, thousands of indigenous people marched in the historic Plaza de Mayo (see Aranda 2011). This sort of second Malón de la Paz began on May 12 in Jujuy, Misiones, and Neuquén and went through ten provinces. The indigenous leaders were received by President Cristina Fernández de Kirchner, with whom they spoke and to whom they delivered three documents, basically demanding "historical reparation for a historical debt": the implementation of the right to prior consultation; cultural/educational reparation; reparation to mother nature and the stopping of the advancement of extractive and polluting industries; the creation of an Indigenous Intercultural Ministry with full participation by indigenous organizations; and economic reparation through the creation of a Permanent Special Fund to implement the life plans defined by each people in their territories, for the purpose of achieving identity-based development (Briones 2014, 179–81). The meeting between the indigenous leaders and the president was not very fruitful: "The President's speech lasted 14 minutes and 57 seconds. Nine times she insisted that they should be 'intelligent' in the negotiations and accept the changes. She also told them to be 'realistic' and 'sensible'" (Aranda 2011). This second historical disagreement derives from a very worrisome reality, far from the multicultural image that the Kirchner administration has portrayed through an enormous media/cultural campaign.[14]

In short, in spite of the multicultural rhetoric, in Argentina indigenous people are almost absent from the public and political agenda. The issue of indigenous peoples in Argentina in the twenty-first century must be understood in terms of long-term memory, because it is the original genocide that casts its shadow over the horizon, evident in the current criminalization and dispossession of territories, once again in the name of "progress" and "development." Part of this reality is described in the report by UN Rapporteur James Anaya, who visited the country in 2011. Published in 2012, this report denounces not only that the international legislation on prior consultation, incorporated in both the National Constitution and those of the various provinces (ILO Convention 169, Article 75 of the National Constitution), is not applied but also that even though there is a law that prohibits evicting indigenous communities and requires a territorial survey (Law 26.160 of 2006), very few provinces have begun such a survey, and the violent evictions continue (in Formosa, Neuquén, Salta, and Jujuy, among other provinces). In addition to the environmental and cultural impacts, the lack of prior consultation, and the violent evictions, there is significant criminalization and repression.

Also, the data included in a report elaborated by Encuentro Memoria, Verdad y Justicia (Memory, Truth, and Justice Meeting; 2012) on the criminalization of protest according to sector is alarming. A survey of 2,198 cases occurring between 2001 and 2012 demonstrates that 31.4 percent of them relate to indigenous people, that is, almost one-third of the total, which is equivalent to the percentage for the sector of trade union struggles. While it is surprising because of its magnitude, it is more so if we consider that in Argentina there are fewer protests by indigenous people than there are trade union struggles, which seems to imply that a large number of the protests by indigenous people are criminalized. While in the south of the country the indigenous question is a penal matter, in the north the situation is directly related to violent death—from direct killings by security forces and landowners to "strange" traffic accidents and "diffuse deaths" (Antonelli 2011), or what appear to be common crimes, resulting in almost two dozen deaths so far. These changes in the forms of state violence point to a growing process of outsourcing of repression (provincial police officers with paramilitary groups, hit men paid by soy farmers and large landowners). Thus, the policy of physical annihilation has gradually shifted to the provinces and their margins, where indigenous and peasant populations have been cornered, and today we see a very significant process of land grabbing.

Regarding prior consultation, one of the most noteworthy cases was the beginning of lithium exploration and exploitation in the north of the country, which led to mobilizations and demands by indigenous communities. In November 2010 Roundtable 33 of Indigenous Communities for the Defense and Management of the Territory (Salta and Jujuy) was created, which filed a lawsuit in Argentina's Supreme Court demanding PFIC. It was precisely this lawsuit, presented to the UN Permanent Forum on Human Rights in Geneva, which enabled the visit of UN Rapporteur James Anaya to the communities in Salinas Grandes, which had a significant impact on the provincial government and the corporations (Göbel 2013). Finally, in January 2013 the Supreme Court rejected the lawsuit filed by the indigenous communities of Jujuy, claiming issues with the form, not the substance. In its sentence the Supreme Court stated, "The actions presented against the Province of Salta and the National State are beyond the competence of the Supreme Court of Justice of the Nation" (Puente and Argento 2015, 134). In light of this, the members of the organizations decided to resort to the IACtHR, which by 2016, when this book was published in Spanish, had not yet made a decision.

The Mapuche communities were not consulted regarding (conventional and nonconventional) hydrocarbon exploitation either. For example, the new hydrocarbon law of 2014, which introduced fracking, does not include any form of prior consultation of indigenous people. The Neuquén basin and the great nonconventional hydrocarbon deposits of Vaca Muerta are seen as an empty territory, a "desert," by provincial and national authorities, which, in addition to reviving ominous memories, ignores the fact that more than twenty Mapuche communities live there and will be affected by the advancement of oil exploitation, and demand their right to be consulted. It is also worth emphasizing the constant process to delegitimize indigenous claims, including the accusation that the Mapuche people are not Argentineans but Chileans, refusing to recognize their presence prior to the formation of the national state.

———

The situation of indigenous people is full of contrasts and contradictions. The recognition of collective rights has led to many debates in Latin America regarding the processes of plural democratization in twenty-first-century Latin American societies, and to especially serious questions regarding the viability and scope of the rights established at the international level and incorporated in all Latin American constitutions today. The dilemma entails a clash between two dynamics. On one hand, on a global scale, since the mid-twentieth century, and in the midst of a decolonization process, the horizon of cultural and political rights of indigenous people expanded. Horizon-concepts such as autonomy, collective rights, and the plurinational state are ever present in Indianist narratives and illustrate the growing political empowerment of indigenous people in various Latin American countries. On the other hand, the dizzying expansion of extractive capital implies a new process to corner indigenous people, threatening the preservation of basic resources for life. *Dispossession* and *recolonization* are some of the terms repeatedly employed by both indigenous referents and socio-territorial movements. In sum, the expansion of the extractive frontier demolishes the very possibility of enforcing the collective rights of indigenous people only recently recognized at the global, national, and local levels.

6

Debates on Development

Do not believe romantic environmentalists, anyone opposed to the country's development is a terrorist.—RAFAEL CORREA, December 2007

Present-day Latin American thought faces many challenges, paradoxes, and ambivalences related both to the process of environmentalization of social struggles and, more precisely, to the most radical and creative branches of critical thought. For that reason, I begin this chapter on the current perspectives on development by examining both the dominant views on the topic and the critique of extractivism. I then examine the various horizon-concepts debated in the context of this new political grammar: the commons, ethics of care, Good Living, and the rights of nature, among others. I also examine the contributions of contemporary anthropology regarding the local models of relating to nature, comparing them to the hegemonic model based on a dualist ontology.

Finally, I conclude with an examination of the notion of ecosocial transition and postextractivism.

Debate 1: Conflicting Views and the Critique of Extractivism

The Dominant Views

Earlier in this work, I observed that since 2000 Latin America has been undergoing an epochal change. Beyond the great expectations generated, especially in countries such as Bolivia, Venezuela, and Ecuador, the beginning of a new political cycle faced serious obstacles and increasing sources of conflict. On one hand, thanks to the boom in the international prices of raw materials, the various governments found themselves in an extremely favorable economic position, a new cycle based on the massive export of commodities, which combined extraordinary profits and comparative economic advantages. On the other hand, the territorial impacts of extractive projects at the service of massive commodity exports led to an exponential increase in socioenvironmental conflicts, which in turn generated significant resistance in the territories. In this increasingly conflictive context, questions arose regarding the meaning of development.

Today there are various political and intellectual trends in Latin America. First, there are the hegemonic positions, which redeploy the notion of development, now associated with a productivist view of indefinite growth and commodification of nature, incorporating concepts with a global resonance (sustainable development or sustainability in its weak version, corporate social responsibility, governance), justified with a presumably industrialist rhetoric. In this line, however, we must distinguish between the neoliberal and the neo-structuralist perspectives.

The neoliberal perspective is based on four fundamental notions: commodities, corporate social responsibility (CSR), weak sustainability, and governance. Natural common goods are of course seen as commodities, that is, standardized products with little added value employed for export, whose price is determined by the international market. Its view of development is based on the idea of a state subordinated to the market and, especially, to supranational regulative bodies (i.e., a "metaregulating state"). A more important element is the CSR discourse, an idea promoted by large corporations and national states, based on two premises: first, that corporations are the quintessential actor of globalized economies; and, second, that those corporations inevitably face conflicts with the local populations, derived from the social, economic, and environmental impacts and risks caused by their economic activities. Further, CSR also goes hand in hand with the notion of governance as a multiactor micropolitical device. This scheme deploys the notion of a presumed "symmetry" between the actors involved, where the state—in its various levels—appears merely as another actor (Svampa 2008). Other actors also intervene—specialists, journalists, and symbolic mediators, among others—contributing to broadening the spectrum of participants in the process of "socio-discursive production" (Antonelli 2014) in order to obtain the communities' acceptance and "social license." Finally, the neoliberal perspective fosters a weak version of sustainable development. By this, we mean, as Eduardo Gudynas argues, that "it accepts the current environmental crisis and posits that it is necessary to foster development in such a way that it does not destroy its ecological base. But this posture considers that development responds directly to economic growth, and that changes take place especially in the market, accepting different forms of commodification of Nature and applying techno-scientific innovations" (2012, 80).

The neo-structuralist perspective in turn is founded on the premise that accumulation depends on the export of commodities or primary goods. This was expressed by Brazilian thinker Luiz Carlos Bresser-Pereira (2010, 27–65), who wrote about the return to neo-development, observing that in the globalization era, export-led growth is the only sensible strategy for developing countries. The Argentineans Mariano Féliz and Emiliano López (2012), as well as Marcelo Saguier and Guillermo Peinado (2014), have associated neo-structuralism with progressive governments, based on the convergence of anti-neoliberal rhetoric and commercial and financial globalization, the latter seen as an opportunity for Latin American economies. In this line, "progressive" neo-structuralism emphasizes the favorable conditions experienced in Latin America today in terms of "natural capital" or strategic natural resources demanded by the international market, especially China. At the same time, it deploys an ambiguous understanding of natural goods that oscillates between the conception of commodities and that of strategic natural resources. While development policies aim at increasing exports, they also seek greater state control of revenues from extractive activities, especially the hydrocarbon and energy industries.

There are, however, clear connections and common topics and frameworks between progressive neo-structuralism and the neoliberal perspective, even though they also differ considerably regarding the state's role and the spheres for democratization. In the progressive view, the state has a different role than it does in neoliberal or conservative governments. In this respect, it is impossible to overlook the state's recovery of certain institutional tools and capacities, once again becoming an important economic actor and sometimes an agent for redistribution. However, this state-centered conception is limited—in the context of world governance theories, founded on the consolidation of a new institutionality based on supranational or metaregulating frameworks, the tendency is not for the national state to become a "mega-actor" or for its interventions to result in substantial changes in regulatory instruments. On the contrary, in the best-case scenario, it is a moderately regulatory state in a multiactor context (a more complex civil society, illustrated by social movements, nongovernmental organizations [NGOs], and other actors) but closely associated with multinational private capital with increasing impact on the national economies. Hence, although the progressive scheme is heterodox and differs from neoliberalism regarding the state's guiding role, it is far from questioning the hegemony of transnational capital in peripheral economies (Féliz 2012, 24–27).

On the other hand, the neo-structuralist view shares the principle of "weak sustainability" with the neoliberal perspective. This is related to the fact that in Latin America most of the lefts and progressive populisms have traditionally held a productivist view of development that tends to focus on the conflict between capital and labor, minimizing the new social struggles focused on the defense of land and territory. In this political/ideological context dominated by a productivist view, so averse to the concern for nature, the current dynamics of dispossession become a blind spot that cannot be conceptualized. Finally, beyond the differences between the political regimes in existence today, whether neoliberal conservative or progressive, there is an evident "consensus" regarding the irresistible nature of extractivism, which thus becomes a threshold or historical-comprehensive horizon regarding the production of alternatives, effectively closing off the very possibility of a debate. The implicit or explicit acceptance of this neo-developmentalist "consensus" contributes to creating a new skepticism or ideology of resignation that reinforces the presumed "soundness and reasonableness" of progressive capitalism, imposing the idea that there are no other alternatives to the current style of extractivist development. As a result, all critical discourses or radical oppositions are seen as antimodern or as rejecting progress, or simply as irrational and an expression of ecological fundamentalism.

In short, the hegemonic notion of development is the product of the convergence of an extractivist paradigm, associated with the reprimarization and commodification of the economy, and a traditional view, whose main features continue to be productivism and competitiveness at all costs, concepts that are renewed by the ever-opportune and malleable use of certain global categories (sustainability, CSR, governance). Thus, the current situation displays a persisting connection not only between extractivism and neoliberalism, emblematically expressed in Peru, Colombia, and Mexico, but also between extractivism and progressive governments, as is the case in Bolivia, Brazil, Ecuador, and Argentina, among others.

The Critique of Extractivism

There are many critical perspectives in Latin America regarding the current development models. Among others, there is the integral environmental perspective, related to the notion of strong sustainability and postdevelopment; the indigenist perspective, which emphasizes Good Living; the ecofeminist perspective, associated with the ethics of care and depatriarchalization; and the eco-territorial perspective, derived from social movements, which emphasizes the concept of territoriality, a critique of maldevelopment, and the defense of the commons. In spite of their differences, all of them are founded on a critique of extractivism.

The category of extractivism or neo-extractivism is present today both in the critical bibliography and in the language of socio-territorial movements. In my opinion, beyond the existing nuances, today's extractivism can be characterized by the presence of several elements. First, it refers to a pattern of accumulation based on the overexploitation of increasingly scarce natural goods, some of them nonrenewable, as well as the expansion of the frontiers of exploitation to territories formerly considered unproductive. Second, it is characterized by the large-scale export of primary goods, among them hydrocarbons (gas and oil), metals and minerals (copper, gold, silver, tin, bauxite, and zinc, among others), agricultural products (corn, soy, wheat), and biofuel. Third, extractivist undertakings are large-scale ventures that are capital-intensive and not labor-intensive, and the actors are usually transnational corporations. Fourth, extractivism tends toward constant advancement and intensive occupation of the territories, through monoculture or monoproduction, with consequences that include displacement and/or destruction of other forms of production (local/regional economies). In effect, what is generally denominated developmentalist neo-extractivism combines enclave dynamics and territorial fragmentation (scarce production of relevant endogenous connections that favor a model of territorial and regional integration) with the dynamics of displacement (dislocation of traditional local economies and expulsion of populations), which tends to position large corporations with a global presence as the total social actor in the context of the local societies. Thus defined, the current form of extractivism encompasses more than those activities traditionally considered extractive. In addition to open-pit megamining, it includes expansion of the oil and energy frontier (through the exploitation of nonconventional hydrocarbons, whether offshore or through the highly questioned fracking method), the construction of large hydroelectric dams (usually at the service of extractive production), the expansion of the fishing and forestry frontier, and the expansion of the agribusiness model (GMO crops such as soy, palm leaf, and biofuel).

Another concept that questions the hegemonic view of development is the *Commodities Consensus* (Svampa 2013), which underscores the arrival in Latin America of a new economic and political/ideological order, maintained by the boom in the international prices of raw materials and consumer goods increasingly demanded by the central countries and the emerging powers. This order is gradually consolidating a neo-extractivist development style that leads to comparative advantages, visible in economic growth, while producing new asymmetries and social, economic, environmental, and political/cultural conflicts. These conflicts mark the beginning of a new cycle of struggles centered on the defense of the territory and the environment and on the discussion of development models and the very frontiers of democracy.

From an economic standpoint, the Commodities Consensus has translated into a reprimarization of the economy, visible in a shift toward extractive primary activities with little value added. This "reprimarization" effect is aggravated by China's fast emergence as an unequal partner in all of Latin America (Svampa and Slipak 2015). From a social standpoint, the Commodities Consensus implies an intensification of the dynamics of dispossession and concentration of land, resources, and territories carried out mainly by large corporations, in a multiscale alliance with the various governments.

A third critical concept is that of *maldevelopment*.[1] Given its scale, extractivism today leads to significant territorial reconfigurations.[2] This occurs in the form of not only the emergence of an exclusionary territoriality relative to other subaltern territorialities but also the degradation of the territories and the quality of life. Its expansion thus implies the consolidation of development models that are not sustainable in the medium and long terms, that is, of models of *maldevelopment* that exacerbate environmental injustice and the expansion of sacrifice areas. With time, what remains for the local communities are the environmental and social and health impacts in territories that become sacrifice areas, where the bodies and the very lives become disposable and sacrificeable.

Finally, one of the consequences of the current extractivist turn in the context of the *Commodities Consensus* is the irruption of socioenvironmental conflicts related to access and control of natural resources or goods, involving different interests and values held by the opposing actors in a context of power asymmetry. One emblematic example is megamining, one of the activities that has met the greatest resistance in the continent. The growing resistances are an expression of the empowerment of ancestral struggles for land carried out by indigenous and peasant peoples, and the emergence of new forms of citizen mobilization and participation centered on the defense of natural resources (defined as common goods), biodiversity, and the environment. This emergence of new languages that focus on the territory has led to an *eco-territorial turn* that is not exclusive to countries with a strong indigenous presence but encompasses most of Latin America, where peasant/indigenous resistances and socio-territorial and environmental movements have multiplied. This has led to the emergence of a new organizational framework involving indigenous/peasant organizations, socioenvironmental movements organized in assemblies, environmental NGOs, networks of critical intellectuals and experts, and cultural collectives. As tends to happen in other fields of struggle, the main actors in this organizational dynamic are women, whose role is crucial both in large organizational structures and in small collectives. This plurality of actors paves the way to the recognition of knowledges and a dialogue between, on one hand, critical expert knowledge, independent of the dominant (economic, political, and media) powers, and, on the other hand, local knowledges, especially peasant/indigenous ancestral knowledges. Thus, eco-territorial struggles point to an expansion of the rights frontier, while expressing a social dispute over what is understood or should be understood as "true development" or "alternative development." They foster a new language that values knowledges and rights, through the enactment of laws, norms, and legal frameworks that point to the construction of a new political and socioenvironmental institutionality.

Hence, the current scenario reflects two opposing tendencies. On one hand, one derives from the hegemonic discourse, through the return of the concept of development as the *grand narrative* in a strong and hegemonic sense, sustained by the discourse of comparative advantages. Whether in the crude language of dispossession (neoliberal perspective) or one that points to the state's control of the surplus (progressive developmentalism or neo-structuralism) in the various countries in Latin America, the development model is founded on an extractivist paradigm, related to the notion of economic opportunities or comparative advantages. On the other hand, the critique of extractivism is related to the eco-territorial turn, visible in the emergence of common frameworks for collective action that operate as schemes of global interpretation and, simultaneously, as producers of an alternative collective subjectivity. At the same time, the critique seeks to foster a debate regarding horizon-concepts: Whether in a language of the defense of the territory and common goods, human rights, the collective rights of native peoples, the rights of nature, or "Good Living," the actions of the mobilized populations are inscribed in the horizon of participatory democracy, which includes, above all, the democratization of decision-making.

Debate 2: The Disputes Surrounding Horizon-Concepts

In this section I would like to present some of the propositional concepts that explicitly abandon the hegemonic idea of development as indefinite growth. These concepts constitute what I have denominated horizon-concepts, among them the commons, ethics of care, Good Living, and the rights of nature. In the following pages, I examine some of the issues present in the discussions.

The Commons, Ethics of Care, or Commodification of Nature

One of the debates regarding development models is the critique of the growing commodification of nature and the proposal to conceive natural goods as common goods. This proposal becomes particularly urgent as the paradigm of sustainable development is replaced by the paradigm of the green economy around the world.

One of the main promoters of the green economy is Brazil, a crucial actor in the subcontinent. During the UN Conference on Sustainable Development (Rio de Janeiro, Brazil, 2012), a final document entitled "The Future We Want" (United Nations 2012) was elaborated, which states that in the context of sustainable development and the eradication of poverty, the green economy is one of the most important tools available to attain sustainable development, providing alternatives in terms of policy creation, but that it should not consist of a set of rigid norms (Svampa and Viale 2014).

The green economy paradigm actually implies a greater commodification of nature, which aggravates harms and inequalities, increasing both the appropriation of territories from local and indigenous communities by transnational corporations and the negative effects of neo-extractivism. As Brazilian researcher Camila Moreno argues, the purpose is to transform nature's elements and processes into objects for trade, initiating a new and unprecedented stage of privatization of nature, beginning with the forests through the mechanisms of REDD+ and gradually expanding to encompass water and biodiversity. In response to the crisis, the capitalist system reverts all common goods of nature, including the right to life; it bolsters its control over the territories and turns carbon into a new commodity (Moreno 2013, 85–86). In addition, by disguising extractivism, green economy tends to exacerbate it, contributing to fostering the process of enclosing the commons, which entails privatization of everything from public goods to all life-forms. It is not by chance that many organizations and social movements have rejected the green economy strategy, renaming it *green capitalism*, arguing that, far from being a positive change, it fosters a greater commodification of nature.

In contrast with this trend, resistance movements in the countries of both the South and the North have been consolidating the concept of the commons, which is key today in the search for an alternative paradigm beyond the market and the state.[3] As Joan Subirats (2011) observes, the reemergence of the interest in the commons from various scientific and disciplinary perspectives—including climate change, cities, digital commons, the protection of water, seeds, scientific production, and cultural heritage, among others—coincided with the recognition of the work of economist Elinor Ostrom (Nobel Prize in Economic Sciences, 2009), who paid special attention to the existence of communal spaces and goods.

However, it is important to highlight the nuances: While in the countries of the North the grammar of the commons is defined in favor of the public, that is, against adjustment and privatization policies (neoliberalism), the expropriation of knowledge, and the new knowledge economy (cognitive capitalism and its forms of appropriation), and only recently against extractivism (especially against fracking), in our peripheral countries this grammar of the commons is directed against the various forms of developmentalist neo-extractivism, which encompasses processes of land grabbing, privatization of seeds, and the overexploitation of natural goods.

On the other hand, in these latitudes the discussion on the concept of the commons takes place at two different levels. The first involves the issue of decommodification. This refers to the need to keep away from the market those resources and goods that, given their character as natural, social, or cultural heritage, belong to the community and have a value that has no price. In Latin America this is closely associated with natural goods and the struggles against extractivism. Natural goods are therefore seen neither as commodities nor exclusively as strategic natural resources. In spite of their differences, both languages impose an exclusively utilitarian conception that disregards other attributes and values—which cannot be represented by a market price. As a result, the notion of the commons not only implies a rejection of the logic of commodities but also questions the state-centered view of "natural resources" from the perspective of the construction of a "type of territoriality" that protects the commons (natural, social, and cultural heritage).[4]

At the second level, the notion of the commons is based on *the production and reproduction of the commons*. This proposes a different understanding of social relations based on the configuration or emergence of spaces and forms of social cooperation, of common use and enjoyment, in the sense of what Mexican thinker Gustavo Esteva (2007) characterized as "realms of community." There are a number of contributions in this respect. For example, Mexican essayist Raquel

Gutiérrez Aguilar (2014) understands it as *a popular/communal political horizon* that aims at "positioning the reproduction of social life as the nucleus for understanding the political, the collective avenues for social conservation and transformation. The point of departure and main focus of communal horizons is the preservation, satisfactory transformation, and deployment of social reproduction." Likewise, from a perspective grounded in Latin America's reality, the Belgian thinker François Houtart associates the commons with *the common good of humanity*, considering its more general character, which implies the fundaments of humanity's collective life on the planet: its relationship with nature, the production of life, collective organization (politics), and the ways of reading, assessing, and expressing the real (culture). However, it is not a matter of heritage but of a "state of being" (well-being, good living) resulting from all the parameters of human life on earth (Houtart 2011, 8). Humanity's common good is without a doubt life and its reproduction.

Another interesting contribution is that of Chilean philosopher Franz Hinkelammert and Costa Rican economist Henry Mora Jiménez, who developed criteria to construct a rationality for the reproduction of life "that neither replaces nor eliminates the means/ends rationality but subordinates it, thus providing elements to create alternatives and construct what they denominate 'economics for life'" (2005, 55). From the perspective of *economics for life*, the purpose of human labor is to produce *use value* or means for life; the systems for the social organization and division of labor are considered rational only if they enable the reproduction of life over time. "The cornerstone is human beings as needful and the necessary reproduction of their material life conditions" (55). When one examines the reproduction of external nature and of human beings, it is important to consider "nonuse values, which are also conditions for existence and for the possibility of reproducing life's system. It requires overcoming the labor-value perspective and examining life-value instead" (Vargas Soler 2008, 173).

Finally, it is worth underscoring the elective affinity between the grammar of the commons, centered on the reproduction of life, and the ethics of care. Ecofeminism and feminist economics highlight the parallel between the exploitation of women and of nature, through invisible and unrecognized reproductive work. By this they refer to the tasks associated with human reproduction, child-rearing, resolution of basic needs, the promotion of health, emotional support, social participation, and everything that has to do with the culture or the labor of care (León 2009). Ecofeminism proposes overcoming women's marginalization through the social recognition of the values attributed to women and the need to extend the social presence of those values, related to the ethics of care, as the foundation of a new paradigm capable of changing the current state of relations between human beings and nature. These values are related to care understood as the basis for a different ethics founded on responsibility and as the quintessential female virtue (Puleo 2011).

There are several currents of ecofeminism, ranging from difference or identity feminism, which naturalizes the relationship between women and nature, to constructivist ecofeminism (Puleo 2011; Svampa 2015b), which conceives that relationship as a historical/social construction related to the sexual division of labor. In my opinion, it is important not to fall into an essentialist view of the "woman-nature" relationship, since the key remains the field of elective affinities deployed by the exploitation of the sexual division of labor and the separation between social production and social reproduction. It is this branch of ecofeminism that interests us when reading ecofeminism of survival, which is closely related to popular ecology in the countries of the South.

In effect, several authors refer to a feminism of the South related to the current of popular ecology, which some of them denominate "ecofeminism of survival" (Shiva [1988] 1995) or eco-territorial feminisms (Svampa 2021), since it relates to women's diverse experience defending health, survival, and territory, which led to the emergence of an awareness of the solid links between gender and the environment, women and environmentalism, and feminism and ecology.

In other words, in the context of today's resistances to neo-extractivism, the language that dignifies women in the context of the culture of care tends to view social relations from a different logic and rationality, questioning capitalism by recognizing our eco-dependence and the importance of social reproduction work. In its anticolonial version, ecofeminism from the South proposes a view of social needs that does not focus on scarcity or misery but on rescuing the culture of care and relational narratives of nature.

Good Living: Controversies and Avatars of a Central Idea

Good Living means recovering our peoples' experience, recovering the Culture of Life, and recovering our life in complete harmony and mutual respect with Mother Nature, with Pachamama, where everything is life, where we are all uywas, creatures of nature and the cosmos. We are all part of nature and there is nothing separate, and all things, from the plants to the hills, are our siblings.—DAVID CHOQUEHUANCA, Minister of Foreign Affairs of the Plurinational State of Bolivia, 2010

Good Living is a plural concept, both because of its cultural matrix and because of the need to adapt it to different environmental contexts.—EDUARDO GUDYNAS AND ALBERTO ACOSTA, "La renovación de la crítica al desarrollo y el buen vivir como alternativa" (The renewal of the critique of development and good living as an alternative), 2011

One of the most appealing topics in Latin American critical thought, which has infused the eco-territorial turn with greater vitality, is that of "Good Living"— *Buen Vivir*, *Sumak Kawsay*, or *Suma Qamaña*, in Spanish, Quechua, and Aymara, respectively. Even though the concept derived from the Andean indigenous worldview, it soon resonated on a continental and global scale. For that reason, it would be impossible to summarize or even systematize the many contributions in existence on the topic of Good Living (GL). Ecuadorian anthropologist David Cortez (2014), who has examined the genealogy of GL—inquiring into when the concept emerged, what its sources are, who its promoters are, and whether or not it represents an alternative to development—argues that there is no explicit record of the term's use prior to 2000, nor are there references in any chronicle or dictionary of the Quechua or Aymara languages. In its different versions, GL is thus a recent historical/social construction but one based on long-term memory, that is, on the logic of indigenous communities, on their relational and communal worldview, in opposition to modern Western logic.

Explicit references to GL appeared in Bolivia in 2000 through indigenous intellectuals such as Simón Yampara and Indianist philosophers such as Javier Medina, and in Ecuador in 2001 through the economist Alberto Acosta and Carlos Viteri, leader of the Kichua people of Sarayaku. One of the most interesting attempts to systematize the various voices and conceptualizations of GL was published in Bolivia in 2011 by Ivonne Farah and Luciano Vasapollo, editors of the work, who in the introduction proposed three approaches to the concept: first, a philosophical definition that confronted the Western and indigenous paradigms but that considered GL as "the complementarity of opposite poles in well-defined territories" (Medina 2014, 128); another that connected GL to the aspirations of subaltern sectors in struggle (Houtart [2011], defining it as "the common good of humanity"); and, finally, one that underscored the environmental dimension by proposing a different view of nature (Gudynas 2009, 2014a; Acosta 2011).[5]

The topic was further promoted by the constituent debates in Bolivia and Ecuador. In this context, GL operates as a broad surface on which different emancipatory meanings are inscribed, with the indigenous/communal as the inspiring framework and common core. However, while in Ecuador the philosophy of GL was re-created as a plural concept with a long lineage (from Aristotle to eco-socialism and ecofeminism), in Bolivia its use was more limited, related only to the worldview of indigenous peoples. For example, for Magdalena León, the notion of GL was based "on reciprocity, cooperation, complementarity" and implied a shift from accumulation to life. The author also relates GL to an ecofeminist view of care for life and for others (León 2009, 4).

Most analysts agree that GL is a "concept under construction" in a disputed space, which from the beginning implied the risk of being emptied of meaning or abused. Examining that dispute allows us to perceive various moments in the first fifteen years of this century. After the constituent processes, and at least until 2010, vindicating GL implied a radical critique of Western modernity and coloniality (of power and knowledge) in defense of Pachamama. There was a certain consensus that GL proposed alternatives to the most conventional development path, which created a possible way out of the primary-export model and, subsequently, of what would be called *extractivism*, despite the difficulties of translating it into concrete public policies. Thus, for example, in Bolivia GL emerged as a sort of aspiration opposed to the dominant Western worldview, as paradigmatically expressed by Foreign Minister David Choquehuanca, a renowned Aymara intellectual with close ties to the NGO world, who promoted the inclusion of GL in the Bolivian Constitution (Albó 2011, 139). In this line, Javier Medina (2014, 127) argues that the concept of development cannot be translated into indigenous languages and that in fact the homeomorphic equivalent to development in the Amerindian system is *Suma Qamaña*, which philosophically must be read from a postrationalist perspective and in relation with deep ecology. But in his opinion, the two paradigms, that of development and that of GL, are antagonistic (133).

In the case of Ecuador, after the constituent debate, the government, through the National Secretariat for Planning and Development (Secretaría Nacional de Planificación y Desarrollo; SENPLADES), developed the Plan for Good Living 2009–2013, which, in addition to a "return of the state," proposed a change in the accumulation model, from a primary-export model to endogenous, biocentered development based on biodiversity, knowledge, and tourism. As was reiterated until a few years ago, "change will not be immediate, but the program for 'Good Living' constitutes a road map" (Ospina 2010, 5). However, by 2010–11 the precarious consensus around GL broke down. In this respect, the Tiquipaya countersummit on climate change was a turning point, by shedding light on the critiques of the Evo Morales administration (Roundtable 18), which portrayed an image of the defense of Mother Earth globally, while silencing the conflicts surrounding extractivism at home. In my opinion, an illustration of the first fissures is the debate prompted by a column published after the summit in the weekly *Página Siete* by Argentine economist and journalist Pablo Stefanoni (2011a), director of *Le Monde Diplomatique* in Bolivia, who at the time was living in La Paz. In that column Stefanoni pointed out several lapses in Evo Morales's speech and his defense of Pachamama, criticizing what was already known as *Pachamamismo*. Provocatively, Stefanoni's thesis pointed to the emptiness of the discourse on Mother Earth, arguing that "the process of change was too important to be left in the hands of *pachamámicos*." By the concept of *pachamámico*, Stefanoni meant "a salon Andean worldview," that is, a certain "pose of ancestral authenticity" that infused nonindigenous and indigenous discourses, which, in his opinion, proposed "a candid reading of the crisis of capitalism and Western civilization" (2011a). In response to the avalanche of criticisms received, the author went even further in a second article (2011b), where he argued that he had never seen "a blockade for Good Living," while wondering how it was possible to apply a communitarian model in a mostly urban and highly hybrid country. He also criticized Foreign Minister Choquehuanca's highly controversial statement "Ants' rights are more important than human rights."

Among the many responses to Stefanoni was that of the legendary Peruvian peasant/indigenous leader Hugo Blanco, who argued that the issue of climate change had not been passed on to indigenous people but that it was they who defended the rights of Mother Earth and struggled against environmental pollution on a daily basis, as the tragic events in Bagua demonstrated. Blanco also argued that there were struggles for GL, such as those against megamining. Finally, he argued that the use of *pachamámico* language by government bodies and NGOs to rein in the indigenous movement did not invalidate "the indigenous spirit, the indigenous worldview, the indigenous language, the indigenous struggle" (2011, 174).

In tune with this line of thought, Colombian thinker Arturo Escobar proposed inverting the terms, arguing that it was "modernism which hinders the discussion" and that "the process of change was too important to leave it in the hands of the moderns" (2011b, 200–201). Escobar's main argument was that the complexity of academic knowledge and the apparent simplicity of the *pachamámico* discourse were discursive effects and therefore derived from power, which meant that they had a beginning, a hegemony, and possibly an end, which could already be underway (200–201). On the other hand, Escobar insisted on the inadequacy of modern knowledge before the current social, ecological, and cultural crisis, arguing that, on the contrary, *pachamámico* knowledge was vital in this context. Finally, without intending to contribute to binary thought, he proposed that it would be more constructive to think of a coexistence between moderns and *pachamámicos*, but with the former's acknowledgment that their knowledge is partial and that, in order to understand pluridiversity, it is necessary to step off the development train and relinquish the Euro-modern episteme.

Uruguayan environmentalist Eduardo Gudynas revived the discussion, reinstating its complexity and context without disqualifying epithets (*pacha-*

mámicos or anti-*pachamámicos*), arguing that it was important to celebrate the discussion in spite of its excesses, since it opened the door to a debate on the ways of conceiving nature and of imagining a new environmental ethic. In his response Gudynas (2014a) lumped together the postures of Evo Morales (his global discourse in defense of Pachamama) and of Foreign Minister David Choquehuanca. In his opinion, both proposals recognized the rights of nature, but while the former aimed at a planetary scale, ignoring local conditions and development styles, the latter did it by recognizing environmental inequality (some living beings enjoyed more rights than others). For that reason, it was difficult for either position to illustrate a consistent environmental ethic. On the other hand, he emphasized that there were other problems in the MAS government, such as dodging the obvious tensions between the environment and development, as vice president Álvaro García Linera had been doing, arguing that economic growth and the exploitation of natural resources was essential in the fight against poverty. In his opinion, these two official discourses contributed little to the construction of a new biocentric environmental ethic, Morales/Choquehuanca because of their generality and lack of elaboration, García Linera because of his productivist stance. Yet both fostered developmentalism. The controversy was brief and intense but was successful in shedding light on the tensions and gaps in the construction of a concept that had significant potential, yet was highly generic and easily manipulable by political interests or academic fads. However, the *pachamámico* epithet remained as a sort of accusatory category, repeatedly invoked by those who defend the "political realism" of progressive governments.

Thus, a second phase of the dispute began in 2010, resulting from the aggravation of the conflicts between governments and anti-extractivist movements. A number of indigenous/peasant actors and organizations started denouncing the manipulation of the concept of GL by the governments of Bolivia and Peru, as well as international bodies. For example, in 2010 René Ramírez, secretary of the National Secretariat for Planning and Development (SENPLADES), defined GL in the long term in terms of distributive socialism and republicanism. For that reason, the secretariat's perspective could not be divorced from that of human development. "They went as far as proposing that the 'abilities' approach (SENPLADES 2007, 18–19) and the theoretical recourse to Aristotle were necessary to achieve a level of legitimacy of 'public reason'" (Bretón et al. 2014, 17).

In Bolivia the aforementioned conflict over the highway in TIPNIS ended up creating divisions. García Linera expressed this in a booklet entitled *Las tensiones creativas de la revolución: La quinta fase del proceso de cambio* (The creative tensions of the revolution: The fifth phase of the change process; 2011), where the fourth tension referred to the "communitarian socialism of Good Living." In the text he revisited Karl Marx's definition of communism, assimilated to the total logic of use value, to conclude, "That is what *Good Living* consists of: using science, technology, and industry to generate wealth; otherwise, how can highways, health clinics, and schools be built, how can food be produced, and how can the basic and growing needs of society be satisfied?" (24).

As Edgardo Lander (2013, 18) argues, in the midst of these increasing tensions there was a shift from the notion of civilizational change and GL to socialism in its modern/Western conception. Also, due precisely to the clash of positions against and in favor of extractivism in both Bolivia and Ecuador in recent years, some thinkers establish a difference—a "bifurcation"—between "Good Living" or "Living Well," to which they attribute government positions, and *Sumak Kawsay* and *Suma Qamaña*, in Amerindian languages, which they associate with indigenous and peasant organizations and subjects. For example, in Ecuador, Atawallpa Oviedo Freire states that Good Living is a "theoretical utopia," while *Sumak Kawsay* is an "experienced utopia with virtues and defects, but with an already trod path" (2014, 159). From this perspective, GL can become a "new fad or adventure" among the many experienced by the left. It is therefore not surprising that the Ecuadorian government's objective seemed to be to instrumentalize GL, that is, to develop new indicators to measure it, which many advocates of GL as a new paradigm consider entirely pointless (Medina, Gudynas, and Acosta, among others).

Javier Medina (2014, 130–31) reflected along the same lines, arguing that the Bolivian regime had "a governmental *pachamámico* side," expressed by the Vice-Ministry of Decolonization, and denounced that the government was attempting to construct a neo-Andean religion to institutionalize GL, while seeking to implement GL public policies, among them low-cost housing baptized as "Productive Housing for Good Living." A new division was thus established, reaffirming the civilizational antagonism between Bolivian society, which is part of Western culture, and indigenous Bolivia, which belongs to the Orient. Finally, for Gudynas (2014a, 33), the image of "bifurcation" reflects a schematic division (developmentalist GL and nondevelopmentalist indigenous *Sumak Kawsay*) that oversimplifies a more complex debate. The Uruguayan environmentalist proposes a substantive use, that is, GL as a plural concept, as a critical platform against development programs that aims at overcoming modernity, thus going beyond both the capitalist and socialist views (43).

Whether or not such a "bifurcation" exists, the fact is that the conflicts unleashed between governments and peasant/indigenous organizations regarding extractive projects tend to reduce GL to an empty, generic, and empirically unsupported discourse. According to some analysts, there is today a radical lack of consensus regarding what was initially presented as a relatively common perspective among those devoted to the search for, formulation of, and implementation of "alternatives to development" (Bretón et al. 2014).

Finally, a number of currents of thought are committed to a North-South dialogue and propose articulating the idea of GL with notions originating in Europe, such as degrowth and postgrowth. It should be noted that the notion of degrowth predates that of GL and was popularized by the Frenchmen Serge Latouche and André Gorz and the Catalan Joan Martínez Alier. The advocates of sustainable degrowth conceive it as a process of democratic and equitable transition toward a smaller-scale economy, with less production and less consumption (Martínez Alier 2009, 2011), or as a "transition model to a stationary state." However, beyond the criticism of the consumption model and the emphasis on scale, the connection between the concept of degrowth and that of GL has few advocates in Latin America because, although the proposal could be viable in the countries of the North, characterized by sustained economic growth and a high standard of living, in Latin America it is more controversial due to the conditions of poverty. In a similar vein, the Basque economist Koldo Unceta Satrústegui (2014) argues that degrowth is a broad concept with a great capacity for impact but with potentially counterproductive effects. It can serve as a motto or element to unify different critical positions regarding the unsustainability of current economic growth, but it has the disadvantage of implying a frontal opposition to all types of growth, especially when conceived from peripheral societies. It is therefore difficult for the concept to constitute a viable alternative.

On the other hand, one of the most interesting proposals in this field of debate is Koldo Unceta Satrústegui's concept of postgrowth, understood in terms of three dimensions: dematerialization, that is, more efficient production with fewer resources; decentralization in the sense of democratization, that is, people's control over the decision-making process; and decommodification, that is, a society less dependent on the market. In particular, Unceta Satrústegui relates decommodification to GL, since it is precisely commodification (or the market society) that exerts pressure on those aspects related to GL and conspires against the construction of a solidary and egalitarian society. In this line, he proposes conceiving a decommodification strategy based on the categories outlined by Karl Polanyi in his analysis of the various forms of social organization. If GL is conceived as a new and plural web of relationalities, that is, as a different system of human relations, a decommodification strategy should be based on reciprocity and redistribution and on resizing the market (Unceta Satrústegui 2014, 195).

In sum, in spite of its manipulation, GL has been constructed as a dynamic, highly disputed, plural, and at times polysemic concept that aims at illuminating a mobilizing utopia and that, unlike other horizon-concepts, was born from the entrails of Latin America.

The Rights of Nature and Relational Ontologies

One of the central axes of GL is humans' relation to nature as an integral part of it.[6] It therefore involves other languages (ecological, religious, aesthetic, cultural) that focus on nature and that posit that economic growth must be subordinated to the preservation of life. This view leads to the recognition of the rights of nature (Gudynas 2011b, 2014b), which does not imply a virgin nature but the integral respect for its existence and the preservation and regeneration of its vital cycles, structure, functions, and evolutionary processes—the defense of life systems. The rights of nature propose a profound civilizational change that questions the dominant anthropocentric logic and becomes a vanguard response to the current civilizational crisis. In line with the GL or *Sumak Kawsay* paradigm, it proposes constructing a society based on harmonious relations between human beings and nature. Thus, while development aims at "Westernizing" life on the planet, GL rescues diversities and values and respects the "other" (Acosta 2011).

From a philosophical standpoint, the concept of Good Living or Living Well proposes a relational holistic view, whether it is related to the indigenous worldview as a paradigm (Javier Medina, Simon Yampara) or whether its greatest strength resides in other views of nature (Acosta, Gudynas). This legal/philosophical perspective, based on deep ecology, is illustrated in the new Ecuadorian Constitution, whose innovative nature accounts for what Gudynas (2009) denominated the "biocentric turn," as a way of emphasizing the shift from an anthropocentric view of nature to one centered on the latter as a subject of rights. Good Living proposes that nature is a subject of law, and as such, its rights and intrinsic values should be recognized.

This has several consequences. First, the new paradigm points to a progressive and essential process of decommodification of nature. Second, the paradigm of the rights of nature also recognizes intrinsic values of nature regardless of human valuation (Gudynas 2011b; Svampa and Viale 2014). Third, nature as a subject of rights demands a relationship of equality and respect. Equality must transcend the human, recognizing in nature a life that must be respected, a necessary interrelationship between humanity and nature that considers the former as part of the latter. Fourth, recognizing the rights of nature calls for another field of justice, ecological justice, whose purpose is not to collect fines for the damage caused but to restore the environment regardless of its economic cost. The criterion of justice focuses on ensuring vital processes, not on economic compensation (Gudynas 2011b, 273–74). It is therefore a matter of expanding and complementing the paradigm of human rights (anthropocentric view) by including the rights of nature (biocentric view). For Alberto Acosta (2011), this transition aims at preserving the integrity of natural processes, guaranteeing the flows of energy and materials in the biospheres, while preserving the planet's biodiversity.

As already mentioned, the debate on the rights of nature entered the political agenda thanks to the new Constitution of Ecuador. In it, nature appears as a subject of rights, defined as "the right to full respect for its existence and the maintenance and regeneration of its vital cycles, structure, functions, and evolutionary processes" (Article 71). However, this trend initiated in Latin America is neither shared worldwide nor adopted by the majority. Just as in the United Nations Conference on the Environment and Development (UNCSD) in 1992, known as Rio 92, the "sustainable development" model triumphed over other forms of conceiving the relationship between humanity and nature, in the UNCSD in 2012, known as Rio +20, the national states elaborated the document "The Future We Want" (United Nations 2012), in which the international community agreed on the notion of the green economy, to the detriment of other concepts such as the rights of nature and GL, which were promoted by different social movements in the continent (Svampa and Viale 2014).

On another level, there is a connection between the idea of the rights of nature and the recognition of other relational ontologies or worldviews. This is not a minor issue, since it implies a different perspective from the dualist ontology derived from the Western viewpoint, which separates society and nature, humans and nonhumans. As Arturo Escobar (2011a) argues, the problem is not the existence of the dualist view but the cultural ways of approaching the binary pair, that is, by establishing hierarchies or asymmetries (man/woman, nature/culture, civilized/barbarian, modern/traditional). This hierarchical classification of differences is one of the features of what in Latin America is called the "coloniality of power," which leads to the suppression or elimination of other forms of knowledge and culture. Escobar argues, "Anthropologists, geographers, and political ecologists have demonstrated with increasing eloquence that many rural communities of the Third World 'construct' nature in ways that are strikingly different from the dominant modern forms—they design, and thus use, natural environments in very particular ways. Ethnographic studies of Third World settings unveil a myriad of significantly different practices of thinking about, relating to, constructing, and experiencing the biological and the natural" (2000, 118).

There is therefore not one single universe but a plurality of them—a pluriverse—each with different cultural perspectives. These forms of relating to and appropriating nature question the constitutive dualisms of modernity and establish a radical difference between worlds, which are nonetheless interrelated (Escobar 2011a). These relational ontologies establish the territory and its communal logics as a condition of possibility. Interrelation generates spaces of synergy between the world of humans and the other worlds that surround the human world. These spaces are materialized in practices; they take the form of mountains or lakes that are believed to be alive, even though it is difficult to demonstrate this from the standpoint of European positivism (Escobar 2011a). An example of this relational view can be found in the works of Brazilian anthropologist Eduardo Viveiros de Castro, who in a renowned essay, *La mirada del jaguar* (The jaguar's gaze), conceptualizes this local model of relationship with nature in terms of Amerindian perspectivism. Unlike relativism, Amerindian perspectivism asserts that the world is populated by many species of beings endowed with consciousness and culture and that each of these beings sees itself as human, perceiving others as nonhuman, that is, as animals or species of spirits (Viveiros de Castro 2013, 16). In contrast to modern mythology, the common background between humans and nonhumans is not animality but humanness. Humanness is not the exception but the rule; each species sees itself as human and therefore under the species of culture. "Humanness is the universal background of the cosmos. Everything is human" (56–57).

In order to account for the clash between different worlds, Escobar replaces the notion of culture with that of ontology, which he borrows from the Canadian-based Argentine anthropologist Mario Blaser. For the latter, "the term political ontology has two interrelated meanings. On one hand, it refers to the negotiations that take place within a field of power in the process of gestation of the entities that conform a certain world or ontology. On the other hand, the term refers to the field of study that focuses on these negotiations, but also on the conflicts that arise when these worlds or ontologies attempt to sustain their own existence while interacting and mixing with different ones" (Blaser 2009, 82). The definition of ontology operates on three levels: The first refers to the ways of understanding the world; the second, to the concrete practices that constitute and generate ontologies; and the third, to the fact that these ontologies are expressed and transmitted through narratives—tales, myths (Escobar 2011a).

The concept of ontologies is very important for environmental or conservation policies, since it expresses a certain view of the nature/society relationship. Thus, an anthropocentric ethic based on a dualist ontology, which operates on the basis not only of dualism but also of hierarchy or asymmetry between opposite poles, constrains certain environmental policies that conceive nature as external to society, and progress as linear (Gudynas 2014b, 109). In contrast, the Pachamama perspective derives from different ontologies. In short, relational ontologies shed light on (a) different view(s) regarding the relationship between worlds and are therefore capable of providing concepts and perspectives that help us conceive a different environmental ethic and environmental policies unlike those derived from the dominant anthropocentric view (109).

Debate 3: Transition and Postextractivism

The discussions regarding alternatives to the dominant development model today in Latin America and its relationship to asymmetrical globalization are not new in the region or unique in the world, but the scope and vertiginous speed of the projects massively implemented today in the continent have raised the alarm among all sorts of organizations, activists, and intellectuals regarding the urgency to elaborate viable alternatives that, while taking into account the exemplary models in existence (sample cases, local and regional economies, experiences of indigenous communities), aim at a more general scale at the national, regional, and global levels.

In several Latin American countries, there are debates on alternatives to extractivism that propose a transition based on a variety of multidimensional intervention scenarios. I examine the contributions of the Permanent Working Group on Alternatives to Development (Grupo Permanente de Trabajo sobre Alternativas al Desarrollo 2012, 2013, 2015), promoted by the Rosa Luxemburg Foundation. For this group, the challenge consists in proposing and elaborating an agenda to put an end to extractivism, which implies conceiving a number of transitional scenarios based on two different levels of action: first, a set of public policies that act at a macrosocial and global level; and, second, interventions at a local and regional scale aiming at identifying, valorizing, and fostering effectively existing cases of alternative development models.

One of the most interesting and comprehensive proposals was developed by the Latin American Center of Social Ecology (Centro Latino Americano de Ecología Social; CLAES) under the direction of the Uruguayan Eduardo Gudynas (2012), who argues that the transition requires a set of public policies that permit a different conception of the relationship between environmental and social questions. The need to move toward a postextractivist strategy is related to the characteristics of maldevelopment models (which the author calls "predatory extractivism"). This proposal underscores that the discussion should be approached in regional terms and in a strategic horizon of change in tune with what indigenous people have called "Good Living." At the same time, it considers that "alternatives" within conventional development are insufficient in the face of extractivism, making it necessary to elaborate "alternatives to development" following a model of superstrong sustainability.[7]

At the public policy level, one of the most problematic elements is the opposition between social debt and environmental debt, that is, between social and economic reform and ecological/environmental reform. In this respect, extractivist progressive thought argues that extractivism is the only avenue capable of generating currency, which is then employed for income redistribution and internal consumption, or for activities with a higher value-added content. Thus, the emphasis is usually placed on increasing social spending, visible in the policies of monetary transfer to the more vulnerable sectors, the very basis of which is extractive income (oil, gas, and mining). First, it is true that the tax revenue obtained through commodity export has made it possible to increase social spending and implement bolder social policies—depending on the country—than in the past, but this also makes it possible to avoid tax reform (most Latin American countries have a regressive tax structure), which would imply other conflicts of interest with powerful economic sectors (Salama 2014). Second, the relationship between extractive income and social spending is also relative and depends on the country (for example, in Bolivia, Ecuador, and Venezuela, social spending depends on extractive income but not in other countries such as Argentina, where social spending is linked to a different tax structure in which the tax on consumption and profit is higher than that on wages). On the other hand, an increase in social spending is not exclusive to the so-called progressive governments; on the contrary, it is a general trend and includes a significant part of Latin American countries. Studies conducted by CEPAL (2012) estimate that currently a total of 19 percent of the Latin American population benefits from bonuses or social plans from the state.

Returning to Gudynas (2012), we could say that transitioning requires a set of public policies that articulate the environmental question, placing limits on production and ostentatious consumption, with the social question, aiming at the eradication of poverty and redistribution of wealth. This implies implementing fiscal reforms, a mostly unexplored territory in the subcontinent in spite of the various progressive governments. Such articulation should emphasize strategic planning and state control of natural goods, decreasing dependence on exports. In this respect, the transition involves different phases. The first phase entails a change from "predatory extractivism" to "sensible extractivism," understood as "that in which each country's social and environmental regulations are complied with, under effective and rigorous controls and internalizing the impacts" (Gudynas 2012, 280). Although this is not the best scenario nor should it become an end in itself (we should not confuse means and ends), it is necessary given the seriousness of the situation in the subcontinent in terms of both environmental harms and social deterioration. The second phase should focus on essential extractive activities, that is, those that aim at satisfying national and regional needs, in pursuit of people's quality of life and in accordance with superstrong sustainability. Therefore, a postextractivist avenue does not imply refraining from exploiting natural goods; rather, it implies "a substantial resizing, maintaining truly necessary projects that meet social and environmental needs and are part of national and regional economic chains" (280). More simply stated, one of the primary objectives is to reorient production to meet regional needs (at the Latin American level). This implies rethinking what we understand by regional integration and the relationship established with the various sectors of the economy: For example, with respect to food, it would mean redirecting agricultural production to satisfy the population's food needs instead of exporting agricultural commodities, thus endowing the concept of food sovereignty with real meaning.

Although these debates have had greater resonance in Ecuador, it was in Peru that a group of organizations participating in the Peruvian Network for Globalization with Equity (Red Peruana por una Globalización con Equidad; RedGE) took a step forward and presented an impact statement to the main political parties before the 2011 presidential elections. The statement proposed a transition scenario toward postextractivism, with measures to make a sustainable use of the territory, to strengthen environmental management instruments, to modify the regulatory framework, and to respect the right to consultation, among other topics (RedGE 2011). In an interesting exercise for the Peruvian case, the economists Vicente Sotelo and Pedro Francke (2011) demonstrated the viability of a postextractivist transition through two simultaneous measures: tax reform (higher taxes on extractive activities or *extraordinary taxes or taxes on mining overprofits*) to obtain greater tax revenues, and a *mining-oil-gas moratorium* on projects initiated between 2007 and 2011. With this exercise, which combines taxes on extraordinary profits and the suspension of extractive projects, the authors demonstrated that, far from losing tax revenues, the national state would obtain much more. This is not a minor issue, because these exercises are far from utopian or *pachamámicos*, which would make them impracticable. On the contrary, they permit advancing with public policies without affecting tax collection.

On the other hand, the environmental and social harms caused by the current model require conceiving alternatives and energy transition models, which is undoubtedly one of the most complex challenges facing our societies. As pointed out by Pablo Bertinat (2013), a specialist in energy and a member of the Ecologist Workshop of Rosario and the Permanent Working Group on Alternatives to Development, the impacts of the current energy model are multiple, ranging from the direct relationship between production and consumption of electric energy and climate change (greenhouse gas emissions) to the impact of large infrastructure projects (on territories, populations, and biodiversity), inequity in the appropriation of energy (only 15 percent of the energy produced is consumed by the residential sector in Latin America; the poorest sectors pay a higher proportion of their income for energy than the richest sectors), and a lack of citizen participation, among other issues. In this context, one of the ways to develop a transition agenda is to diversify the energy matrix through clean and renewable energy sources (such as wind and solar). But the continuity and reinforcement of the current model, promoted by the powerful oil lobby, seeks to minimize the role of other energy sources, for example, asserting that a model based on alternative energies is economically unfeasible.

Two fundamental topics should be part of any postextractivist energy agenda: deconcentration and energy efficiency. On one hand, the postextractivist energy model requires decentralization and regionalization of energy generation, transport, and consumption, as well as increasing community control over the energy system (Acosta et al. 2013, 335). Generalized decentralization is a necessary condition to democratize the access and distribution systems. This implies that profits are more dispersed and less concentrated, contrary to what happens with the large monopolies that dominate hydrocarbons. On the other hand, energy efficiency must be established as a requirement. A reform that involves modifying the wasteful policies in effect in the current transportation system (basically, automobile transportation) and the inefficiency present in residential consumption would result in significant savings or reductions in energy use.[8] Finally, it is necessary to reflect on the construction of energy sustainability from the perspective of a superstrong sustainability model, which implies consolidating the notion of energy as a natural heritage and as a right. In other words, as Bertinat argues, energy is also part of the commons. Thus, one of the great challenges is "the social construction of energy as a right and the decommodification of the energy sector" (2013, 167–70).

As we can see, the discussion goes well beyond the issue of extraordinary profits. It is a discussion on how to conceive the relationship between the economy and society in the middle and long term, as well as the relationship between human beings and nature from the standpoint of other paradigms; on how to advance on the path of what is understood as development and strong sustainability in social and environmental terms; on the need to include civil society in the collective decision-making processes; and even more so on the creation of models for a possible and desirable society.

7

Dependency as
a "Compass"

In this chapter I examine the current relevance of the dependency category through two debates. The first one is theoretical and consists in inquiring to what extent certain theories on globalization dialogue with dependency theory. The second one dives fully into Latin America's reality, inquiring into whether it is pertinent to analyze facts and data on the growing relationship between China and Latin America in terms of a "new dependency." Finally, I examine the category of marginality, which is now dissociated from the field of dependency and whose main characteristic is the diversity of paths to which its evolution and subsequent problematization have led.

Debate 1: New Theoretical Approaches and Dependency Theory

Social theory coined several categories to conceptualize society in the globalization era: "network society" (Castells 1999), "world-system" (Wallerstein 2001), "risk society" (Beck 1998), "advanced modernity" (Giddens 1993), and "Empire" (Hardt and Negri 2000), among others. Beyond the theoretical differences between these categories, most authors agree on the depth of transformations and on the significant differences between the periods before and after the fall of the Berlin Wall (in terms of the "social contract" and modes of participation).

Globalization arrived together with the consolidation of a neoliberal order that strengthened the dominant role of the United States as a guarantor of free trade and the free flow of capital, and of the legal and institutional regulations that constitute its pillars. This trend was further consolidated with the end of the bipolar world after the collapse of real socialisms, and was aggravated by the events of September 11, 2001, and the beginning of the crusade against "international terrorism." Also, the emergence of new economic blocks and political units that concentrated the activity of developed nations led to new processes of regionalization and fragmentation of the world economy, while illustrating the growing asymmetries between the nations of the center and those of the periphery. Finally, these processes weakened the national state as a regulating agent of economic relations and led to the emergence of new frontiers and new forms of sovereignty beyond the nation-state.

In peripheral countries, the dynamics of globalization further fueled the processes of transnationalization of economic power already analyzed by dependency theorists in the 1960s and 1970s, leading to an increase in asymmetries, to a radical dismantlement of the welfare state in its "populist/developmentalist" version, and to the emergence of an "exclusionary modernity" (Barbeito and Lo Vuolo 1992). As a result, in Latin America the transition to neoliberal globalization through the so-called structural reforms aggravated preexisting inequalities and led to the emergence of new political, economic, social, and cultural divisions, evident, on one hand, in the fragmentation and loss of power of popular sectors and a significant part of the middle classes and, on the other hand, in political and economic concentration in the hands of the elites of international power. The arrival of the new socioeconomic order included an opening and deregulation of the economy and a profound reform of the state apparatus, together with a highly exclusionary modernizing discourse. This twofold process, experienced to a significant extent by all Latin American countries, led to the institutionalization of a "new dependency," whose common feature was the power conferred on financial capital through its main economic institutions (the International Monetary Fund, the World Bank).

There were two lines of interpretation in this regard, which attempted to characterize globalization processes in Latin America and reflected specifically on the decline of the nation-state. On one hand, one line asserted that there had been a break with the previous period and understood globalization as the "era of globalism," that is, as a geohistorical configuration resulting from the intensive and extensive development of capitalism. This was the position of Brazilian thinker Octavio Ianni (1996), who in a renowned text proposed that we were in the midst of a "fundamental epistemological moment" (1–12), since the classical paradigm based on the national society was subsumed effectively and formally by the new paradigm based on the global society. The notions of interdependence, dependency, and imperialism associated with the nation-state were brought into question and had to be reformulated in the new global context, without overlooking the fact that these new global processes were marked by unequal and combined development (Falero 2006, 164). Hence, the concept of dependency was left aside, since it was related to the diagnoses of the 1960s prior to asymmetrical globalization and the consolidation of a supranational institutionality that significantly conditioned peripheral national states.

A second line of reading emphasized the continuities, rather than the changes, present in what was denominated globalization processes. Among other authors, the political scientist Atilio Borón, then executive secretary of the influential Latin American Council of Social Sciences (Consejo Latinoamericano de Ciencias Sociales; CLACSO), understood globalization as a higher phase of imperialism, providing an alibi for the dominant groups that attempted to increase their profits by lowering wages in a context of structural adjustment, generating dramatic situations in Latin America. He also considered that the diagnoses that announced the "disappearance" of the national state should be relativized because, while the recipes of the Washington Consensus had weakened the national states in Latin America and eastern Europe, in the developed countries of the West the state had grown, and public spending had increased (Borón 1999).[1] Using the Argentine case as a reference, Borón argued that globalization aggravated the countries' mechanisms of dependency.

Other analysts focused on the ways in which the so-called structural reforms were applied in each country and the changes fostered by those processes in the various national societies. In this line, from a comparative perspective, analysts such as Juan Carlos Torre (1998) underscored the emergence of a new socioeconomic order in its contingent and conflictive dimension, as a result of the convergence and radicalization of the new pressures exerted by capital derived from the opening of the markets and the increasing penetration of financial capital; they underscored the crisis of the populist/developmentalist state and the shock of hyperinflation, the weight of the presidentialist tradition, and the consolidation of delegative democracies.

In the late 1990s, the debates on the consequences and scope of globalization relative to the national state and the new forms of protest multiplied. From a critical perspective, there were at least three different lines of interpretation that critically dialogued with dependency theory. The first is the world-systems thesis proposed by US historian and sociologist Immanuel Wallerstein, who made a general reading of the origins and evolution of international capitalism, with a long-term perspective in line with Fernand Braudel's studies. Wallerstein argued that globalization was an older phenomenon that had existed since the sixteenth century, when capitalism emerged as a world system. A number of analysts have noted the connections between dependency theory (especially in the version proposed by Andre Gunder Frank and Theotônio dos Santos) and the world-systems theory. Wallerstein himself referred to dependency theory when he stated that he had reexamined the center/periphery cleavage proposed by the Economic Commission for Latin America and the Caribbean (Comisión Económica para América Latina y el Caribe; CEPAL) and further developed by dependency theorists. But to this division Wallerstein added the concept of semiperiphery as a third stratum that configured the productive spatial structure of the capitalist world-system, which allowed us to understand those regions located somewhere between the center and the periphery. He also emphasized the hegemonic role of the central economies in the organization of the capitalist system. However, in his opinion, dependency theory had two limitations. First, its perspective was not sufficiently historical because it failed to analyze long-term cycles; and, second, its unit of analysis, the nation-state, fostered the idea of separating from the capitalist economy in order to attain autonomous development. The concept of world-system, on the other hand, posited that the world economy as a whole was the only comprehensible unit of analysis (Wallerstein 1998).

Another reading of globalization that critically dialogues with the dependency tradition was the one proposed by Italian philosopher Antonio Negri. In *Empire* (2000), coauthored with Michael Hardt, the authors argued that the current process of recomposition of capitalism inevitably and irreversibly erodes the nation-state and leads to the emergence of a postnational sovereignty characterized as a diffuse economic and political network without a clear seat of power, understood through the notion of Empire. This notion replaced both that of imperialism and that of the nation-state, alluding to an unlimited totality without a center, which encompasses all of life and all social relations (Hardt and Negri 2000). Consequently, the forms of resistance (and counter-power) it generates tend to develop both at the local and at the supranational levels, as was the case in Seattle (1999) when demonstrations successfully disrupted the talks of the World Trade Organization. While Negri and Hardt's reading was quite potent in its characterization of the new forms of resistance and political subjectivation, as a general theory it emptied and simplified the role of the nation-state in its modality in the globalization process, and failed to develop a more complex theory of political mediations. Finally, the notion of the emergence of a deterritorialized and decentralized structure not only challenged the theory of imperialism but also seemed to contradict the facts at a time when, after the collapse of the Soviet Union, the United States was consolidated as a hegemonic power.

In Latin America Hardt and Negri's book was critiqued by Atilio Borón (2002), who responded to the authors' thesis in an acerbic and disqualifying manner, reaffirming a continuity in terms of the "persistence of imperialism." In spite of the unfriendly tone, which closed the door to any fruitful dialogue, Borón was right in reproaching Hardt and Negri for their complete ignorance of the Latin American reality and bibliography on the topic, which was not a minor issue when examining the global reach of "Empire." Perhaps in an attempt to overcome this weakness, years later, together with Brazilian thinker Giuseppe Cocco, Negri wrote an essay from a Latin American perspective: *GlobAL: Biopoder y luchas en una América Latina globalizada* (GlobAL: Bio-power and struggles in a globalized Latin America; Negri and Cocco 2006), where the authors criticized the state matrix and referred to the limits of the developmentalist model and those of dependency theory. For Negri and Cocco, the neoliberal aperture to the flows of globalization redefined the terms of dependency, transforming and expanding it as interdependence between the center and the periphery (48), thus closing the door to the possibility of a national development (or national-popular) project. The authors insisted on the idea that Empire did not have a specific national base but a transnational one (multilateral bodies, multinational corporations) and that it did not conform to the rules of imperialism and colonialism, thus becoming a sort of "universal no-place" (66). Finally, they proposed a new deal between emerging Latin American progressive governments and oppositional social movements, based on the primacy and mobilization of production over the forces of capital (71–75). Other important authors associated with the autonomist perspective, such as John Holloway, observed that no national state, whether rich or poor, could be understood independently of its existence as a moment of the international relations of capital. From this standpoint, the distinction between dependent and nondependent states broke down, since "the nation-states are defined, historically and persistently, through their relationship with the totality of social capitalist relations" (Holloway 1993, quoted in Rey and Castillo 2008, 28).

Finally, although this is often denied, there are connections between the decolonial approach and dependency theory. What is known as the decolonial turn underscores the distinction between colonialism and coloniality—while colonialism is a political and military fact, coloniality is a more complex historical phenomenon that refers to a pattern of power that operates through the naturalization of territorial, racial, cultural, and epistemic hierarchies (Restrepo and Rojas 2010, 22). Colonial difference is therefore not only racial but also epistemic—it refers to what has been denominated the coloniality of knowledge (Lander 2000). This critical approach points to the elaboration of a new paradigm, the decolonial paradigm, which refers to both an ethic and a politics of pluriversality, as an epistemology that questions Eurocentric models of knowledge. Sociologists such as the aforementioned Aníbal Quijano, Edgardo Lander, and Ramón Grosfoguel; essayists such as Walter Mignolo and Catherine Walsh; and even philosophers such as Enrique Dussel, from the Latin American philosophical current, are among its representatives.

In this line, the decolonial perspective proposes going beyond dependency theory as well as Marxism, the world-systems theory, and postcolonial studies (Grosfoguel and Castro Gómez 2007, 13). Regarding dependency theory, it had an influence on decolonial thinkers but mainly through the world-systems theory. It is true that Aníbal Quijano constitutes a direct link between both approaches—not by chance does the author argue that "the coloniality of power implies, in international relations of power and in the countries' internal relations, what in Latin America has been denominated historical/structural dependency" (2007, 121). However, other authors point to the shortcomings of dependency theory, among which is the tendency to focus on economic and political relations to the detriment of cultural and ideological issues. For these authors, the dependency perspective thus shares a tendency toward economic reductionism with orthodox Marxism. According to the editors of the book *El giro decolonial: Reflexiones para una diversidad epistémica más allá del capitalismo global* (The decolonial turn: Reflections toward epistemic diversity beyond global capitalism), this has led to two problems: on one hand, an underestimation of the role of the symbolic in the configuration of modern/colonial hierarchies and, on the other hand, an analytic impoverishment unable to account for the complexities of the "hierarchical processes of the world-system" (Grosfoguel and Castro Gómez 2007, 16–17). Santiago Castro Gómez

(2000, 97) had previously pointed to the need to avoid the binary categories proposed by dependency theorists to analyze the mechanisms of the production of difference in the globalization era, which implied reformulating critical theory in Latin America. Other authors also pointed to the binary logic based on the distinctions of underdevelopment/development, center/periphery, and autonomy/dependency, indicative of a mindset that continued to appeal to the hierarchies imposed by modernity (Flórez Flórez 2015, 250).

From a world-systems theory perspective, Ramón Grosfoguel critically synthesized dependency theory as follows:

> A peripheral nation-state may experience transformation in its form of incorporation into the capitalist world-economy, a minority of which might even move to a semiperipheral position. However, to break with or transform the whole system from a nation-state level is completely beyond their range of possibilities. Therefore, a global problem cannot have a national solution. . . . The dependentistas overlooked this issue due, in part, to their tendency to privilege the nation-state as the unit of analysis. . . . This had terrible political consequences for the Latin American left and the credibility of the dependentista political project. The political failure contributed to the demise of the dependentista school [and] enabled the reemergence of old developmentalist ideas in the region. (2003, 161)

In sum, beyond the critique of the weakness or absence of the cultural/symbolic dimension, the major difference between dependency theory, on one hand, and the world-systems theory, the empire theory, and the decolonial paradigm, on the other, resides in the (im)possibility for political/economic action by peripheral nation-states.

Between the Semiperiphery and Subimperialism

An interesting dialogue emerged with the subimperialism category elaborated by Ruy Mauro Marini ([1969] 1974). This category has the ability to reflect intermediate situations regarding the emergence of "medium-sized centers of accumulation" or "medium-sized powers." In the 1980s and 1990s, there was little room for the notion of "antagonistic cooperation" associated with subimperialism, in the context of Latin America's alignment with the United States. However, beginning in 2000, with the challenges to the neoliberal consensus and the arrival of a new Latin American scene, some authors saw the possibility of employing this category to explain Brazil's new situation, without, however, reiterating prior situations.

Two lines of interpretation emerged in this context. The first one alludes to the pertinence or not of applying the subimperialism thesis in the current Brazilian context as a medium-sized or regional power with a (new) capacity for negotiation. This perception of Brazil as a global (and not only regional) power seemed to be confirmed not only by Brazil's continuous reluctance to consolidate counterhegemonic proposals emerging from Latin America's progressive block—such as the Bank of the South—but also by the growing importance of the new block of emerging powers consolidated through BRICS.[2] Among those who considered this thesis useful and pertinent to explain the current situation is the political scientist Mathias Seibel Luce (2007, 2011), who developed it at length, applying it to Luiz Inácio Lula da Silva's government, and who argues that the difference between imperialist and subimperialist countries is that the latter are merely capital importers and are unable to become exporters, which is a determining factor. Brazil's dependency derives primarily from the role of agribusiness, since Cargill and Monsanto use Brazil as a platform to expand to Paraguay and Bolivia. Also, he returns to the category to reflect on the country's new role beyond the stereotypical notion of "Brazil power" as the natural leader for integration, as well as a simplistic anti-imperialism (Seabra and Bueno 2012).

A second reading proposes a dialogue between the category of subimperialism and that of semiperiphery, proposed by Wallerstein in the context of the world-systems theory. It is worth recalling that for this author semiperipheries function both as peripheries for the central countries and as the center for some peripheries. In addition, according to Wallerstein, although during periods of international decline or crisis of the hegemonic economy there is a certain room for autonomy, only some of these medium-sized powers can turn that advantage into opportunities, that is, into a real change in their economic positions. In Latin America, Brazil and Mexico constitute semiperipheral nations. Does this mean that these two countries, given their level of industrialization and regional geopolitical importance, have the conditions to "develop" not only in economic but also in social terms? Revisiting the notion of semiperiphery, Alfredo Falero argues, "The author's [Wallerstein's] response is that this is impossible in the system's peripheral zones. 'Second-hand industrialization' through displacement may occur, but not in the sense of the central countries" (2006, 252).

Comparing the concepts of semiperiphery and subimperialism, Brazilian authors Raphael Lana Seabra and Fabio Marvulle Bueno argue, like Wallerstein, that the latter is limited because it does not break with the binary center/periphery model deployed by dependency theorists, nor does it explain the complex role of semiperipheral states within the system, which is by definition trimodal. "The world-system operates through *two types of exploitation*. First, the proletariat is exploited by the bourgeoisie; second, the periphery and semi-periphery are exploited by the center. These are not really two different types of exploitation but complementary processes that characterize the complexity of the world-economy. In this regard, semiperipheries act paradoxically as 'means of balance' for the world-system and, given their intermediate nature, imply a specific social class division in those countries, which also makes them more politically and economically unstable from the system's standpoint" (Seabra and Bueno 2012, 80).

In the context of progressive governments, and from the perspective of critical geopolitics, Mexican sociologist Jaime Preciado Coronado proposed returning to Wallerstein's tripartite system to account for the emergence of a Latin American semiperiphery and establish its relationship with the "return" of the nation-state. Thus, the new realignment of the map of alliances and rivalries encompassed new spaces for negotiation and regional blocks between the center and the periphery. While the free trade agreements and the Puebla-Panama-Colombia Plan were part of North-South negotiations, the infra-structure and energy projects proposed by the Initiative for the Integration of the Regional Infrastructure of South America (Iniciativa para la Integración de la Infraestructura Regional Suramericana; IIRSA), the Union of South American Nations (USAN) / Unión de Naciones Sudamericanas (UNASUR), and the Bolivarian Alliance for the Peoples of Our America (Alianza Bolivariana para los Pueblos de Nuestra América; ALBA) were part of the South-South cooper-ation axis, led mainly by Brazil. The creation of the Community of Latin Amer-ican and Caribbean States (Comunidad de Estados Latinoamericanos y Cari-beños; CELAC) in 2010 also went in that direction (Preciado Coronado 2013). In this context, Brazil emerged in the international arena as a *post-neoliberal semiperiphery* by questioning the central world powers, aiming at becoming a world power; Mexico in turn did so as a *semiperiphery subordinated* to the US strategic project, and Venezuela promoted itself (until Hugo Chávez's death) as an emerging semiperiphery that sought a continental projection as an *antihege-monic semiperiphery* (Preciado Coronado 2013).

In sum, the panorama presented entails two different positions. On one hand, in the name of globalization and neoliberalism, the Washington Con-sensus implied a series of structural reforms that led to immense reconfigu-rations in the national societies. This resulted in the consolidation of a nearly unprecedented *new* economic and financial *dependency* in Latin America. In this context, some thinkers return to the notion of dependency as a common feature, though with little theoretical consistency. On the other hand, there are those who assume dependency theory as a critical tradition but believe that given its theoretical shortcomings (the state-centered matrix), there is no point in attempting to preserve its theoretical/methodological relevance.

In my opinion, the critical readings that criticize the state-centered matrix in the name of globalization and its changes run the risk of falling prey to the metonymic temptation, that is, of viewing a part as the whole, committing the mistake popularly known as throwing the baby out with the bathwater. There is no doubt that the concept of dependency must be disassociated from the 1960s diagnosis, closely related to the notion of the inevitability of revolution, economic stagnation, and the centrality of the nation-state as an agent for change. But we must remember that from its origins dependency was never a static category; rather, it was conceived and applied as a dynamic and recursive notion, as its main authors underscored at the time, when analyzing the great global transformations and the changes in the relationship between the center and the periphery. From the periphery, looking backward in the medium and long term, dependency theory has the virtue of shedding a different light on the successive economic and political cycles, with a perspective that critiques and/or complements the classical theory of imperialism. Looking ahead, the situation of dependency should be related in a more general manner to the global transformations of capitalism, which implies recognizing that the mechanisms of dependency themselves change over time.

In this context, although the notion of dependency is evoked by various authors, it is undertheorized and disconnected from the theoretical/critical field that originated it. Furthermore, it is reduced to a "situation," instead of being conceived as a theoretical approach. It could be said that we are before a paradox: Dependency theory has not been updated, even though the notion was (re)incorporated into critical language. However, dependency remains a *compass* (in the sense that José Carlos Mariátegui conceived Marxist dogma), that is, a guiding category applicable to the new processes of capital accumulation and the new forms of the relationship between the center, the semiperiphery, and the periphery, especially in the current context of hegemonic transition. In short, to restore complexity to the dependency hypothesis and endow it with new analytic dimensions, it must be updated in terms of both a "situation" and a theoretical approach—that is, restoring the recursive and procedural character that dependency theorists themselves assigned to it decades ago, in a more general frame of interpretation.

Debate 2: China and Latin America:
Strategic Cooperation or New Dependency?

When the relationship was started, the idea that China would become an economic competitor of the United States seemed unimaginable. But what was the alternative? If a country of one billion people organizes itself, it is bound to turn into a huge competitor. The fiscal imbalance is not caused by the opening but by unwise American policies. US Secretary of State Hillary Clinton once expressed her frustration with China by saying: "How do you deal toughly with your banker?"—HENRY KISSINGER, "Mao Might Consider Modern China to Be Too Materialistic," 2011

China's emergence as a great economic power elicits today intense historiographic and political debates on the hegemonic succession.[3] For some, it is evident that we are before important geopolitical changes, visible in the decline of the United States as the hegemonic power and the emergence of new global powers, among which stands out the People's Republic of China. There is no doubt that between 1989 and 2012, China emerged as a great economic world power. Its expansion is also related to the new geopolitical configuration that emerged from the collapse of the bipolar world (1989–91), which, in a context of US hegemony, resulted in a decrease in power asymmetries between China, on one hand, and Russia and the United States, on the other; the end of the colonial process that had implied China's physical expansion; and its admission to the World Trade Organization (2000), among other important factors. In addition, there was an economic/commercial shift from the Atlantic to the Pacific, involving a significant number of Asian countries (Japan, Taiwan, Indonesia, and Korea, among others) (Bolinaga 2013, 27).

However, the theory of the decline of the United States and the inevitable hegemonic succession of China contains ingredients of determinism. The first element that must be underscored is that China's global ascension has been peaceful and is the product of a strategy of collaboration, not opposition or confrontation, with the United States. The growing commercial and financial interdependence has served as a "restraint belt," in spite of readings regarding the "Chinese threat" from the standpoint of US strategic interests or triumphalist interpretations by Chinese think tanks, which forecast that the clash between the United States and China will be "the duel of the century" (Bolinaga 2013, 150–51). Reflecting on the characteristics of this relationship, Wallerstein (2012) wonders, "Are China and the United States rivals? Yes, up to a point. Are they enemies? No, they are not enemies. Are they collaborators? They already are more than they admit, and will be much more so as the decade proceeds."

Second, transitions or successions of hegemony are highly conflictive periods. Wallerstein analyzed three cases from a historical perspective—Holland (sixteenth century), England (nineteenth century), and the United States (twentieth century)—demonstrating that to gain access to the respective cycles of world hegemony, global military conflicts were unleashed that involved all the powers in existence at the time. In addition, the People's Republic of China is facing serious internal problems, in part related to its immense internal heterogeneity and its fast-paced urbanization processes. In this line, Wallerstein considers that US hegemony could be replaced by a chaotic struggle between the powers, in addition to a systemic—that is, civilizational—crisis that includes the planet's ecological limits. Likewise, there are those who argue that the international system will evolve toward a multipolar world where the different economic and political regions will play a role, for example, through the alliance between China, Russia, and India—or through BRICS more generally—which currently represent 45 percent of the world's population and 30 percent of the world's gross domestic product (GDP).

For Argentine specialist Eduardo Oviedo (2014), the end of the bipolar world with the collapse of the Soviet Union did not lead to either a unipolar or a multipolar order, as many people believe, but to a new *oligopoly*, with the hegemonic primacy of the United States, between 1991 and 2003. In addition to the Unites States, the oligopoly included other countries that concentrated the world's wealth, such as Japan, Germany, France, Italy, and the United Kingdom. In this context, Japan was the only non-Western country until China's arrival in 1998 (shortly before its admission to the World Trade Organization). The end of this period of hegemonic primacy took place in 2003 with the Iraq War, during which, far from enjoying a consensus, the United States faced disagreements and resistance from various countries, in contrast with the first stage of full hegemony. The rise of China, India, and Brazil signaled a reorganization of the oligopoly. While the superpower regressed to the role of a great power, China, India, and Brazil grew from midsized economies to great economic powers. This decentralization, however, has been economic, not military (since US military capacity largely exceeds that of other powers), but has implied changes in the power relations between the great powers (less concentrated economic strength, greater civilizational heterogeneity), which does not mean, however, that the current order has changed (bringing about a new world order) (Oviedo 2014).

Today China is the second-largest economy and the most dynamic and important economic pole in the world. It is the greatest exporter of goods on the planet; the greatest consumer of energy and automobiles; the main consumer of aluminum, copper, tin, soy, and zinc; the second-largest consumer of sugar and oil; and the fifth-largest exporter of services. It has the largest population on the planet—1.3 billion inhabitants with increasing access to the world of consumption, in a process strongly promoted by official plans in the context of a growing and accelerated urbanization. China is the world's greatest factory, whose commercial insertion depends not only on exports with little technology added but also on high-tech products. As consumption rises, its increasingly high-tech industry requires more energy resources and raw materials. For that reason, it has become the world's leading consumer of most commodities, which in turn drives up commodity prices. On the other hand, China is not only a productive power but also a financial power. Large trade surpluses and a high rate of domestic savings have led to a large part of this surplus being used to purchase treasury bonds from the United States, for which China is the main lender. It also has consolidated its position as the world's leading holder of international reserves, and today some forty central banks around the world use the yuan as their reserve currency. Two facts illustrate China's financial power: it is the third-largest global issuer of foreign direct investment flows, and in 2014 ninety-five out of the five hundred firms with the highest turnover in the world originated in this Asian country (Slipak 2014a).

In sum, no one can doubt that China is one of the main candidates to become the new hegemon in the international power structure, whether in the form of an oligopoly or hegemonic primacy, which may or may not translate into civilizational changes. After all, as Henry Kissinger (2011) reflected when asked whether he thought the Chinese believe they are returning to past glories, "The Chinese are often described as a 'rising power.' But they do not think of themselves as a rising power because, for 18 of the last 20 centuries, their GDP was the largest in the world."

In recent years, trade between Latin America and China has increased considerably. China has displaced the United States as a trading partner—so much so that it ranks first as an export destination for countries such as Brazil, Chile, and Peru; second for Uruguay, Venezuela, and Colombia; and third for Argentina. It is also the main source of imports for Brazil and Paraguay and the second for Argentina, Bolivia, Chile, Colombia, Costa Rica, Ecuador, Honduras, Mexico, Peru, Panama, and Venezuela. However, this trade is asymmetrical. While 84 percent of exports from Latin American countries to China are commodities, 63.4 percent of Chinese exports to the region are manufactured goods (Svampa and Slipak 2015). To mention a few cases: Argentina basically exports soy, oleaginous fruits, and vegetable oils; Chile, copper; Brazil, soybeans and iron ore; Venezuela and Ecuador, oil; and Peru, iron ore and other minerals.

Furthermore, the presence of Chinese capital is increasingly important in the region. Some examples serve to illustrate this. In the hydrocarbon sector, four large companies of Chinese origin are present in the region: Sinopec, the China National Petroleum Corporation, the China National Offshore Oil Company, and Sinochem. In 2010 these four companies participated in some fifteen extraction projects in Peru, Venezuela, Ecuador, Colombia, Brazil, and Argentina. Regarding mining and metals, China is present in most Latin American countries, even though the main destination for mining investments is Peru and, more recently, Ecuador.

Two of the countries that have expanded their economic relation with China the most are Argentina and Ecuador. China arrived in Ecuador attracted by oil and other strategic products such as minerals and energy. Today it is involved in seven hydroelectric projects and two large-scale mining projects, as well as oil extraction, since two of the five companies that signed new oil contracts with Ecuador are Chinese. China has also invested in the construction of a refinery on the Pacific coast and hydroelectric, transportation, communications, agricultural cooperation, military, and other projects. Today Ecuador is the country with the greatest Chinese investment in Latin America relative to its GDP (Chicaiza 2014, 48–49). Finally, regarding loans granted by China, in addition to their high interest rates, they are guaranteed with oil or raw materials (loans conditioned by commodities) and include an investment policy with the participation of Chinese companies. The loans and prepayments commit no less than 50 percent of the country's crude oil (52).

In the case of Argentina, relations began under the Néstor Kirchner administration in 2004, when Chinese president Hu Jintao visited the country and signed letters of intent to invest US$19.71 billion in housing, hydrocarbons, railroads, communications, and telecommunications over a decade. In recent years, the state-owned China National Offshore Oil Company acquired 50 percent of Bridas Corporation (Argentina). It is worth recalling that Bridas owns 40 percent of the shares of Pan American Energy and exploits Cerro Dragón, the most important oil field in Argentina, in the province of Chubut. Chinese capital is also present in the Neuquén basin, where the Vaca Muerta field is located and unconventional hydrocarbons are exploited through fracking technology. China also acquired Nidera, a multinational corporation based in Argentina that ranks fourth in the world in grain production, which assured China the control of seeds and entry into the GMO business. China has been investing in mining, and it will soon invest in dams, in addition to the huge railroad business and other important areas, to which are added the loans promoted by the Cristina Fernández de Kirchner government. Trade relations with China were further strengthened after the official visit by the then president of Argentina in February 2015 to establish all sorts of economic, commercial, and investment agreements that commit the country for decades, in areas ranging from energy, mining, and railway infrastructure to telecommunications. Argentina's Parliament, with a pro-government majority, approved the agreements without disclosing the fine print.

Latin American Views on China

The interest in China's dazzling rise and the questions regarding the type of commercial and financial relationship currently under development between Latin America and the Asian giant have increased significantly in recent years. As is well known, the People's Republic of China has been employing a language that emphasizes South-South cooperation, such as that used in the White Book, published in 2008 (People's Republic of China 2008), especially addressed to Latin America. This book argues for the need to continue to expand the ties between China and Latin America on the basis of the complementarity of their economies. It also expresses China's fascination with Latin America's natural wealth, proposing a trade integration based on a classical static comparative advantages approach, which further consolidates Latin America's role as a global commodity supplier.

In the progressive field, the prevailing interpretation is that the relationship with China allows increasing the margins for autonomy from US hegemony in the region. It was former Venezuelan president Hugo Chávez himself who led this posture, implementing a strong policy of rapprochement with China. Thus, out of the seven Venezuelan presidential visits to China in thirty-nine years of diplomatic relations between the two nations, six occurred during Chávez's term in office. Supported by oil wealth, Chávez saw in China the ideal commercial and political ally to distance himself from the hegemony of the United States and its constant threats to the Venezuelan regime. In this context, for some, the relationship with China acquires strategic political significance in terms of South-South cooperation, in a context that points to a prompt passage from a bipolar to a multipolar world where China, India, and Russia play a very important role in the region's geopolitical balance. This line of interpretation is supported by some intellectuals connected to progressive governments, who consider that the new geopolitical context and the natural wealth and biodiversity of Latin America create an opportunity to establish strategic alliances with China, which should be adopted at the regional level, employing the regional spaces or blocks created in recent years (USAN, CELAC). This position is illustrated by the former executive secretary of CLACSO, Atilio Borón (2012), who argues that the rise of the Asian giant is taking place in a context of growing multipolarity but that neither China nor any other power can bring together the combination of factors that enabled US hegemony after the end of World War II. There is therefore a geopolitical transition underway from undisputed hegemony (the United States) to multilateralism and concert among nations. Nonetheless, the role of the United States will remain crucial as guarantor of global capitalist development and, at the same time, as imperial enforcer. At the regional level, US military bases, the reactivation of the US Fourth Fleet, and the recent coup attempts in Latin America, with US approval, should be closely monitored.

In tune with this view, decolonial thinker Walter Mignolo (2012) celebrates the emergence of BRICS and reads China's rise as "de-Westernization and the racial distribution of knowledge," which, while it does consolidate economic coloniality (capitalism), points to the constitution of a polycentric order. Mignolo clarifies that this de-Westernization dynamic occurs in the political/economic sphere and does not imply questioning capitalism or development. In this process of de-Westernization of capitalism, the author includes China but also countries such as Ecuador, Bolivia, Brazil, Argentina, India, Turkey, Indonesia, Russia, and South Africa, that is, "strong economies and progressive governments in South America" (Mignolo 2012, 2013).

I believe, however, that these analyses are insufficient. In my opinion, the relationship between China and Latin America should be analyzed in terms of three major issues: The first is related to the notion of hegemonic transition, experienced less as dislocation and much more as the entry into a period characterized by polycentrism and plurality—albeit conflictive—in civilizational terms. Also, as Wallerstein argues, the transition is indicative of an immense systemic crisis related to both the crisis of capitalism and the ecological crisis. In this world in transition, it is worth examining the asymmetries in the new relationship between Latin American countries and the Asian giant. For example, Eduardo Oviedo argues that even though Latin America is a peripheral region for China, the conjunction of Chinese and Latin American interests has endowed the relationship with greater density, associated with the arrival of Chinese investments in the extractive sectors (2014, 16). In this context, peripheral countries like Argentina or Ecuador cannot establish the same type of relationship with China as Brazil has. In a trimodal line of interpretation, it is important to include the notion of semiperiphery to allude to the role of Brazil, which plays in other global leagues (BRICS), in addition to its ascendancy in Latin America. In spite of this, the relationship between China and Brazil remains asymmetrical and can be read in terms of "early deindustrialization," especially because of the government's inability to counter the effects of the "Dutch disease," that is, the massive export of raw materials linked to the exploitation of natural resources (Salama 2012).

The second issue is the scope of Latin American regionalism. It could be said that since 2000 we have witnessed the emergence of a "defiant Latin American regionalism" (to use Jaime Preciado Coronado's [2014] expression) with an anti-imperialist position relative to traditional US hegemony. Among the most important milestones was the Mar del Plata summit in 2005, where Latin American countries closed the door to the Free Trade Area of the Americas proposed by the United States, creating instead the Bolivarian Alliance for the Peoples of Our America (ALBA), promoted by the charismatic Hugo Chávez. Ambitious projects were conceived from a Latin Americanist perspective, such as the creation of a single currency (Sucre) and the Bank of the South, which failed to prosper partly because of Brazil's disinterest—a country that, given its role as an emerging power, plays in other global leagues. The creation of the Union of South American Nations (USAN) in 2007, and later of the Community of Latin American and Caribbean States (CELAC) in 2010, initially as a forum to process conflicts in the region outside of Washington, further bolsters this regional integration process. Yet the direction taken by the relations between China and the various Latin American countries seems to refute the thesis of defiant regionalism, which seems to have more to do with wishful thinking than with the actual economic and trade practices of the different progressive Latin American governments. On one hand, beyond certain achievements, regional integration is part of an emancipatory rhetoric that seems to be increasingly disconnected from the economic and trade policies adopted by Latin American countries. Among the commercial ties established with China, unilateral agreements by the different Latin American governments (many of which commit the economies of their nations for decades) are far from being the exception. On the contrary, they seem to be a relatively general phenomenon in recent times, which, instead of strengthening Latin American integration, increases competition between the states.

Finally, it is worth examining the destination of investments from China. All analyses in this regard agree that they go mostly to extractive activities (mining, oil, agribusiness, megadams), which reinforces the reprimarization effect on economies that operate under the so-called *Commodities Consensus*. In some cases, they focus on the tertiary sector to support extractive activities. This is aggravated by the policy of commodity-backed loans. These represent a threat even to clusters made up of small and medium-sized companies, either because of environmental pollution or because of the possibility of exporting products that were processed by local small and medium-sized enterprises directly to China. The

Argentine and Ecuadorian cases examined above may help answer the question. While Ecuador's main export is oil, Argentina exports mostly soybeans and their derivatives. It is therefore in a context of increasing commodity exports and hence greater extractivism that the discussions on Latin America's relationship with China should be located. Thus, while it is true that the irruption and quick consolidation of the influence of the People's Republic of China in Latin America appears as an opportunity to attain greater autonomy from the United States, all of the above—a purely rhetorical Latin Americanism, de facto competition between the various countries in the region, an increase in exports of raw materials—ends up consolidating asymmetries, fueling the trend toward neo-dependent extractivism, which increasingly positions China as a hegemonic pole.

In this context, a privileged commercial relationship with China based on the demand for commodities and the vertiginous consolidation of unequal trade signals the emergence of new relations of dependency, with characteristics defined by that country's unilateral negotiations with each of its Latin American partners. From an economic standpoint, this asymmetry has been translating into a process of reprimarization of the economy, visible in the shift toward primary extractive activities with little value added.

In short, the question of China's role in Latin America and the emergence of a "new dependency" must be read in terms of the dominant extractivism. In addition, many analysts believe that we are reaching the end of the "commodity super cycle" (Canutto 2014), which some thinkers relate above all to China's slower growth rate. Not only are most Latin American governments ill prepared for a fall in commodity prices, but the consequences can already be seen in the trends observed in trade deficits (Martínez Alier 2015). In other words, Latin American exports to China are quite large, yet insufficient to offset the cost of imports from that country. All of this leads not only to an increase in debt but also to an exacerbation of extractivism, that is, a tendency to increase exports of raw materials in order to cover the trade deficit, thus entering into a sort of perverse cycle (an increase in extractive projects, greater socioenvironmental conflicts, displacement of populations, and the like).

In sum, even in a context that can be characterized as one of global hegemonic transition, Latin America is heading toward a new situation of dependency. Everything seems to indicate that we are witnessing the consolidation of new and vertiginous asymmetrical relations between Latin America and China, which signal the passage from the Commodities Consensus (large-scale export of primary products) to what we propose calling the Beijing Consensus

(China as a hegemonic pole) (Svampa and Slipak 2015), whose extent cannot yet be fully assessed, even if the new economic, social, and political forms of neo-dependency are already beginning to take shape.

Debate 3: The Long Life of Marginality and Its Metamorphoses

The access of the marginalized to the goods and services market has to do with conditionings that go beyond marginal income and that, as a whole, configure a network of mutual aid relations, which can be denominated a "survival structure" and is an important part of the economic relations of the marginalized.—ANÍBAL QUIJANO, "La constitución del 'mundo' de la marginalidad urbana" (The constitution of the 'world' of urban marginality), 1972

Few categories have been as fertile in the field of Latin American social sciences as that of marginality. I do not intend to trace its evolution, much less to give an account of the immense bibliography on the subject. However, I cannot close this chapter without mentioning the different research avenues that emerged in Latin America related to the issue of marginality and its consequences, as well as some of the debates regarding an issue that touches the core of subalternity in its urban/popular expression.

In several articles, Aníbal Quijano refers to marginalized groups that developed as a stratum present in all of society, "about whose social interests and inherent conflicts we have conjectured a great deal without effectively knowing much" (1972, 138). He also proposed speaking of a "survival structure" to refer to "a network of relations of mutual aid" (94). In 1973 Larissa Lomnitz (1998), a Chilean anthropologist living in Mexico, revisited Quijano's reflection, positing that there were still unexplored mechanisms of reciprocity and inquiring into how the marginalized survived. Lomnitz set out to answer this question through a study that established a relationship among marginality, migration, and reciprocity networks, with ethnographic research conducted in a shantytown in Mexico City. The author argued that the survival of the marginalized did not depend on the market but on their ability to create a system of exchange based on kinship and friendship, which differed entirely from the rules of the market.

The study also proposed an approach to the subaltern world that went beyond the miserabilist description of scarcity and the scourges of the "surplus population" (Aníbal Quijano) or the "culture of poverty" (Oscar Lewis). Central to this was the notion of reciprocity as a form of interchange, on which Karl Polanyi and many authors of anthropological literature reflected. Lomnitz's pioneering work was followed by a series of studies devoted to describing and analyzing survival networks, understood as networks of reciprocity and interchange in the popular world, from an ethnographic and sociological perspective. Four decades later, we could say that social networks, the set of social and institutional mediations, and even more, their relations with the state in their various scales, are among the central themes of anthropological and sociological studies of the popular classes in Latin America.

In a similar vein, oriented to an inquiry into social sectors from below, the concept of social economy or popular economy arose in the early 1980s, related to the consolidation of economic relations of reciprocity or interchange of labor power outside of the market, and the resulting forms of communal organization. The studies indicated that, far from being the result of a temporary crisis, these organizational forms were a constituent part of Latin America's reality. It was also Quijano (1998) who, decades after reflecting on the marginal pole, wondered about the passage from it to the "popular economy" and, more precisely, about whether the sector of economic units organized on the basis of the community and reciprocity instead of the logic of capital could constitute the foundation for an alternative economy. The work of researchers on "popular economic organizations" developed among *pobladores* (members of a housing social movement) in Chile, led by Luis Razeto (2009), and later those of Argentinean José Luis Coraggio (2011) on social or popular economy, were among the most representative of this perspective. Another line of studies that focused on the survival economy is condensed by the concept of the urban informal sector, introduced by the International Labour Organization (ILO). In its 1972 report on Kenya, the ILO drew attention to the existence of a broad sector outside the formal channels of the economy. Years later, the Regional Employment Program for Latin America and the Caribbean, under the aegis of the ILO, with headquarters in Chile, defined the informal sector as "workers and/or enterprises in nonorganized activities that use simple technological procedures and work in competitive markets or at the base of economic structures characterized by oligopolistic concentration" (PREALC 2006, quoted in Salas 2006, 195). From then on, the category of the urban informal sector became part of the vocabulary of Latin American technicians and officials. This success was not unrelated to the fact that the notion seemed to appeal to a sort of value neutrality, unlike the much-debated and "ideologized"—according to some thinkers—category of marginality. For that reason, some authors posited that the category of marginality had been replaced by the concept of informal sector (Salas 2006). This is, however, only a half-truth because while it is true that a whole area of studies on informal sectors and public policies has been consolidated in Latin America (including renowned authors such as Víctor

Tokman, Alejandro Portes, and Bryan R. Roberts, among others), it is also true that the category of marginality is continuously revisited by different branches of critical thought related to subaltern studies, as evidenced by the many academic works elaborated since the 1990s.

Another important approach on the subject of urban marginality and its *socio-spatial dimensions* led to a series of studies on the forms of organization and mobilization of the urban poor in their demand for goods and services. In effect, the emergence of new struggles in urban spaces (land occupation) related to living conditions, and therefore to the demand for land, housing, and public services, gave rise to "urban social movements." Thus, the vast contingent of marginalized people occupying urban peripheries not only broke loose from the invisibility and apathy that some attributed to them but also became one of the main actors in the new social mobilizations, which ranged from direct action (illegal settlements) to institutional action (demands for land titles and various services from the state), adopting long-lasting organizational forms (such as neighborhood councils).

The dynamics of urban struggles illustrated the emergence of a new matrix of territorial action, with a strong focus on demands addressed to the state. This led to different interpretations. On one hand, urban social movements were included in the category of new social movements (Calderón and Jelin 1987), arousing expectations in some analysts. This was the case for Spanish thinker Manuel Castells, author of several books on the subject, including on dependent urbanization (1973) and on urban social movements (1974), who predicted a conjunction between (urban) social struggles and (trade union, political party) political struggles. However, the expected conjunction did not occur. Other works had more pessimistic prognoses, considering the pragmatic character of urban social movements, as well as the process of co-optation and institutionalization of action within the framework of "local development" (R. Cardoso 1983). Accompanying this diagnosis, Theotônio dos Santos, reflecting on social movements in the mid-1980s, wrote the following in a most somber tone:

> The issue of social movements is relevant today because capitalism is developing into state monopoly capitalism. There is no longer capitalism without the state; it cannot function without it. Insofar as it functions through the state, all social categories (from social classes, strata, social groups, etc.) are in direct relation with it. . . . Due to the more encompassing role of the state, the projects and actions of social movements tend to be redefined by the capitalist state. If it is a question of housing, it immediately becomes an item of housing policy, of industrial civil construction

policy, encompassing landownership, the financial system, etc., all of it* inevitably related to state policies. (1985, 50)

The distrust regarding the potential of these urban masses as a political actor and the stigma of a previously configured class weakness were in fact present from the beginning, subsiding only occasionally. It is not by chance that Lúcio Kowarick ([1979] 1996, 737) argued that it seemed to him more analytically promising to inquire into the meaning of these collective experiences by linking them not so much to the vicissitudes of the expansion of capitalism but to the revaluation of a social subjectivity, from approaches that emphasized the question of dignity or a political analysis of the dynamics of insubordination or obedience, introducing the problematic of moral economy and justice.

In the 1990s the transition to a new type of society, characterized by the association between globalization and neoliberalism, had a significant impact on collective action, evident in the limited efficacy of the traditional repertoires of action (marches, demonstrations, strikes) and, later, in the (re)emergence of new forms of direct action (looting, social outbursts, uprisings, roadblocks, and public shame actions, among others). Collective action systems went through a moment of inflection—of crisis and weakness—visible in the fragmentation of struggles, the focus on specific demands, local pressure, or spontaneous and semi-organized actions. As in other latitudes, these dizzying changes called into question analytic approaches associated with the social movement paradigm, employed up to that time to read collective actions, gradually paving the way to a different type of perspective related to the political model and the theory of strategic interaction. The context of social reconfiguration led certain authors who adhered to the identity paradigm of collective action to point out that social movements seemed to be "the big losers," underscoring "their inability to become actors" (Touraine 1988, 15–21); others referred to the "centrality of the marginalized," visible in the decomposition of the populist model (and its political mediations) and the emergence of a direct relationship between the leader and the masses (Zermeño 1989). Both authors emphasized the fragmentary character of collective action, its growing diversification, and, even more, the disarticulation of stable collective identities.

The inflection in the system of collective action therefore led to the displacement of the category of social movements—which had been hegemonic in studies on the subject—and enabled the use of the social protest category, which quickly went beyond the academic field, becoming a sort of a commonplace in both the journalistic and political fields. In this context, the category of marginality, associated with the theoretical developments of the 1960s, also made a strong comeback. It is important to examine at greater depth this reemergence before turning to the perspective associated with collective mobilization.

Marginality and the (New) Social Question

At the beginning of the twenty-first century, in a review of the literature on marginality, thirty years after the dependency debates on the marginal mass, as well as the marginality derived from the industrial model, Argentine sociologist Javier Auyero (2001, 52) stressed that several Latin American countries (among them Argentina) were experiencing a *new marginality* derived from the globalized post-Fordist economy, early and nonmodern tertiarization, and the implementation of neoliberal adjustments by the state. In my opinion, what was noteworthy was not the (re)emergence of an issue that was in fact never absent from the academic agenda but its magnitude, visible in a rise in unemployment and in the aggravation of different forms of job insecurity and social vulnerability. In addition, in the context of the flexible accumulation model, there was a growing consensus that the new faces of marginality and the resulting social fracture were not exclusive to the peripheral countries and that the problem of "exclusion" also affected the central countries, where it surfaced in various themes such as "the end of labor" and "the world's misery"—in short, what in French sociological terms would soon be called "the new social question."

The discussion was particularly important in Argentina, where, in the context of the implementation of neoliberal reforms, unemployment and underemployment rates rose exponentially. In this context, much of sociology and anthropology drew on the contributions of French sociology (especially Robert Castel and Pierre Rosanvallon, among others), as well as on the category of marginality coined in previous decades. As we mentioned, José Nun reprinted his 1969 article on the marginal mass ([1969] 2001) in order to debate the simple and direct use of the notion in certain works produced in the central countries that affirmed the "end of labor" in its different versions. Nun criticized the sociological view of the end of stable and well-paid wage labor (which included Claus Offe, Ulrich Beck, and Pierre Rosanvallon), conceiving it in historical terms from the perspective of the central countries. For Nun, from a broader historical perspective, marginality was part of the operation and reproduction of the capitalist system (and not merely its dysfunction) and therefore could not be read as a transitional form. However, he acknowledged that the profound transformations in the occupational structure in the previous fifty years had made it more heterogeneous and unstable, a situation further aggravated by the crisis of the large Fordist factory, which displaced unskilled laborers and generated uncertainty among skilled workers, for whom the notion of a "career" no longer made sense. In short, far from being a transitional process, the marginal mass had diversified; its effects varied depending on the sector, evincing the crisis of the wage society, which is a particular form adopted by capitalism, especially in the central countries. On the other hand, Nun argued that in the end, his views had proved to be correct in spite of Fernando H. Cardoso's criticism of the notion of marginal mass three decades earlier, due to its broad and unspecific character. For that reason, he insisted that the category did not apply exclusively to the phenomenon of unemployment, as some authors believed, but also to a diverse and plural series of modalities relative to the dominant sector of the economy, which can be analyzed through the successive changes in the occupational structure. Thus, the forms of precariousness present in the current system of labor relations were included in the category, but so were the forms of self-employment and informality.

On the other hand, there were several differences between the Latin American approach to marginality and the more contemporary approach to exclusion and vulnerability. On one hand, the notion of marginality was closely related to a society analyzed according to social classes, associating the categories of exclusion and exploitation (Perona 2001). On the other hand, the reflections emerging from the central countries were related to a sociology of social decay, as demonstrated by the successful book of interviews organized by Pierre Bourdieu, *La misère du monde* (The misery of the world; 1993), or the texts by Castel, who was unable to conceive other forms of social solidarity that did not involve the world of labor (in crisis) or protection by the state. In this context, the excluded or nonaffiliated were negatively defined by their difficulties in mobilizing or constituting a social subject or, as the Frenchmen Pierre Rosanvallon and Jean-Paul Fitoussi argued in *La nouvel âge des inégalités* (The new age of inequalities; 1998), expressing a flaw in the social fabric.

The thinker who went the furthest in both his historical examination of the preindustrial world and his rejection of the notion of a dual society based on the static notion of social exclusion was Robert Castel. In his renowned book, *Les métamorphoses de la question sociale: Une chronique du salariat* (The metamorphoses of the social question: A chronicle of wage workers; 1995), he associated the social question with the crisis of the wage society, visible in the destabilization of the stably employed, the establishment of job insecurity, and a deficit in available spaces in the social structure (the floating surplus population). From his standpoint, the phenomenon derived from the loss of the state's integrating dimension but also, at a different level, of the companies' integrating dimension. Thus, a form of targeted state intervention (a policy of insertion and not integration) and a policy of labor flexibilization and entrepreneurial competitiveness converged, disqualifying the least apt and excluding the young, who became "workers without work" or "the useless of the world." Castel also proposed a theory of social integration based on a processual approach. His point of departure was the general hypothesis of the "correlation between the place occupied in the social division of labor" (greater or lesser integration through work) and the density of relational participation in family and sociability networks (proximity support). There were therefore three different zones of social cohesion: those characterized by integration (stable employment and solid relational insertion), zones of nonaffiliation (lack of productive activity and relational isolation), and intermediate or unstable zones of social vulnerability, characterized by job insecurity and relational fragility. The zone of exclusion and vulnerability also reflected the way in which European social welfare societies had dissolved the community and social integration structures (proximity supports) that existed at least until the late 1930s (Castel 1995, 17).

Things were quite different in Latin America, where historically the deficit of systemic integration had been offset by the development of other social ties based on popular self-organization, as demonstrated by a number of anthropological and sociological studies on marginality. In any case, beyond the visible differences, reflections on the new processes of decollectivization pointed to the need to build a common ground between Argentine and French sociologies on the topic of marginality. However, this turned out to be an asymmetrical interchange. The self-referential character of European literature, embodied by its French sociologist representatives, contrasted with the search for a true dialogue proposed by Argentine sociologists and anthropologists, who insisted on establishing a comparative North-South perspective regarding the new processes of exclusion and marginality. The dialogue ended up being one-sided: In its self-centeredness, French sociology entirely ignored Latin American (past and present) intellectual elaborations, while, in a sort of renewed act of intellectual and epistemic dependency, Argentine social sciences adopted the presumably new categories emerging from the center, in an attempt to combine them with those derived from the Latin American sociological and anthropological tradition.

Finally, at present, the marginal pole thesis has been recovered by the Argentine Social Debt Observatory (Observatorio de la Deuda Social Argentina; ODSA), directed by Argentine sociologist Agustín Salvia, who in various texts has drawn attention to the existence of a socioeconomic context that accumulates two or more generations of members without access to effective opportunities for social mobility (see Salvia 2005, 32). Since 2007 ODSA has played a more important role in Argentina due to the low credibility of the official figures disseminated by the National Institute of Statistics and Censuses (Instituto

Nacional de Estadística y Censos; INDEC) after the Kirchner administration's intervention that year. For Salvia and his team, in spite of the economic growth experienced in the past decade, a marginal pole was consolidated, mainly made up of workers with unstable employment below the indigence line and beneficiaries of employment plans. In addition, there are the underemployed and "discouraged" unemployed, who are not included in official numbers (cited in Kessler 2014, 83).

The fact is that in a context of a traditional deficit of systemic integration such as that experienced in Latin America, the creation of other social supports for integration—networks of reciprocity, social economy, collective action—is a constituent part of the subcontinent's reality.

From Urban Social Movements to the New
Socio-Territorial Movements

There seems to be a certain consensus today among different Latin American analysts regarding two matters. The first has to do with the return of the notion of social movements. The beginning of a new cycle of struggles against neoliberal globalization since 1994 illustrates this solid return of social movements. There is no doubt that the challenges to neoliberal adjustment did not emerge from institutional politics but from organizations and sectors that were traditionally excluded or considered marginal, from indigenous and peasant peoples to the unemployed. The cycle began with the irruption of the Zapatista movement in Chiapas, which, as we mentioned in a previous chapter, was the first movement against neoliberal globalization, which in turn appealed strongly to the new Latin American lefts and had a significant influence on the alter-globalization groups and collectives that were emerging in Europe and the United States. A second moment, with a progressive accumulation of struggles against neoliberal reforms, began in 2000 with the Cochabamba Water War and experienced new inflections in Argentina in December 2001, in Ecuador in 2005, and again in Bolivia in 2003 and 2006, among others. The main protagonists of this new cycle were therefore social organizations and movements, which, through their struggles and claims, and even insurrectional practices, were able to broaden the political agenda and include in it new issues, thus contributing to legitimizing other ways of conceiving politics and social relations: the crisis of representation in the current systems; the demands in response to the violation of the most elementary rights; the defense of natural resources, conceived as common goods; and the vindication of indigenous autonomies.

The second point of consensus has to do with the importance that socio-territorial movements acquired. While in the 1960s and 1970s the process of territorialization was associated with the habitat and living conditions, since the late 1980s the territory gradually became the main focus of struggles due to the implementation of new localized social policies designed from above to control and contain poverty. More recently, in the twenty-first century, the disputes over the territory have experienced other inflections due to the new modalities adopted by the logic of capital in spaces considered strategic in terms of natural resources. Thus, one of the constituting dimensions of Latin American social movements is *territoriality*. Generally speaking, for both urban and rural movements, the territory is a space of resistance and also, increasingly, a place to resignify and create new social relations. In sum, for a significant and representative part of Latin American social sciences, Latin American social movements must be understood as socio-territorial movements.[4]

We should recall that Latin America continues to be the most unequal continent. Marginality is therefore one of the main issues that remind us of the consolidation and scope of social inequalities (Kessler 2014). According to CEPAL (2012), 19 percent of Latin America's population is on social plans (bonus policies or income transfer programs), that is, about 113 million people in fifteen Latin American countries, regardless of ideology, most of whom are women heads of households. This is undoubtedly a disturbing fact that confirms the consolidation of a marginal pole and forces us to reflect on the consequences of the consolidation of a welfare/participatory citizenship model highly dependent on the state, which offers subjects few possibilities to develop with (political, social, and economic) autonomy.

In sum, beyond the disciplinary specificity and epistemological nuances of the various approaches, anthropological, economic, and sociological studies have uncovered a dense web of local cooperation networks linked to the world of poverty and basic needs. They have demonstrated that, historically, due to their peripheral and dependent condition, territories in Latin America have been and continue to be factories of collective solidarity. Located outside the formal market and in the absence of the state, a large part of popular sectors have had to develop and reproduce through structures of reciprocity and self-managed forms of cooperation. In the Andean world, the persistence of the "community" is often key to explain the relevance of cooperation and interdependence networks, but in urban contexts of uprootedness, with unequal modernization and a plebeian culture, the popular/communal ethos must be generated from other places of interconnection and articulation, thus requiring the development of new solidarities.

Thus, the self-organization of popular sectors fosters a cyclic return to the first level of socio-territorial movements, recurrently raising the question of the scope of politicization of the marginal sectors, whether they are seen as potential bearers of a popular communal ethos or of a solidarity economy that allows conceiving an alternative society based on reciprocity, or whether they are seen as the confirmation of the fragmentation and polarization of the sociopolitical matrix and the consolidation of ties with the state through compensatory social policies, in a context of impoverishment and increasing inequalities. As a result, a variety of approaches were developed regarding this reality, associated with the persistence and reproduction of "marginality": on one hand, those that privilege collective dynamics and relate the process of territorialization of the popular classes to the possibility of reconstituting social bonds, of developing a popular economy, and of social movements questioning the existing order (albeit temporarily); and, on the other hand, those that tend to emphasize the negative aspects of the phenomenon, seeing in marginality the expression of a political economy of poverty, of a fragmented popular matrix, and of the consolidation of a marginal pole or structural poverty, highly dependent on the state.

This is a recurrent and unceasing debate for which there is no general or univocal answer, beyond the—often circumstantial or epochal—extremes, which go from the miserabilist pole to the celebratory pole, without excluding other possibilities of interpretation, illustrating the complexity and ambivalence of the issue. Whatever the interpretation, whether seen as possible agents of change or as structurally poor, dependent on the state and lacking political autonomy, or as both dimensions combined in an ontic perspective, these forms of subaltern solidarity generated from the margins of society have persistently challenged Latin American critical thought and political imagination.

8

Twenty-First-Century
Populisms

From 2000 onward, some countries of Latin America experienced an epochal change. Although many authors spoke early on of "post-neoliberalism" and even of a "turn to the left" or "pink tide," other analysts returned to the controversial and slippery category of populism. Furthermore, toward the end of the first decade of the twenty-first century, when conducting a necessary assessment of the so-called progressive governments, many of them fully consolidated and quite a few in their second or even third mandates, the category of populism started regaining strength, to the point of becoming commonplace once again. It is true that for some analysts (such as Ernesto Laclau), this characterization is not incompatible with the former; however, for many others—as I attempt to demonstrate—it is a very different phenomenon than it was at the beginning of the cycle.

Once again, populism as a theoretical category became a political and interpretative battlefield. But unlike earlier times, when a negative view predominated, its current return takes place in more complex and disputed political and intellectual scenes. For that reason, in the first part of this final chapter, I propose reviewing the theoretical perspectives on populism present today in the academic field and presenting my hypothesis on the subject, synthesized in the concept of high-intensity populisms. I also include a review of the main critiques of progressive populisms today. In the second part, I examine in greater depth the distinction between different types, basically between plebeian populisms and middle-class populisms, exemplified by the cases of Bolivia and Venezuela and of Argentina and Ecuador, respectively.

Debate 1: Theoretical and Critical
Perspectives on Populisms

Three Theoretical Readings

There are currently three theoretical positions on populism. The first approaches it from a mode of heteronomous appropriation and returns to several of the critical and disqualifying themes that mark the long history of negative readings on the subject. A second position does it from a mode of positive appropriation, viewing populism as a democratizing political phenomenon identified with the inclusion of excluded or abused sectors of society. In this line, the works of Argentine thinker Ernesto Laclau and several of his followers are particularly noteworthy. Finally, a third interpretative path differs from the first two, tending to read populism in its radical ambivalence or intrinsic duality, which allows conceptualizing it as a complex political phenomenon with both democratic and nondemocratic elements. An unavoidable question in the discussion of specific positions is whether there is an ontological predominance of either of these two aspects, or whether it is merely the situation, the context—the ontic—that determines which takes priority over the other.

Among the negative views are those academic readings that posit the recurrence of populism as a myth, as well as those, much publicized by the media, that insist on reducing it to a macroeconomic policy (squandering, social spending, and inflationary tendencies, among others) and political clientelism. My intention is to avoid those stigmatizing and simplistic readings and to focus on academic readings, that is, those that associate populism with myth, understanding it as a phenomenon somewhere between religion and politics, opposed to the democratic ethos.

This topic has been reexamined by Loris Zanatta (2015), an Italian historian who specializes in Peronism, who considers that populism evokes above all the idea of an organic community, is apolitical (it does not associate social justice with democracy), embodies the will to return to the people the sovereignty they have been denied, and, finally, proposes a sort of return to prepolitical values that it associates with a harmonious world. Zanatta (who examines several of the topics presented in chapter 4 in the first part of this book) replaces the idea of myth with that of an "imaginary populist ethos" and stresses that it "appeals to a view of the world that precedes and contrasts with an enlightened tradition in which liberal constitutionalism and the rule of law are its historical products" (2015, 34–35). According to him, populists thus reject liberal democracy, becoming the most powerful antiliberal and intolerant force of the democratic era (35). These definitions include many political experiences, from those that can generically be considered center-left or left-wing, such as the governments of Cristina Fernández de Kirchner and Hugo Chávez, to those clearly identified with the right, such as Lega Nord (Northern League) and the government of the media czar Silvio Berlusconi in Italy. It should be noted, however, that although current populisms still yearn for a homogeneous community typical of a prepolitical view, Zanatta believes that unlike "old" populisms, they are not strong enough to become regimes, combining that tendency with a more institutionalist and parliamentarian logic. They thus configure a "hybrid phenomenon," a sort of "populist animal imprisoned in a narrow institutionalist cage, that of the rule of law, from which it cannot escape" (238). In other words, the development of liberal institutions ends up functioning as a democratic corset that limits the expansion of the organicist yearnings of populist leaders.

The Argentine political scientist Aleardo Laría (2011, 242–43) further develops this line of thought, associating populism with mobilizing myth and archetype, two notions that the author relates to the Goffmanian concept of frame to designate the mental structures that shape the way that subjects understand the institutional and symbolic reality of the political world and that emotionally motivate them. In his meticulous journey, the author includes revolutionary myths, racist mythology, reactionary myths about the role of the masses, and the myth of the invisible hand of the market. Beyond ideological differences, which range from the left to the right, the common element in all of these myths is their imperviousness to debate or rational argumentation (305); this explains why Laría speaks of the "populist religion."

Beyond the fact that these disqualifying critiques tend to amalgamate politically opposite phenomena, in my opinion, their main problem is the fact that, far from conducting a critical/comprehensive analysis, they tend to reduce democracy to its liberal form, thus precluding the possibility of understanding it in terms of "demo-diversity" (an expression coined by Boaventura de Sousa Santos [2005]); that is, it is a profoundly liberal critique that questions the legitimacy of other forms of democracy, among them participatory, communal, deliberative, and direct democracy, which many collective forces postulate today.

Second, with an opposite perspective and based on notable theoretical work, a reading with very significant repercussions in the past decade is that of Argentine thinker Ernesto Laclau, whose work on populism led to political positions in support of progressive governments as a whole, especially the successive governments of the Kirchner couple (2003–15). In 2005 Laclau published his book *On Populist Reason*, where he developed the premise that populism constitutes a logic inherent to the political and, as such, is a privileged platform to observe the political sphere. As mentioned in a previous chapter, far from the ethical censure deployed by the heteronomous view, Laclau proposed conceiving populism as a rupture based on the dichotomization of the political space (two opposing blocks) and an articulation of popular demands through the logic of equivalence. For example, he stressed that while there have been important social mobilizations and movements, such as the Landless Workers' Movement (Movimento dos Trabalhadores Rurais Sem Terra; MST) in Brazil or *piquetero* (unemployed workers' movement) organizations in Argentina and Zapatismo in Mexico, they were horizontal protest movements without vertical integration (logic of difference). Popular subjectivity, on the other hand, emerged as a product of the chains of equivalence between subaltern demands. In sum, "populism is a matter of degree, of the proportion in which the logic of equivalence prevails over the logic of difference" (Laclau 2009, 59, 62–64).

On the other hand, for Laclau, the specificity of the Latin American situation was determined by the context: the traumatic past of the military dictatorships in the 1970s, the destructive neoliberal policies in recent decades. Also, although the notion of the twofold character of the national-popular does not disappear entirely, since Laclau affirms that the populist rupture can adopt different ideological stances (from communism to fascism, they are all contingent postures), in his later works populism tends to be identified broadly with the political (a theory of identities constituted through antagonism), in opposition to the institutional, which refers to politics as administration. Populism is important for democracy because it allows constituting the people, a sine qua non condition for democracy to function; it can therefore not be conceived or read as an anomalous form of democracy. Moreover, if something endangers democracy, it is not populism but neoliberalism.

Laclau's reading has had a profound influence on the current problematization of Latin American populism, without the prior and almost universal ethical condemnation it used to receive from the academy. Some of the readings on current populism either dialogue with or attempt to distance themselves from Laclau's pro-populist views. And yet it is important to recognize that his proposals have more followers in Argentina than in other countries. The dialogue has also resulted in criticisms in his own field. For example, Gerardo Aboy Carlés has pointed out Laclau's difficulty in accounting for populism's twofold character, that is, the displacements that locate it between rupture and the communitarian temptation. Taking refuge in an analysis that distinguishes between the ontological plane (that of being) and the ontic plane (the really existing populisms), Laclau radicalizes certain topics that were already present in his first reflections on populism, which he finally understands as synonymous with the political, "impermeable to being disproved by the political experiences themselves" (Aboy Carlés 2010, 31).

This assimilation between populism and politics has also been questioned by other authors. In a compilation including works by Laclau and Chantal Mouffe and others who dialogue critically with Laclau, the Uruguayan Francisco Panizza (2009) distances himself from the arguments of his Argentine peer, arguing that in his eagerness to differentiate politics from administration, Laclau concludes that the only form of politics is that which constantly creates and re-creates the space of division and antagonism. In this context, "permanent revolution" becomes a necessary condition for politics. On the other hand, if populism as antagonism is politics par excellence, it is also the negation of politics, since in the populist imaginary, the people's identification with their leader also defines the end of history, as well as "the liberal illusion of a society without conflict, the social order of Hobbes' Leviathan or Marx's classless society" (Panizza 2009, 46).

Finally, a third line of interpretation underscores the twofold nature of populism. Although this reading stands out for its critical/comprehensive aspiration, there are very different emphases within it. Thus, Paraguayan political scientist Benjamín Arditi defines populism as a recurrent feature of modern politics, which can be expressed in both democratic and nondemocratic contexts (2009, 104). In his more relevant works, he dialogues with the text of English thinker Margaret Canovan and revisits Jacques Derrida, to reflect on populism more as a "specter" than as the shadow of democracy, suggesting the idea of "visitation," "an unsettling return," which refers to "the undecidability that is inbuilt into populism, for it can be something that both accompanies democracy and haunts it" (Arditi 2009, 122). Along the same lines, Panizza (2009) reflects that a characteristic of populism in its ever-controversial relationship with democracy is that "by raising awkward questions about modern forms of democracy, and by often representing the ugly face of the people, populism is neither the highest form of democracy nor its enemy, but a mirror in which democracy may contemplate itself, warts and all, in a discovery of itself and what it lacks" (Arditi 2004, 86–99). Finally, the reflections of the Argentinean Gerardo Aboy Carlés (2010, 2012), although indebted to Laclau's perspective, open up to other speculative horizons insofar as he proposes conceiving populism as the coexistence of two contradictory tendencies: foundational rupture (which allows for the inclusion of the excluded) and the hegemonic pretension of representing the community as a whole (the tension between *plebs* and *populus*, that is, between the part and the whole).

At the other extreme, entirely unsympathetic to the populist phenomenon, are the readings of the Ecuadorian Carlos de la Torre and Venezuelan Margarita López Maya, who nonetheless underscore populism's bivalent aspects. López Maya, who has analyzed rentier populism in Venezuela (López Maya and Panzarelli 2012), adopts certain elements from Laclau (e.g., populism as a form of articulation of unsatisfied needs through empty signifiers) while analyzing the passage to more direct forms of relationship between the masses and the leader. De la Torre in turn does not consider populism an inherent danger to democracy, but neither does he see it as its redeemer: "Populism simultaneously represents a regeneration of democracy's participatory and egalitarian ideals and the possibility of denying the plurality of the social" (2013a). From a perspective that recognizes populism's radical ambiguity and the various models of democracy in existence, the author examines the populist experience through the government styles of Chávez in Venezuela, Correa in Ecuador, and Evo Morales in Bolivia, and their relationship with grassroots movements. These three presidents had similar discursive styles, portraying themselves as the people's saviors or redeemers after a long history of exclusion. He also argues that in Latin America there were different models of democracy (liberal, Marxist, and populist) and that populism shared with the Marxist model a distrust of representative democracy, while maintaining a view of democracy from a majoritarian perspective, privileging the rights of the excluded or what the leaders consider to be their interests, while the rights of minorities are considered enemies of the people (de la Torre 2010, 174; 2013a). However, the idea that populism can lead to authoritarian practices, although true, should also include the other two models of democracy (liberal and Marxist).

Toward High-Intensity Populisms

Paradoxically, in the early 1990s, as I mentioned in a previous chapter, with the arrival of the Washington Consensus, rivers of ink flowed in Latin American social sciences, speaking of a *new populism*. Uses and abuses made the category slipperier and more ambiguous, nearing distortion and conceptual vacuity. The aforementioned Argentine sociologist Aníbal Viguera (1993) rightly proposed an ideal type, distinguishing two dimensions: one, according to the type of participation; the other one, according to its social and economic policies. Thus, from his perspective, the neopopulism of the 1990s had a populist political style, but unlike classical populisms, it did not follow a particular economic program (nationalist or state centered). Adopting this analytic distinction, I propose calling that phenomenon *low-intensity populism*, given its unidimensional character (political style and leadership disconnected from a nationalist or state-centered economic program).

In contrast, beyond the obvious differences, today we face more typical political configurations that have points in common with the classical populisms of the twentieth century (those of the 1940s and 1950s). Throughout the first decade of the new century, the political inflections adopted by the governments of Hugo Chávez in Venezuela (1999–2013), Néstor Kirchner and Cristina Fernández de Kirchner in Argentina (2003–7 and 2007–15, respectively), and Evo Morales in Bolivia (2006–19), all of them countries with notorious and persistent populist traditions, enabled a return of the concept *in a strong sense*, that is, a *high-intensity populism* based on the vindication of the state (as the builder of the nation after the passage of neoliberalism), the exercise of politics as a permanent contradiction between two opposing poles (the new popular block vs. sectors of the regional oligarchy or the dominant media), and the centrality of the leader.

The reading of populisms I propose is of a critical/comprehensive sort and entails processual analysis, since the Latin American governments we characterize in those terms did not become populist overnight. In this twenty-first century, the return of the populist matrix was timid and gradual at first, becoming firmer and developing faster in the dynamics of construction of hegemony. While the Venezuelan process was promptly mired in social and political polarization, in Argentina the political scene was polarized only in 2008 due to the conflict between the government and agrarian enterprises over the distribution of soybean income, exacerbated to unbearable levels in the following years. In Bolivia polarization has occurred since the beginning of the Movement for Socialism (Movimiento al Socialismo; MAS) government (2007), due to the confrontation with the regional oligarchies, but this stage of "hegemonic standoff" ended around 2009, giving way to a long period of hegemonic consolidation of the party in power. However, in this second period, alliances with various movements and oppositional social organizations were broken (2010–11). In other words, the populist inflection took place in a context of a break with indigenist sectors but with a more limited or circumstantial social polarization. In the same period, Rafael Correa's mandate occurred in a context of growing polarization that involved both the sectors of the political right and, increasingly, a part of the left and important social organizations and indigenist movements. The counterpart to the consolidation of presidential authority and the growing establishment of Alianza PAIS (Proud and Sovereign Homeland Alliance) was the government's increasing distance from the directives established by the Constituent Assembly, as well as its direct confrontation with the most important indigenous organizations (the Confederation of Indigenous Nationalities of Ecuador; Confederación de Nacionalidades Indígenas del Ecuador [CONAIE]) and the socioenvironmental movements and organizations that had accompanied its rise.

Four clarifications are necessary, however, regarding this characterization. First, I define populism as a complex and contradictory political phenomenon that exhibits a constitutive tension between democratic and nondemocratic elements. What characterizes populism—we said in a text written with Danilo Martuccelli in 1993 and republished in 1997—is a dual conception of legitimacy, which goes beyond democratic legitimacy but falls short of authoritarian imposition. In effect, populism implies an unavoidable tension between acceptance of democratic legitimacy and the search for a source of legitimacy that exceeds it; a supplement of meaning or excess that in a way resides at the heart of all democratic projects but that generally fails to replace procedural and representative democracy entirely. Also, it is in terms of other forms of democracy (especially forms of plebeian democracy) that populism is best understood, since it largely responds to the (historical) need to repair offenses and shorten the distance between representatives and the represented, a gap consolidated during the long period of liberal/conservative domination, under military dictatorships, or, more recently, after the neoliberal reforms of the 1990s.

Second, as has been repeatedly observed, populism understands politics in terms of polarization and binary schemes, which has several consequences: On one hand, it implies constituting a dichotomous space divided into two opposing blocs; on the other hand, the binary reconfiguration of the political field implies selecting certain antagonisms and establishing a hierarchy among them, to the detriment of others. As a result, other conflicts are concealed or obscured, denying or minimizing their relevance and/or validity, excluding them from the political agenda to a significant extent.

Third, the constitutive tension inherent to populisms sooner or later brings to the fore a disturbing question—actually, the fundamental question in politics: What type of hegemony is being built in this dangerous and unavoidable tension between the democratic and the nondemocratic, between a pluralistic and an organicistic conception of democracy, between the inclusion of demands and the denial of differences?

Fourth, we must take into account the existence of different types of populisms, related to social class conditions and/or interpellation, as demonstrated by the extensive literature on the subject. In this respect, I propose establishing a distinction between, on one hand, plebeian populisms more closely related to the actions of popular sectors, which have developed more innovative and radical policies, thus leading to processes of grassroots redistribution of social power (Bolivia, Venezuela), and, on the other hand, middle-class populisms, which have empowered—even at the cost of interclass fragmentation—the middle sectors (Argentina, Ecuador). Even if both Argentine and Ecuadorian populisms emerged out of plebeian mobilizations, they are far from having resulted in a redistribution of social power; nor were they anti-elitist populisms that challenged the so-called legitimate culture (they instead reinforced middle-class values, whether progressive or technocratic-meritocratic), nor did they attempt to promote a paradigm of participation, as was the case—at least in part—in Venezuela and Bolivia.

In sum, my hypothesis is that we are witnessing a return of high-intensity populism, since current experiences are oriented toward building a certain type of hegemony whose structure of political intelligibility is based on bipolarity and the undisputed role of the leader. The polarization processes implied a reconfiguration of the populist matrix, which, through a recursive dynamic, established itself through opposition and, at the same time, the absorption and rejection of elements from other oppositional matrices—the indigenous/peasant narrative, various classical or traditional lefts, the new autonomist lefts—which played an important role at the beginning of the epochal change. Thus, double reference or constitutive tension, polarization and reading grid, construction of hegemony, and the existence of different types are interconnected aspects that, in my opinion, constitute the unavoidable point of departure for understanding today's populisms in Latin America.

Criticisms of Really Existing Progressive Populisms

Criticisms of populism reveal multiple ideological differences, not only between the right and populism, but also between really existing lefts, including both the traditional left and ecologist, Indianist, and autonomist lefts. In Latin America there are different lines of historical accumulation, with their organizational forms and their ways of conceiving politics and social change, which have attempted to articulate—successfully or not—the national-popular in counter-hegemonic terms. For that reason, there are various oppositional sociopolitical matrices, including the populist matrix, the indigenous/peasant communal matrix, the classical Marxist or partisan left, and, more recently, the "new" autonomist narrative.

Yet in spite of this plurality of matrices, in Latin America the national-popular, far from being related to the socialist alternative, as Juan Carlos Portantiero analyzed in an article mentioned in chapter 4 (1991), is—recurrently and predominantly—associated with the populist hypothesis. Since 1940 really existing populisms have articulated most national-popular experiences in the region, giving rise to a specific political/cultural tradition, a memory of struggles, and a stock of narratives and available organizational forms in each country, which over time delineated what I call here the *sociopolitical matrix*. On one hand, beyond the differences, the sociopolitical matrix of populism manifests certain common topics: It is inscribed in "middle-term memory" (the populist experiences of the 1930s, 1940s, and 1950s) and tends to stand on the triple axis of the affirmation of the nation, a redistributive and conciliatory state, and the relationship between a charismatic leader and the organized masses (the people). The nationalization of the worker and peasant masses and their transformation into citizens was the result of this political process, which led to the consolidation of a statist—some would say "state-centered"—matrix embodied in the leader. On the other hand, while each matrix has a certain configuration, the various national contexts and internal tensions endowed each particular case with a specific dynamism and historicity.

Thus, each matrix has a specific national history in accordance with the country's organizational developments, its encounters and differences with other sociopolitical matrices, and its role in the various contexts of resistance, crises, and opportunities derived from new political situations. Sociopolitical matrices therefore do not exist in a pure state, since the different political dynamics have resulted in processes of intersection and conjunction (between Indianism and Marxism, Indianism and the populist matrix, Indianism and the narrative of autonomy, and Marxism and autonomism, to cite a few examples), as well as conflict, collision, and disjunction, which can heighten differences in terms of conceptions and ways of thinking and of doing politics.

The critiques of really existing populisms can be summarized according to three main aspects: a political/institutional aspect that emphasizes the authoritarian/totalitarian temptation of the various populist regimes; a political and economic aspect that underscores the absence of an alternative model and its distance from a leftist approach; and an eco-territorial one that criticizes extractivism and the lack of alternative development models.

The first perspective (1) emerges in the context of political polarization and questions populism's democratic nature. Insofar as populism expresses itself through an extreme antagonism and dichotomy of the political space, the critiques underscore the persistence or reinforcement of its authoritarian features; the consolidation of plebiscitary and *caudillista* leaderships, bolstered by the extreme concentration of presidential power; a disregard for the division of state powers; and the clientelist use of the state apparatus (redistributive populism)—in sum, a concern over the ever-controversial relationships between populism and the republican ethos.

The second criticism (2) is political and economic and questions populism's presumed turn to the left as well as its scope, based on the lack of an alternative economic program or model. It criticizes the fact that Latin American populist governments accepted the process of asymmetrical globalization, and with it the rules of the game, which places limits on any income and wealth redistribution policy. This critique raised questions regarding the Venezuelan case in particular, which explicitly wagered on the construction of an alternative model—"twenty-first-century socialism"—through the reproduction of communal councils and other structures that illustrate participatory democracy or popular power.

On the other hand, critiques from the left point out that while social welfare policies have reduced poverty, they consolidated an assistentialist model that fosters clientelism and dependence on the state. Furthermore, really existing populisms have implemented only minor reforms to the tax system, if at all, taking advantage of the Commodities Consensus but failing to tax the most powerful sectors. Finally, in spite of nationalization processes (whose scope must be analyzed in each particular case) and their relevance, or lack thereof, in terms of a "turn to the left," the critiques tend to focus on the economic alliances established with large transnational corporations (agribusiness, industry, extractive sectors).

The third critique (3), which I call eco-territorial, is of a systemic nature, focusing on the relationship with the global environmental crisis, arguing that Latin American populisms not only maintain the productivist matrix of hegemonic modernity but have been implementing a state-centered policy that consolidates extractivism, in spite of the eco-communal narratives initially deployed by the Bolivian and Ecuadorian governments or Chavismo's critical statements regarding the rentier and extractive nature of Venezuelan society. The eco-territorial critique also exhibits an elective affinity with the autonomist critique regarding the construction of power and the empowerment of social subjects, while establishing an inherent relationship between (mal)development models, environmental issues, and democratic regression.

It is important to underscore that the three critiques are rarely intercon-nected. Rather, they tend to be deployed in isolation—although there are connections between critiques 2 and 3, the relationships between them can be conflictive (as has always been the case between *indigenismo* and Marxist lefts and between the new ecologist left and the classical left). On the other hand, al-though critiques 2 and 3 tend to include critique 1 (hyperpresidentialism, statism, corruption, and the emergence of a new political oligarchy, the failure to separate state powers), critique 1 is less likely to include 2 or 3, even though in the context of certain conflicts they have sometimes converged (as in the case of the Isiboro Sécure National Park and Indigenous Territory; Territorio Indígena y Parque Nacional Isiboro-Sécure [TIPNIS] in Bolivia), resulting in long-lasting dis-cords due to the opportunistic appropriation of arguments from critique 3 by sectors of the right. Also, although critique 1 is not exclusive of institutionalist sectors, since it encompasses all political opposition, it tends to be related to a more liberal/conservative perspective. Furthermore, both perspectives 1 and 2, the latter associated with the classical left, are part of the repertoire of traditional criticisms of populism. Such is not the case with critique 3, which reflects the emergence of a new ethos associated with socioenvironmental mobilizations, an eco-communal narrative, the defense of other languages that value nature, and the proposal of alternatives and transitional configurations to overcome ex-tractivism. Far from focusing only on technical issues, the critique of extractiv-ism denounces a logic of regional dispossession beneficial to rapacious capital-ism on a global scale, which consolidates vertical processes at the local/national level related to rent seeking that run counter to democratizing processes.

In response to those critiques, the advocates of progressive/populist govern-ments have developed a number of strategies. The most common is to group together the three types of criticism, denouncing their conservative nature and their connection with right-wing positions. There are plenty of arguments that point to the governments' anti-imperialist dynamics (their opposition to the United States) and a conspiratorial perspective (criticisms can only favor the political right). They also highlight the emergence of a defiant and anti-imperialist regionalism (evident in the various regional bodies, from USAN to CELAC). More specifically, regarding critique 1, the arguments point to the opposition's conservative and reactionary character (regional oligarchies, hege-monic media, other economic actors) in response to the inclusive and egalitar-ian policies proposed by the new governments.

Regarding critique 2 (that populism does not represent a true turn to the left), populism attempts not only to portray itself as the only leftist option that is possible, viable, realistic, and truly revolutionary but also to marginalize those criticisms by underscoring the "testimonial" character of the classical (Marxist) left. Finally, regarding critique 3, the response also resorts to the discourse of (political, instead of economic) realism, proposing that the social question (redistribution, social justice) runs counter to the environmental question (environmental justice, protection of the commons). Álvaro García Linera (2012) has developed an emblematic critique of the critique of extractivism, reducing the latter to "a technical relation with nature." In addition, in some contexts (Argentina, Bolivia), the consolidation of hyperleadership or hyperpresidentialism is justified with arguments that posit that the demands for autonomy/self-determination have more to do with the political positions of radical intellectuals than with a demand for democratization and empowerment of subaltern sectors.

Debate 2: Types of Really Existing Populisms

What are the most noteworthy features and political particularities of really existing populisms in twenty-first-century Latin America? To begin with, we should bear in mind that the governments characterized today as populist were preceded by intense anti-neoliberal social mobilizations; they all initiated a cycle of political stability; they all brought the (regulatory, mediating) state to the forefront; they all deployed important social policies (social welfare programs) to alleviate the crisis and reduce poverty; they all implied extraordinary processes of concentration of power in the executive branch; and, regarding the construction of power and their relations with social organizations, they all sought to consolidate a model of social participation controlled by the state.

In any case, in my opinion, a real characterization requires looking beyond the similarities, examining the specificities of the different historical processes. One way of doing so is to ask what models of democracy they advocate, which social sectors are empowered, and what the characteristics of the relationship between the governing party and social organizations are. In this regard, I propose distinguishing between, on one hand, plebeian populisms that aim at redistributing social power by empowering popular sectors and, on the other hand, middle-class populisms led by the middle sectors through different means (cultural/media apparatus or technocratic/meritocratic model). While the former corresponds to Bolivia and Venezuela, the latter refers to Argentina and Ecuador. In what follows, I attempt to characterize these two types of populisms in existence today.

While in expressive and discursive terms the plebeian entails a process of self-affirmation of the popular as a denied and excluded being, in cultural and political terms it implies an iconoclastic and anti-elitist challenge to the dominant culture, and especially to the cultural ethos of the middle classes. It is not by chance that subaltern class movements that combine the popular, ethnic miscegenation, the working class, and the marginal tend to be unanimously repudiated by the dominant classes and broad middle-class sectors.

Also, as Margarita López Maya (2000, 2005) argues, the process of politicization of the plebeian is associated with occupying the streets and public spaces. Thus, in general, when speaking of the plebeian in Latin America, certain cultural features of the excluded are highlighted, but when speaking specifically of the irruption of the plebeian, this cultural and symbolic dimension is linked to powerful processes of social change and protagonism of the lower classes in the streets. Historically, given the highly heterogeneous nature of the popular in Latin America, the notion of the plebeian is present in many popular social movements and organizations, without, however, being exclusively associated with workers' organizations or a specific political party. In Argentina in the 1950s, for example, Peronism was the political and countercultural incarnation of the workerist plebeian, but in the late 1990s, in the midst of structural adjustment, these plebeian elements reappeared in the new socio-territorial movements (unemployed or *piquetero* organizations), rather than in grassroots organizations linked to the Partido Justicialista (Justicialist Party), which at the time had shifted to neoliberalism. Likewise, in Bolivia the closure of the mines (1985) led to a crisis of the mineworker narrative linked to the populist-nationalist model. However, other forms of plebeian protest emerged from a conglomerate of rural and urban organizations—peasants, indigenous people, urban and informal workers—giving rise to a new popular and emancipatory narrative. This new emergence of the popular conceived as a "plebeian irruption," with its different "lines of historical accumulation and structures of rebellion," was the focus of the political/sociological analyses of Grupo Comuna (Commune Group) (Raquel Gutiérrez, Álvaro García Linera, Luis Tapia, Raúl Prada, and Oscar Vega). In the same line, Chavismo's plebeian character has often been underscored, among others by the aforementioned Margarita López Maya, who spoke of the origins of Chavismo as a "second plebeian wave" (the first one having occurred from 1945 to 1948), "a new incarnation of politics as one of the main means for upward social mobility along with the army" (quoted in Saint-Upéry 2008a,

131). Finally, in the case of Ecuador, the plebeian emergence has also been a subject of reflection (Saint-Upéry 2008b; F. Ramírez 2010).

It is clear that plebeian protagonism is an important variable in current populisms. However, even though current populisms have plebeian social bases and political and cultural elements, in their dynamics of political construction and accumulation they do not necessarily remain as such. Moreover, within populism, the disruptive presence of the plebeian can be conceived either as central or defining or as episodic or circumstantial, depending on the situation, without necessarily assuming a decisive role in the process of construction of national-state hegemony.

From this standpoint, even under different modalities, Bolivia and Venezuela ended up consolidating as populisms "from below," unlike Argentina and Ecuador. Otherwise stated, unlike the Bolivian and Venezuelan experiences, which reflect different types of plebeian populisms, which partly explains their radicalism, the Argentine and Ecuadorian cases articulate the plebeian in an episodic or circumstantial manner, or tend to appeal to it only in the process of plebiscitary and decisionist construction of leadership.

The Bolivian political process is without a doubt one of the richest and most exciting in the current Latin American scene. Three main elements mark its uniqueness in the region: First, a process of change emerged from the entrails of social movements. In the context of a crisis of the old political parties, social organizations and movements developed a significant capacity for mobilization and political/social self-representation. Thus, the horizon of possibilities, and even more Evo Morales's presidential candidacy, was forged in the context of the struggles against neoliberal reforms, which gained momentum in 2000 with the Water War in Cochabamba. The instituting corollary was the "October agenda" in 2005, shared by an important group of social organizations and movements, synthesized in two slogans: "nationalization of hydrocarbons" and "Constituent Assembly."

Second, this process of change brought to the presidency, for the first time in Bolivian history, a trade unionist from the peasant movement. His uniqueness can only be compared to that of another Latin American leader, Luiz Inácio Lula da Silva, a labor leader from the militant industrial union movement, twice president of Brazil. Evo Morales not only participated in the trade union movement but was also of indigenous origin. In a country with a very significant presence of historically marginalized and excluded indigenous peoples and nations, Morales's election implied a revolution from a political and symbolic standpoint. However, his rise to power and the opening of a new political context inevitably implied a reconfiguration of the difficult relationship between social movements and the new government, whose dynamics gradually shaped the specific contours and tenor of the project for change.

Third, the process of political/state construction required overcoming many challenges. In a previous chapter I referred to the conflicts and tensions experienced in Evo Morales's first years in power. Without reiterating them, it is worth recalling that his government (2006–10) can be understood from the standpoint of two conflicts: an external one, with regional oligarchies; and an internal one, regarding the two dimensions of the project for change, the indigenous/peasant communal line and the populist/statist line. The confrontation between, on one hand, the new block in power, led by MAS and accompanied by a number of social organizations, some leftist parties, and independent leaders, and, on the other hand, the regional oligarchies of the Media Luna region (Santa Cruz, Tarija, Beni, and Pando), marked Morales's first mandate, leading to an apparent "catastrophic impasse," finally settled in favor of the government in 2009. After this stage the MAS focused on consolidating the new political project. In this context, the twofold dynamics of the decolonizing project acquired more specific features, and the country entered a new period characterized by the growing hegemony of the MAS and the beginning of a specifically populist phase.

The government's flagships were the policy of bonuses (social programs), land distribution (a new agrarian reform), economic growth and stability, and nationalization of strategic companies, together with the advancement of the hydrocarbon frontier and the expansion of agribusiness. However, in 2011 the TIPNIS conflict over the construction of a highway without consulting the indigenous populations reconfigured the political scene and unveiled the government's realpolitik, which ran counter to the eco-communal discourse in defense of Pachamama and the criticism of the ecological debt of the more developed countries. The government's indigenist and more autonomous wing thus gradually succumbed to the statist wing, more akin to a traditional populist domination scheme. It was the sociologist and vice president Álvaro García Linera who was in charge of defending extractivism, accusing the TIPNIS movement of "colonial environmentalism," a characterization he applied to international cooperation agencies, leftist nongovernmental organizations (NGOs), and critical indigenous organizations alike.

Therefore, TIPNIS became a "revealing moment," as Luis Tapia has stated.[1] Recently, many thinkers have argued that in recent years the MAS has gradually shifted toward a closure of pluralistic channels of expression, visible in the displacement of rebellious indigenous organizations and the creation of parallel structures, the only ones recognized by the state, as well as the suffocation of critical journalism by manipulating official communications, leading to a growing process of self-censorship in nonofficial media; and, finally, through threats of expelling critical and leftist NGOs (the Center for Studies on Labor and Agrarian Development, Centro de Estudios para el Desarrollo Laboral y Agrario [CEDLA]; the Bolivian Center for Documentation and Information, Centro de Documentación e Información Bolivia [CEDIB], Fundación Tierra), as occurred in August 2015, in addition to the elaboration of a new regulatory law for disciplinary purposes.

The populist turn therefore occurred in the second stage of Evo Morales's government, which began in 2009–10, reflecting the political primacy of the statist narrative over the indigenous-communal narrative. In other words, the MAS's populist evolution is related not only to the reinstatement of a populist tradition, very present in coca growers' organizations and other areas of Bolivian society, but also to the process of building hegemony. This statist and centralist tendency, which runs counter to the recognition of the plurinational state and the advancement of indigenous autonomies, gradually configured a more classical domination model, in terms of both development models and the state-centered matrix. In the context of the new national-state hegemony, the social energy that paved the way to a new historical cycle gradually lost its strength and capacity for transformation. At the same time, the citizenship models and the forms of participation of the popular tend to be circumscribed to a narrower definition of democracy (representative, and only partially communitarian or plurinational).

The Venezuelan case presents much more controversial features. From the beginning, Chavismo seemed to contain all the elements of classical populism, constituting a high-intensity populism: the constant oscillation between democratic opening and authoritarian closure, the dichotomization of the political space to unimaginable levels, and the state as the central tool for social and economic redistribution, among others. The process of plebeian democratization that characterized Venezuela during the Hugo Chávez government can only be compared to Latin American populisms between the 1940s and 1960s. As in Argentina under the first Peronist government (1946–55), Chavismo allowed the entry of traditionally excluded social sectors, achieving a real and effective process of empowerment of the popular sectors through tense and contradictory means. In its first phase, this was exemplified by the missions to reduce poverty, universal access to education (Robinson Mission), access to health care (Barrios Adentro Mission), a reduction of the infant mortality rate, the construction of popular housing, and land distribution, among others.

On the other hand, the centrality of Hugo Chávez's leadership, his charisma and political ability, had a significant impact not only at the national level but also throughout the continent. Chávez reactivated the anti-imperialist tradition and led the process of creating a "defiant regionalism." One of the risks of plebeian democracy has always been its articulation with decisionist processes marked by strong personalistic leaderships (F. Ramírez 2010). Thus, the growing political polarization signaled a shift toward plebiscitary and direct democracy as well as the consolidation of what has been termed *hyperleadership*, which increases the direct contact between the leader and the masses without mediation (through both street demonstrations and the intense television communications developed by Chávez in his weekly speeches—"Aló Presidente" [Hello President]—and national broadcasts).

However, as has been observed by several authors, the most radical element of Chavista populism is the centrality of participatory democracy, which became the paradigm par excellence of the transformation of politics and its legitimizing device. Much has been written on this subject. The contributions of Margarita López Maya on the origins of participatory democracy, who argues that it is neither an invention of Chavismo nor of the Marxist lefts, are undoubtedly enlightening. Her conceptual source is the Catholic Church's social doctrine, which refers to the French Catholic philosophers (Jacques Maritain and Emmanuel Mounier, among others) and the Medellín Conference (1968) and its option for the poor.

Regarding the contents of participatory democracy during the Chávez administration, it is worth examining the contributions of Chilean researcher Marta Harnecker, former adviser to Chávez, who participated in drafting the Communal Council Law, approved in 2006. In her description of these councils, the author argues that they are "a form of autonomous and grassroots organization in a small space ideal for popular participation. They are an unprecedented form of territorial organization today in Latin America because of their small number of participants: between 150 and 400 families in densely populated urban areas, more than twenty families in rural areas, and even fewer families in remote, mainly indigenous areas. The point was to favor citizen participation in small spaces as much as possible to facilitate the protagonism of the participants, making them feel comfortable and uninhibited" (2009, 25).[2]

In 2009 Chávez announced that the process would be further developed, and one year later, in 2010, the Organic Law of Popular Power and the Law of Communes were sanctioned, as regulations aimed at creating a communal state.[3] The areas of work of the communal councils are popular economy, integral social development, housing, infrastructure and habitat, education and sports, culture, communications, information and training (alternative community media and the like), and security and defense (defense units). Thus, as the political and social processes developed, participatory democracy gradually acquired new dimensions: First understood as "participatory and protagonist democracy," later renamed as "popular power," and finally redefined as "communal power," popular participation acquired a more radical character, hindered, however, by various economic and political obstacles.[4] The Communal Council Law was undoubtedly a turning point, since, together with the later creation of the single party (United Socialist Party of Venezuela; Partido Socialista Unido de Venezuela [PSUV]), it illustrated the Venezuelan government's shift toward the "socialism of the twenty-first century."

We are probably still far from being able to make an objective assessment of the results of this democratizing experiment. As is usually the case, diving into reality reveals important nuances. In a recent assessment, Edgardo Lander (2015) argued that although there is an important popular experience in Venezuela that remains active in many places, when the Venezuelan process declared itself socialist (2005–6), a more rigid organization started to be institutionalized under the aegis of a state bent on controlling and directing the processes in a vertical manner in its relationship with society.

Chávez's death in 2013 and the beginning of a phase of profound political crisis and economic shortage have jeopardized the achievements made during almost fifteen years and revealed the regime's increasingly authoritarian tendencies in a context of deepening sociopolitical polarization. Post-Chavismo is thus facing all sorts of problems, among them the economic and political crisis: the inherited hyperpresidentialism; the limitations of the rentier model, increasingly based on oil extractivism and strengthened by the new development programs introduced in 2012; and the growing trend of repressive closure against political dissidence.

In closing, it is necessary to dwell for a moment on the differences between the plebeian populism experienced in Bolivia and in Venezuela. While in Bolivia populism led to a reduction of the structures of rebellion, with the populist narrative subordinating the indigenist narrative, which appealed to plurinationality and criticized extractivism, in Venezuela populism and the beginning of a stage of polarization fostered a radicalization of participatory democracy during the fourteen years of Chavismo. These differences are not coincidental: In Bolivia social protagonism preceded and made possible Evo Morales's rise to power. Morales rose from the entrails of social movements, but that did not turn his administration—as some thinkers argue—into a "government of social movements." The sharpest criticisms of the Bolivian process therefore point to two major issues: On one hand, as in the case of Ecuador, the government's unfulfilled promises regarding indigenous autonomy and the politics of Good Living (based on an eco-communitarian vision); on the other hand, the dynamics of concentration of power in the hands of the president, whose counterpart is the subalternization of social actors, and hence the appropriation of the autonomous social energy expressed between the Water War (2000) and the Gas War (2004). In contrast, the rise to power of Hugo Chávez—a mestizo military man from the lower middle classes—was the result not so much of a growing cycle of social struggles but of the crisis and exhaustion of traditional political forces. The process of mobilization and social empowerment came later, once he was in power. However, Chavismo gave expression to a demand that had been present in Venezuela's society for twenty years, fostering a renewal of democracy through the creation of new forms of participatory democracy. On the other hand, the Bolivian case is the least polarized of all populist governments, while Venezuela under Nicolás Maduro, in a context of economic crisis and a worrisome suppression of political freedoms, is approaching the end of its cycle at a vertiginous pace.

Middle-Class Populisms: Argentina and Ecuador

The high-intensity populisms of the twenty-first century in Latin America also illustrate the vitality of processes of empowerment of leaderships and elites from the middle classes. Both the Argentine and the Ecuadorian cases reflect this condition: They have not entailed a change in the distribution of social power to the lower classes and are neither anti-elitist nor iconoclastic. They are governments that, despite having been built on plebeian mobilizations, have a profound distrust of the potentially autonomous mobilizations of the masses, which they aim at guarding and incorporating in various manners, whether through decorporatization (Ecuador) or inclusion (Argentina).

Kirchnerism emerged as a local instance of progressivism around 2003 after the end of the great 2001–2 crisis. The political turn was in line with the antineoliberal character of social mobilizations and the changes at the national and Latin American levels. As a result, postconvertibility Argentina started to be associated with economic and industrial reactivation, also in line with the commodities boom (especially soy and its derivatives). However, Kirchnerism's populist evolution was gradual. During the Néstor Kirchner government (2003–7), tactical movements in search of a progressive identity organized around two major axes: the vindication of human rights as a state policy and a Latin Americanist discourse. There was also an attempt to build a transversal progressive force outside of Peronism. This latter attempt, which was rather erratic and was soon discarded, provided a space for *piquetero* organizations indebted to the populist matrix, which were integrated into the government under the politically correct name of "social organizations." Finally, the conflict of the newly appointed Cristina Fernández de Kirchner government with agrarian producers in 2008 was the turning point that led to a full update of the populist legacy: In this context, the government obtained the active support of a broad group of progressive intellectuals and scholars, who defended the institutional framework and read the agrarian mobilizations as a "destituent conflict" and a "coup without a subject."[5] Months later, the government revived the initiative, and the binary scheme was significantly strengthened by the conflict caused by the Audiovisual Media Law (2009), which this time led to a direct clash with the multimedia daily *Clarín*. In this context, the government promoted the most progressive measures, among them, the Law on Equal Marriage, the nationalization of the pension system, and especially the Universal Child Allowance, a measure sanctioned by presidential decree, which had been advocated for years by progressive opposition parties and social organizations.

Néstor Kirchner's sudden death fully opened the doors to populism in its classical statist version. This had two major consequences: On one hand, it consolidated the binary discourse as the "grand narrative" that refounded Kirchnerism, synthesized in the opposition between a popular block and concentrated power sectors (monopolies, corporations, gorillas, anti-Peronists). As in other periods of Argentine history, the dichotomous schemes, which began as principles that reduced complexity in times of conflict, ended up operating as a structure to read the political reality. On the other hand, they mobilized a sector of the youth. In this context, groups such as La Cámpora, founded by the son of the Kirchner couple, grew enormously and started to spread throughout the country with a twofold militancy: both from high positions in the state apparatus and from the grassroots. Far from manifesting a social polarization between the upper and lower sectors, the struggle illustrated a sort of fissure at the very heart of the middle classes.[6] This was aggravated by the dissolution of the government's alliance with trade unionist Hugo Moyano, which led the government to abandon classical populism (the "trade union leg" as the backbone) to focus on its middle-class allies. Kirchnerism's social base was thus reduced to a sector of the Argentine Workers' Central Union (Central de Trabajadores de la Argentina; CTA) linked to middle sectors (teachers and state employees), together with a traditionally Peronist General Confederation of Labor (Confederación General del Trabajo; CGT), purged of dissident voices. Finally, faithful to the Peronist legacy in Latin American politics, the strong encapsulation of the executive power led to an extreme presidentialist model, not very prone to democratic debate. In this context of takeover of the state apparatus by the young members of La Cámpora and narrower social alliances, Kirchnerism became a middle-class populism that sought to monopolize the progressive language in the name of the popular classes, while simultaneously disqualifying other mobilized middle-class sectors. Toward the end of the Cristina Fernández de Kirchner administration, the government also sought to advance to other areas (e.g., the judiciary).

As a result, Argentina entered a phase of political and social polarization, albeit differently from other twenty-first-century Latin American populisms—in the first place, because the Kirchnerist model is profoundly Peronist, capable of combining political audacity and a traditional organizational legacy, revealing a pragmatic conception of social change and construction of hegemony. Thus, the populist inflection not only is the result of a historical relationship or of enduring ties between the Partido Peronista (Peronist Party) and social organizations but also responds to a certain conception of social change, which views transformation as a result of a shift in the government's political orientation rather than in the possibility of a new balance of power through social struggles. This primacy of the political party system tends to express itself in strong efforts to subordinate the organized masses to the leader's authority (as clearly illustrated by the trade unions of the once-powerful CGT and by today's official unemployed, peasant, and human rights organizations), through the model of "controlled social participation." This organizational primacy contributes to explaining the fact that Kirchnerism was never interested in fostering potentially autonomous participatory dynamics, as was the case in Venezuela, or processes of institutional renewal, as in Bolivia and even Ecuador, which broadened the frontier of rights in those countries, at least during the presidents' first terms of office.

As in other countries in the region, Rafael Correa's rise to power in Ecuador was related to the great economic crisis and the collapse of traditional parties, whose greatest expression was a popular uprising, especially in Quito, in April 2005, with *cacerolazos* (pot-banging protests), *escraches* (public shaming actions), and other forms of protest, which brought down the neoliberal government of Lucio Gutiérrez and paved the way to a tumultuous electoral transition.[7] Also in the background of this rebellion was a growing indigenous protagonism, a line of historical accumulation embodied since the mid-1990s by CONAIE, one of the most important indigenous organizations in Latin America, whose political agenda signaled an eco-territorial turn in the struggles (plurinationality, defense of the territories, and shortly afterward a critique of extractivism). Correa, who had been minister of the economy in the transition government (2005–6), presented himself as an outsider candidate with a new party, Alianza PAIS, with a strong anti-neoliberal and anti–International Monetary Fund discourse.

In this context, the Citizens' Revolution raised enormous expectations at the beginning, since it articulated several sociopolitical matrices and critical narratives that echoed the demands of indigenous movements and various sectors of the left. In this line, the people's emergence had a corollary in the Constituent Assembly of Montecristi (2008), where various social, indigenous, rural, and urban movements converged, together with leftist and ecologist sectors and intellectuals, adopting a clear position in favor of a plurinational state and participatory democracy.[8] The new Constitution also proposed several innovations, among them, the rights of nature and Good Living as goals of the new development program. The president of the Constituent Assembly was the renowned economist and ecologist Alberto Acosta, who was forced to step down, however, before the end of the process.

One of the most noteworthy changes introduced by Correa was the role of the state, which, unlike in the neoliberal era, became the engine that spearheaded the Citizens' Revolution. As in Venezuela, there was a recovery of oil activities by the state, accompanied by an increase in tax revenue and a series of social plans (*bonos*) aimed at reducing poverty and increasing access to health and education (Ospina 2013). The program's success, in a context of booming oil prices, gave legitimacy to Correa's government, as demonstrated by subsequent electoral results.

The process of construction of hegemony of the Citizens' Revolution followed a twofold strategy. On one hand, presidential authority, which had clearly been weakened after the long period of political instability, was reinforced. This was further fueled—for the same reasons—by the presidentialist elements of the new Constitution. Presidentialism was also accompanied by high doses of decisionism. On the other hand, this process was complemented by a strategy of "decorporatization" of society, which, although it aimed at neutralizing the political pressure exerted by different groups in a context of crisis and a necessary construction of presidential authority and at fostering citizenship or republican values, also constituted the primary means to discredit the leaders of social movements, which were described "as elites that defend their corporate privileges" (de la Torre 2013b), and hence any attempt at autonomous social mobilization. With this strategy, the government sought to undermine the CONAIE, which had been the great political protagonist of resistance movements against neoliberal adjustment, thenceforth considered a "pressure group," and to confront other reluctant sectors, such as teachers with ties to Maoism and other public unions.

On the other hand, one of the fronts of conflict with respect to extractivism has been the resistance against the entry of megamining. The Constituent Assembly at one point proposed declaring Ecuador "free of polluting mining." In April 2008 the government declared the expiration of thousands of illegal mining concessions, jeopardizing millionaire extractive projects, but in January 2009 the Parliament approved the new Mining Law, which further fueled the extractivist model.

At the beginning of the Correa administration, one of the most noteworthy changes was the importance that the National Secretariat for Planning and Development (Secretaría Nacional de Planificación y Desarrollo; SENPLADES) acquired in the new government, which elaborated a National Development Plan following the general lines of the Montecristi Constitution, involving an integral conception of development, that is, not only in terms of a productive and social logic but also as "the achievement of Good Living in harmony with nature and the indefinite continuance of human cultures" (SENPLADES 2007, 54). The plan's elaboration included roundtable discussions in which different sectors of Ecuadorian society participated, as well as an arduous process of systematization and consensus on its components. The next plan, the 2009–13 Plan for Good Living, proposed, in addition to the "return of the state," a change in the model of accumulation, from primary-export to endogenous, bio-centered development based on biodiversity, knowledge, and tourism. However, the Plan for Good Living was far from being implemented; on the contrary, the president's decisions and the neo-extractivist developmentalist course taken reduced the Constitution and its promises to a dead letter, only demanded by indigenous organizations and environmentalist sectors. Finally, the centrality of SENPLADES accounted for one of the characteristics of Correa's government: the appeal to expert knowledge "as one of the axes of its rituals of political justification" (F. Ramírez 2015).

In this line, one noteworthy aspect is the increasing importance of the meritocratic model, embodied by young, middle-aged, middle-class professionals with doctoral degrees, who have even been called "the PhD cabinet" (F. Ramírez 2015). The counterpart of this emphasis on higher education is the distrust toward other dynamics or forms of legitimization. Thus, under the decorporatization banner and with the meritocratic emphasis, the government attempted to limit autonomous spaces and place them under state tutelage.

On the other hand, much of the public debate that has confronted Correa in the right-wing sectors is related to the weight of the state in the public sector (which went from less than 25 percent in 2006 to almost 50 percent in 2011) and the "disproportionate" public spending (Ospina 2013, 156–57). The polarization also placed the media at one of the poles. As in other Latin American countries, the media have openly political agendas that tend to substitute those of the discredited political parties, combining the defense of the status quo (in economic terms) with the defense of political freedoms. Thus, in order to engage in the cultural battle, as in other countries (Venezuela, Argentina, and Bolivia in part), the government created its own media structure and implemented an intense and aggressive publicity campaign, making excessive use of national TV (President Correa also has a weekly TV program called *Enlace Ciudadano* [Citizen liaison]). In other words, it deployed the typical repertoire of action in the communication battle with large and medium-sized media, which is today standard practice for polarization among twenty-first-century Latin American populisms.

Correa's conflict with the media resulted in measures that are difficult to defend, which weakened him politically and discredited his government internationally. Correa also faced a police rebellion that resulted in a chaotic coup attempt in 2011. Immediately afterward, he called for a popular consultation consisting of ten questions, five of which involved amendments to the recently approved Constitution, and several of which were regressive in nature. "The first two seek to replace the expiration of pretrial detention and to restrict alternatives to deprivation of liberty with the argument of combating crime. . . . The fourth and fifth questions modify the integration of the highest judicial bodies, allowing the Executive and Parliament to interfere in their appointment" (Zibechi 2011). These restrictions on freedom also reached the field of political expression and demands. Finally, the response to socioenvironmental conflicts was the criminalization and judicialization of protest, which led to criminal prosecutions of spokespersons of organizations, as well as the withdrawal of the legal status of NGOs and their expulsion.

The above weakened and hindered the autonomy of social organizations (especially indigenous, ecologist, and student organizations), which, together with the beginning of an era of greater social control and restriction of freedoms, resulted in a concentration of power in the president. While references to the Montecristi Constitution are increasingly weaker, the model that gradually consolidated is closer to a conservative Catholic regime than the ecologist and national left that accompanied Correa in his rise to power. Also, with time, hyperpresidentialism and the meritocratic model obtained greater autonomy, as the spaces for independent participation of social organizations and the citizenry in general diminished, under the scheme of controlled participation overseen by the state.

In sum, although Argentine and Ecuadorian populisms have different features, they nevertheless illustrate a common typology, insofar as the process of constructing hegemony exhibits a sort of expropriation/resignification of the mobilized social energy in favor of a leading sector of the middle classes, with a visibly meritocratic side in Correaism, not present in Kirchnerist populism, which instead deployed a cultural/media apparatus in its discursive battle with opposition media. On the other hand, while Ecuador put in power an academic and economist outsider, Rafael Correa, who moved past the crisis of traditional political parties by building his own political force (Alianza PAIS), in Argentina the return to "political normality" came from the traditional Partido Peronista with Néstor Kirchner, who appealed to broad sectors of society, with some innovative policies in a context of rebounding economic growth (commodity boom). But while Kirchnerism has sought to legitimize itself through history, appealing to the imaginary of infinite Peronism (the photographs of Juan Perón and Eva Perón, as well as the presidential couple—Néstor and Cristina Kirchner—have multiplied since 2008–10), Correaism portrayed itself as a point of departure, with Correa as a sort of absolute demiurge, the maker of history.

There are other differences regarding the radical nature of the Ecuadorian experience and the innovative discussions that took place (Good Living, the rights of nature, other developments), which did not occur in the Argentine experience, where the critique of extractivism was never part of the political and public agenda. In the context of "really existing populisms," in Argentina the populist matrix tends to deliberately reject or erase other conflicts—as well as other forms of popular expression—that do not fit the binary categorization. In Ecuador doing so is not as easy, due to the important presence of indigenous and socioenvironmental issues in the political and media agenda, hence the feeling of "betrayal" or "unfulfilled promises" regarding Correaism, relative to both the postextractivist development model and the demands for participation and expansion of the plurinational state. On the other hand, in Argentina Kirchnerism never encouraged this type of promises; as a result, the issue of extractivism—due to the presence of movements of assemblies against megamining—always constituted a blind spot for the ruling party and its intellectual spokespersons. Finally, in both cases, the process of empowerment and leadership of the middle classes is not unrelated to the social origin of their leaders—the Kirchner couple, middle-class professionals; Rafael Correa, a university professor. The centrality of the leader further bolsters the importance of these biographical or individual elements.

———

With few exceptions, the return to high-intensity populism operates in an academic context that does not easily accept the traditionally pejorative use of the concept. It is quite likely that Ernesto Laclau's theoretical work influenced this change, but it would be naive, of course, to imagine that it explains it all. The twofold nature of populism has prompted a more complex view of the phenomenon, which is also reflected in theoretical work—otherwise stated, we have gone from different forms of heteronomous appropriation of the concept of populism, dominated by disqualifying views, to an (often conflictive) coexistence of different modes of appropriation: positive, negative, and ambivalent. This explains the existence of a plurality of readings, by virtue of not only Latin America's variegated political history but also the conceptual and political turns we have experienced.

The flip side has been a recurrent political/media reductionism, whether in the form of exultant apologies or of angry rejections. In other words, all attempts at greater complexity, depth, and sharpness of analysis made from the field of political/academic research weaken or die once they enter the political/media arena, where only one-dimensional answers are admitted, loaded with value judgments—whether negative or positive—highly dependent on the context of polarization in force. It is true that the tension at the heart of the populist project once again reveals what Arditi denominated "the undecidable structure of populism" (2009); however, this undecidability should not prevent us from developing a critical/comprehensive view, which requires examining national trajectories and understanding historical processes.

It is for this reason that I proposed the distinction between plebeian populisms and middle-class populisms, which by no means implies establishing a difference between good and bad populisms. While plebeian populisms wagered on participation from below, often in a disorderly or anarchic manner (especially in Venezuela, and with more corporatist features in Bolivia), or sought to create a new political/legal structure to account for a plural reality (the plurinational state), middle-class populisms have made participation merely a rhetorical device, replacing institutional innovation and the search for equality with the more ambiguous and narrow paradigm of "social inclusion."

Final Reflections

The debates examined in this book illustrate an intersection between various disciplines, including social theory, the history of ideas, and Latin American political and economic thought. The purpose was, on one hand, to conduct a sociology of absences (Boaventura de Sousa Santos), revisiting certain topics and debates that have been present throughout the history of Latin American social and human sciences, which—as we have observed—have been characterized by a deficit of accumulation, which hinders the possibility of a real recognition and a necessary transmission, both in the continent and abroad. Thus, in the first part of our voyage, the reconstruction attempted to shed light on some of the fundamental debates of our Latin American history, examining a set of explanatory categories and theoretical views that tend to be forgotten or simply undervalued in the languages of the dominant Latin American social sciences. We therefore saw the emergence of both critical concepts and horizon-concepts, which provide other avenues beyond the hegemonic discourse. Currently, critical categories such as postdevelopment, extractivism, and post-neoliberalism, and horizon-categories such as plurinational state, common goods, and Good Living, among others, are concepts under construction that sustain the new twenty-first-century Latin American thought, which is elaborated together with the mobilization processes of subaltern sectors, their demands for social change, and their political grammars.

A second objective was to account for the current reality, examining not only the resurgence of those debates but the relationship between them: the role of the indigenous, development, dependency, and populism. To that end, I propose a finale in two movements: first, a brief voyage through the disciplines and approaches that are revisiting those topics today and, second, an examination of the current debates and articulations.

Approaches and Languages

In Latin America the social sciences emerged imbued in a constitutive tension, marked by a tendency toward professionalization and the search for solutions to the great social problems. The fact that their focus was the analysis of concrete processes does not mean that they did not foster more global understandings. On the contrary, a considerable part of those sciences (e.g., political sociology and political economics) was structured around the larger questions regarding the characteristics of peripheral capitalism and its impacts on the process of domination and the expectation—or lack thereof—of social change. Furthermore, the possibility of having an effect on the problems of the respective societies fostered, according to Gerónimo de Sierra, Manuel Antonio Garretón, Miguel Murmis, and Hélgio Trindade, "a greater relative incidence of ideological discourses in the academy, as well as a tendency to engage with politics, political parties, and governments" (Garretón et al. 2005; de Sierra et al. 2007, 21).

Today there are a number of critical perspectives in tune with the approaches of the coloniality of knowledge (Aníbal Quijano, Edgardo Lander, Santiago Castro Gómez), internal colonialism (Silvia Rivera Cusicanqui), and epistemology of the South (Boaventura de Sousa Santos), which posit the need for other analytic views. In the following pages, I attempt to summarize those approaches and disciplines in Latin America today that revisit most of the debates I have presented in this book.

One of the most innovative approaches is that of political ecology. There are several leading authors on the subject in the region, among whom Enrique Leff stands out; for him, political ecology raises a question regarding the most recent processes of change in human beings' existential condition, in terms not only of the conflicts of ecological distribution but also of the relationships between peoples' lives and the globalized world. Leff (2006) argues that ecology's main contribution is political, not only epistemological, insofar as it points, on one hand, to the denaturalization of nature, of the "natural" conditions of existence, of "natural" disasters; and, on the other hand, to the ecologization of social relations. In short, for Leff, political ecology is a disputed territory where new cultural identities are in the process of construction around the defense of a culturally resignified nature, through today's resistance struggles.[1] As we have seen, these struggles stand against the different forms of extractivism in the continent and in defense of other languages that value the territory. Also, political ecology has become a new political epistemology, whose efforts at integrating and complementing knowledges go beyond the interdisciplinary project, "recognizing the strategies at play in the field of power and leading to the idea of a dialogue and a meeting of knowledges" (Leff 2014, 136). Finally, political ecology proposes a new environmental rationality centered on the defense of the production and reproduction of life, challenging the sociological imagination and examining social imaginaries of sustainability, which confront established knowledge through a change in beliefs and values, in favor of other ways of understanding and inhabiting the world (136).

It is also important to include the contributions of environmental history, which studies "topics such as human societies' adaptation to the ecosystems, their transformation through technology, or the various conceptions of nature" (Alimonda 2011, 28–30). According to Héctor Alimonda, the field of environmental history has grown considerably in Latin America thanks to the Latin American and Caribbean Society of Environmental History (SOLCHA). In its intersection with political ecology, Alimonda proposes a definition of environmental history that points to its affinity with the modernity/coloniality program, by complementing the "decolonial turn" with a natural-colonial turn (or the coloniality of nature). Concepts such as asynchrony and eccentricity (which the author borrows from Colombian Germán Palacio) were features derived from coloniality (36).

On the other hand, for several decades a number of specialists have developed an innovative viewpoint from the perspective of ecological economics, studying these new conflicts marked by an unequal distribution of environmental risks, most especially the Catalonian Joan Martínez Alier, who maintains a permanent and fluid dialogue with critical intellectuals and perspectives in Latin America. Early on, Martínez Alier baptized these movements for environmental history in the countries of the South or the periphery as "popular ecology" or "ecology of the poor." This unequal distribution of labor, which has an effect on the distribution of environmental conflicts, affects above all the most vulnerable populations. Finally, this growing connection between ecological struggles and the struggles of the popular sectors makes anticapitalist struggles become ecologist struggles, even if inadvertently (Martínez Alier 2004).

In this line of thought, which problematizes the issues of space, territory, and social relations, are the contributions of Brazilian critical geographers, among whom stand out Milton Santos, Carlos Porto Gonçalves, and Bernardo Mançano Fernandes. As the latter argues, "We coexist with several types of territories that produce and are produced by different social relations and that are disputed on a daily basis" (Fernandes 2009). This dispute takes place in a complex space where logics of action and rationalities that entail different value assessments meet. The expansion of the extractive frontier through large-scale metal mining, the advancement of hydrocarbon exploitation, and agribusiness in its various forms, among others, can be conceived as a paradigmatic example that generates not only a "tension of territorialities" (Porto Gonçalves 2001) but also a view of territoriality that excludes current (or potentially existing) territorialities. In this context, the "geography of dissent" must also be included, developed for decades by Henri Acselrad (2004b), to identify environmental conflicts that, from civil society, question the development model spatially configured by the state.

In tune with these perspectives is critical political sociology, which aims at elaborating concepts with an intermediate scope and the necessary analytic tools to study the dynamics established between the social structure and social subjects, that is, between the forms of accumulation of capital and the changes in social subjectivities, the transformations of the state's role, the characteristics and dynamics of the political system, and socio-discursive production from spaces of power. It was undoubtedly in the 1960s, with the debate on marginality, and later with the analysis of urban social movements, that the territory became the primary battlefield, resulting from the implementation of focalized compensatory social policies designed by power for the sake of the control and containment of poverty. However, more recently, the territory also became the focus of demands by peasant, indigenous, and socioenvironmental movements, in response to the new modalities of appropriation of capital in spaces considered strategic. In this interpretive line are several critical contributions by authors such as Norma Giarracca, Miguel Teubal, Raúl Zibechi, Horacio Machado Aráoz, Mirta Antonelli, Pablo Ospina, Mina Lorena Navarro, and Raphael Hoetmer, among many other approaches that, like those of the author of this book, underscore the importance of the territory and territoriality, in both urban and rural movements, since the territory appears as a space for resistance and also, increasingly, as a place for resignification and creation of new social relations. Thus, Latin American social movements must be understood as socio-territorial movements. From this standpoint, the process of environmentalization of social struggles (Leff 2006) can be read in terms of an eco-territorial turn in the struggles (Svampa 2012). It is also important to recognize that this analytic approach to social movements must be related to the perspective of autonomy, related to the demand for "self-determination," which today means especially the recognition of diversity and difference but also the possibility of constructing the commons independently from the market and the state.

Finally, these critical views converge with the interdisciplinary postdevelopmentalist perspective, which includes theoretical and analytic contributions by environmentalists such as Eduardo Gudynas, by critical economists such as Alberto Acosta, by anthropologists such as Arturo Escobar, by political scientists such as Luis Tapia and Raúl Prada, and by sociologists such as Edgardo Lander and many others, who propose an original line of thought that paves the way to other perspectives and languages to conceive possible transitions to postextractivism, through an epistemological framework different from the dominant one, developing powerful concepts such as Good Living and the rights of nature, as well as hyperstrong sustainability, environmental rationality, and environmental ethics.

In short, political ecology, ecological economics, critical geography or the geography of dissent, political sociology, and the postdevelopmentalist perspective converge in an effort to develop a paradigm on the basis of a different relationship between society and nature, space and social relations, collective subjects and democracy. In my opinion, this inter-multidisciplinary field under construction, which develops in debate with the dominant perspectives (those that advocate both neoliberalism and progressive neo-developmentalism), has a very significant potential, since it seeks to articulate critical thought, collective subjects, and the defense of life.

Second, although it is hard to relate it to a specific current or school, there is an important Indianist perspective in several Latin American countries, which actively fosters contemporary theoretical and political debates, especially those related to the various dimensions of decolonization, from both a political and an epistemological standpoint. The Indianist perspective is associated with the indigenous reemergence in Latin America since the 1970s, after the evident failure of the integrationist project deployed by national-developmentalist governments, and later of the neoliberal project, together with multiculturalism. This perspective has had and has different political and social expressions, among which the Katarist movement in Bolivia stands out due to its reelaboration and reinvention of the indigenous.

As we saw in the chapter on the problematization of the indigenous, this vindication or reinvention of the indigenous is also related to the consolidation of the paradigm of collective rights in the international agenda. In other words, the Indianist perspective emerges from the conjunction of two scenarios: a national-regional one that entails the advancement of indigenous struggles, which are also political and cultural struggles; and an international one after the creation of the United Nations following World War II, where the decolonization perspective gradually gives way to a new agenda of recognition and enunciation of collective rights and, increasingly, of peoples' autonomy. The conjunction of these two scenarios and the failure of assimilationist projects paved the way to a new context in Latin America, visible in the work of reinvention of identities, as well as the empowerment of indigenous organizations and intellectuals through novel legal tools related to concepts such as autonomy, territory, and the plurinational state.

Finally, I would like to underscore the emergence of a thought process derived from feminisms of the South, or popular feminisms, especially related to an alternative paradigm regarding the relationship between society and nature. It is well known that in Latin America—and in general in the countries of the South—women have a greater protagonism in social struggles and processes of collective organization. This has been called the process of feminization of struggles, which alludes to the central role of women, especially those from the lower and middle sectors, as well as cultural collectives that participate in indigenous organizations, socio-territorial movements, and environmentalist nongovernmental organizations. In my opinion, these dynamics of feminization of struggles must be compared to the process of environmentalization of social struggles. This popular evolution of feminism, which at first was not recognized as explicitly feminist, proposes continuities and ruptures with prior feminist currents or with classical feminism, more strongly related to the middle classes. In terms of ruptures, popular feminisms imply an expansion of the topics under discussion relative to classical liberal feminism, debating about lands, territories, bodies, and representations. In addition, eco-dependency is another element of rupture.

In this line, there has been a progressive development and valuation of the ecofeminist perspective. Although the term *ecofeminist* emerged in the 1970s, and many authors operate in this field, in recent years it has become more pervasive. Two topics contributed to the development of ecofeminist theory. The first is the ecological crisis, understood as an anthropological social crisis: Domination as a formula for affirmation of the human is reflected at the level of interpersonal relations and in the relationships between the human and the natural. Based on this, ecofeminism drew a parallel between domination of one gender over another and domination of human beings over nature, with expressions such as logic of domination, or identity logic, reflecting the same basic idea: the justification of domination and marginalization based on a devaluation of those considered different, in this case women relative to men, and the natural relative to the human. The second topic is the critical and liberating character of ecology, which questions the dualist/Cartesian view of mind and body and aims at eliminating the hierarchical relation between human and nonhuman nature. Ecofeminism thus attempts to take advantage of this emancipatory aspect of ecology (Ramírez García 2012).

On the other hand, as has already been mentioned in this book, ecofeminism and feminist economics underscore the parallels between exploitation of women and exploitation of nature, through invisibilized and unrecognized reproductive work. Ecofeminism proposes eliminating female marginalization through the social recognition of the values attributed to women and the need to broaden the social presence of those values, related to the ethics of care, as the foundation of a new paradigm capable of changing the current state of relations between human beings and nature. These values have to do with care, which is considered the basis of a different ethics founded on responsibility, reciprocity, and solidarity. From this perspective, ecofeminism is, as Alicia Puleo (2011) argues, a wager for "the universalization of the ethics of care toward humans and nature." This does not mean that women must adopt a sacrificial standpoint but that men must adopt such an ethic.

To paraphrase the Ecuadorian philosopher Bolívar Echeverría (2002), popular feminisms and ecofeminism entail a defiant ethos that, unlike the structuring principle of capitalism, based on the market value of things, proposes a pro-communal and popular-communitarian ethos (Gutiérrez Aguilar 2014), which aims at structuring life in terms of a qualitatively defined telos that acts based on the use value of things, on the dynamics of their practical consistency. Today, before the advancement of enclosures and the seizure of the commons, the new resistances point to the creations of spaces of community and forms of sociability, that is, fields of collective experimentation that vindicate the production and reproduction of the commons, outside of the state and the market. Hence, the idea of a pro-communal ethos serves to reflect on both the preexisting communitarian dimensions in Latin America and the current political dimensions of resistances, focused on protecting the commons and on radical democracy.

In short, many approaches, languages, and disciplines in Latin America today question epistemological colonialism and converge on a critique of the advancement of the commodification of life and the commons in the region. This is not by chance, since the critique of extractivism and the new positions regarding progressive governments shed light on other issues and classical debates in Latin American thought, such as the topic of the role of indigenous peoples in the context of the current development models, the constant re-creation of dependency, and the return of infinite populisms.

Interrelationships between Debates

One general consideration, often reiterated in this book and maintained by several authors, is that Latin America does not respond to the "canonical" model observed in Western societies (Europe and the United States). Maladjustment, asymmetries, structural heterogeneity, variegation, dislocation, and especially dependency as the great master frame and populism as a specificity are categories that reflect this difficulty in comprehending Latin America's reality, its social classes and processes of social mobilization, and its political regimes from a "normalizing" perspective or through preestablished patterns, as both the theory of modernization and orthodox Marxism intended.

That is how some of the debates examined in this book must be understood. One of them is the problematization of the indigenous question, since a common feature has been the denial of indigenous people's condition as full-fledged political actors, based on classist or modernizing readings that understood ethnic and cultural aspects as social, economic, and of course class backwardness. Both the multiplication of scissions and conflicts and a reassessment of ethnicity in recent decades, as well as the political empowerment of indigenous sectors, have weakened the explicative capacity of these classical reading schemes, which are nonetheless far from having disappeared. Furthermore, the incomplete character of social classes does not refer exclusively to subaltern sectors (urban, rural, formal, marginal, peasant, indigenous) but also to the dominant classes (traditional oligarchies and local bourgeoisies), which are incapable of becoming true leading classes or national bourgeoisies—without forgetting, of course, the not-so-"progressive" middle classes.

There are many debates today surrounding decolonization that imply a positive reassessment of the indigenous, its political dynamics, and its emancipatory horizons. One of the most mobilizing mottos present in the debates is that of Good Living—*Buen Vivir, Sumak Kawsay*, or *Suma Qamaña*—related to the Andean indigenous worldview. At the moment, Good Living is a broad surface on which various emancipatory values are inscribed. Among them, communitarianism is the inspiring framework and common core, in spite of the difficulties of translating it into experiences (we should not idealize the indigenous communitarian world or ignore the different incarnations of the communitarian in Latin America), or into concrete public policies, in the face of the extractivism in place. The threat is that it will become hollowed of meaning in the hands of governmental legitimation rhetoric—as is partially the case in Bolivia—or possibly be "parasitized" by international bodies, as has happened with other notions with great political potential.

Something different happens with the dependency approach, centered on one of the leading categories of Latin American thought. Rather than a class approach, dependency proposes an articulation between the international and the national (center/periphery), insofar as it attempts to explain structural deficiencies and social inequalities through formulas of accumulation of international capitalism and its modes of intervention in peripheral economies. For that reason, some authors have underscored the contributions that anticipated the dependency approach in the theories on globalization, while also pointing out their limitations, in particular their tendency toward an economistic perspective and the lack of intermediate categories, unsuited for a more thorough geopolitical analysis.

However, one common element for reflection among the advocates of dependency theory was to consider dependency a dynamic category that must be read differently according to the various and successive cycles of change in the modes of capital accumulation. In this line, the current emergence of a new configuration of dependency, which in this book has been read relative to the People's Republic of China, must be analyzed in terms of three major questions: The first one, in geopolitical terms, refers to the situation of *hegemonic transition*, interpreted as the beginning of a period characterized by—still conflictive—polycentrism and plurality in civilizational terms. The second one, in regional terms, assesses the scope of *Latin American defiant regionalism*, whose most important anti-imperialist milestone regarding traditional US hegemony was the rejection of the Free Trade Area of the Americas in the Mar del Plata summit in 2005, promoted by Hugo Chávez, Luiz Inácio Lula da Silva, and Néstor Kirchner. The third and last question refers to the *expansion of extractivism* visible at a regional scale, that is, the increase in commodity exports in the context of a vertiginous dynamic of consolidation of economic ties with the People's Republic of China. The most salient aspect, however, is not the—inevitable and necessary—ties with China but the way these are developed. Far from the rhetoric of regional unity and integration in the name of Mercosur, the Union of South American Nations, or the Community of Latin American and Caribbean States, each country has unilaterally signed commercial and financial agreements with China, which tend to fuel extractivism in all its variants (commodity loans, commodity exports, and infrastructure related to extractive projects).

Thus, through the vicissitudes of history, new ties of dependency with China become evident ten years after the demise of the Free Trade Area of the Americas, which still resonates in the anti-imperialist Latin American imaginary. The turning point was 2015, which began with the establishment of many commercial agreements between Argentina and China, after a much-publicized trip by then President Cristina Fernández de Kirchner, which among other things included infrastructure and dams, as well as many agreements with secret clauses that committed the country for decades; and it ended with the agreements signed by Bolivia, through Vice President Álvaro García Linera, obtaining a multimillion-dollar loan to finance eleven important infrastructure projects (megahighways) linking the Amazon, the valleys, and the Altiplano, as well as railroads and electric energy projects. China thus became Bolivia's foremost creditor, displacing financial institutions controlled by the United States and the European Union. In spite of the enthusiasm this has awakened in Bolivia, few people seem to be wondering what will happen to the peasant and indigenous populations that reject these megaprojects, or whether they will affect protected areas and biodiversity. In any case, everything seems to indicate that the increasingly closer relations with China will entail the demise of any other development model inspired by indigenous Good Living. Paradoxically, that Mar del Plata summit of 2005 ended up becoming the high point of Latin American defiant regionalism, when in fact it should have been the point of departure for a new, truly integrative Latin Americanist construction that included the creation of a new platform for regional negotiation to open the doors to more symmetrical relations with the new and powerful commercial partners.

Finally, the return of infinite populisms in Latin America reinstates the constitutive tension present in Latin American social sciences, between the affirmation of deficit and excess, between the zeal for normality and the temptation of anomaly. Far from the categorizations at the beginning of the epochal change that alluded to a "turn to the left," in 2015 the reflections on really existing populisms in Latin America inscribe us in a more pessimistic political scenario that once again sheds light on the inevitable tension present in them: Hence, the various national cases today illustrate the conflictive relations between models of democracy, the increasingly harsh confrontations between progressive governments and social movements, the growing limitations of the economic projects in the context of current neo-extractivism, and the renewed hegemonic temptations of the regimes in power.

Everything seems to indicate that the return of high-intensity populism and the end of the progressive cycle are related. From an economic standpoint, it is related to the fall of commodity prices, affecting especially oil, minerals, and, to a lesser extent, soybeans. Beyond the expressions of good intentions, it has been demonstrated that current extractivism (which some people euphemistically call "neo-developmentalism") does not lead to an industrial development model or to a rise in production but to a greater primarization and the consolidation of maldevelopment models, which are unsustainable at various levels and dimensions. As Martínez Alier (2015) points out, the fall in the prices of primary products leads not only to greater debt but also to more extractivism, in an attempt to compensate for the commercial deficit, leading the countries to a perverse cycle. It is therefore not by chance that new explorations are announced in frontier zones and/or natural parks. Furthermore, the "reprimarization effect" has been aggravated by the arrival of China, which has become the foremost destination for exports from Chile and Brazil; the second-biggest destination for exports from Argentina, Peru, Colombia, and Cuba; and the third-biggest for exports from Mexico, Uruguay, and Venezuela (Svampa and Slipak 2015).

On the other hand, neo-extractivism inaugurated a new phase of criminalization and violation of human rights that includes not only conservative and neoliberal governments but also progressive populisms. In recent years, there have been many socioenvironmental and territorial conflicts that went beyond the local and acquired national visibility, such as the Isiboro Sécure National Park and Indigenous Territory conflict (Bolivia), the construction of the Belo Monte megadam (Brazil), the Famatina mining protests and the resistances against megamining (Argentina), and the definitive suspension of oil extraction in Yasuní (Ecuador) and of the Nicaragua Canal megaproject. It is clear that the expansion of the frontier of rights (collective, territorial, environmental) has been limited by the growing expansion of the frontiers of exploitation by capital, in its search for goods, lands, and territories, shattering the emancipatory narratives that had raised such high expectations, especially in countries such as Bolivia and Ecuador. Otherwise stated, the end of the commodity boom confronts us with the consolidation of the "more extractivism/less democracy" equation, illustrated by the criminalization of socioenvironmental struggles and the distortion of the available institutional devices (public audiences, prior consultation of indigenous populations, public consultation), a scenario shared today by both progressive and conservative or neoliberal governments.

From a strictly political standpoint, we observe a reconfiguration of high-intensity populism that affirms a model of subordination of social actors (social movements and indigenous organizations) and attempts to annul differences, underscoring the threat to and restriction of political liberties. The most recent examples are those of Bolivia and Ecuador, where the promises of creating "other development models" or "Good Living" outside of an extractivist matrix are a thing of the past. Today's high-intensity populism, with its national specificities in the various countries in the region, confronts us once again with the oscillation between democratic opening (the incorporation of the excluded) and the hegemonic temptation (the closure of the channels for freedom of expression and the leaders' intention to remain in power). Thus, one of the common elements is the concentration of power in the executive branch and the subordination of (previously mobilized) social actors as a result of the fetishization of the state embodied by the president.

One example can help assess the importance of the leader's role. Several years ago, in 2007, a documentary about Bolivia entitled *Hartos Evos aquí hay* (There are many Evos here) premiered, which narrated the process of mobilization from below from an ethnographic standpoint (Ulloque Franco and Ruiz Montealegre 2007). The significant title alluded to the existence of multiple leaderships, implying that Evo Morales was one more among them. However, in 2015 it would be difficult to defend that thesis. As Bolivian historians Vincent Nicolas and Pablo Quisbert (2014) argue, the idea that Evo Morales was one more peasant among many, who reached the presidential palace, evolved into the idea of his exceptionality, of the person destined to be a leader—an idea behind the new constitutional reform to enable Morales's "candidacy" for a fourth presidential term beginning in 2020.

The topic of "reelections" is not new in Latin America and has always been a motive for social polarization. Hugo Chávez went down that controversial path, achieving, a few years before his death (2009), the constitutional approval of indefinite election. In 2013 Cristina Fernández de Kirchner played with the possibility of reelection, but Argentine society put an end to her aspirations. Likewise, confronted with social resistance in 2015, the Ecuadorian Rafael Correa backed down from modifying the Constitution to enable a third presidential term. In spite of their differences, the governments cited tend to employ the same arguments: the need to give continuity to the changes and the always imminent threat of regression. They thus foster a messianic reading of history, believing that transformations are the result of a change in the leader's orientation, rather than the possibility of a new balance of power through social struggles.

There are currently quite a few intellectuals engaged in political processes led by progressive governments in the continent, who promote new obstacles and blind spots in the face of the risk of a "return of the right" or the "imperialist threat." While no one can deny the existence of conservative or retrograde forces, both in our societies and elsewhere, which promote a return to an economic and political context closer to the Washington Consensus, this permanent threat in the subcontinent does not justify demonizing social struggles and intellectual views that question the current Commodities Consensus, nor does it legitimize the conspiratorial readings and binary understandings present in a significant part of extractivist progressivism and its intellectual spokespersons, when building the barricades of the new political pragmatism.

In my opinion, we would be ill advised as the Latin American left to believe that these criticisms are an exclusive domain of the political right, since neither the defense of pluralism nor the condemnation of the concentration of power—visible in the fetishization of the leaders—has an ideological copyright. Furthermore, as Roberto Gargarella (2014) argues, it is almost impossible to believe that the expansion and promotion of popular participation and the concentration of power can come together—and reelection is clearly an expression of concentration of power. Finally, we should not forget that it is precisely the most vulnerable sectors and the lefts that are the recurrent victims of the closure of political spaces and the processes of human rights violations.

Hence, these debates and new positions regarding the relationship among neo-extractivism, the commodity boom, and the return of populism created a fissure in critical Latin American thought. Unlike in the 1990s, when the continent seemed to have been reformatted in a unidirectional manner by the neoliberal model, the new century is mired in a series of tensions and contradictions that are difficult to process. The passage from the Washington Consensus to the Commodity Consensus and the return of high-intensity populism created new problems and paradoxes that gradually reconfigured the horizon of critical thought, confronting us with theoretical and political fissures that progressively crystallize in increasingly antagonistic ideological positions.

In short, much has happened between 2000 and 2015. In this context, we might ask ourselves whether the tension between transformation and restoration typical of this *epochal change* has led us to the *end of a cycle*, which could be characterized as a *passive revolution*, as Massimo Modonesi (2013) argues—a category for historical analysis that, associated with transformism and democratic Caesarism, expresses a reconstitution of social relations in a new order of hierarchical domination. This would constitute a sad and deplorable end for our progressive governments, which entailed so much collective energy and political expectations, which of course includes not only populist experiences in their various matrices but also others such as the Brazilian Workers' Party (Partido dos Trabalhadores; PT), which in Dilma Rousseff's second term has experienced its darkest moment, marked by corruption and economic adjustment, while relinquishing its promises of social transformation.

What is clear is that the end of the cycle signals important changes in both economic and political terms, since speaking of a *new Latin American left* is not the same as speaking of *twenty-first-century populisms*. In the passage from one characterization to the next, something important was lost—something that evokes abandonment, the loss of the emancipatory dimension of politics, and signals an evolution toward traditional domination models based on the cult of the leader, their identification with the state, and the aspiration to remain in power forever. In this line, the perverse equation established today of "more extractivism/less democracy" raises the question of the always tense and contradictory relationship between populisms and democracies, and demonstrates the dangerous slippage toward political closure, questioning pluralism and increasingly criminalizing dissidence.

The end of the progressive cycle also confronts us with a greater supply of conservative politics and the possible return of the right in the region—as was already the case in Argentina through elections—and reinstates the challenge of reinventing plural and democratic leftist movements with an emancipatory vocation.

Notes

INTRODUCTION

1. All quotations originally in Spanish are translated into English, except when there is an English version available, in which case we employ the text of the English translation published. [Trans.]

2. Although strictly speaking the term *campesino* differs from the term *peasant*—which refers to agricultural laborers in a European context—we chose to translate it as such for the sake of clarity and simplicity. [Trans.]

3. Postcolonial critique has been developed by other authors from the South, that is, Ranajit Guha, Partha Chatterjee, and Gayatri Spivak, among others. The inaugural manifesto of subaltern studies was published in 1993, promoted by Latin American scholars living in the United States. The manifesto argued for the need to reflect not only on the new dynamics or problematics derived from globalization but also on the subaltern sectors in Latin America. It proposed finding the locus from where such subalterns speak as political and social subjects. See Castro Gómez and Mendieta (1998, 70–83).

4. The proposal of these critical dialogues is outlined in his interview/conversation with Silvia Rivera. See Rivera Cusicanqui and Santos (2015).

5. The encounter was organized by the Costa Rican Jorge Rovira.

CHAPTER I. THE DEBATE ON THE INDIGENOUS AND *INDIANIDAD*

1. In 2012 a new census conducted in Bolivia resulted in different data on the indigenous population, that is, that only 40 percent of the population over fifteen years of age considered itself a member of Indigenous Peasant Native Peoples. In this regard, see the chapter on the topic in Nicolas and Quisbert (2014). For a historic perspective on the topic, see Lavaud and Lestage (2009).

2. In 2006 Toledo counted 671 indigenous peoples "directly or implicitly recognized by States" in public policy instruments (CEPAL 2007, 160, citing Toledo 2006). As mentioned above, by 2012 the number had risen to 826 peoples.

3. The Amazon, with 11 percent of the Peruvian population, is home to innumerable indigenous peoples, many of them isolated from Western culture. Historically, the feeling of social and cultural superiority over Amazonian peoples has not been exclusive to the elites and urban middle classes—especially in Lima—but has also been shared by indigenous and peasant peoples in the Andean region.

4. When a page number cannot be given for a cite of an English edition because an electronic source was consulted, the Spanish edition is also cited in order to provide a page number. [Trans.]

5. This was also the case for women, as the feminist movement denounced, since their claims were not understood as belonging to the field of rationality and politics but to that of irrationality or the private sphere.

6. Saavedra was later president of Bolivia from 1921 to 1925.

7. "In 1899, Venezuelan author César Zumeta published a booklet entitled *El continente enfermo*; the same year, Argentine essayist Agustín Álvarez wrote his *Manual de patología política*; in 1905, another Argentine, Manuel Ugarte, published *Enfermedades sociales*; and in 1909, the Bolivian Alcides Arguedas published his renowned essay *Pueblo enfermo*. Evidently, these authors did not share the same ideas regarding Spanish American reality, but there is a striking similarity in their terminology. All of them agreed that the continent—or the country—was seriously ill, and many were convinced that the cause of the illness was race" (Stabb 1968, 182–83).

8. Domingo Faustino Sarmiento's view of Civilization and Barbarism, as expressed in *Facundo* ([1845] 1988) and further developed in *Conflictos y armonías de las razas en América* (Conflicts and harmonies of the races in America; [1883] 1915), with a clearly racialist/positivist perspective, was one of the main sources of inspiration. See Svampa (1994, 1998).

9. The Argentine state and the army thus inaugurated the sinister method of "appropriation": Women and children, violently separated from their families, were handed over to white families, where they ended up working for the rest of their lives as domestic personnel. Although there are no linear continuities, this incites us to reflect on later applications of certain sinister methods of extermination (their appropriation in the long term), applied first to indigenous people and, a century later, to the children of forcefully disappeared persons during the latest military dictatorship in Argentina (1976–83).

10. The authors examined include Claudia Briones, Morita Carrasco, Gastón Gordillo, Diana Lenton, Silvia Hirsch, Mónica Quijada, Rita Segato, Carlos Martínez Sarasola, Walter Delirio, and Liliana Tamagno, among others.

11. The campaign to return the indigenous remains to their communities of origin began in 1998 with the return of the cacique Inacayal, but the museum continued to display human remains until 2006, when it was ordered to remove them.

12. Bolivia lost its access to the sea, and Peru lost a part of the Arica province in the south.

13. The culturalist thesis developed in Germany in opposition to the French notion of civilization, more closely associated with the idea of material progress and meeker customs (see Elías 1989).

14. *Eurindia* was more influential in the world of art than in the world of ideas.

15. A legendary character characterized by Mariátegui as "the Don Quixote of Latin America's politics and literature" (quoted in Melgar Bao 2012). His most important

works on the indigenous question are *La justicia del inca*, published in 1926 in Belgium, and *La tragedia del Altiplano*, written in Europe and published in Buenos Aires in 1935.

16. An edited version of the text can be found at https://www.ensayistas.org/antologia/XXA/marof/divisiones.htm.

17. Far from Tamayo's moralist critiques or even Arguedas's racialism, Marof does not discard mestizos—whom he does not consider a dominant class, even though they can serve as an instrument of the dominant class.

18. We shall speak of *congresos indigenales* later in this text, in the context of integrationist *indigenismo*.

19. The later accusation of populism against Mariátegui in 1942 by the Cuban Communist Party did not help to understand the indigenous question and its relationship to the national question. José María Aricó (1978) developed this topic at length. I return to this in chapter 4, on populism.

20. The controversy also entailed the issue of the name. One year earlier, Mariátegui and his friends had founded the Socialist Party of Peru. The Third International equated "socialist" to reformist social democracy and even "treason" and demanded that the name be changed to Communist Party.

21. I return to this in chapter 4, on populism.

22. In addition to other anthropologists and archaeologists such as Moisés Sáenz, Gastón Aguirre Beltrán, and Alfonso Caso.

23. Vasconcelos held several government offices, especially in education as rector of the National Autonomous University of Mexico (Universidad Nacional Autónoma de México) and secretary of public education from 1921 to 1924. He also coined the famous slogan inscribed on the university's main building: "For my race the spirit shall speak."

24. *Arielismo* refers to the book *Ariel* ([1900] 2021), by Uruguayan author José Enrique Rodó, where he inverted William Shakespeare's famous metaphor that associated Caliban (barbarism) with America, while also criticizing the United States for its materialism and identifying Latin America with a spiritualist (and elitist) legacy or mission.

25. In Mexico an ejido is a rural property for collective use, which implies a cooperative exploitation of land.

26. During this period, Che Guevara was murdered (October 1967). Interestingly, in his notes, Guevara speaks of peasants, not of Indians.

27. In 1950, 6 percent of the country's hacienda owners held 92 percent of all tillable lands. At the same time, 60 percent of landowners possessed only 0.2 percent of the land. Out of a total of thirty-six million tillable hectares, eight million were reassigned from 1954 to 1968 (Gotkowitz 2007; 2011, 361).

28. Vincent Nicolas and Pablo Quisbert's work reconstructs the topic of Tiwanaku as the original source of nationality, starting in 1930.

29. The peasant federations, guided by Marxist principles, in turn subordinated peasants (Indians) to the urban proletariat (mestizos) (de la Cadena 2000; 2004, 209–11).

30. This process of racialization of native subaltern sectors took place earlier in the Yrigoyen administration. However, under Peronism it reached unprecedented levels. I analyzed these issues in my 1994 book *El dilema argentino: Civilización o Barbarie* (The Argentine dilemma: Civilization or barbarism).

31. The clause was reestablished after the 1955 coup, which revoked the Peronist Constitution. To consult the Constitution sanctioned in 1853, see "Constitución de la Nación Argentina de 1853," InfoLEG, https://www.infoleg.gob.ar/?page_id=3873.

32. For a detailed account of the events, see Valko (2013).

33. According to anthropologist Carlos Martínez Sarasola (2011, 587–88), Peronism began a policy of land distribution around 1949, effective in 1952, that benefited indigenous communities in Jujuy.

34. The massacre was finally recognized by Argentina's justice system as a crime against humanity in October 2015. See Agencia Farco 2015.

35. I would like to thank Juan Carlos Torre for informing me of this incredible episode.

36. For a detailed account of the first indigenous census, see Martínez Sarasola (2011, 607–11).

37. Although José Bengoa (2009) places the first indigenous emergence in the 1980s and its pinnacle in the 1990s, there was already a radical turn in the 1970s in terms of how indigenous people were conceived.

38. Thus, once the concept of race is at least formally rejected, the category of ethnicity emerges, which emphasizes cultural practices and viewpoints that distinguish a certain community of people: language, history, real or imagined ancestry, religion, imaginaries, dress (Giddens 2000, 277–315). While ethnic differences are culturally learned and passed on and are conceived dynamically, race emphasizes physical or phenotypical variations that communities or societies consider socially significant.

39. Excerpt of *Manifiesto del Movimiento Indio Tupak Katari: MITKA* (Manifesto of the Tupak Katari Indian Movement: MITKA), reproduced in full in N. Rodríguez and Varese (1981b).

40. A number of these manifestos, documents, and conclusions of different national and continental congresses in the 1970s were collected by Nemesio Rodríguez and Stefano Varese in two volumes—*El pensamiento indígena contemporáneo en América Latina* (Contemporary indigenous thought in Latin America; 1981a) and *Experiencias organizativas indígenas en América Latina* (Indigenous organizational experiences in Latin America; 1981b).

41. See also the documents of the second meeting of Barbados, compiled in the book *Indianidad y descolonización en América Latina* (Indianidad and decolonization in Latin America; see "Documentos" 1979).

42. In the same line, Bonfil published a critical text in 1970, *De eso que llaman antropología mexicana* (That which they call Mexican anthropology, with Arturo Warman and Margarita Armas), and *México profundo: Una civilización negada* (Deep Mexico: Reclaiming a civilization) in 1987.

43. García Linera develops the category of "ethnic capital" to analyze the relationship between social class and race in Bolivian society. For an elaboration of the concept, see García Linera (2007). For an overview of the author's sociological work, see *La potencia plebeya* (Plebeian power; 2008d).

44. For this reconstruction, we referred to Anaya (2006), Stavenhagen (2006a, 2006b), and González (2010).

45. It was precisely at the beginning of the twenty-first century that, for the first time in its twenty years of existence, the Inter-American Court of Human Rights dealt with a case of violation of the collective rights of an indigenous community (Hale 2002, 486).

46. See chapter 3, where I discuss the various theories on globalization and their dialogue with dependency theory.

47. The issue of multiculturalism rekindled the debate between the universalist and the particularist (or culturalist) perspectives, illustrated in the eighteenth and nineteenth centuries by French rationalist philosophers, who advocated for a universalist perspective of "civilization," on one hand, and the German tradition represented by romantic historicism (Johann Gottfried Herder, among others), which asserted the particularism of "culture," on the other. On the opposition between culture and civilization, see Elías (1989); for a Latin American reading, see Díaz Polanco (2006b).

48. On the topic of the emergence and evolution of MAS, see Do Alto (2007) and Do Alto and Stefanoni (2010).

49. We took these two stereotypes created by the elite from Albó (2008).

50. According to Araceli Burguete Cal y Mayor (2010), the multicultural paradigm arose precisely to counter the actions related to the paradigm of autonomy.

51. See the works of Brazilian critical geography, among them those of the aforementioned Bernardo Mançano Fernandes, Milton Santos, and Carlos Porto Gonçalves.

52. On this topic, we reviewed the positions of Carlos Degregori (1995), Marisol de la Cadena (2000), Ramón Pajuelo Teves (2007), José Antonio Lucero and María Elena García (2006), Rodrigo Montoya Rojas (2006), and Carmen Salazar Soler (2014).

53. One of the rare exceptions is Hugo Blanco, who considers himself an "Indian" and not only a peasant, as emphasized in *We the Indians* ([2010] 2018).

54. See the analysis by Pajuelo Teves (2007, 108–25). Pajuelo Teves argues that both Alberto Fujimori and Alejandro Toledo invoked the ethnic factor but created an anti-indigenous government (110).

55. An interesting reflection on this process can be found in Tamagno (2009, 105–13).

56. There is a thin line between incorporation and co-optation; in the twelve years of consecutive government with Néstor Kirchner and Cristina Fernández de Kirchner, the tendency leans clearly toward co-optation and a complete lack of independence from government politics.

CHAPTER 2. BETWEEN THE OBSESSION WITH DEVELOPMENT AND ITS CRITIQUE

1. For a general discussion of the topic of capitalism, see Gutiérrez Garza (1994), Mallorquín (1994), Sztulwark (2003), Nahón et al. (2006), Brieva et al. (2002), Pécaut (1989), Mathias and Salama (1983), and Gutiérrez Garza and González Gaudiano (2010).

2. In Spanish, *idea-fuerza*. The expression was coined by Octavio Rodríguez and revisited by Estela Gutiérrez Garza (1994, 126).

3. According to Carlos Mallorquín (1994, 71), conceptual elements can be found in this text that would be revisited by dependency theory later, especially in the book

Dependency and Development in Latin America (1979a), by Fernando Henrique Cardoso and Enzo Faletto, who were in Chile at the time and participated in the discussions.

4. *Revista de la CEPAL*, first quarter of 1976, https://repositorio.cepal.org/server/api/core/bitstreams/3e3e0bb3-2cb7-4f6d-8129-5884610beb96/content. It also includes papers by Marshall Wolfe and Prebisch, among others.

5. In her book *Imperial Eyes: Travel Literature and Transculturation*, Canadian essayist Mary Louise Pratt ([1992] 2007) undertook a detailed analysis of the images deployed by Europeans about America, especially those of nature and the continent's landscapes, through naturalists such as Linnaeus, Buffon, and Alexander von Humboldt. But it was above all Antonello Gerbi's monumental work, *The Dispute of the New World* ([1982] 2010), that traced the uninterrupted history of the thesis of America's inferiority, from Georges Buffon, through Cornelio de Paw, to its most forceful expression with Georg Wilhelm Friedrich Hegel.

6. The model of the "ideal" society was based on a radical change in the world's social organization in order to free humanity from underdevelopment and oppression. According to Gilberto Gallopín (2004), the basic elements for any desirable society are (a) equity at all levels based on the satisfaction of basic needs—food, housing, health, education; (b) nonconsumerism, that is, production must be determined by social needs instead of profit, and the structure and growth of the economy must be compatible with the environment; and (c) recognition that social needs—beyond basic needs—are differently defined at different moments by different cultures and different forms of social organization. Finally, the priority was social *participation* in decision-making, both as an end in itself and as the main mechanism to establish the legitimacy of needs in the new society.

7. See the next chapter, devoted to the field of dependency.

8. According to Escobar, in the 1960s and 1970s there were tendencies with a critical position to development, even though they were not sufficient to articulate a rejection of the discourse on which it was founded. Among them, he mentions the "pedagogy of the oppressed" (Paulo Freire [1970] 2005), liberation theology, and the critiques to "intellectual colonialism" (Fals Borda 1970), as well as dependency theory. He also observes that the most incisive cultural critique of development was articulated by Ivan Illich, who created the notion of conviviality, which exerted a great influence in Latin America, especially in Mexico (Escobar [1990] 2005, 22).

9. For an analysis of the origins of European environmentalism, see Offe ([1988] 1996) and Melucci ([1977] 1990).

10. Alimonda compiled two important books on the topic: *Ecología política: Naturaleza, sociedad y utopía* (Political ecology: Nature, society and utopia; 2002) and *Los tormentos de la materia: Aportes para una ecología política latinoamericana* (The torments of matter: Contributions toward a Latin American political economy; 2006). A more recent book that engages with the debates on extractivism is *La naturaleza colonizada: Ecología política y minería en América Latina* (Colonized nature: Political ecology and mining in Latin America; 2011).

11. See "Primer Encuentro Nacional de la Red Brasilera de Justicia Ambiental" [First National Meeting of the Brazilian Environmental Justice Network], Observatorio Latinoamericano de Conflictos Ambientales (OLCA), December 2004, www.olca.cl/oca/justicia/justicia02.htm, and Rede Brasileira de Justiça Ambiental, https://rbja.org/.

1. I employ the frame alignment theory freely in its four types of moments, as proposed by David Snow (bridging, amplification, extension, and transformation). See Snow (2004).

2. On the sources of dependency, see Osorio (1994), Domingo Ouriques (1994), and Bambirra (1978).

3. These ten years separated the first edition of *Dependency and Development* and the postscript, elaborated specifically for the English edition and later included in subsequent editions of the book in both English and Spanish.

4. The theory of unequal and combined development refers to Leon Trotsky. Its purpose is to understand capitalist evolution in colonial and semicolonial countries.

5. We employed here the 2001 edition.

6. The texts of the controversy can be found in www.elortiba.org/old/pdf/Debate_Puiggros_Gunder_Frank.pdf.

7. For a review of approaches regarding the bourgeoisie, see Acuña (1994).

8. Class unity occurs when a sector (agrarian, industrial or financial, exporters or internal market providers) imposes itself over the other sectors, maintaining the contradictions, while imposing "social domination" on society.

9. Book review published in the *New York Review of Books* in 1967 (157).

10. Emphasis added.

CHAPTER 4. POPULISMS, POLITICS, AND DEMOCRACY

1. There are many texts and compilations on populism. The first one was *Populism: Its Meaning and National Characteristics*, by Ghita Ionescu and Ernest Gellner (1969). Margaret Canovan's book *Populism* (1981) represented a turning point by questioning the very use of the concept of populism. Several works published in Spain approached the topic from a critical/pejorative perspective, among them José Álvarez Junco's *Populismo, caudillaje y discurso demagógico* (Populism, *caudillaje*, and demagogical discourse; 1987). See also the compilation by Frank Adler et al., *Populismo posmoderno* (Postmodern populism; 1996). Two excellent compilations were published in Argentina: Carlos Vilas's *La democratización fundamental: El populismo en América Latina* (The fundamental democratization: Populism in Latin America; 1994) and Moira Mackinnon and Mario Petrone's *Populismo y neopopulismo en América Latina: El problema de la Cenicienta* (Populism and neopopulism in Latin America: The Cinderella problem; 1998). Detailed reviews of the main interpretations on the issue are also found in Carlos Moscoso Perea's *El populismo en América Latina* (Populism in Latin America; 1990) and, recently, Aleardo Laría's *La religión populista: Una crítica al populismo posmarxista* (The populist religion: A critique of postmarxist populism; 2011). The return of populism in recent years produced new works, among them Flavia Freidenberg's *La tentación populista: Una vía de acceso al poder en América Latina* (The populist temptation: A path to power in Latin America; 2007) and Carlos de la Torre and Enrique Peruzzotti's compilation *El retorno del pueblo: Populismo y nuevas democracias en América Latina* (The return of the people: Populism and new democracies in Latin America; 2008).

2. I revisit previous works here: Martuccelli and Svampa (1997) and Svampa (2005).

3. I would like to thank Pablo Ospina for comments and suggestions regarding the Ecuadorian case.

4. The true culprits, however, were not the masses. "The culprits are the caudillos of the civil war, who, for the sake of the victory of their appetites and ambitions, unscrupulously incite the resentments and primitive forces of misery, even knowing that with such convulsive movements no social and historical improvement is possible" (Americo Ghioldi, *Alpargatas y Libros en la historia argentina* [1946], 24–25, quoted in Svampa 1994, 325).

5. Another text by Cueva, with an in-depth analysis of the relationship between the leader and the masses in Velasquismo, is *El proceso de dominación política en Ecuador* (The process of political domination in Ecuador; 1988). A more thorough review of the various readings on Velasquismo can be found in de la Torre (1993).

6. I return to this subject when examining current debates.

7. Their article was republished in a compilation edited by Vilas (1994).

8. Laclau later acknowledged the rupture between populism and socialism and did not insist on the subject in his later works.

9. E. P. Thompson's concept of the "moral economy of the crowd" and Raymond Williams's "structure of feeling" inspire this plebeian perspective.

10. With this concept, Williams (1978) refers to an effectively social and material type of feeling and thought in an embryonic state, without ever truly giving rise to fully articulated and well-defined forms; that is, a specifically qualitative dimension, never completely incorporated into fixed institutional forms.

11. For a review of the literature, see Martuccelli and Svampa (1997).

CHAPTER 5. THE WAYS OF *INDIANISMO*

1. "The so-called 'Cocopa Law' was elaborated in December 1996 by the legislators from the Concord and Pacification Commission (Cocopa). The legislators belonged to the four most important political parties: PRI, PAN, PRD, and PT." "Basically, the 'Cocopa Law' provides constitutional recognition of a reality: indigenous people are a part of Mexico and have their own forms of social and political organization; that is, they have the right to be both indigenous and Mexican" (EZLN 2001).

2. Strictly speaking, there are three levels: the community, the municipality, and the *caracol*, which administers several municipalities. But the autonomous territories are not closed to the outside world and establish relationships with non-Zapatistas, especially in terms of mediation and justice. For a detailed analysis of the evolution of autonomies, based on fieldwork conducted from 2005 to 2007, see Baronnet et al. (2011).

3. On this topic, see also Baschet (2014).

4. For an analysis of these and other de facto autonomies, see the edited volume by Giovanna Gasparello and Jaime Quintana Guerrero (2010), which in the first part examines various aspects of autonomy in Guerrero and Oaxaca.

5. I return to the issue of those dilemmas in chapter 8, on populism.

6. On the vicissitudes of the Constituent Assembly, see Prada Alcoreza (2010).

7. This conceptualization was elaborated by the Guarani people and enriched by the various organizations that participated in the process (June 7, 2006). The new Bolivian Constitution recognizes the preexistence of "indigenous-native-peasant" nations and

peoples, a triple characterization that, according to Fernando Mayorga (2011, 84), corresponds to the combination of three different codes: "native nations" (*naciones originarias*), a denomination employed by organizations in the highlands; "indigenous peoples" (*pueblos indígenas*), employed by ethnic groups in the lowlands; and "peasants" (campesinos), employed by rural workers' organizations assembled in rural unions since 1952.

8. Text of the decree: "Bolivia: Decreto Supremo N° 212, 15 de julio de 2009," accessed November 27, 2024, https://www.lexivox.org/norms/BO-DS-N212.html.

9. I return to this topic in the next section.

10. Pueblo Indígena Kichwa de Sarayaku vs. Ecuador, Corte Interamericana de Derechos Humanos, sentence, June 27, 2012, https://www.corteidh.or.cr/docs/casos/articulos /seriec_245_esp.pdf.

11. Based on interviews I conducted that year in La Paz.

12. Available at "Pueblo Indígena Kichwa de Sarayaku vs. Ecuador," Corte Interamericana de Derechos Humanos, https://corteidh.or.cr/docs/casos/articulos/seriec_245_esp.pdf.

13. On the topic of the *rondas campesinas*, see Hoetmer et al. (2013). For a legal reading of the pertinence of the *rondas campesinas* regarding the right to prior consultation, see Yrigoyen Fajardo (2002).

14. The first disagreement was the Malón de la Paz in 1946, examined earlier in this book.

CHAPTER 6. DEBATES ON DEVELOPMENT

1. On the topic of maldevelopment, see Tortosa (2011) and Svampa and Viale (2014).

2. Given its importance in the new processes of accumulation, the notion of territory became a sort of social analyzer. In this respect, the main conceptual contributions have come from Brazilian critical geography, through authors such as Milton Santos, Carlos Porto Gonçalves, and Bernardo Mançano Fernandes, among others. We have synthesized these contributions in Svampa and Viale (2014).

3. Internationally, the works of David Bollier and Silke Helfrich, in the context of the Commons Strategies Group, are essential (see Bollier and Helfrich 2012).

4. For a discussion of the various nuances surrounding the notion of strategic natural resources, see Fornillo (2014).

5. Another collection with contributions on the topic was compiled by Gian Carlos Delgado Ramos (2014) in Mexico, as well as the collection published by Fundación F. Ebert (Endara 2014) and the one by Salvador Schavelzon (2015).

6. I would like to thank Eduardo Gudynas for underscoring the importance of the rights of nature and relational worldviews in a seminar that we attended together in Santiago de Chile in 2013, which inspired me to explore this avenue. This section owes much to his contributions.

7. "*Superstrong* sustainability maintains that the environment must be valued in ways that go well beyond its economic utility: There are also cultural, ecological, religious, or aesthetic values that are as important or more" (Gudynas 2011a, 85).

8. It is also necessary to answer more basic questions regarding the current energy model. For example, for what purpose and for whom do we produce energy? Energy production is still at the service of the extractive model, and this has not changed in any way with progressive governments.

CHAPTER 7. DEPENDENCY AS A "COMPASS"

1. A number of collective texts were produced within CLACSO that analyzed the new problematic (see Borón et al. 1999).

2. The term *BRIC* was coined by Goldman Sachs in 2001 to refer to the emerging economies that would mark the economic and political developments in the twenty-first century. The first BRIC meeting was held in 2006 with the presence of Brazil, Russia, India, and China. In 2010 South Africa was invited to join the group.

3. This section partially draws on an article I elaborated together with Ariel Slipak (Svampa and Slipak 2015). I also took the liberty of employing information generously shared by Edgardo Lander (2014), with whom I participated in the Permanent Working Group on Alternatives to Development.

4. This characterization is employed, among others, by Bernardo Mançano Fernandes and other renowned Brazilian geographers (Milton Santos, Carlos Porto Gonçalves, Jorge Montenegro); Norma Giarracca, Miguel Teubal, Horacio Machado Aráoz, and myself in Argentina; Marielle Palau in Paraguay; and Raúl Zibechi in Uruguay.

CHAPTER 8. TWENTY-FIRST-CENTURY POPULISMS

1. Plural Reflections on the Experience of Progressive Governments in Latin America, seminar at Universidad Mayor de San Andrés, La Paz, October 2015.

2. On this subject, in addition to her 2009 text, Harnecker wrote *Herramientas para la participación* (Tools for participation) together with Luis Bonilla and Haiman El Troudi (El Troudi et al. 2005). My gratitude to Margarita López Maya, Edgardo Lander, and Emiliano Terán Mantovani for the bibliographic suggestions.

3. The smallest unit is the communal council; several communal councils together constitute a commune, which can be united through "territorial corridors"; and the highest body for self-government is the communal parliament, made up of two speakers from each communal council, from the communal bank, and from the socio-productive organizations.

4. On these limitations, see Lander (2004, 2013).

5. For an interesting analysis, see Sarlo (2011).

6. A similar reading to the one presented here, which understands Kirchnerism as "middle-class Peronism," can be found in Altamirano (2013).

7. On the subject, see the excellent reconstruction by F. Ramírez (2005).

8. The plurinational state had already been sanctioned in the 1988 Constitution.

FINAL REFLECTIONS

1. In 2000 a pioneer in this field in Latin America was the study group on political ecology coordinated by Héctor Alimonda, where several of the best-known representatives of ecology in the continent were present, among them Enrique Leff, Henri Acselrad, Guillermo Castro Herrero, Roberto Guimarães, and Arturo Escobar. Today the field of political ecology is very broad and includes a large number of women.

References

Aboy Carlés, G. 2001. *Las dos fronteras de la democracia Argentina: La reformulación de las identidades políticas de Alfonsín a Menem*. Rosario, Argentina: Homo Sapiens.

Aboy Carlés, G. 2010. "Las dos caras de Jano: Acerca de la relación compleja entre populismo e instituciones políticas." *Pensamento Plural*, no. 7, 21–40. https://periodicos-old.ufpel.edu.br/ojs2/index.php/pensamentoplural/article/view/3642.

Aboy Carlés, G. 2012. "El populismo entre la ruptura y la integración." *Revista de Ciencia Política* 15 (10): 87–98.

Aboy Carlés, G. 2014. "La democratización beligerante del populismo." *Revista de la Asamblea Nacional de Panamá*, no. 12, 46–57.

Acosta, A. 2011. "Hacia la declaración universal de los derechos de la naturaleza: Reflexiones para la acción." Alta alegremia, January 13. https://www.altaalegremia.com.ar/contenidos/declaracion_universal_derechos_naturaleza.html.

Acosta, A., E. Martínez, and W. Sacher. 2013. "Salir del extractivismo: Una condición para el Sumak Kawsay; Propuesta sobre petróleo, minería y energía en Ecuador." In *Alternativas al capitalismo/colonialismo del siglo XXI*, by Grupo Permanente de Trabajo sobre Alternativas al Desarrollo. Quito: Fundación Rosa Luxemburgo.

Acselrad, H., ed. 2004a. *Conflitos ambientais no Brasil*. Rio de Janeiro: Relume-Dumará, Heinrich Böll Foundation.

Acselrad, H. 2004b. "Movimiento de justicia ambiental: Estrategia argumentativa y fuerza simbólica." In *Ética ecológica: Propuestas para la reorientación*, edited by J. Riechmann. Montevideo: Nordman.

Acuña, C. 1994. "El análisis de la burguesía como actor politico." *Realidad Económica*, no. 128, 45–77.

Adamovsky, E., C. Albertani, B. Arditi, et al. 2011. *Pensar las autonomías: Alternativas de emancipación al capital y el Estado*. Mexico City: Bajo Tierra–Sísifo.

Adler, F., T. Fleming, P. Gottfried, et al. 1996. *Populismo posmoderno*. Buenos Aires: Universidad Nacional de Quilmes.

Agencia Farco. 2015. "La justicia confirmó que la Masacre de Rincón Bomba fue un crimen de lesa humanidad." October 13. https://agencia.farco.org.ar/noticias/la-justicia-confirmo-que-la-masacre-de-rincon-bomba-fue-un-crimen-de-lesa-humanidad/.

Albó, X. 2002. *Pueblos indios en la política.* La Paz: Cuadernos de Investigación y Promoción del Campesinado (CIPCA).

Albó, X. 2008. *Movimientos y poder indígena en Bolivia, Ecuador y Perú.* La Paz: Cuadernos de Investigación y Promoción del Campesinado (CIPCA).

Albó, X. 2011. "Suma qamaña = convivir bien: ¿Cómo medirlo?" In *Vivir bien: ¿Paradigma no capitalista?*, edited by I. Farah and L. Vasapollo. La Paz: CIDES-UMSA. https://biblioteca.clacso.edu.ar/clacso/engov/20131216115814/VivirBien.pdf.

Alimonda, H., ed. 2002. *Ecología política: Naturaleza, sociedad y utopía.* Buenos Aires: CLACSO.

Alimonda, H. 2006. *Los tormentos de la materia: Aportes para una ecología política latinoamericana.* Buenos Aires: CLACSO.

Alimonda, H. 2011. *La naturaleza colonizada: Ecología política y minería en América Latina.* Buenos Aires: CLACSO.

Almeyra, G. 2008. "Los vaivenes de los movimientos sociales en México." *Revista OSAL*, no. 24, 87–101. https://bibliotecavirtual.clacso.org.ar/ar/libros/osal/osal24/05almeyra.pdf.

Altamirano, C. 2013. "El kirchnerismo es el peronismo de las clases medias." Interview, Agencia Paco Urondo, Buenos Aires, September 13. https://www.agenciapacourondo.com.ar/cultura/el-kirchnerismo-es-el-peronismo-de-las-clases-medias.

Altamirano, C., and B. Sarlo. 1983. *Ensayos argentinos: De Sarmiento a la vanguardia.* Buenos Aires: CEPAL.

Altvater, E. 2000. "El lugar y el tiempo de lo político bajo las condiciones de la globalización económica." *Zona Abierta*, nos. 92–93, 7–61.

Álvarez Junco, J., ed. 1987. *Populismo, caudillaje y discurso demagógico.* Madrid: Siglo XXI.

Alvizuri, V. 2009. *La construcción de la aymaridad.* Santa Cruz de la Sierra: Editorial El País.

AméricaEconomía. 2014. "Bolivia tendrá una ley de consulta a indígenas sobre proyectos económicos." May 12. https://www.americaeconomia.com/politica-sociedad/politica/bolivia-tendra-una-ley-de-consulta-indigenas-sobre-proyectos-economicos.

Amin, S. 1973. *Le développement inégal: Essais sur les formations sociales dans le capitalisme périphérique.* Paris: Minuit.

Amin, S. 1976. *Unequal Development: An Essay on the Social Formations of Peripheral Capitalism.* New York: Monthly Review Press.

Amin, S. 1990. *Maldevelopment: Anatomy of a Global Failure.* London: Zed Books.

Anaya, S. J. 2006. "Los derechos de los pueblos indígenas." In *Pueblos indígenas y derechos humanos*, edited by N. Berraondo. Bilbao: Instituto de Derechos Humanos, Universidad de Deusto.

Anaya, S. J. 2012. *Informe definitivo del Relator Especial de los pueblos indígenas de la ONU, sobre la situación de los pueblos indígenas en Argentina.* United Nations. https://acnudh.org/wp-content/uploads/2012/09/Informe-del-Relator-sobre-derechos-de-pueblos-ind%C3%ADgenas-misi%C3%B3n-a-Argentina-2012.pdf.

Andrade, O. de. 1928. "Manifiesto antropófago." *Revista de Antropofagia*, no. 1, 3–7.

Ansaldi, W. 1991. *La búsqueda de América Latina.* Cuadernos, no. 1. Instituto de Investigaciones Sociales, UBA. http://geshal.sociales.uba.ar/wp-content/uploads/sites/110/2014/11/Ansaldi-1991-La-b%C3%BAsqueda-de-Am%C3%A9rica-Latina-1.pdf.

Antkowiak, T., and A. Gonza. 2010. "El derecho a la consulta en las Américas: Marco legal internacional." *Revista Aportes: Revista de la Fundación para el debido proceso legal* 3 (14): 2–5.

Antonelli, M. 2011. "Megaminería, desterritorialización del Estado y biopolítica." *Astrolabio*, no. 7, 3–22. https://revistas.unc.edu.ar/index.php/astrolabio/article/view/592.

Antonelli, M. 2014. "Megaminería transnacional e invención del mundo cantera." *Nueva Sociedad*, no. 252, 72–86. https://nuso.org/articulo/megamineria-transnacional-e -invencion-del-mundo-cantera/.

Aranda, D. 2011. "Laclau, el doble discurso y el verdadero kurso." *Taringa!*, October. https://www.taringa.net/+offtopic/laclau-el-doble-discurso-y-el-verdadero-kurso _15lzjr. No longer available.

Araujo, O. (1968) 2013. *Venezuela violenta*. Caracas: Colección Venezuela y su petróleo, Banco Central de Venezuela.

Arditi, B. 2004. "El populismo como espectro de la democracia: Una respuesta a Canovan." *Revista Mexicana de Ciencias Políticas y Sociales* 47 (191): 86–99.

Arditi, B. 2009. "El populismo como periferia interna de la democracia." In *El populismo como espejo de la democracia*, edited by F. Panizza. Buenos Aires: FCE.

Arguedas, A. (1909) 1999. *Pueblo enfermo*. Cochabamba, Bolivia: Librería La Juventud.

Argumedo, A. 2009. *Los silencios y las voces en América Latina: Notas sobre el pensamiento nacional y popular*. Buenos Aires: Ediciones de Pensamiento Nacional.

Aricó, J. 1978. *Mariátegui y los orígenes del marxismo latinoamericano*. Mexico City: Cuadernos de Pasado y Presente.

Aricó, J. 1988. *La cola del diablo: Itinerario de Gramsci en América Latina*. Buenos Aires: Siglo XXI.

Asamblea Permanente de Derechos Humanos and FIDH. 2013. *Bolivia: Informe de verificación de la consulta realizada en el territorio indígena Parque Nacional Isiboro-Sécure*. CEDIB, Bolivia. https://www.cedib.org/post_type_titulares/bolivia-informe -de-verificacion-de-la-consulta-realizada-en-el-territorio-indigena-parque-nacional -isiboro-secure-apdh-y-fidh-04-13.

Auyero, J. 2001. *La política de los pobres*. Buenos Aires: Manantial.

Bagú, S. (1949) 1992. *Economía de la sociedad colonial: Ensayo de historia comparada de América Latina*. Mexico City: Grijalbo/Conaculta.

Bagú, S. (1949) 2007. "Índole de la economía colonial y la economía como capitalismo colonial." *Rebelión*, May 2. https://www.rebelion.org/indole-de-la-economia-colonial -y-la-economia-como-capitalismo-colonial. Originally published in *La economía de la sociedad colonial*.

Bagú, S. 1952. *Estructura social de la colonia: En sayo de historia comparada de América Latina*. Buenos Aires: El Ateneo.

Bambirra, V. (1974) 1999. *El capitalismo dependiente latinoamericano*. 15th ed. Mexico City: Siglo XXI.

Bambirra, V. 1978. *Teoría de la dependencia: Una anticrítica*. Mexico City: Era.

Barbeito, A., and R. Lo Vuolo. 1992. *La modernización excluyente*. Buenos Aires: UNICEF–Ciepp–Losada.

Bárcena, A. 2012. *Informe anual 2012: Los bonos en la mira; Aporte y carga para las mujeres*. Santiago de Chile: CEPAL–Naciones Unidas.

Baronnet, B., M. Mora Bayo, and R. Stahler-Sholk, eds. 2011. *Luchas "muy otras": Zapatismo y autonomía en las comunidades indígenas de Chiapas*. Mexico City: Universidad Autónoma Metropolitana, Centro de Investigaciones y Estudios Superiores en Antropología Social, Universidad Autónoma de Chiapas. https://zapatismoyautonomia.files.wordpress.com/2013/12/luchas-muy-otras-2011.pdf.

Barragán, R. 1992. "Identidades indias y mestizas: Una intervención al debate." *Autodeterminación*, no. 10, 14–77.

Bartolomé, M. A. 2006. "Los laberintos de la identidad: Procesos identitarios en las poblaciones indígenas." *Avá*, no. 9, 28–48.

Bartra, A. 2012. "Reabriendo el debate latinoamericano sobre el campesinado como clase social." Interview by Arisbel Leyva Remó. *Rebelión* 59 (September 22): 9–32. https://rebelion.org/reabriendo-el-debate-latinoamericano-sobre-el-campesinado-como-clase-social/.

Baschet, J. 2014. *Adiós al capitalismo: Autonomía, sociedad del buen vivir y multiplicidad de mundos*. Buenos Aires: Ned-Futuro Anterior.

Beck, U. 1998. *What Is Globalization?* Cambridge, UK: Polity.

Beigel, F. 2003. *El itinerario y la brújula: El vanguardismo estético-político de José Carlos Mariátegui*. Buenos Aires: Biblos.

Beigel, F. 2006. "Vida, muerte y resurrección de las 'teorías de la dependencia.'" In *Crítica y teoría en el pensamiento social latinoamericano*, by F. Beigel, A. Falero, J. C. Garandilla, et al. Buenos Aires: CLACSO. https://biblioteca.clacso.edu.ar/clacso/becas/20140227054137/C05FBeigel.pdf.

Belvedere, C. 1997. "El inconcluso 'proyecto marginalidad.'" *Apuntes de Investigación*, no. 1, 97–115.

Bengoa, J. 2009. "¿Una segunda etapa de la emergencia indígena en América Latina?" *Cuadernos de Antropología Social*, no. 29, 7–22. http://revistascientificas.filo.uba.ar/index.php/CAS/article/view/2789.

Bennett, D., ed. 1998. *Multicultural States: Rethinking Difference and Identity*. London: Psychology Press.

Bergel, M. 2009. "En torno al autonomismo argentino." In *La autonomía posible: Reinvención de la autonomía y emancipación*, edited by C. Albertani, G. Rovira, and M. Modonesi. Mexico City: UACM.

Bertinat, P. 2013. "Un nuevo modelo energético para la construcción del Buen Vivir." In *Alternativas al capitalismo/colonialismo del siglo XXI*, by Grupo Permanente de Trabajo sobre Alternativas al Desarrollo. Quito: Fundación Rosa Luxemburgo.

Birnbaum, P. 1979. *Le peuple et les gros*. Paris: Pluriel.

Blanco, H. (2010) 2018. *We the Indians: The Indigenous Peoples of Peru and the Struggle for Land*. London: Merlin. Originally published as *Nosotros los indios*. Buenos Aires: La Minga and Ediciones Herramienta.

Blanco, H. 2011. "Reivindicando el espíritu y las luchas indígenas." In "Dossier: El debate sobre el pachamamismo." *Revista Tierra Socialista: Papeles sobre democracia, socialismo y ecología política* 2 (2): 169–74.

Blaser, M. 2009. "La ontología política de un programa de caza sustentable." *Red de Antropologías del Mundo—World Anthropologies Network*, no. 4, 81–107.

Boccara, G. 2011. "Le gouvernement des 'autres': Sur le multiculturalisme néolibéral en Amérique Latine." *Actuel Marx*, no. 50, 191–206.

Bolinaga, L. 2013. *China y el epicentro del Pacífico Norte*. Buenos Aires: Teseo.

Bollier, D., and S. Helfrich, eds. 2012. *The Wealth of the Commons: A World Beyond Market and State*. The Commons Strategies Group. Amherst, MA: Levellers Press.

Bonfil Batalla, G. 1972. "El concepto del indio en América: Una categoría de la situación colonial." *Anales de antropología* 9:105–24. http://www.journals.unam.mx/index.php/antropologia/article/view/23077.

Bonfil Batalla, G. 1987. *México profundo: Una civilización negada*. Mexico City: Grijalbo.

Bonfil Batalla, G. 1996. *México Profundo: Reclaiming a Civilization*. Austin: University of Texas Press.

Bonfil Batalla, G., A. Warman, M. Nolasco Armas, M. Oliveira Bustamante, and E. Valencia. (1970) 2022. *De eso que llaman antropología mexicana*. Mexico City: Fondo de Cultura Económica.

Borón, A. 1999. "Pensamiento único y resignación política." *Nueva Sociedad*, no. 163, 139–51.

Borón, A. 2002. *Imperio, imperialismo*. Buenos Aires: CLACSO.

Borón, A. 2012. *América Latina en la geopolítica del imperialismo*. Buenos Aires: Ediciones Luxemburgo.

Borón, A., J. Gambina, and N. Minsburg, eds. 1999. *Tiempos violentos: Neoliberalismo, globalización y desigualdad en América Latina*. Buenos Aires: CLACSO.

Bourdieu, P. 1993. *La misère du monde*. Paris: Seuil.

Bravo Ahuja Ruiz, M. M., E. Víctor, and M. A. Michel. 1994. "Alianza de clases y dominación: México, 1936–1940." In *La democratización fundamental: El populismo en América Latina*, edited by C. Vilas. Mexico City: Consejo Nacional para la Cultura y las Artes.

Bresser-Pereira, L. C. 2010. *Globalización y competencia: Apuntes para una macroeconomía estructuralista del desarrollo*. Buenos Aires: Siglo XXI.

Bretón, V., D. Cortes, and F. García. 2014. "En busca del Sumak Kawsay: Presentación del dossier." *Íconos: Revista de Ciencias Sociales*, no. 48, 9–24.

Briceño León, R., and H. R. Sontag. 1998. "La sociología de América Latina entre pueblo, época y desarrollo." *Zona Abierta*, nos. 82–83, 245–66.

Brieva, S., A. Castellani, M. F. Fernández Vila, and P. Laría. 2002. *El concepto de desarrollo en las ciencias sociales: Pasado y presente de una categoría central en el análisis de las sociedades latinoamericanas*. Buenos Aires: FLACSO.

Briones, C. 2005. *Cartografías argentinas: Políticas indigenistas y formaciones provinciales de la alteridad*. Buenos Aires: Geaprona.

Briones, C. 2008. "Formaciones de alteridad: Contextos globales, procesos nacionales y provincials." In *Cartografías argentinas: Políticas indigenistas y formaciones provinciales de alteridad*, edited by C. Briones. Buenos Aires: Antropofagia.

Briones, C. 2014. *Los derechos territoriales de los pueblos indígenas en Argentina: Un balance de los reconocimientos y las políticas*. Popayán, Colombia: Universidad del Cauca.

Briones, C. 2015. "Políticas indigenistas en Argentina: Entre la hegemonía neoliberal de los años noventa y la 'nacional y popular' de la última década." *Antípoda: Revista de Antropología y Arqueología*, no. 21, 21–48.

Bunge, C. O. 1903. *Nuestra América, ensayo de psicología social*. Introduction by José Ingenieros. Buenos Aires: Talleres Gráficos Argentinos L. J. Rosso.

Burbano de Lara, F. 1998. *El fantasma del populismo: Aproximación a un tema (siempre) actual*. Caracas: Nueva Sociedad.

Burguete Cal y Mayor, A. 2010. "Autonomía: La emergencia de un nuevo paradigma en las luchas por la descolonización en América Latina." In *La autonomía a debate: Autogobierno indígena y Estado plurinacional en América Latina*, edited by M. González, A. Burguete Cal y Mayor, and P. Ortiz. Quito: FLACSO–GTZ–IWGIA–CIESAS–UNICH.

Calderón, F., and E. Jelin. 1987. *Clases y movimientos sociales en América Latina: Perspectivas y realidades*. Buenos Aires: Centro de Estudios de Estado y Sociedad.

Camacho, D., ed. 1979. *Debates sobre la teoría de la dependencia y la sociología latinoamericana*. 2 vols. San José, Costa Rica: Educa.

Canovan, M. 1981. *Populism*. Boston: Houghton Mifflin Harcourt.

Canutto, O. 2014. "The Commodity Super Cycle: Is This Time Different?" *Economic Premise*, no. 150. Washington, DC: World Bank.

Cárdenas, L. 1940. "Discurso del Presidente de la República en el Primer Congreso Indigenista Interamericano." Pátzcuaro, Michoacán, April 14. Memoria Política de México. https://www.memoriapoliticademexico.org/Textos/6Revolucion/1940PCM.html.

Cardoso, C. 1973. "Sobre los modos de producción coloniales en América." In *Modos de producción en América Latina*, by C. Sempat Assadourian, C. F. Santana Cardoso, H. Ciafardini, J. C. Garavaglia, and E. Laclau. Mexico City: Cuadernos de Pasado y Presente.

Cardoso, F. H. (1971) 2001. "Comentario sobre los conceptos de sobrepoblación relativa y marginalidad." In *Marginalidad y exclusión social*, by J. Nun. Buenos Aires: FCE. Originally published in *Revista Latinoamericana de Ciencias Sociales*.

Cardoso, F. H. (1973) 1977. "Eppur si muove." In *Clases sociales y crisis política en América Latina*. Mexico City: UNAM–Siglo XXI.

Cardoso, F. H. 1974. "Notas sobre el estado actual de los estudios sobre dependencia." In *Desarrollo latinoamericano, ensayos críticos*, edited by José Serra. Mexico City: FoCoEo.

Cardoso, F. H., and E. Faletto. (1969) 2003. *Dependencia y desarrollo en América Latina*. Buenos Aires: Siglo XXI.

Cardoso, F. H., and E. Faletto. 1979a. *Dependency and Development in Latin America*. Berkeley: University of California Press.

Cardoso, F. H., and E. Faletto. 1979b. "Post scriptum a 'Dependencia y desarrollo en América Latina.'" In *Debates sobre la teoría de la dependencia y la sociología latinoamericana*, edited by D. Camacho. San José, Costa Rica: Educa. Available in English at https://doi.org/10.1525/9780520342118-009.

Cardoso, R. 1983. "Movimentos sociais urbanos." In *Sociedade e política no Brasil pós-64*, by B. Sorj and M. H. Tavares. São Paulo: Brasiliense.

Carrasco, M. 2002. "El movimiento indígena anterior a la reforma constitucional y su organización en el programa de participación de pueblos indígenas." University of Texas, working paper. http://lanic.utexas.edu/project/etext/llilas/vrp/carrasco.pdf.

Carson, R. (1962) 2022. *Silent Spring*. Boston: Mariner Books Classics.

Castel, R. 1995. *Les métamorphoses de la question sociale: Une chronique du salariat*. Paris: Fayard.

Castells, M. 1973. *La cuestión urbana*. Madrid: Siglo XXI.

Castells, M. 1974. *Movimientos sociales urbanos*. Buenos Aires: Siglo XXI.

Castells, M. 1999. *La era de la información*. Vol. 1. Madrid: Siglo XXI.

Castoriadis, C. 1997. *Un mundo fragmentado*. Buenos Aires: Altamira.

Castoriadis, C. 2005. *Une société à la derive: Entretiens et débats 1974–1997*. Paris: Seuil.

Castro Gómez, S. 2000. "Ciencias sociales, violencia epistémica y el problema de la invención del otro." In *La colonialidad del saber: Eurocentrismo y ciencias sociales; Perspectivas latinoamericanas*, by E. Lander. Buenos Aires: Consejo Latinoamericano de Ciencias Sociales (CLACSO).

Castro Gómez, S. 2012. "Los avatares de la crítica de colonial." Interview by Grupo de Estudios sobre Colonialidad (GESCO). *Tabula Rasa*, no. 16, 213–30.

Castro Gómez, S., and E. Mendieta. 1998. *Teorías sin disciplina (latinoamericanismo, poscolonialidad y globalización en debate)*. Mexico City: Miguel Ángel Porrúa.

Ceceña, A. E. 2003. "20, 10 y la historia infinita de la utopía de la reconstrucción." *Revista OSAL: A diez años del levantamiento zapatista*, September–December. https:// biblioteca-repositorio.clacso.edu.ar/handle/CLACSO/13448.

CEPAL. 2007. *Social Panorama of Latin America 2006*. Santiago de Chile: CEPAL.

CEPAL. 2014. *Guaranteeing Indigenous People's Rights in Latin America: Progress in the Past Decade and Remaining Challenges*. Santiago de Chile: CEPAL. https://www.cepal .org/en/publications/37051-guaranteeing-indigenous-peoples-rights-latin-america -progress-past-decade-and.

CEPAL, Observatorio de igualdad de género de América Latina y el Caribe (OIG). 2012. *Informe anual 2012: Los bonos en la mira, aporte y carga para las mujeres*. Santiago de Chile: CEPAL. https://www.cepal.org/es/publicaciones/35401-observatorio-igualdad -genero-america-latina-caribe-oig-informe-anual-2012-bonos.

Chang Rodríguez, E. 2009. "José Carlos Mariátegui y la polémica del indigenismo." *América sin Nombre*, nos. 13–14, 103–12. http://rua.ua.es/dspace/handle/10045/13375.

Chávez León, M. 2008. "Autonomías indígenas y Estado plurinacional." *Revista OSAL*, no. 24, 135–71.

Chicaiza, G. 2014. *Mineras chinas en Ecuador: Nueva dependencia*. Quito: Agencia Ecologista de Información Tegantai.

Choque Canqui, R. 2010. "El manifiesto de Tiwanaku (1973) y el inicio de la descolonización." *Revista de la Biblioteca y Archivo Histórico de la Asamblea Legislativa Plurinacional* 4 (11): 11–15.

Colectivo Guías, Grupo de Investigación en Antropología Social, F. M. Pepe, M. A. Suárez, and P. Harrison. 2010. *Antropología del genocidio, identificación y restitución: "Colecciones de restos humanos en el Museo de La Plata."* Prologue by Alberto Rex González and Walter Delrio. La Plata: De la Campana.

Comandanta Ramona. 1996. "Mensaje del Ejército Zapatista de Liberación Nacional en la celebración del 12 de octubre de 1996." Accessed November 27, 2024. https:// palabra.ezln.org.mx/comunicados/1996/1996_10_12.htm.

Coraggio, J. L. 2011. *Economía social y solidaria: El trabajo antes que el capital*. Quito: Abya-Yala.

Córdova, A. 1975. "Empleo, desempleo y marginalidad." In *Problemas del subdesarrollo latinoamericano*, by S. Bagú, A. Córdova, and F. H. Cardoso. Mexico City: Nuestro Tiempo.

Coronil, F. 1997. *The Magical State: Nature, Money, and Modernity in Venezuela*. Chicago: University of Chicago Press.

Cortez, D. 2014. "Genealogía del sumak kawsay y el buen vivir en Ecuador: Un balance." In *Poscrecimiento y buen vivir*, edited by G. Endara. Quito: Fundación Ebert.

Cueva, A. (1972) 2007. "El velasquismo: Ensayo de interpretación." In *Entre la ira y la esperanza y otros ensayos de crítica latinoamericana*. Bogotá: Pensamiento Crítico Latinoamericano, CLACSO.

Cueva, A. (1975) 2010. "El uso del concepto de modo de producción en América Latina: Algunos problemas teóricos." *Ola Financiera* 3 (5): 235–60.

Cueva, A. 1979. "Problemas y perspectivas de la teoría de la dependencia." In *Debates sobre la teoría de la dependencia y la sociología latinoamericana*, edited by D. Camacho. 2 vols. San José, Costa Rica: Educa.

Cueva, A. 1988. *El proceso de dominación política en Ecuador*. Quito: Planeta.

Cunill Grau, P. 1999. "La geohistoria." In *Para una historia de América, I: Las estructuras*, edited by M. Carmagnani, A. Hernández Chávez, and R. Ruggiero. Mexico City: FCE.

David, G. 2008. *El indio deseado: Del Dios Pampa al santito gay*. Buenos Aires: Las Cuarenta.

"Declaration of Barbados. For the Liberation of the Indians." 1971. International Work Group for Indigenous Affairs. https://www.iwgia.org/images/publications/0110 _01Barbados.pdf.

Degregori, C. 1995. "El estudio del otro: Cambios en los análisis sobre etnicidad en el Perú." In *Perú 1964–1994: Economía, sociedad y política*, edited by J. Cotler. Lima: IEP.

de Imaz, J. L. 1979. "¿Adiós a la teoría de la dependencia?" In *Debates sobre la teoría de la dependencia y la sociología latinoamericana*, edited by D. Camacho. San José, Costa Rica: Educa.

de Ípola, E. 1983. *Ideología y discurso populista*. Mexico City: Folios.

de Ípola, E., and J. C. Portantiero. (1987) 1994. "Lo nacional popular y los populismos realmente existentes." In *La democratización fundamental: El populismo en América Latina*, edited by C. Vilas. Mexico City: Consejo Nacional para la Cultura y las Artes.

de la Cadena, M. 2000. *Indigenous Mestizos: The Politics of Race and Culture in Cuzco, Peru, 1919–1991*. Durham, NC: Duke University Press.

de la Cadena, M. 2004. *Indígenas mestizos: Raza y cultura en Cuzco*. Lima: IEP.

de la Torre, C. 1993. "Región, clase y discurso: Análisis crítico de varias obras recientes sobre el proceso social y político ecuatoriano entre 1930 y 1950 (debates)." *Revista Ecuatoriana de Historia*, no. 4. Quito: Universidad Andina Simón Bolivar.

de la Torre, C. 2008. "Populismo, ciudadanía y estado de derecho." In *El retorno del pueblo: Populismo y nuevas democracias en América Latina*, by C. de la Torre and E. Peruzzotti. Quito: FLACSO.

de la Torre, C. 2010. "Populismo y democracia." Interview. *Cuadernos del Cendes*, 3rd ser., 27 (7): 171–84.

de la Torre, C. 2013a. "El populismo latinoamericano, entre la democratización y el autoritarismo." *Nueva Sociedad*, no. 247, 120–37. https://nuso.org/articulo/el-populismo -latinoamericano-entre-la-democratizacion-y-el-autoritarismo/.

de la Torre, C. 2013b. "Rafael Correa, un populista del siglo XXI." In *Rafael Correa, balance de la Revolución Ciudadana*, edited by S. Mantilla Baca and S. Mejía Ribadeneira. Quito: Centro Latinoamericano de Estudios Políticos (CELAEP).

de la Torre, C., and E. Peruzzotti. 2008. *El retorno del pueblo: Populismo y nuevas democracias en América Latina*. Quito: FLACSO.

Delfino, A. 2012. "La noción de marginalidad en la teoría social latinoamericana: Surgimiento y actualidad." *Universitas Humanística*, no. 74, 17–34.

Delgado Ramos, G. C., ed. 2014. *Buena vida, buen vivir: Imaginarios alternativos para el bien común de la humanidad*. Mexico City: UNAM.

Delrio, W., D. Lenton, M. Musante, M. Nagy, A. Papazian, and P. Pérez. 2010. "Del silencio al ruido en la historia: Prácticas genocidas y pueblos originarios en Argentina." Paper presented at III Seminario Internacional Políticas de la Memoria, Recordando a Walter Benjamin: Justicia, Historia y Verdad. Escrituras de la Memoria, Centro Cultural de la Memoria Haroldo Conti, Buenos Aires, October 28–30.

Demélas, M. D. 1981. "Darwinismo a la criolla: El darwinismo social en Bolivia, 1880–1910." *Historia Boliviana* 1 (2): 55–82.

De Sierra, G., M. A. Garretón, M. Murmis, and H. Trindade. 2007. "Las ciencias sociales en América Latina en una mirada comparativa." In *Las ciencias sociales en América Latina en perspectiva comparada*, edited by H. Trindade, 17–52. Mexico City: Editorial Siglo XXI.

Devés Valdés, E. 2003. *El pensamiento latinoamericano en el siglo XX*. 3 vols. Buenos Aires: Editorial Biblos.

Díaz Polanco, H. 1978. "Indigenismo, populismo y marxismo." *Nueva Antropología: Revista de Ciencias Sociales*, no. 9, 7–32.

Díaz Polanco, H. 1991. *Autonomía regional: La autodeterminación de los pueblos indios*. Mexico City: Siglo XXI.

Díaz Polanco, H. 2006a. *El laberinto de la identidad*. Mexico City: Coordinación de Difusión Cultural, Dirección General de Publicaciones y Fomento Editorial.

Díaz Polanco, H. 2006b. *Elogio de la diversidad: Globalización, multiculturalismo y etnofagia*. Mexico City: Siglo XXI.

Díaz Polanco, H. 2008. "La insoportable levedad de la autonomía: La experiencia Mexicana." In *Estados y autonomías en democracias contemporáneas (Bolivia, Ecuador, España, México)*, by N. Gutiérrez Chong. Mexico City: Plaza y Valdés.

DIP (Dirección de Información Parlamentaria). 1991. *Tratamiento de la Cuestión Indígena*. Estudios e Investigaciones 2. Buenos Aires: Dirección de Información Parlamentaria del Congreso de la Nación.

Di Tella, T. 1966. "La formación de una conciencia nacional en América Latina." *Desarrollo Económico* 6 (22–23): 417–42.

Di Tella, T. 1983. *Política y clase obrera*. 2nd rev. ed. Buenos Aires: CEPAL.

Di Tella, T., G. Germani, and O. Ianni. 1973. *Populismo y contradicciones de clase*. Mexico City: Era.

Do Alto, H. 2007. "Cuando el nacionalismo se pone el poncho: Una mirada retrospectiva de la etnicidad y la clase en el movimiento popular boliviano, 1952–2007." In *Bolivia: Memoria, insurgencia y movimientos sociales*, edited by M. Svampa and P. Stefanoni. Buenos Aires: El Colectivo–OSAL (CLACSO).

Do Alto, H., and P. Stefanoni. 2010. "El MAS, un partido en tiempo heterogéneo." In *Mutaciones del campo político en Bolivia*, by L. A. García Orellana and F. L. García Yapur. La Paz: PNUD-Bolivia.

"Documentos de la segunda reunión de Barbados." 1979. In *Indianidad y descolonización en América Latina*. Mexico City: Editorial Nueva Imagen.

Domingo Ouriques, N. 1994. "Hacía una teoría marxista de la dependencia." In *La teoría social latinoamericana*, edited by R. M. Marini and M. Millán. Mexico City: El Caballito.

dos Santos, T. 1972. *Socialismo o fascismo: El nuevo carácter de la dependencia y el dilema latinoamericano*. Buenos Aires: Periferia.

dos Santos, T. (1978) 2011. *Imperialismo y dependencia*. Prologue by C. E. Martins. Caracas: Biblioteca Ayacucho.

dos Santos, T. 1985. "La crisis y los movimientos sociales en Brasil." *Política y Administración* 1 (2).

dos Santos, T. 2002. *La teoría de la dependencia: Balance y perspectivas*. Mexico City: Plaza & Janés.

dos Santos, T. 2003. "Argentina puede negociar hoy mejor que Brasil." Interview by José Natanson. *Página/12*, July 19. https://www.pagina12.com.ar/diario/elmundo/4-22914 -2003-07-19.html.

Dumont, R., and M. F. Mottin. 1982. *El mal desarrollo en América Latina (México, Colombia, Brasil)*. Mexico City: Panorama.

Echeverría, B. 2002. "La clave barroca de la América Latina." Lecture at the Latin-Amerika Institute of the Freie Universität Berlin, November 2002.

Elías, N. 1989. *El proceso de civilización*. Mexico City: FCE.

El Troudi, H., M. Harnecker, and L. Bonilla. 2005. *Herramientas para la participación*. Caracas: Editorial Servi-K. https://rebelion.org/docs/15385.pdf.

Encuentro Memoria, Verdad y Justicia. 2012. *Informe sobre criminalización de la protesta*. Buenos Aires: Anred. https://www.anred.org/wp-content/uploads/2012/03/Informe _Criminalizacion_de_la_Protesta.pdf.

Endara, G., ed. 2014. *Poscrecimiento y buen vivir: Propuestas globales para sociedades equitativas y sustentables*. Quito: Fundación F. Ebert.

Escobar, A. (1990) 2005. "El post-desarrollo como concepto y práctica social." In *Políticas de economía, ambiente y sociedad en tiempos de globalización*, edited by D. Mato. Caracas: Facultad de Ciencias Económicas y Sociales, Universidad Central de Venezuela.

Escobar, A. 2000. "El lugar de la naturaleza y la naturaleza del lugar: ¿Globalización o postdesarrollo?" In *La colonialidad del saber: Eurocentrismo y ciencias sociales; Perspectivas latinoamericanas*, edited by E. Lander, 113–43. Buenos Aires: CLACSO.

Escobar, A. 2011a. "Epistemologías de la naturaleza y colonialidad de la naturaleza: Variedades de realismo y constructivismo." In *Aproximaciones a propósito del bicentenario de la independencia de Colombia*, edited by L. Montenegro Martínez. Bogotá: Jardín Botánico de Bogotá José Celestino Mutis.

Escobar, A. 2011b. "¿Pachamámicos contra modérnicos?" In "Dossier: El debate sobre el pachamamismo." *Revista Tierra Socialista: Papeles sobre democracia, socialismo y ecología política* 2 (2): 198–207.

Escobar, A. 2012. "Cultura y diferencia: La ontología política del campo de cultura y desarrollo." *Wale'keru: Revista de Investigación en Cultura y Desarrollo*, no. 2, 7–16. https://dugi-doc.udg.edu/bitstream/handle/10256/7724/WALEKERU-Num2-p7 -16.pdf.

Esteva, G. (1992) 2002. "Development." In *The Development Dictionary: A Guide to Knowledge as Power*, edited by W. Sachs. New York: Zed Books.

Esteva, G. 1996. "Desarrollo." In *Diccionario del desarrollo: Una guía del conocimiento como poder*, edited by W. Sachs. Lima: PRATEC.

Esteva, G. 2007. "'*Commons*: Más allá de los conceptos de bien, derecho humano y propiedad'; Entrevista con Gustavo Esteva sobre el abordaje y la gestión de los bienes communes." Interview by A. Becker, International Conference on Citizenship and the Commons, Mexico, December.

Exeni Rodríguez, J. L. 2015. "Autogobierno indígena y alternativas al desarrollo." In *El proceso de las autonomías indígenas en Bolivia: La larga marcha*, edited by J. L. Exeni Rodríguez. La Paz: Fundación Rosa Luxemburgo.

EZLN. 2001. "El EZLN responde a preguntas que han llegado a través de la página web y correo electrónico." *Enlace Zapatista*. https://enlacezapatista.ezln.org.mx/2001/02/09/el-ezln-responde-a-preguntas-que-han-llegado-a-traves-de-la-pagina-web-y-correo-electronico/.

Falero, A. 2006. *El paradigma renaciente de América Latina: Una aproximación sociológica a legados y desafíos de la visión centro-periferia*. Buenos Aires: CLACSO.

Fals Borda, O. 1970. "La crisis, el compromiso y la ciencia." In *Ciencia propia y colonialismo intelectual*. Mexico City: Editorial Nuestro Tiempo.

Fanon, F. (1961) 1963. *The Wretched of the Earth*. New York: Grove.

Farah, I., and L. Vasapollo, eds. 2011. *Vivir bien: ¿Paradigma no capitalista?* Universidad Mayor de San Andrés (CIDES-UMSA) and Economics Department of the Sapienza University of Rome.

Favre, H. 1998. *El indigenismo*. Mexico City: FCE.

Féliz, M. 2012. "Proyecto sin clase: Crítica al neoestructuralismo como fundamento del neodesarrollismo." In *Más allá del individuo: Clases sociales, transformaciones económicas y políticas estatales en la argentina contemporánea*, by M. Féliz, E. López, P. E. Pérez, et al. Buenos Aires: El Colectivo.

Féliz, M., and E. López. 2012. *Proyecto neodesarrollista en la Argentina: ¿Modelo nacional-popular o nueva etapa en el desarrollo capitalista?* Buenos Aires: El Colectivo.

Fernandes, B. M. 2005. "Movimentos socioterritoriais y movimentos socioespaciais: Contribuição teórica para uma leitura dos movimentos sociais." *Revista OSAL*, no. 16, 273–85.

Fernandes, B. M. 2009. "Sobre la tipología de los territorios." Córdoba: Universidad Nacional de Córdoba. http://web.ua.es/es/giecryal/documentos/documentos839/docs/bernardo-tipologia-de-territorios-espanol.pdf.

Fernandes, B. M. 2012. "Movimentos socioterritorias e movimientos socioespaciais: Contribucao teórica para uma leitura geográfica dos movimientos sociais." *Revista Nera* 6:24–34.

Fernandes, F. 1973. "Problemas de conceptualización de las clases sociales en América Latina." In *Las clases sociales en América Latina*, edited by F. Fernandes and R. Benitez Zenteno. Mexico City: UNAM, Instituto de Investigaciones Sociales, Siglo XXI.

Fernández Fernández, J. 2009. "Indigenismo." In *Diccionario crítico de ciencias sociales: Terminología científico-social*, edited by R. Reyes. Madrid: Plaza y Valdés.

Flores Galindo, A. 1977. "Movimientos campesinos en el Perú: Balance y esquema." *Cuaderno Rural*, no. 18. Marxists Internet Archive, August 2012. https://www.marxists.org/espanol/floresgalindo/1977/movcam.htm.

Flores Galindo, A. 1980. *La agonía de Mariátegui: La polémica con el Komintern.* Lima: Centro de Estudios y de Promoción del Desarrollo.

Flórez Flórez, J. 2015. *El giro decolonial de los movimientos sociales.* 2nd ed. Bogotá: Universidad Javeriana.

Fornillo, B. 2014. "¿*Commodities,* bienes comunes o recursos estratégicos? La importancia de un nombre." *Nueva Sociedad,* no. 252, 101–17.

Franco, R. 1979. "La sociología en América Latina: Panorama de 25 años." In *Debates sobre la teoría de la dependencia y la sociología latinoamericana,* edited by D. Camacho. 2 vols. San José, Costa Rica: Educa.

Frank, A. G. 1965. *Capitalismo y subdesarrollo en América Latina.* Santiago de Chile: Centro de Estudios Miguel Enríquez. https://www.archivochile.cl/Ideas_Autores /gunderfa/gunderfa0006.pdf.

Frank, A. G. 1966. "The Development of Underdevelopment." *Monthly Review* 18 (4): 17–31.

Frank, A. G. 1967a. *Capitalism and Underdevelopment in Latin America: Historical Studies of Chile and Brazil.* New York: Monthly Review Press.

Frank, A. G. 1967b. "El desarrollo del subdesarrollo." *Pensamiento Crítico,* no. 7, 159–72.

Frank, A. G. 1968. "Latinoamérica: Subdesarrollo capitalista o revolución socialista." *Pensamiento Crítico,* no. 13, 3–41.

Frank, A. G. 1969. "Sociología del desarrollo y subdesarrollo de la sociología." In *La sociología subdesarrollante,* by A. G. Frank, C. Real de Azúa, and P. González Casanova. Montevideo: Aportes.

Frank, A. G. (1969) 1973. *Lumpenburguesía: Lumpendesarrollo; Dependencia, clase y política en Latinoamérica.* Buenos Aires: Periferia.

Frank, A. G. 1972a. "La dependencia ha muerto: Viva la dependencia y la lucha de clases." *Sociedad y Desarrollo,* no. 3, 35–51.

Frank, A. G. 1972b. *Lumpenbourgeoisie: Lumpendevelopment; Dependence, Class, and Politics in Latin America.* New York: Monthly Review Press.

Frank, A. G. 1974. "Dependence Is Dead, Long Live Dependence and the Class Struggle: An Answer to Critics." *Latin American Perspectives* 1 (1): 87–106.

Freidenberg, F. 2007. *La tentación populista: Una vía de acceso al poder en América Latina.* Madrid: Síntesis.

Freire, Paulo. (1970) 2005. *Pedagogy of the Oppressed.* New York: Continuum.

Fuentes, C. 1969. *La nueva novela hispanoamericana.* Mexico City: Cuadernos de Joaquín Mortiz.

Fundación Bariloche. 1976a. *Catastrophe or New Society? A Latin American World Model.* Ottawa: International Development Research Centre.

Fundación Bariloche. 1976b. "Modelo mundial latinoamericano." *Nueva Sociedad,* no. 22, 16–29.

Funes, P., and W. Ansaldi. 2006. "Cuestión de piel: Racialismo y legitimidad política en el orden oligárquico latinoamericano." In *Caleidoscopio latinoamericano: Imágenes históricas para un debate vigente,* edited by W. Ansaldi. Buenos Aires: Ariel.

Furtado, C. 1966. *Subdesarrollo y estancamiento en América Latina.* Buenos Aires: Eudeba.

Furtado, C. 1974. *El mito del desarrollo económico y el futuro del tercer mundo*. Buenos Aires: Periferia.

Furtado, C. 1981. "Modernización versus desarrollo." *Crítica y Utopía*, no. 4, 4–16.

Furtado, C. 1985. *La fantasía organizada*. Bogotá, Colombia: Eudeba–Tercer Mundo.

Furtado, C. 2020. *The Myth of Economic Development*. Cambridge, UK: Polity.

Gallopín, G. C. 2004. "El Modelo Mundial Latinoamericano ('Modelo Bariloche'): Tres décadas atrás." In *¿Catástrofe o nueva sociedad? Modelo Mundial Latinoamericano 30 años después*, by A. O. Herrera, H. D. Scolnick, G. Chichilinsky, et al. Ottawa: International Development Research Centre. https://idrc-crdi.ca/en/book/catastrofe-o-nueva-sociedad-modelo-mundial-latinoamericano-30-anos-despues-segunda-edicion.

Gamio, M. 1916. *Forjando patria*. Mexico City: Librería Porrúa Hermanos. https://archive.org/details/forjandopatriaproogamiuoft.

Gandarillas, M. 2015. "Últimas medidas sobre consulta a pueblos indígenas y áreas protegidas." Presentation at CEDIB, La Paz.

García Linera, Á., ed. 2004. *Sociología de los movimientos sociales, estructuras de movilización, repertorios culturales y acción política*. With M. Chávez León and P. Costas Monje. La Paz: Diakonia-Oxfam.

García Linera, Á. 2007. "Marxismo e indianismo: El desencuentro entre dos razones revolucionarias." In *Bolivia: Memoria, insurgencia y movimientos sociales*, edited by M. Svampa and P. Stefanoni. Buenos Aires: El Colectivo-CLACSO.

García Linera, Á. 2008a. "Autonomías indígenas y Estado multinacional." In *La potencia plebeya: Acción colectiva e identidades indígenas, obreras y populares en Bolivia*, edited by P. Stefanoni. Buenos Aires: CLACSO-Prometeo.

García Linera, Á. 2008b. "Marxismo y mundo agrario: Introducción al *Cuaderno Kovalevsky*." In *La potencia plebeya: Acción colectiva e identidades indígenas, obreras y populares en Bolivia*, edited by P. Stefanoni. Buenos Aires: CLACSO-Prometeo.

García Linera, Á. 2008c. "Narrativa colonial y narrativa comunal." In *La potencia plebeya: Acción colectiva e identidades indígenas, obreras y populares en Bolivia*, edited by P. Stefanoni. Buenos Aires: CLACSO-Prometeo.

García Linera, Á. 2008d. *La potencia plebeya: Acción colectiva e identidades indígenas, obreras y populares en Bolivia*. Edited by P. Stefanoni. Buenos Aires: CLACSO-Prometeo.

García Linera, Á. 2011. *Las tensiones creativas de la revolución: La quinta fase del proceso de cambio*. La Paz: Vicepresidencia del Estado Plurinacional de Bolivia. https://www.rebelion.org/docs/134332.pdf.

García Linera, Á. 2012. "Geopolítica de la Amazonía, poder hacendal y acumulación capitalista." *America Latina en Movimiento*, September 9. https://www.alainet.org/es/articulo/160819.

García Linera, Á., L. Tapia, and R. Prada. 2007. *La transformación pluralista del Estado*. La Paz: Muela del Diablo.

Gargarella, R. 2014. *La sala de máquinas de la Constitución: Dos siglos de constitucionalismo en América Latina (1810–2010)*. Buenos Aires: Katz.

Garretón, M., M. Murmis, G. de Sierra, and H. Trindade. 2005. "Social Sciences in Latin America: A Comparative Perspective—Argentina, Brazil, Chile, Mexico and

Uruguay." *Social Science Information* 44 (2–3): 557–93. https://doi.org/10.1177
/0539018405053297.

Gasparello, G., and J. Quintana Guerrero, eds. 2010. *Otras geografías: Experiencias de
autonomías indígenas en México*. 2nd rev. ed. Mexico City: Redez Tejiendo la Utopía.
https://www.rebelion.org/docs/132466.pdf.

Gerbi, A. 1982. *La disputa del nuevo mundo: Historia de una polémica, 1750–1900*. Mexico
City: Siglo XXI.

Gerbi, A. 2010. *The Dispute of the New World: The History of a Polemic, 1750–1900*. Pittsburgh: University of Pittsburgh Press.

Germani, G. 1965. *Política y sociedad en una época de transición*. Buenos Aires: Paidós.

Germani, G. 1973. *El concepto de marginalidad: Significado, raíces históricas y cuestiones teóricas, con particular referencia a la marginalidad urbana*. Buenos Aires: Nueva Visión.

Giddens, A. 1993. *Consecuencias de la modernidad*. Madrid: Alianza Universidad.

Giddens, A. 2000. *Sociología*. 3rd rev. ed. Madrid: Alianza.

Gilly, A. (1971) 2006. *The Mexican Revolution*. New York: New Press.

Gilly, A. 1997. *Chiapas la razón ardiente: Ensayo sobre la rebelión del mundo encantado*.
Mexico City: Era.

Göbel, B. 2013. "La minería del litio en la Puna de Atacama: Interdependencias transregionales y disputas locales." *Revista Iberoamericana*, no. 49, 135–50. https://journals.iai
.spk-berlin.de/index.php/iberoamericana/article/view/363.

González, M. 2010. "Autonomías territoriales indígenas y regímenes autonómicos (desde
el Estado) en América Latina." In *La autonomía a debate: Autogobierno indígena y
Estado plurinacional en América Latina*, edited by M. González, A. Burguete Cal y
Mayor, and P. Ortiz. Quito: FLACSO–GTZ–IWGIA–CIESAS–UNICH.

González Casanova, P. (1965) 1970. *Democracy in Mexico*. Oxford: Oxford University Press.

González Casanova, P. (1969) 2006. "Colonialismo interno (una redefinición)." In *La
teoría marxista hoy: Problemas y perspectivas*, edited by A. A. Borón, J. Amadeo, and
S. González. Buenos Aires: CLACSO.

González Casanova, P. 1974. "América Latina: La evolución de las críticas a las ciencias
sociales." In *Debates sobre la teoría de la dependencia y la sociología latinoamericana*,
edited by D. Camacho. San José, Costa Rica: Educa.

González Prada, M. 1989. *Horas de lucha*. Lima: Peisa.

Gordillo, G., and S. Hirsch. 2010. *Movilizaciones indígenas e identidades en disputa en la
Argentina*. Buenos Aires: ICRJ–La Crujía.

Gotkowitz, L. 2007. *A Revolution for Our Rights: Indigenous Struggles for Land and
Justice in Bolivia, 1880–1952*. Durham, NC: Duke University Press.

Gotkowitz, L. 2011. *La revolución antes de la revolución: Luchas indígenas por tierra y
justicia en Bolivia, 1880–1952*. La Paz: Plural.

Graciarena, J. 1976. "Poder y estilos de desarrollo en América Latina." *Revista de la
CEPAL*, no. 1.

Gramsci, A. 1975. *Notas sobre Maquiavelo, sobre política y sobre el Estado moderno*. Mexico
City: Juan Pablos.

Gros, C. 2006. "Nationaliser l'indien, ethniciser la nation: L'Amérique Latine face au
multiculturalisme." In *Etre indien dans les Amériques*, by C. Gros and M. C. Strigler.
Paris: Éditions de l'IHEAL, La Documentation Française.

Grosfoguel, R. 2003. "Cambios conceptuales desde la perspectiva del sistema-mundo: Del Cepalismo al neoliberalismo." *Nueva Sociedad*, no. 183, 151–66.

Grosfoguel, R., and S. Castro Gómez. 2007. "Prólogo: Giro decolonial, teoría crítica y pensamiento heterárquico." In *El giro decolonial: Reflexiones para una diversidad epistémica más allá del capitalismo global*, edited by R. Grosfoguel and S. Castro Gómez. Bogotá: Siglo del Hombre Editores, Universidad Central, Instituto de Estudios Sociales Contemporáneos and Pontificia Universidad Javeriana, Instituto Pensar.

Grupo Permanente de Trabajo sobre Alternativas al Desarrollo. 2012. *Más allá del desarrollo*. Quito: Fundación Rosa Luxemburgo.

Grupo Permanente de Trabajo sobre Alternativas al Desarrollo. 2013. *Alternativas al capitalismo/colonialismo del siglo XXI*. Quito: Fundación Rosa Luxemburgo.

Grupo Permanente de Trabajo sobre Alternativas al Desarrollo. 2015. *¿Cómo transformar? Instituciones y cambio social en América Latina y Europa*. Quito: Fundación Rosa Luxemburgo.

Gudynas, E. 1992. "Los múltiples verdes del ambientalismo latinoamericano." *Nueva Sociedad*, no. 22, 104–15.

Gudynas, E. 2004. *Ecología, economía y ética del desarrollo sostenible*. 5th rev. ed. Montevideo: Coscoroba.

Gudynas, E. 2009. "Diez tesis urgentes sobre el nuevo extractivismo." In *Extractivismo, política y sociedad*, by J. Schuldt, A. Acosta, A. Barandiarán, et al. Quito: CAAP–CLAES. https://www.rosalux.org.ec/pdfs/extractivismo.pdf.

Gudynas, E. 2011a. "Desarrollo, derechos de la naturaleza y buen vivir después de Montecristi." In *Debates sobre cooperación y modelos de desarrollo: Perspectivas desde la sociedad civil en el Ecuador*, edited by G. Weber. Quito: Centro de Investigaciones CIUDAD y Observatorio de la Cooperación al Desarrollo.

Gudynas, E. 2011b. "Imágenes, ideas y conceptos sobre la naturaleza en América Latina." In *Cultura y naturaleza: Aproximaciones a propósito del bicentenario de la independencia de Colombia*, edited by L. Montenegro. Bogotá: Jardín Botánico de Bogotá José Celestino Mutis. http://www.ceapedi.com.ar/imagenes/biblioteca/libreria/279.pdf.

Gudynas, E. 2012. "Desarrollo, extractivismo y buen vivir: Debates sobre el desarrollo y sus alternativas en América Latina; Una breve guía heterodoxa." In *Más allá del desarrollo*, by M. Lang and D. Mokrani, Grupo Permanente de Trabajo sobre Alternativas al Desarrollo. Quito: Fundación Rosa Luxemburgo–Abya-Yala.

Gudynas, E. 2014a. "Buen vivir: Sobre secuestros, domesticaciones, rescates y alternativas." In *Bifurcación del Buen Vivir y Sumak Kawsay*, edited by A. Oviedo Freire. Quito: Sumak.

Gudynas, E. 2014b. *Derechos de la naturaleza: Ética biocéntrica y políticas ambientales*. Lima: RedGE, PDTG–CLAES–CooperAcción. https://gudynas.com/wp-content/uploads/GudynasDerechosNaturalezaLima14r.pdf.

Gudynas, E., and A. Acosta. 2011. "La renovación de la crítica al desarrollo y el buen vivir como alternativa." *Utopía y Praxis Latinoamericana* 16 (53): 71–83.

Güiraldes, R. 1926. *Don Segundo Sombra*. Buenos Aires: Editorial Proa.

Gutiérrez Aguilar, R. 2006. "Dignidad como despliegue de soberanía social: Autonomía como fundamento de transformación." In *Movimiento indígena en América Latina: Resistencia y proyecto alternativo*, edited by R. Gutiérrez Aguilar and F. Escárzaga. Mexico City: Universidad Autónoma Metropolitana.

Gutiérrez Aguilar, R. 2014. "Horizontes comunitarios de la política." Pueblos en Camino, January 20. https://pueblosencamino.org/?p=636.

Gutiérrez Garza, E. 1994. "Economía, teoría e historia: La CEPAL y los estilos de desarrollo." In *La teoría social latinoamericana*, edited by R. M. Marini and M. Millán. Mexico City: El Caballito.

Gutiérrez Garza, E., and E. González Gaudiano. 2010. *De las teorías del desarrollo al desarrollo sustentable*. Mexico City: UANL–Siglo XXI.

Hale, C. 2002. "Does Multiculturalism Menace? Governance, Cultural Rights and the Politics of Identity in Guatemala." *Journal of Latin American Studies* 34 (3): 485–524.

Hardt, M., and A. Negri. 2000. *Empire*. Cambridge, MA: Harvard University Press.

Harnecker, M. 2009. "De los consejos comunales a las comunas: Construyendo el socialismo del siglo XXI." April 1. Caracas.

Haya de la Torre, V. 1936. *El antiimperialismo y el Apra*. Santiago de Chile: Ercilla.

Hernández, J. 1897. *El gaucho Martín Fierro*. Buenos Aires: Librería Martín Fierro.

Herrera, A. O., H. D. Scolnick, G. Chichilinsky, et al. 2004. *¿Catástrofe o nueva sociedad? Modelo Mundial Latinoamericano, 30 años después*. Ottawa: International Development Research Centre. https://idrc-crdi.ca/en/book/catastrofe-o-nueva-sociedad-modelo-mundial-latinoamericano-30-anos-despues-segunda-edicion.

Hinkelammert, F., and H. Mora Jiménez. 2005. *Hacia una economía para la vida: Preludio a una reconstrucción de la economía*. San José de Costa Rica: Dei.

Hirsch, J. 2001. "Globalización y el futuro del Estado nación." Paper presented at a seminar, translation by Instituto Goethe, Buenos Aires, July 2–3.

Hirsch, S., and G. Gordillo. 2010. "La presencia ausente: Invisibilizaciones políticas estatales y emergencias indígenas en Argentina." In *Movilizaciones indígenas e identidades en disputa en la Argentina*, edited by S. Hirsch and G. Gordillo. Buenos Aires: FLACSO.

Hiruelas, N. 2015. "La consulta previa en su laberinto." *El Gran Angular*, June 22. https://elgranangular.com/blog/reportaje/la-consulta-previa-en-su-laberinto/.

Hobsbawm, E. J. 1965. *Pre-Capitalist Economic Formations*. New York: International Publishers.

Hoetmer, R., M. Castro, Mar Daza, et al. 2013. *Minería y movimientos sociales en el Perú: Instrumentos y propuestas para la defensa de la vida, el agua y el territorio*. Lima: Programa de Democracia y Transformación Global.

Holloway, J. 1993. "La reforma del Estado: Capital global y Estado nacional." *Doxa: Cuadernos de Ciencias Sociales*, nos. 9–10.

Houtart, F. 2011. *De los bienes comunes al bien común de la humanidad*. Quito: Fundación Rosa Luxemburgo.

Hylton, F. 2003. *Ya es otro tiempo el presente: Cuatro momentos de insurgencia indígena*. Potosí, Bolivia: Muela del Diablo.

Ianni, O. 1965. "Sociología de la sociología en América Latina." *Revista Latinoamericana de Sociología* 1 (3): 414–28.

Ianni, O. 1975. "Populismo y capitalismo." In *La formación del Estado populista en América Latina*. Buenos Aires: Era.

Ianni, O. 1996. *Teorías de la globalización*. Mexico City: Siglo XXI.

IELA. 2022. "Primera declaración de Barbados: Por la liberación del indígena." March 3.
https://iela.ufsc.br/primera-declaracion-de-barbados-por-la-liberacion-del-indigena/.

Impemba, M. 2013. ¿Los otros invisibles? La cultura mapuche en el expansionismo de San Martín de los Andes. Buenos Aires: Ferreyra Editor.

Ingenieros, J. 1913. Sociología argentina. Madrid: Daniel Jorro.

Ionescu, G., and E. Gellner. 1969. Populism: Its Meaning and National Characteristics. New York: Macmillan.

James, D. 1987. "17 y 18 de octubre de 1945: El peronismo, la protesta de masas y la clase obrera Argentina." Desarrollo Económico 27 (107): 445–61.

James, D. 1988. "October 17th and 18th, 1945: Mass Protest, Peronism and the Argentine Working Class." Journal of Social History 21 (3): 441–61.

James, D. (1988) 1994. Resistance and Integration: Peronism and the Argentine Working Class, 1946–1976. Cambridge: Cambridge University Press.

Jiménez, B. 2015. "Consulta previa en minería no avanza por no reconocer a pueblos andinos." La República, October 1.

Katsiaficas, G. 2009. "El significado de los autónomos." In La autonomía posible: Reinvención de la autonomía y emancipación, edited by C. Albertani, G. Rovira, and M. Modonesi. Mexico City: UACM.

Kessler, G. 2014. Controversias sobre la desigualdad. Buenos Aires: FCE.

Kissinger, H. 2011. "Mao Might Consider Modern China to Be Too Materialistic." Spiegel International, June 7. https://www.spiegel.de/international/world/spiegel-interview-with-henry-kissinger-mao-might-consider-modern-china-to-be-too-materialistic-a-772292.html.

Knight, A. 1998. "Cardenismo, ¿coloso o catramina?" In Populismo y neopopulismo en América Latina: El problema de la Cenicienta, edited by M. M. Mackinnon and M. A. Petrone. Buenos Aires: Eudeba.

Korsbaek, L., and M. Á. Sámano Rentería. 2007. "El indigenismo en México: Antecedentes y actualidad." Ra Ximhai 3 (1): 195–224.

Kourí, E. 2010. "Manuel Gamio y el indigenismo de la Revolución Mexicana." In Historia de los intelectuales en América Latina II: Los avatares de la "ciudad letrada" en el siglo XX, edited by C. Altamirano. Buenos Aires: Katz.

Kowarick, L. (1979) 1996. "Expoliación urbana, luchas sociales y ciudadanía: Retazos de nuestra historia reciente." Estudios Sociológicos 14 (42): 729–43.

Kush, R. 1976. Geopolítica del hombre americano. Buenos Aires: Garcia Cambeiro.

Kymlicka, W. 1996. Multicultural Citizenship: A Liberal Theory of Minority Rights. Oxford: Oxford University Press.

Laclau, E. 1973. "Feudalismo y capitalismo en América Latina." In Modos de producción en América Latina, by C. Sempat Assadourian, C. Flamarión, H. Ciafardini, J. C. Garavaglia, and E. Laclau. Mexico City: Cuadernos de Pasado y Presente.

Laclau, E. 1978. Política e ideología en la teoría marxista: Capitalismo, fascismo, populismo. Madrid: Siglo XXI.

Laclau, E. 2005. On Populist Reason. London: Verso.

Laclau, E. 2006. "La deriva populista y la centroizquierda latinoamericana." Nueva Sociedad, no. 205. https://nuso.org/articulo/la-deriva-populista-y-la-centroizquierda-latinoamericana/.

Laclau, E. 2009. "¿Qué nos dice el nombre?" In *El populismo como espejo de la democracia*, edited by F. Panizza, 51–70. Buenos Aires: FCE.

Laclau, E., and C. Mouffe. (1985) 2014. *Hegemony and Socialist Strategy: Towards a Radical Democratic Politics*. London: Verso.

Lander, E. 2000. *La colonialidad del saber: Eurocentrismo y ciencias sociales; Perspectivas latinoamericanas*. CLACSO.

Lander, E. 2004. "Izquierda y populismo: Alternativas al neoliberalismo en Venezuela." *Mimeo*, October 25. https://www.tni.org/es/publicaci%C3%B3n/izquierda-y-populismo-alternativas-al-neoliberalismo-en-venezuela.

Lander, E. 2013. "Tensiones/contradicciones en torno al extractivismo en los procesos de cambio: Bolivia, Ecuador y Venezuela." In *Promesas en su laberinto: Cambios y continuidades en los gobiernos progresistas de América Latina*, by C. Arze, J. Gómez, P. Ospina, and V. Álvarez. Quito: Cedla.

Lander, E. 2014. "La (re)emergencia de China como potencia global y las presiones extractivistas en Sudamérica." Compiled and systematized for the Grupo Permanente de Trabajo sobre Alternativas al Desarrollo. Quito. https://www.slideserve.com/duman/la-re-emergencia-de-china-como-potencia-global-y-las-presiones-extractivistas-en-sudam-rica#google_vignette.

Lander, E. 2015. "El tejido solidario devino en un bachaqueo individualista y competitivo (Venezuela)." Interview by Hugo Prieto. *Kavilando* 7 (2): 147–56. https://dialnet.unirioja.es/servlet/articulo?codigo=5476438.

Lang, M. 2015. "México: Desde abajo todo, desde arriba nada." In *¿Cómo transformar? Instituciones y cambio social en América Latina y Europa*, by Grupo Permanente de Trabajo sobre Alternativas al Desarrollo. Quito: Fundación Rosa Luxemburgo.

Laría, A. 2011. *La religión populista: Una crítica al populismo posmarxista*. Buenos Aires: Nuevo Hacer, Grupo Editor Latinoamericano.

Lavallé, B. 2011. *Eldorados d'Amérique: Mythes, images et réalités*. Paris: Payot.

Lavaud, J. P., and F. Lestage. 2009. "Contar a los indígenas (Bolivia, México, Estados Unidos)." In *El regreso de lo indígena: Retos, problemas y perspectivas*, edited by V. R. Azevedo and C. S. Soler. Lima: IFEA/CBC/CRPA.

Leff, E. 1993. "Cultura democrática, gestión ambiental y desarrollo sustentable en América Latina." *Ecología Política* 4:47–55.

Leff, E. 2006. "La ecología política en América Latina: Un campo en construcción." In *Los tormentos de la materia: Aportes para una ecología política latinoamericana*, edited by H. Alimonda. Buenos Aires: CLACSO. https://biblioteca.clacso.edu.ar/clacso/gt/20101002070402/3Leff.pdf.

Leff, E. 2014. *La apuesta por la vida: Imaginación sociológica e imaginarios sociales de los territorios ambientales del sur*. Mexico City: Siglo XXI.

Lenin, V. I. (1899) 2004. *The Development of Capitalism in Russia*. Forest Grove, OR: University Press of the Pacific.

Lenton, D. 2011. "El Estado se construyó sobre un genocidio." Interview by Darío Aranda. *Página/12*, October 10. https://www.pagina12.com.ar/diario/dialogos/21-178560-2011-10-10.html.

Lenton, D., and M. Lorenzetti. 2005. "Neoindigenismo de necesidad y urgencia: La inclusión de los pueblos indígenas en la agenda del Estado neoasistencialista." In *Car-*

tografías argentinas: Políticas indigenistas y formaciones provinciales de alteridad, edited by C. Briones. Buenos Aires: Antropofagia.

León, M. 2009. "Cambiar la economía para cambiar la vida: Desafíos de una economía para la vida." In *El buen vivir: Una vía para el desarrollo*, edited by A. Acosta and E. Martínez. Quito: Abya-Yala.

León Pesantez, C. 2013. *El color de la razón: Pensamiento crítico en las Américas*. Cuenca, Ecuador: Universidad Andina, Corporación Editorial Nacional.

Lévi-Strauss, C. 1968. *Elogio de la Antropología*. Córdoba, Argentina: Pasado y Presente.

Lewis, O. (1959) 1975. *Five Families: Mexican Case Studies in the Culture of Poverty*. New York: Basic Books.

Lewis, O. (1961) 2011. *The Children of Sanchez: Autobiography of a Mexican Family*. New York: Vintage.

Leyva Remón, A. 2012. "Entrevista a Armando Bartra, reabriendo el debate latinoamericano sobre el campesinado como clase social." *Textual*, no. 59, 9–32.

Lomnitz, L. 1998. *Cómo sobreviven los marginados*. Mexico City: Siglo XXI.

López Bárcenas, F. 2011. "Las autonomías indígenas en América Latina." In *Pensar las autonomías: Alternativas de emancipación al capital y el Estado*, by E. Adamovsky, C. Albertani, B. Arditi, et al. Mexico City: Bajo Tierra-Sísifo.

López Maya, M. 2000. "La protesta popular en la Venezuela contemporánea: Enfoque conceptual, metodológico y fuentes." In *Visiones del oficio: Historiadores venezolanos en el siglo XXI*, edited by J. Rodríguez. Caracas: Academia Nacional de la Historia–FHE–UCV.

López Maya, M. 2005. "La protesta popular venezolana: Mirando al siglo XX desde el siglo XXI." In *Venezuela, visión plural*, by CENDES. Caracas: Bid and Co. Editor, Cendes–UCV.

López Maya, M., and A. Panzarelli. 2012. "Populismo, rentismo y socialismo del siglo XXI: El caso venezolano." In *Qué democracia en América Latina?*, edited by I. Chereski. Buenos Aires: CLASCO-Prometeo. https://pensamientolatinoamericanounmdp .files.wordpress.com/2012/08/lc3b3pez-maya-y-panzarelli_venezuela-chavez.pdf.

López y Rivas, G. 2011. "Autonomías indígenas, poder y transformaciones sociales." In *Pensar las autonomías: Alternativas de emancipación al capital y el estado*, by E. Adamovsky, C. Albertani, B. Arditi, et al. Mexico City: Bajo Tierra-Sísifo.

Lorini, I. 2006. *El nacionalismo en Bolivia de la pre y posguerra del Chaco (1910–1945)*. La Paz: Plural.

Lucero, J. A., and M. E. García. 2006. "Reflexiones sobre la autenticidad indígena, los movimientos sociales y el trabajo de campo en el Perú contemporáneo." *Red Voltaire*, December 28. https://www.voltairenet.org/article144504.html.

Lugones, L. (1913) 1980. *El payador*. In *Antología de poesía y prosa*. Caracas: Biblioteca Ayacucho.

Machado Aráoz, H. 2012. "Naturaleza mineral: Una ecología política del colonialismo moderno." PhD diss., Universidad Nacional de Catamarca.

Machado Aráoz, H. 2014. *Potosí, el origen*. Buenos Aires: Mardulce.

Mackinnon, M. M., and M. A. Petrone, eds. 1998. *Populismo y neopopulismo en América Latina: El problema de la Cenicienta*. Buenos Aires: Eudeba.

Maiguashca, J., and L. North. 1991. "Orígenes y significado del velasquismo: Lucha de clases y participación política en el Ecuador, 1920–1972." In *La cuestión regional y el poder*, vol. 29, edited by R. Quintero. Quito: York University, CERLAC.

Máiz, R. 2004. "El indigenismo político en América Latina." *Revista de Estudios Políticos*, nueva epoca, no. 123 (January–March), 129–74.

Máiz, R. 2008. "XI tesis para una teoría política de la autonomía territorial." In *Estados y autonomías en democracias contemporáneas*, edited by N. Gutiérrez Chong. Mexico City: Plaza y Valdés.

Mallorquín, V. C. 1994. "Lucha, poder y desencanto: Los primeros tiempos de Celso Furtado." In *La teoría social latinoamericana*, edited by R. M. Marini and M. Millán. Mexico City: El Caballito.

Malloy, J. 2003. "La revolución inconclusa." In *Memorias de la Conferencia internacional: Revoluciones del siglo XX: Homenaje a los cincuenta años de la revolución boliviana; Tenemos pecho de bronce . . . pero no sabemos nada*. La Paz: PNUD–FES–ILDIS/ASDI/Plural.

Mariátegui, J. C. (1928) 1988. *Siete ensayos de interpretación sobre la realidad peruana*. Lima: Amauta.

Mariátegui, J. C. (1928) 1994. "El problema de las razas en la América Latina." In *Mariátegui total*. Lima: Amauta.

Mariátegui, J. C. 1971. *Seven Interpretive Essays on Peruvian Reality*. Austin: University of Texas Press.

Mariátegui, J. C. 1972a. *Aniversario y balance*. Lima: Amauta.

Mariátegui, J. C. 1972b. *Defensa del marxismo*. Lima: Amauta.

Mariátegui, J. C. 2010. *La tarea americana*. Selected and introduced by Héctor Alimonda. Buenos Aires: CLACSO-Prometeo.

Marini, R. M. (1969) 1974. *Subdesarrollo y revolución*. 6th ed. Mexico City: Siglo XXI. https://www.archivochile.com/Ideas_Autores/maurinirm/02tex_teo/maurini_texte000002.pdf.

Marini, R. M. 1973. *Dialéctica de la dependencia*. Mexico City: Era.

Marini, R. M. 1978. "Las razones del neodesarrollismo (respuesta a F. H. Cardoso y J. Serra)." *Revista Mexicana de Sociología* 40:57–106.

Marini, R. M. 2008. *América latina, dependencia y globalización*. Edited by C. E. Martins. Bogotá: Siglo del Hombre Editores; Buenos Aires: CLACSO.

Marini, R. M. 2022. *The Dialectics of Dependency*. New York: Monthly Review Press.

Marof. T. 1926. *La justicia del inca*. Brussels: Librería Falk Fils.

Marof, T. 1935. *La tragedia del Altiplano*. Buenos Aires: Editorial Claridad. *Proyecto Ensayo Hispánico*. https://www.ensayistas.org/antologia/XXA/marof/divisiones.htm.

Marroquín, A. D. 1977. *Balance del indigenismo: Informe sobre la política indigenista en América*. México City: Instituto Indigenista Interamericano.

Martí i Puig, S. 2004. "Sobre la emergencia e impacto de los movimientos indígenas en las arenas políticas de América Latina: Algunas claves interpretativas desde lo local y lo global." Barcelona: CIDOB.

Martínez, F. 2010. *"Régénérer la race": Politique éducative en Bolivie (1898–1920)*. Paris: Éditions de l'IHEAL.

Martínez Alier, J. 2004. *El ecologismo de los pobres: Conflictos ambientales y lenguajes de valoración*. Barcelona: Icaria Antrazo–FLACSO Ecología.

Martínez Alier, J. 2009. "Hacia un decrecimiento sostenible en las economías ricas." *Revista de Economía Crítica* 1 (8): 121–37. https://revistaeconomiacritica.org/index .php/rec/article/view/426.

Martínez Alier, J. 2011. "La justicia ambiental y el decrecimiento económico: Una alianza entre dos movimientos." *Ecología Política: Cuadernos de debate internacional*, no. 41, 45–54.

Martínez Alier, J. 2015. "Sudamérica: El triunfo del post extractivismo en el 2015." *Sinpermiso*, February 28. https://www.sinpermiso.info/textos/sudamrica-el-triunfo-del-post -extractivismo-en-el-2015.

Martínez Cobo, J. R. 1986. *Estudio del problema de la discriminación contra las poblaciones indígenas*. Naciones Unidas. https://cendoc.docip.org/collect/cendocdo/index/assoc /HASHe3ed/3187d77a.dir/RapCobo_v2_ch5defIP_es.pdf.

Martínez Sarasola, C. 2011. *Nuestros paisanos los indios: Vida historia y destino de las comunidades indígenas en América Latina*. Buenos Aires: Del Nuevo Extremo.

Martins, C. E. 1998. "Theotonio dos Santos: Introducción a la vida y obra de un intelectual planetario." In *Los retos de la globalización: Ensayos en homenaje a Theotonio dos Santos*, by T. Dos Santos and F. L. Segrera. UNESCO–Unidad Regional de Ciencias Sociales. Buenos Aires: CLACSO.

Martuccelli, D. 1995. *Décalages*. Paris: Puf.

Martuccelli, D. 2008. "Para abrir la reflexión: Etnicidades modernas; Identidad y democracia." In *Revisitar la etnicidad: Miradas cruzadas en torno a la diversidad*, edited by D. Gutiérrez Martínez and H. Balslev Clausen. Mexico City: Siglo XXI.

Martuccelli, D., and M. Svampa. 1993. "Notas para una historia de la sociología latinoamericana." *Sociológica*, no. 23, 75–95.

Martuccelli, D., and M. Svampa. 1997. *La plaza vacía: Las transformaciones del peronismo*. Buenos Aires: Losada.

Martuccelli, D., and M. Svampa. 1998. "Las asignaturas pendientes del modelo nacional-popular: El caso peruano." In *Populismo y neopopulismo en América Latina: El problema de la Cenicienta*, edited by M. M. Mackinnon and M. A. Petrone. Buenos Aires: Eudeba.

Marx, K. (1852) 1994. *The Eighteenth Brumaire of Louis Bonaparte*. New York: International Publishers.

Marx, K. (1867) 2024. *Capital: Critique of Political Economy, Volume 1*. Princeton, NJ: Princeton University Press.

Mathias, G., and P. Salama. 1983. *El Estado sobredesarrollado: De la metrópolis al tercer mundo*. Mexico City: Era.

Max-Neef, M., A. Elizalde, and M. Hopenhayn. 1986. "Desarrollo a escala humana: Una opción para el futuro." Special issue, *Development Dialogue*, 7–94.

Mayorga, F. 2003. "La revolución boliviana y la participación política." In *Memorias de la Conferencia internacional: Revoluciones del siglo XX; Homenaje a los cincuenta años de la revolución boliviana; Tenemos pecho de bronce . . . pero no sabemos nada*. La Paz: PNUD–FES–ILDIS/ASDI/Plural.

Mayorga, F. 2011. *Dilemas: Ensayos sobre democracia intercultural y estado plurinacional*. La Paz: SESU–UMSS–Plural.

Meadows, D., J. Randers, and W. Behrems. 1972. *The Limits to Growth: A Report for the Club of Rome's Project on the Predicament of Mankind*. New York: Universe Books.

Medina, J. 2014. "Suma Qamaña, Vivir Bien y de Vida Beata." In *Bifurcación del Buen Vivir y Sumak Kawsay*, edited by A. Oviedo Freire. Quito: Sumak.

Medina Echavarría, J. 1963. *Social Development of Latin America in the Post-War Period*. Mar del Plata, Argentina: CEPAL. https://repositorio.cepal.org/bitstream/handle /11362/14734/S6400013_en.pdf.

Melgar Bao, R. 2012. "El exilado boliviano Tristán Marof: Tejiendo redes, identidades y claves de la autoctonía política." *Pacarina del Sur* 3 (12): 301–33.

Melucci, A. (1977) 1990. *Sistema politico, partiti e movimenti sociali*. Milan: Feltrinelli.

Méndez, C. 1996. "Incas sí, indios no: Apuntes para el estudio del nacionalismo criollo en el Perú." *Documentos de trabajo*, no. 56, 1–36.

Mignolo, W. 2012. "Dheli 2012: La desoccidentalización, los BRICS y la distribución racial del capital y del conocimiento." Personal blog. No longer available.

Mignolo, W. 2013. "Re-emerger: El retorno del Este global y del Sur global." Interview by Norma Giarracca. *Causa Sur*, February.

Modonesi, M. 2010. *Subalternidad, antagonismo, autonomía: Marxismos y subjetivación política*. Buenos Aires: CLACSO-Prometeo.

Modonesi, M. 2011. "El concepto de la autonomía en el marxismo contemporáneo." In *Pensar las autonomías: Alternativas de emancipación al capital y el estado*, by E. Adamovsky, C. Albertani, B. Arditi, et al. Mexico City: Bajo Tierra-Sísifo.

Modonesi, M. 2013. "Gobiernos progresistas y desmovilización: ¿Revoluciones pasivas en América Latina?" *Anuario del Conflicto Social*, no. 2, 1367–84. https://revistes.ub.edu /index.php/ACS/article/view/6367.

Montenegro, C. (1944) 2005. *Nacionalismo y coloniaje*. La Paz: Librería Editorial La Juventud.

Montoya Rojas, R. 2006. "¿Por qué no hay en Perú un movimiento político indígena como en Ecuador y Bolivia?" In *Movimiento indígena en América Latina: Resistencia y proyecto alternativo*, edited by R. Gutiérrez and F. Escárzaga. Mexico City: Centro de Estudios Andinos y Mesoamericanos.

Morales Martín, J. J. 2013. "José Medina Echavarría y la sociología del desarrollo." *Íconos: Revista de Ciencias Sociales*, no. 36, 133–46.

Moreno, C. 2013. "La economía verde: Una nueva fuente de acumulación primitiva." In *Alternativas al capitalismo/colonialismo del siglo XXI*, edited by M. Lang, C. López, and A. Santillana. Grupo Permanente de Trabajo sobre Alternativas al Desarrollo. Quito: Fundación Rosa Luxemburgo.

Mosco Perea, C. 1990. *El populismo en América Latina*. Mexico City: Centro de Estudios Constitucionales, Suprema Corte de Justicia de la Nación.

Muñoz Ramírez, G. 2009. "Contra viento y marea." *Ojarasca* 150, supplement of the daily *La Jornada*, October 12. https://www.jornada.unam.mx/2009/10/12/oja150 -autonomiazapa.html.

Murmis, M. 1969. "Tipos de marginalidad y posición en el proceso productivo." *Revista Latinoamericana de Sociología* 5 (2): 413–21.

Murmis, M., and J. C. Portantiero. 1971. *Estudios sobre los orígenes del peronismo*. Vol. 1. Buenos Aires: Siglo XXI.

Nagy, M. 2013. "La gente letrada fue beneficiada para quedarse con mano de obra gratis." Interview. *Agassaganup*, October 11. https://agassaganup.wordpress.com/2013/10/11/la-gente-letrada-fue-beneficiaria-de-quedarse-con-mano-de-obra-gratis/.

Nahón, C., K. Rodríguez, and M. Schorr. 2006. "El pensamiento latinoamericano en el campo del desarrollo del subdesarrollo: Trayectoria, rupturas y continuidades." In *Crítica y teoría en el pensamiento social latinoamericano*, edited by F. Beigel, A. Falero, J. G. Gandarilla Salgado, et al., 327–88. Buenos Aires: CLACSO.

Naredo, J. M. 2006. *Raíces económicas del deterioro ecológico y social*. Madrid: Siglo XXI.

Negri, A., and G. Cocco. 2006. *GlobAL: Biopoder y luchas en una América Latina globalizada*. Buenos Aires: Paidós.

Nicolas, V., and P. Quisbert. 2014. *Pachakuti: El retorno de la nación; Estudio comparativo del imaginario de la nación de la revolución nacional y del estado plurinacional*. La Paz: PIEB.

North, L. 1985. "Orientaciones ideológicas de los dirigentes militares peruanos." In *El gobierno militar*, edited by C. McClintock and A. F. Lowenthal. Lima: IEP.

Nun, J. 1969a. "La marginalidad en América Latina." *Revista Latinoamericana de Sociología* 5 (2): 174–78.

Nun, J. 1969b. "Superpoblación relativa, ejército industrial de reserva y masa marginal." *Revista Latinoamericana de Sociología* 5 (2): 178–236.

Nun, J. (1969) 2001. "Nueva visita a la teoría de la masa marginal." In *Marginalidad y exclusión social*. Buenos Aires: FCE.

Nun, J. 2001. *Marginalidad y exclusión social*. Buenos Aires: FCE.

Nun, J., M. Murmis, and J. C. Marín. 1968. *La marginalidad en América Latina: Informe preliminar*. Buenos Aires: Instituto Torcuato Di Tella, Centro de Investigaciones Sociales.

Ocantos, C. M. 1891. *Quilito*. Paris: Librería Española de Garnier Hermanos. https://www.ocmal.org/wp-content/uploads/2017/03/libro_mineria.pdf.

O'Donnell, G. 1972. *Modernización y autoritarismo*. Buenos Aires: Paidós.

O'Donnell, G. 1973. *Modernization and Bureaucratic-Authoritarianism*. Berkeley: University of California, Institute of International Studies.

O'Donnell, G. 1978a. "Apuntes para una teoría del Estado." *Revista Mexicana de Sociología* 40 (4): 1157–99.

O'Donnell, G. 1978b. "Notas para el estudio de la burguesía local, con especial referencia a sus vinculaciones con el capital transnacional y el aparato estatal." *Estudios Sociales*, no. 12. Buenos Aires: CEDES. http://repositorio.cedes.org/handle/123456789/3311.

O'Donnell, G. 1992. "¿Democracia delegativa?" *Cuadernos del CLAEH* 17 (61): 5–20.

Offe, C. (1988) 1996. *Partidos políticos y nuevos movimientos sociales*. Madrid: Sistema.

OLCA (Observatorio Latinoamericano de Conflictos Ambientales). 2004. "Primer encuentro Nacional de la red Brasilera de Justicia Ambiental." December. https://www.olca.cl/oca/justicia/justicia02.htm.

Osorio, J. 1994. "Fuentes y tendencias de la teoría de la dependencia." In *La teoría social latinoamericana*, edited by R. M. Marini and M. Millán. Mexico City: El Caballito.

Ospina, P. 2010. "Significados de la radicalización: Análisis de coyuntura." Comité Ecuménico de Proyectos (CEP). Quito: Mimeo.

Ospina, P. 2013. "Estamos haciendo mejor las cosas con el mismo modelo antes que cambiarlo." In *Promesas en su laberinto: Cambios y continuidades en los gobiernos progresistas de América Latina*, by C. Arze, J. Gómez, P. Ospina, and V. Álvarez. Quito: CEDLA.

Ospina, P. 2022. "'Nada solo para los indios': ¿Por qué la Conaie sigue liderando las protestas en Ecuador?" *Nueva Sociedad*, June. https://nuso.org/articulo/protestas -Ecuador-conaie/.

Oteiza, E. 2004. "El modelo mundial latinoamericano: Scriptum—Post scriptum." In *¿Catástrofe o nueva sociedad? Modelo mundial latinoamericano, 30 años después*, by A. O. Herrera, H. D. Scolnick, G. Chichilinsky, et al. Ottawa: International Development Research Centre, 7–13. https://idrc-crdi.ca/en/book/catastrofe-o-nueva -sociedad-modelo-mundial-latinoamericano-30-anos-despues-segunda-edicion.

Oviedo, E. 2014. "América Latina: Entre la hegemonía estadounidense y la influencia china." In *FLACSO-ISA Joint International Conference: Global and Regional Powers in a Changing World*. http://web.sanet.org/Web/Conferences/FLACSO-ISA%20Bueno- sAres%202014/ Archive/19a9b824-087d-4788-a429-a1a572d6846a.pdf.

Oviedo Freire, A. 2014. "Ruptura de dos paradigmas." In *Bifurcación del Buen Vivir y Sumak Kawsay*, edited by A. Oviedo Freire. Quito: Sumak.

Pacheco Medrano, K. 2007. *Incas, indios y fiestas: Reivindicaciones y representaciones en la configuración de la identidad cuzqueña*. Cuzco, Peru: Instituto Nacional de Culturas, Dirección Regional de Cultura de Cuzco.

"Pacto de Unidad, Propuesta de las Organizaciones Indígenas, Originarias, Campesinas y de Colonizadores hacia la Asamblea Constituyente." (2006) 2007. In *Bolivia: Memoria, insurgencia y movimientos sociales*, edited by M. Svampa and P. Stefanoni. Buenos Aires: El Colectivo–CLACSO.

Pajuelo Teves, R. 2007. *Reinventando comunidades imaginadas: Movimientos indígenas y procesos sociopolíticos en los países centroandinos*. Lima: Instituto Francés de Estudios Andinos (IFEA)-IEP.

Panizza, F. 2009. "Introducción: El populismo como espejo de la democracia." In *El populismo como espejo de la democracia*, edited by F. Panizza. Buenos Aires: FCE.

Park, R. E. 1928. "Human Migration and the Marginal Man." *American Journal of Sociology* 33 (6): 881–93.

Pécaut, D. 1989. *Entre le peuple et la nation: Les intellectuels et la politique au Brésil*. Paris: Édition de la Maison des Sciences de L'homme.

Peña, M. 2012. *Historia del pueblo argentino*. Definitive ed. Buenos Aires: Emecé.

Penchaszadeh, P., and M. de Asúa. 2010. *El deslumbramiento: Aimé Bonpland y Alexander Von Humboldt en Sudamérica*. Buenos Aires: Museo Argentino de Ciencias Naturales Bernardino Rivadavia.

Pengue, W. 2009. *Fundamentos de economía ecológica*. Buenos Aires: Kaicron.

People's Republic of China. 2008. "Documento sobre la política de China hacia América Latina y el Caribe." Xihua University, November 5. https://www.eumed.net/rev/china /09/documento.pdf.

Pepe, F. M., M. A. Andolfo, and M. A. Suárez. 2014. "Prisioneros de la ciencia: Entrevista al Colectivo GUIAS." Interview by Ana Gutiérrez. *Analítica del Sur, Psicoanálisis y Política*, no. 1. http://analyticadelsur.com.ar/prisioneros-de-la-ciencia.

Pereira, M. 2012. "Encuentro en la sal." Video on James Anaya's visit to Salinas Grandes. Accessed January 7, 2025. https://www.youtube.com/watch?v=seRH49ngEnc.

Perona, N. 2001. "Desde la marginalidad a la exclusión social: Una revisión de los conceptos." *Revista Venezolana de Economía y Ciencias Sociales* 7 (2): 35–48.

Pessin, A. 1992. *Le mythe du people.* Paris: PUF.

Petra, A. 2008. "Los intelectuales latinoamericanos y el imperialismo cultural: El caso del proyecto marginalidad." *Revista Políticas de la Memoria*, no. 8/9, 249–60.

Pierri, N. 2005. "Historia del concepto de desarrollo sustentable." In *¿Sustentabilidad?*, edited by G. Foladori and N. Pierri. Mexico City: Colección América Latina y el Nuevo Orden Mundial, Miguel Ángel Porrúa–UAZ–Cámara de Diputados LIX Legislatura.

Piñeiro Iñiguez, C. 2006. *Pensadores latinoamericanos del siglo XX: Ideas, utopía y destino.* Buenos Aires: Siglo XXI, Instituto di Tella.

Pinto, A. (1976) 2008. "Notas sobre los estilos de desarrollo en América Latina." *Revista de la CEPAL*, no. 96, 73–93. Original edition, first quarter of 1976, *Revista de la CEPAL.* https://hdl.handle.net/11362/11281.

Portantiero, J. C. 1991. "Gramsci en clave latinoamericana." *Nueva Sociedad*, no. 115, 152–57. https://nuso.org/articulo/gramsci-en-clave-latinoamericana/.

Porto Gonçalves, C. 2001. *Geo-grafías: Movimientos sociales, nuevas territorialidades y sustentabilidad.* Mexico City: Siglo XXI.

Postero, N. G., and L. Zamosc. 2005. "La batalla de la cuestión indígena en América Latina." In *La lucha por los derechos indígenas en América Latina*, edited by N. G. Postero and L. Zamosc, 11–53. Quito: Abya-Yala.

Prada Alcoreza, R. 2010. "Al interior de la Asamblea Constituyente." Interview. In *Balance y perspectivas: Intelectuales en el primer gobierno de Evo Morales*, by M. Svampa, P. Stefanoni, and B. Fornillo. La Paz: Le Monde Diplomatique, F. F. Ebert.

Pratt, M. L. (1992) 2007. *Imperial Eyes: Travel Writing and Transculturation.* New York: Routledge.

Pratt, M. L. 2010. *Ojos imperiales: Literatura de viaje y transculturación.* Buenos Aires: FCE.

Prebisch, R. (1948) 2013. "El desarrollo de América Latina y algunos de sus principales problemas." Santiago de Chile: CEPAL. http://prebisch.cepal.org/sites/default/files/2013/prebisch_el_desarrollo_eco.pdf.

Preciado Coronado, J. 2013. "Paradigma social en debate: Aportaciones del enfoque geopolítico crítico; La Celac en la integración autónoma de América Latina." In *América Latina en la crisis global: Problemas y desafíos*, edited by M. N. Ruiz. Buenos Aires: CLACSO.

PROA. n.d. "La polémica sobre la obra Arquetipo Símbolo." https://www.proa.org/exhibiciones/pasadas/-vitullo/sala1/1.html.

Puente, F., and M. Argento. 2015. "Conflictos territoriales y construcción identitarias en los salares del noroeste argentino." In *Geopolítica del litio: Industria, ciencia y energía en Argentina*, edited by B. Fornillo. Buenos Aires: El Colectivo–CLACSO.

Puiggrós, R., and A. G. Frank. 1966. "Los modos de producción en Iberoamérica." *Izquierda Nacional*, no. 3.

Puleo, A. 2011. "Ecofeminismo para otro mundo posible: Hablamos con Alicia Puleo de su nuevo libro." Interview by Montserrat Boix. *Mujeres en Red*, May. https://www.mujeresenred.net/spip.php?article1921.

Quijada, M. 2004. "De mitos nacionales definiciones cívicas y clasificaciones grupales: Los indígenas en la construcción nacional argentina, siglos XIX a XXI." In *Caleidoscopio latinoamericano: Imágenes históricas para un debate vigente*, edited by W. Ansaldi. Buenos Aires: Ariel.

Quijano, A. 1966. *Notas sobre el concepto de marginalidad social*. Santiago de Chile: CEPAL.

Quijano, A. (1970) 1977. *Imperialismo y marginalidad en América Latina*. Lima: Mosca Azul Ediciones.

Quijano, A. (1970) 2014. "Polo marginal de la economía y mano de obra marginada." Lima: Universidad Católica. In *Cuestiones y horizontes: Antología esencial; De la dependencia histórico-estructural a la colonialidad/descolonialidad del poder*, edited by D. Assis Clímaco. Buenos Aires: CLACSO.

Quijano, A. 1972. "La constitución del 'mundo' de la marginalidad urbana." *Revista EURE—Revista de Estudios Urbano Regionales* 2 (5): 89–106.

Quijano, A. 1998. "Populismo y Fujimorismo." In *El fantasma del populismo: Aproximación a un tema (siempre) actual*, edited by F. Urbano de Lara. Caracas: FLACSO–Nueva Sociedad.

Quijano, A. 2007. "Colonialidad del poder y clasificación social." In *El giro decolonial: Reflexiones para una diversidad epistémica más allá del capitalismo global*, edited by R. Grosfoguel and S. Castro Gómez. Bogotá: Siglo del Hombre Editores, Universidad Central, Instituto de Estudios Sociales Contemporáneos and Pontificia Universidad Javeriana, Instituto Pensar.

Quijano, A. 2014a. *Cuestiones y horizontes: Antología esencial; De la dependencia histórico-estructural a la colonialidad/descolonialidad del poder*. Edited by D. Assis Clímaco. Buenos Aires: CLACSO.

Quijano, A. 2014b. "José Carlos Mariátegui: Reencuentro y debate." Prologue to *Siete ensayos de interpretación de la realidad peruana*. In *Cuestiones y horizontes: Antología esencial; De la dependencia histórico-estructural a la colonialidad/descolonialidad del poder*, by A. Quijano, edited by D. Assis Clímaco. Buenos Aires: CLACSO.

Quintero, R. (1972) 2014. *Antropología del petróleo*. Caracas: Colección Venezuela y su petróleo, Banco Central de Venezuela.

Quintero, R. 1980. *El mito del populismo en Ecuador: Análisis de los fundamentos del Estado ecuatoriano moderno (1895–1934)*. Quito: FLACSO. https://biblio.flacsoandes.edu.ec/libros/6052-opac.

Quintero, R. 2009. *Nueva crítica al populismo*. Quito: Abya-Yala. https://repository.unm.edu/bitstream/handle/1928/12148/nueva%20 cr%c3%adtica%20al%20populismo.pdf?sequence=1.

Ramírez, F. 2005. *La insurrección de abril no fue solo una fiesta*. Quito: Taller del Colectivo.

Ramírez, F. 2010. "Decisionismos transformacionales, conflicto político y vínculo plebeyo: Poder y cambio en la nueva izquierda sudamericana." In *América Latina: 200 años y nuevos horizontes*, by Á. García Linera, M. A. Garcia, R. Forster, et al. Buenos Aires: Secretaría de Cultura de la Nación.

Ramírez, F. 2015. "La defección correísta." In "El pensamiento crítico y los gobiernos de izquierda: Dossier especial sobre intelectuales y el poder." *Revista Brecha*, April.

Ramírez, G. C. 2013. "Imaginarios de pueblos indígenas y nación a fines del México revolucionario: Forjando patria; Génesis del ideario del indigenismo del siglo XX." *Margen: Revista de Trabajo Social y Ciencias Sociales*, no. 70, 5–10.

Ramírez García, H. S. 2012. *Biotecnología y ecofeminismo: Un estudio de contexto, riesgos y alternativas.* Mexico City: Tirant Lo Blanch.

Razeto, L. 2009. *Las organizaciones económicas populares, 1973–1990.* Santiago de Chile: PET.

RedGE: Red Peruana por una Globalización con Equidad. 2011. "El Perú y el modelo extractivo: Agenda para un nuevo gobierno y necesarios escenarios de transición." http://www.redge.org.pe/node/637.

Reinaga, F. 1970. *La revolución india.* La Paz: PIB.

Reinaga, F. 1971. *Tesis india.* La Paz: PIB.

Restrepo, E., and A. Rojas. 2010. *Inflexión decolonial: Fuentes, conceptos y cuestionamientos.* Popayán, Colombia: Editorial Universidad del Cauca. https://www.ram-wan.net/restrepo/documentos/Inflexion.

Retamozo, M. 2006. "Populismo y teoría política: De una teoría hacia una epistemología del populismo para América Latina." *Revista Venezolana de Economía y Ciencias Sociales* 12 (2): 95–113.

Rey, M. T., and J. Castillo. 2008. "Desarrollo, dependencia y Estado en el debate latinoamericano." *Araucaria: Revista Iberoamericana de Filosofía, Política y Humanidades*, no. 19, 24–45.

Rivera Cusicanqui, S. (1984) 1987. *Oppressed but Not Defeated: Peasant Struggles Among the Aymara and Qhechwa in Bolivia, 1900–1980.* Geneva: United Nations Research Institute for Social Development.

Rivera Cusicanqui, S. (1984) 2003. *Oprimidos pero no vencidos: Luchas del campesinado aymara y qhechwa, 1900–1980.* La Paz: Yachaywasi.

Rivera Cusicanqui, S., and B. de Sousa Santos. 2015. "Conversa del mundo." In *Revueltas de indignación y otras conversas*, by B. de Sousa Santos. La Paz: Alice, Cex, Oxfam.

Rodó, J. (1900) 2021. *Ariel.* Portland, OR: Mint Editions.

Rodríguez, I., and L. Pinto. 1999. Review of *El fantasma del populismo: Aproximación a un tema (siempre) actual*, edited by F. Burbano de Lara. *Espacio Abierto* 8 (3): 408–11. www.redalyc.org/pdf/122/12208310.pdf.

Rodríguez, N., and S. Varese. 1981a. *El pensamiento indígena contemporáneo en América Latina.* Mexico City: Dirección General de Educación Indígena de la SEP.

Rodríguez, N., and S. Varese. 1981b. *Experiencias organizativas indígenas en América Latina.* Mexico City: Dirección General de Educación Indígena de la SEP.

Rodríguez, S. 2007. "Modos de producción en América Latina: Anatomía de un debate en el espejo de la academia contemporánea." *Revista de Ciencias Sociales* 11 (15): 1–18.

Rodríguez Garavito, C., ed. 2010. *La consulta previa a los pueblos indígenas: Estándares del derecho internacional.* Bogotá, Colombia: Universidad de los Andes, Programa de Justicia Global.

Rodríguez Garavito, C. 2012. "El derecho en los campos minados." In *Etnicidad.gov: Los recursos naturales, los pueblos indígenas y el derecho a la consulta previa en los campos sociales minados*, 8–24. Bogotá: Dejusticia.

Roig, A. (1981) 2009. *Teoría y crítica del pensamiento latinoamericano.* Buenos Aires: Una Ventana.

Roitman, M. 2008a. *Pensamiento sociológico y realidad nacional en América Latina*. Mexico City: Instituto de Estudios Educativos y Sindicales de América.

Roitman, M. 2008b. *Pensar América Latina: El desarrollo de la sociología latinoamericana*. Buenos Aires: CLACSO. http://biblioteca.clacso.edu.ar/clacso/formacion-virtual/20100721012022/roitman.pdf.

Rojas, R. 1924. *Eurindia*. Buenos Aires: Librería La Facultad.

Rojas Piérola, R. R. 2009. *Estado, territorialidad y etnias andinas: Lucha y pacto en la construcción de la nación boliviana*. La Paz: UMSA.

Rosanvallon, P., and J.-P. Fitoussi. 1998. *La nouvel âge des inégalités*. Paris: Points.

Rostow, W. W. 1960. *The Stages of Economic Growth: A Non-Communist Manifesto*. Cambridge: Cambridge University Press.

Sachs, I. 1980. "Estrategias de desarrollo con requerimientos energéticos moderados." *Revista de la CEPAL*, no. 12 (December).

Sachs, I. 1981. "Ecodesarrollo: Concepto, aplicación, beneficios y riesgos." *Agricultura y Sociedad*, no. 18, 9–32.

Sachs, I. 1994. "Interview." *Science, Nature, Societé* 2 (3): 258–65.

Sachs, W., ed. (1992) 2002. *The Development Dictionary: A Guide to Knowledge as Power*. London: Zed Books.

Saguier, M., and G. Peinado. 2014. "Minería transnacional y desarrollo en el kirchnerismo." Paper presented at Decimonovenas Jornadas "Investigaciones en la Facultad" de Ciencias Económicas y Estadística, Universidad Nacional de Rosario, November 27.

Saint-Upéry, M. 2008a. *El sueño de Bolívar: El desafío de las izquierdas sudamericanas*. Barcelona: Paidós.

Saint-Upéry, M. 2008b. "¿Hay patria para todos? Ambivalencia de lo público y emergencia plebeya en los nuevos gobiernos progresistas." *Revista Íconos*, no. 32, 75–87. http://revistas.flacsoandes.edu.ec/iconos/ article/view/284.

Salama, P. 2012. "China-Brasil: Industrialización y 'desindustrialización temprana.'" *Cuadernos de Economía* 31 (56): 223–52. https://www.researchgate.net/publication/260766264_China-brasil_Industrializacion_y_desindustrializacion_temprana.

Salama, P. 2014. "¿Es posible otro desarrollo en los países emergentes?" *Nueva Sociedad*, no. 250, 88–101.

Salas, C. 2006. "El sector informal: Auxilio u obstáculo para el conocimiento de la realidad social en América Latina." In *Teorías sociales y Estudios del Trabajo: Nuevos Enfoques*, edited by Enrique de la Garza Toledo. Barcelona: Anthropos.

Salazar, C., J. M. Rodríguez Franco, and A. Sulcata Guzmán. 2012. *Intelectuales aymaras y nuevas mayorías mestizas: Una perspectiva post-1952*. Informes de Investigación. La Paz: PIEB.

Salazar Soler, C. 2014. "¿El despertar indio en el Perú andino?" In *De la política indígena: Perú y Bolivia*, edited by G. Lomne. Lima: IFEA-IEP.

Salvia, A. 2005. "Crisis del empleo y nueva marginalidad: El papel de las economías de la pobreza en tiempos de cambio social." In *Los nuevos rostros de la marginalidad: La supervivencia de los desplazados*, edited by F. Mallimaci and A. Salvia. Buenos Aires: Biblos–Instituto Gino Germani.

Sánchez Vázquez, A. 1999. *De Marx al marxismo en América Latina*. Mexico City: Editorial Itaca–Universidad de Puebla.

Sanjinés, J. 2005. *El espejismo del mestizaje.* La Paz: IFEA.

Santos, B. de Sousa. 2005. *Reinventar la democracia, reinventar el Estado.* Buenos Aires: CLACSO.

Santos, B. de Sousa. 2009a. "Las paradojas de nuestro tiempo y la plurinacionalidad." In *Plurinacionalidad: Democracia en la diversidad.* Quito: Abya-Yala.

Santos, B. de Sousa. 2009b. *Una epistemología del sur.* Buenos Aires: CLACSO. In English: *Epistemologies of the South: Justice Against Epistemicide.* New York: Routledge, 2014.

Santos, B. de Sousa. 2010. *Refundación del Estado en América Latina: Perspectivas desde una epistemología del sur.* Quito: Ediciones Abya-Yala.

Santoul, C. 1988. *Racismo, etnocentrismo y literatura: La novela indigenista andina.* Buenos Aires: Serie Antropolítica, Ediciones del Sol.

Sarlo, B. 2011. *La audacia y el cálculo: Kirchner 2003–2010.* Buenos Aires: Sudamericana.

Sarmiento, D. F. (1845) 1988. *Facundo: Or, Civilization and Barbarism.* New York: Penguin Classics.

Sarmiento, D. F. (1883) 1915. *Conflictos y armonías de las razas en América.* Buenos Aires: La Cultura Argentina.

Schavelzon, S. 2015. *Plurinacionalidad y vivir bien/buen vivir: Dos conceptos leídos desde Bolivia y Ecuador post-constituyentes.* Quito: Abya Yala–CLACSO.

Seabra, R. L., and F. M. Bueno. 2012. "El protagonismo brasileño en el siglo XXI: ¿Subimperialismo o semiperiferia?" *Rebela* 2 (1): 75–86. https://core.ac.uk/download/pdf/185255809.pdf.

Segato, R. L. 2007. *La nación y sus otros: Raza, etnicidad y diversidad religiosa en tiempos de políticas de la identidad.* Buenos Aires: Prometeo.

Seibel Luce, M. 2007. "O imperialismo hegemônico e o subimperialismo brasileiro: Diagnóstico e alternativas." Paper presented at the 26th Congress of the Latin American Association of Sociology, Guadalajara, August 13–17.

Seibel Luce, M. 2011. "A teoria do subimperialismo em Ruy Mauro Marini." BA thesis, Universidade do Rio Grande do Sul, Porto Alegre, Brazil.

Sempat Assadourian, C., C. F. Santana Cardoso, H. Ciafardini, J. C. Garavaglia, and E. Laclau. (1973) 1979. *Modos de producción en América Latina.* Mexico City: Cuadernos de Pasado y Presente.

Sen, A. 2000. *Desarrollo y libertad.* Buenos Aires: Editorial Planeta.

SENPLADES (Secretaría Nacional de Planificación y Desarrollo). 2007. *Plan Nacional de Desarrollo 2007–2010.* Quito: SENPLADES. https://www.planificacion.gob.ec/wp-content/uploads/downloads/2013/09/Plan-Nacional-Desarrollo-2007-2010.pdf.

Serra, J., and F. H. Cardoso. 1976. "As desventuras da dialética da dependência." *Estudos CEBRAP,* no. 23, 33–80. São Paulo: Editora Brasileira de Ciências Sociais.

Serra, J., and F. H. Cardoso. 1978. "Las desventuras de la dialéctica de la dependencia." *Revista Mexicana de Sociología* 40:9–55.

SERVINDI. 2013. "Bolivia: Indígenas exigen que propuesta de ley marco para la consulta previa sea consensuada." June 11. http://servindi.org/actualidad/89197.

Shiva, V. (1988) 1995. *Staying Alive: Women, Ecology and Survival in India.* London: Zed Books.

Sichra, I. 2009. *Atlas sociolingüístico de pueblos indígenas en América Latina.* Cochabamba, Bolivia: FUNPROEIB Andes–UNICEF.

Sigal, S., and E. Verón. 1986. *Perón o muerte: Los fundamentos discursivos del fenómeno peronista*. Buenos Aires: Legasa.

Sikkink, K. 2009. *El proyecto desarrollista en la Argentina y Brasil: De Frondizi y Kubitschek*. Buenos Aires: Siglo XXI.

Slipak, A. 2014a. "América Latina y China: ¿Cooperación Sur-Sur o Consenso de Beijing?" *Nueva Sociedad*, no. 250, 102–13.

Slipak, A. 2014b. "La expansión de China en América Latina: Incidencia en los vínculos comerciales argentino-brasileros." Paper presented at the Congreso de Economía Política Internacional, Universidad Nacional de Moreno (UNM), Moreno, Buenos Aires, November 5–6.

Snow, D. A. 2004. "Framing Processes, Ideology, and Discursive Fields." In *The Blackwell Companion to Social Movements*, edited by D. A. Snow, S. A. Soule, and H. Kriesi. Oxford: Blackwell.

Soruco Sologuren, X. 2011. "Apuntes sobre el Estado plurinacional." In *Descolonización, Estado plurinacional, economía plural y socialismo comunitario: Debates sobre el cambio*. La Paz: Vicepresidencia del Estado Plurinacional de Bolivia.

Sotelo, I. 1972. *Sociología de América Latina: Estructuras y problemas*. Madrid: Tecnos.

Sotelo, V., and P. Francke. 2011. "Es economicamente viable una economia postextractivista en el Peru?" In *Transiciones: Post extractivismo y alternativas al extractivismo en el Perú*, edited by A. Alayza and E. Gudynas, 115–41. Lima: CEPES.

Sotelo Valencia, A. 2005. *América Latina, de crisis y paradigmas: La teoría de la dependencia en el siglo XXI*. Mexico City: Plaza y Valdés.

Stabb, M. 1968. "La Argentina y el continente enfermo: Positivismo y racismo en el ensayo argentino, 1898–1910." Paper presented at Terceras jornadas de investigación de la historia y la literatura rioplatense y de los Estados Unidos: Situaciones conflictivas en la historia y la literatura argentina y/o norteamericana entre 1880 y 1910, Universidad Nacional de Cuyo, Mendoza, October 10–11.

Stalin, J. (1938) 1985. *Dialectical and Historical Materialism*. London: Taylor and Francis.

Stavenhagen, R. (1965) 1981. "Siete tesis equivocadas sobre América Latina." In *Sociología y subdesarrollo*. Mexico City: Nuestro Tiempo.

Stavenhagen, R. 1967. *Seven Erroneous Theses About Latin America*. Boston: New England Free Press.

Stavenhagen, R. 1969. *Las clases sociales en las sociedades agrarias*. Mexico City: Siglo XXI.

Stavenhagen, R. 1991. "Los conflictos étnicos y sus repercusiones en la sociedad internacional." *Revue Internationale de Sciences Sociales* 43 (1): 131–55. http://unesdoc.unesco.org/images/0008/000881/088134so.pdf.

Stavenhagen, R. 2006a. "La emergencia de los pueblos indígenas como nuevos actores políticos y sociales en América Latina." In *Movimiento indígena en América Latina: Resistencia y proyecto alternativo*, edited by R. Gutiérrez and F. Escárzaga. Mexico City: Centro de Estudios Andinos y Mesoamericanos.

Stavenhagen, R. 2006b. "Los derechos de los pueblos indígenas: Esperanzas, logros y reclamos." In *Pueblos indígenas y derechos humanos*, edited by M. Berraondo. Bilbao: Instituto de Derechos Humanos, Universidad de Deusto.

Stavenhagen, R. 2018. *Derecho indígena y derechos humanos en América Latina*. Instituto Interamericano de Derechos Humanos. Alicante: Biblioteca Virtual Miguel de

Cervantes. https://www.cervantesvirtual.com/obra/derecho-indigena-y-derechos
-humanos-en-america-latina-924449/.

Stefanoni, P. 2010a. "¿Pueblo enfermo o raza de bronce? Etnicidad e imaginación
nacional en Bolivia (1900–2010)." In *Debatir Bolivia: Los contornos de un proyecto de
descolonización*, by M. Svampa, P. Stefanoni, and B. Fornillo. Buenos Aires: Taurus.

Stefanoni, P. 2010b. *"Qué hacer con los indios . . .": Y otros traumas irresueltos de la colonialidad*. La Paz: Plural.

Stefanoni, P. 2011a. "¿Adónde nos lleva el pachamamismo?" In "El debate sobre el pachamamismo." *Revista Tierra Socialista: Papeles sobre Democracia, Socialismo y Ecología
Política* 2 (2): 166–67.

Stefanoni, P. 2011b. "Indianismo y pachamamismo." In "El debate sobre el pachamamismo." *Revista Tierra Socialista: Papeles sobre Democracia, Socialismo y Ecología
Política* 2 (2): 167–69.

Stefanoni, P. 2014. *Los inconformistas del Centenario: Intelectuales socialismo y nación en
una Bolivia en crisis (1925–1939)*. La Paz: Plural.

Subirats, J. 2011. "Algunos apuntes sobre la relación entre los bienes comunes y la
economía social y solidaria/Some Thoughts on Commons and Social Economy." *Otra
Economía* 5 (9): 195–204.

Sunkel, O., and P. Paz. 1970. *El subdesarrollo latinoamericano y la teoría del desarrollo*.
15th ed. Mexico City: Siglo XXI.

Svampa, M. 1994. *El dilema argentino: Civilización o barbarie*. Buenos Aires: El Cielo por
Asalto.

Svampa, M. 1998. "La dialéctica entre lo nuevo y lo viejo: Sobre los usos y nociones del
caudillismo en Argentina durante el siglo XIX." In *El caudillismo en el Río de La Plata*,
edited by N. Goldman and R. Salvatore. Buenos Aires: Eudeba.

Svampa, M. 2005. *La sociedad excluyente: La Argentina bajo el signo del neoliberalismo*.
Buenos Aires: Taurus.

Svampa, M. 2008. *Cambio de época: Movimientos sociales y poder politico*. Buenos Aires:
Siglo XXI.

Svampa, M. 2010a. "El 'laboratorio boliviano': Cambios, tensiones y ambivalencias del
gobierno de Evo Morales." In *Debatir Bolivia: Contornos de un proyecto de descolonización*, by M. Svampa, P. Stefanoni, and B. Fornillo. Buenos Aires: Taurus.

Svampa, M. 2010b. "Movimientos sociales, matrices socio-políticas y nuevos contextos
en América Latina." In *One World Perspectives*. Working Paper 01/2010, University of
Kassel.

Svampa, M. 2011. "Argentina, una década después: Del 'que se vayan todos' a la exacer-
bación de lo nacional-popular." *Nueva Sociedad* 235 (September–October). https://
www.nuso.org/articulo/argentina-una-decada-despues-del-que-se-vayan-todos-a
-la-exacerbacion-de-lo-nacional-popular/.

Svampa, M. 2012. "Extractivismo neodesarrollista y movimientos sociales: ¿Un giro
eco-territorial hacia nuevas alternativas?" In *Más allá del desarrollo*, by M. Lang and
D. Mokrani, Grupo Permanente de Trabajo sobre Alternativas al Desarrollo. Quito:
Fundación Rosa Luxemburgo.

Svampa, M. 2013. "Consenso de los *commodities* y lenguajes de valoración en América
Latina." *Nueva Sociedad*, no. 244, 30–46.

Svampa, M. 2015a. "El desarrollo en cuestión." In *Ensayos políticos: Debates en torno al poder la organización y la etapa*, by E. Lucita, F. Orchani, F. N. Martín, et al. Buenos Aires: El Colectivo.

Svampa, M. 2015b. "Feminismos del sur y ecofeminismo." *Nueva Sociedad*, no. 256, 127–31.

Svampa, M. 2021. "Feminismos ecoterritoriales en América Latina: Entre la violencia patriarcal y extractivista y la interconexión con la naturaleza." Working paper 59, Fundación Carolina, Madrid.

Svampa, M., and A. Slipak. 2015. "China en América Latina: Del consenso de los *commodities* al consenso de Beijing." *Revista Ensambles*, no. 3, 34–63.

Svampa, M., and P. Stefanoni, eds. 2007. *Bolivia: Memoria, insurgencia y movimientos sociales*. Buenos Aires: El Colectivo-OSAL (CLASCO).

Svampa, M., and E. Viale. 2014. *Maldesarrollo: La Argentina del extractivismo y del despojo*. Buenos Aires: Katz.

Sztulwark, S. 2003. *El estructuralismo latinoamericano: Fundamentos y transformaciones del pensamiento económico de la periferia*. Buenos Aires: UNGS.

Taguieff, P. A. 1996. "La ciencia política frente al populismo: De un espejismo conceptual a un problema real." In *Populismo posmoderno*, by F. Adler, T. Fleming, P. Gottfried, et al. Bernal, Buenos Aires: Universidad de Quilmes.

Tamagno, L. 2009. "Saberes, ética y política: La restitución de restos humanos en el museo de La Plata." In *Pueblos indígenas: Interculturalidad, colonialidad, política*, edited by L. Tamagno. Buenos Aires: Biblos.

Tamayo, F. 1910. *Creación de la pedagogía nacional*. Capítulo XVII. https://www.ensayistas.org/antologia/XXA/tamayo/tamayo17.htm.

Tamayo, F. 1979. *Obra escogida*. Caracas: Bibliotecas Ayacucho.

Tapia, L. 2006. *La invención del núcleo común: Ciudadanía y gobierno multisocietal*. La Paz: Muela del Diablo.

Tapia, L. 2008. *Una reflexión sobre la idea de Estado plurinacional*. Oxford: Oxfam.

Tapia, L. 2011. "Consideraciones sobre el Estado plurinacional." In *Descolonización, Estado Plurinacional, economía plural y socialismo comunitario: Debates sobre el cambio*, edited by G. Gosálvez and J. Dulon. La Paz: Vicepresidencia del Estado Plurinacional de Bolivia.

Tapia, L. 2013. *De la forma primordial a América Latina como horizonte epistemológico*. La Paz: CIDES–UMSA.

Taylor, C. 1992. *Multiculturalism and the Politics of Recognition*. Princeton, NJ: Princeton University Press.

Ticona Alejo, E. 2003. "La revolución boliviana y los pueblos indígenas." In *Revoluciones del siglo XX: Homenaje a los cincuenta años de la Revolución Boliviana; Tenemos pecho de bronce . . . pero no sabemos nada*, by PNUD-FES. La Paz: PNUD–FES–ILDIS/ASDI/Plural.

Toledo, Víctor. 2006. "Pueblos indígenas, territorios, derechos y políticas públicas en América Latina." Fifth Congress of the Latin American Network of Legal Anthropology, Oaxetepec, Mexico, October 16–20.

Torre, J. C. 1991. *La vieja guardia sindical y Perón*. Buenos Aires: Sudamericana.

Torre, J. C. 1998. *El proceso político de las reformas económicas en América Latina*. Buenos Aires: Paidós.

Tortosa, J. M. 2011. *Maldesarrollo y mal vivir: Pobreza y violencia a escala mundial*. Quito: Abya-Yala.

Touraine, A. 1988. *La parole et le sang*. Paris: Odile Jacob.

Trindade, H. 1982. "El tema del fascismo en América Latina." *Revista de Estudios Políticos*, no. 30, 111–42.

Ulloque Franco, H., and M. Ruiz Montealegre, dirs. 2007. *Hartos Evos aquí hay: Los cocaleros del Chapare*. Film. Colombia: Medio de Contención.

Unceta Satrústegui, K. 2009. "Desarrollo, subdesarrollo, maldesarrollo y posdesarrollo: Una mirada transdisciplinar sobre el debate y sus implicaciones." *Carta Latinoamericana: Contribuciones en desarrollo y sociedad en América Latina*, no. 7. Montevideo: CLAES.

Unceta Satrústegui, K. 2014. *Desarrollo, postcrecimiento y buen vivir: Debates e interrogantes*. Quito: Abya-Yala.

United Nations. 1972. *Report of the United Nations Conference on the Human Environment, Stockholm, 5–16 June 1972*. New York: United Nations. https://digitallibrary.un.org/record/523249.

United Nations. 1987. *Report of the World Commission on Environment and Development. Our Common Future*. New York: United Nations. https://digitallibrary.un.org/record/139811.

United Nations. 2012. "The Future We Want." *Sustainable Development Knowledge Platform*. https://sustainabledevelopment.un.org/futurewewant.html.

Uslar Pietri, A. (1936) 2005. "Sembrar el petróleo." *Revista de Artes y Humanidades UNICA* 6 (12): 231–33.

Valcárcel, L. 1927. *Tempestad en los Andes*. Lima: Populibros Peruanos.

Valenzuela, E. 1991. "La experiencia nacional-popular." *Proposiciones*, no. 20, 12–33.

Valko, M. 2013. *Los indios invisibles del Malón de la Paz*. Buenos Aires: Sudestada.

Vargas Soler, J. C. 2008. "Reseña del libro Hacia una Economía para la vida." *Otra Economía* 2 (2): 172–76.

Vasconcelos, J. (1925) 1997. *The Cosmic Race/La raza cósmica*. Baltimore, MD: Johns Hopkins University Press.

Vega Centeno, I. 1991. *Aprismo popular, cultura, religión y política*. Lima: Cisepa Puc.

Venturi, F. 1981. *El populismo ruso*. Vol. 1. Madrid: Alianza.

Vicepresidencia del Estado Plurinacional de Bolivia. 2010. *Descolonización, estado plurinacional, economía plural, socialismo comunitario: Debate sobre el cambio*. La Paz: Vicepresidencia del Estado Plurinacional de Bolivia.

Vidal Molina, P. 2013. "Theotonio dos Santos en el Chile de la Unidad Popular." *Cuadernos de Historia* (Santiago), no. 39, 185–200.

Viguera, A. 1993. "'Populismo' y 'neopopulismo' en América Latina." *Revista Mexicana de Sociología* 55 (3): 49–66.

Vilas, C. M., ed. 1994. *La democratización fundamental: El populismo en América Latina*. Mexico City: Consejo Nacional para la Cultura y las Artes.

Vilas, C. M. 2003. "¿Populismos reciclados o neoliberalismo a secas?" *Revista Venezolana de Economía y Ciencias Sociales* 9 (3): 13–36. https://www.researchgate.net/publication/307723730_Populismos_reciclados_o_neoliberalismo_a_secas_El_mito_del__neopopulismo_latinoamericano.

Viñas, D. 1982. *Indios, ejército y frontera*. Buenos Aires: Siglo XXI.

Viola, E. 1992. "El ambientalismo brasileño: De la denuncia y concientización a la institucionalización y el desarrollo sustentable." *Nueva Sociedad*, no. 122, 138–55.

Viveiros de Castro, E. 2013. *La mirada del jaguar: Introducción al perspectivismo amerindio (entrevistas)*. Buenos Aires: Tinta Limón.

Volmer, A. 2009. *Ricardo Rojas y su obra literaria*. University of Koeln. https://lateinamerika.phil-fak.uni-koeln.de/fileadmin/sites/aspla/bilder/ip_hausarbeiten_koeln_2009/Andrea_Volmer.pdf.

Walicki, A. 1969. "Russia." In *Populism: Its Meanings and National Characteristics*, edited by G. Ionescu and E. Gellner. New York: Macmillan.

Wallerstein, I. (1974) 2011. *The Modern World-System*. Vol. 1, *Capitalist Agriculture and the Origins of the European World-Economy in the Sixteenth Century*. Berkeley: University of California Press.

Wallerstein, I. 1998. "1968: Entrevista con Immanuel Wallerstein." Interview by Andrés Cisneros Sosa. *Sociológica* 13 (38): 205–13.

Wallerstein, I. 2001. *Capitalismo histórico y movimientos antisistémicos*. Madrid: Akal.

Wallerstein, I. 2012. "China and the United States: Rivals, Enemies, Collaborators?" *I.W*, January 15. https://iwallerstein.com/china-and-the-united-states-rivals-enemies-collaborators/.

Weffort, F. 1974. "Los sindicatos en la política (Brasil 1955–1964)." In *Movimiento obrero, sindicatos y poder en América Latina*, by CEIL-CONICET. Buenos Aires: El Coloquio.

Weffort, F. 1978. *O populismo na política brasileira*. Rio de Janeiro: Paz e Terra.

Weffort, F. 1994. "Los sindicatos en la política: Brasil (1955–1964)." In *La democratización fundamental: El populismo en América Latina*, edited by C. Vilas. Mexico City: Consejo Nacional para la Cultura y las Artes.

Williams, R. 1978. *Marxism and Literature*. Oxford: Oxford University Press.

Yrigoyen Fajardo, R. 2002. "Hacia un reconocimiento pleno de las rondas campesinas y el pluralismo legal." *Alpanchis* 34 (59–60): 31–81.

Zanatta, L. 2015. *El populismo*. Buenos Aires: Katz.

Zavaleta Mercado, R. (1986) 2009. *Lo nacional-popular en Bolivia*. La Paz: Plural.

Zavaleta Mercado, R. 2006. "Formas de operar del Estado de América Latina." In *Ensayos, testimonios y revisions*. Buenos Aires: Miño y Dávila.

Zea, L. 1965. *El pensamiento latinoamericano*. Mexico City: Formaca.

Zermeño, S. 1989. "El regreso del líder: Crisis, neoliberalismo y desorden." *Revista Mexicana de Sociología* 51 (4): 115–50.

Zibechi, R. 2011. "Ecuador: El estado fuerte y la criminalización a los movimientos." *MIRA: Feminismos y democracias*, March 9. https://www.americas.org/es/ecuador-el-estado-fuerte-y-la-criminalizacion-a-los-movimientos/.

Zibechi, R. 2013. "La libertad según los zapatistas." *Rebelión*, September 4. https://rebelion.org/la-libertad-segun-los-zapatistas/.

Žižek, S. 1997. *Multiculturalism, or, The Cultural Logic of Multinational Capitalism*. Ljubljana: New Left Review.

Index

delegative democracy, 212
Deleuze, Gilles, 223
Delrio, Walter, 84
Demélas, Marie D., 23
democracy (discussion of), 177–78, 181–84, 194–95, 202, 206–8, 212, 230, 253, 303–13, 317–22. *See also* fascism (discussion of); populism; socialism (discussion of)
demographic data, 15–17, 27, 78, 343nn1–2
demonstrative effect, 184
de Paw, Cornelio, 348n5
Dependencia y desarollo en América Latina (Cardoso and Faletto), 134–37, 161–63, 166, 172
dependency theory, 2–5, 9–10, 96–97, 110, 114, 125–41, 166–75, 276–82, 336–37, 348n8. *See also* center/periphery; globalization; historical-structural perspective; marginality; national bourgeoisie; new dependency
Dependency Theory (Bambirra), 141
dependent industrialization, 136–37
dependentism, 188
Derrida, Jacques, 305
Descartes, René, 106
de Sierra, Gerónimo, 330
destituent moment, 225
Deutsch, Karl, 183
development (discussion of), 87–90, 98, 108–9, 115–18, 131, 136, 249–54, 267. *See also* center/periphery; extractivism; maldevelopment; postdevelopment; underdevelopment
developmentalism, 93–94, 106, 116, 127, 133, 162, 166, 187–89, 261
Development Dictionary, The (Sachs), 117
development economics, 90
Development of Capitalism in Russia, The (Lenin), 198
"Development of Underdevelopment, The" (Frank), 137–38
development styles, 96, 164–65
Devés Valdés, Eduardo, 2–3
Devil's Tail, The (Gramsci), 201
Dialéctica de la dependencia (Marini), 169–71
Dialectical and Historical Materialism (Stalin), 200
dialogue of knowledges, 122
Díaz, Porfirio, 178

Díaz Polanco, Héctor, 70, 76–77, 85, 199, 226
"Discurso del Presidente de la República en el Primer Congreso Indigenista Interamericano" (Cárdenas), 43
Dispute of the New World, The (Gerbi), 348n5
Di Tella, Torcuato, 183–84, 187
Dobb, Maurice, 155, 158
Domingo Ouriques, Nildo, 127
Don Segundo Sombra (Güiraldes), 33
Donzelot, Jacques, 147
dos Santos, Theotônio, 2, 125–28, 132–34, 138–40, 151, 153, 162, 168–70, 172–74, 188, 276, 293–94
Dumont, René, 114
Durkheim, Émile, 37
Dussel, Enrique, 6, 278

Echeverría, Bolívar, 335
Echeverría, Luis, 110
ecodevelopment, 110–11
ecofeminism, 115, 121, 251, 256–58, 334–35. *See also* feminism; women
Ecología politica (Alimonda), 348n10
Ecological Notebooks, The (Marx), 196
Economía de la sociedad colonial (Bagú), 155
Economic Commission for Asia and the Far East, 89
Economic Commission for Latin America and the Caribbean, 88–97, 130–31, 237, 276
ecosocial transition, 248
eco-territorial turn, 253, 310–12, 322–24
Eighteenth Brumaire of Louis Bonaparte, The (Marx), 152
El antiimperialismo y el Apra (Haya de la Torre), 197–98
El capitalismo dependiente latinoamericano (Bambirra), 140–41
"El concepto del indio en América" (Bonfil Batalla), 62
El continente enfermo (Zumeta), 344n7
"El desarrollo de la América Latina y algunos de sus principales problemas" (Prebisch), 91
El deslumbramiento (de Asúa and Penchaszadeh), 97
El Dorado myth, 98, 101, 103
El fantasma del populismo (Quintero), 213

marginal pole, 148–49

Mariano Rosas, 82

Mariátegui, José Carlos, 3, 6, 32–33, 35–43, 52, 196–99, 282, 345nn19–20

Mariátegui y los orígenes del marxismo latino-americano (Aricó), 43, 198

Marín, J. Carlos, 144, 151

Marini, Ruy Mauro, 2, 127–28, 134, 140–43, 154, 162, 167, 169–71, 279

Maritain, Jacques, 318

Marof, Tristán, 36–38, 345n17

Marroquín, Alejandro, 44, 47

Martí, José: and Latin American thought, 10–11; and social theory, 3, 6

Martínez Alier, Joan, 122–23, 263, 331

Martínez Cobo, José, 65

Martuccelli, Danilo, 210, 308

Marvulle Bueno, Fabio, 280–81

Marx, Karl, 127, 132, 146–47, 149, 152, 189, 196–200, 222

Marxism: crisis of, 207; and the Cuban Revolution, 58, 128; and the decolonial perspective, 278; and the definition of communism, 262; and democracy, 306, 318; and dependency theory, 130, 133, 166, 278; and *indianismo*, 60, 199–200, 310; and the indigenous question, 42; Latin American, 36, 38, 40, 43, 132–33, 144, 198–99; in literature, 133, 156, 159, 165–66, 199–200; and postdevelopment, 118

"Marxismo e indianismo" (García Linera), 63

Massacre of Mohoza (1899), 22–23

massacres, 55. *See also* genocide

Max-Neef, Mandref, 116–17

Mayan people, 30

Mayorga, Fernando, 236, 350n7

Meadows Report, 107, 111–12

Medellín Conference, 59, 318

Medina, Javier, 258–59, 262, 264

Medina Echavarría, José, 95, 125, 131

megamining, 80, 142–43, 236, 242–43, 251–53, 324. *See also* extractivism

Memory, Truth, and Justice Meeting, 244

Mendes, Chico, 120

Méndez, Cecilia, 30

Mendoza, Jamie, 34

Menem, Carlos, 210–13

Mercado, René Zavaleta, 5

mestizaje, 40, 44–45, 49, 52, 57

mestizo baroque, 51

mestizos, 17–18, 24–25, 28–34, 46, 54–57, 345n17

Mexican Revolution, 44, 49

Mezzadra, Sandro, 223

Mignolo, Walter, 6, 278, 288

Minstrel, The (Lugones), 33

miscegenation, 18, 24–25, 29–35, 44–46, 49, 51–52, 57, 314

mode of production, 128

Modernización y autoritarismo (O'Donnell), 171–72

modernization (theory of), 145, 150

Modern World-System, The (Wallerstein), 160

Modonesi, Massimo, 223, 341

Modos de producción en América Latina (Cardoso), 159

monogenist view, 99

Montenegro, Carlos, 51

Mora Jiménez, Henry, 256

Morales, Evo, 64, 73–74, 77, 80, 217, 225, 229–31, 239–41, 259, 261, 306–7, 315–20, 340

Moreira, Roberto, 121

Moreno, Camila, 254

motley societies, 5

Mottin, M. F., 114

Mouffe, Chantal, 203, 207, 305

Mounier, Emmanuel, 318

Movimiento al Socialismo—Instrumento Político por la Soberanía de los Pueblos, 73, 230, 234–35, 261, 307, 316–17

Movimiento Indio Tupac Katari, 64

Movimiento Nacional Revolucionario, 48–51

Movimiento Revolucionario Tupac Katari, 64

Moyano, Hugo, 321

multiculturalism, 68–74, 79–81, 83, 85–86, 347n47. *See also* social theory (discussion of)

Murmis, Miguel, 144–45, 148–49, 151, 192, 330

Museum of Natural Sciences of La Plata, 9, 29, 82

Myrdal, Gunnar, 90

mythmaking, 98, 101, 103, 111, 178, 180–82, 193, 205, 224, 302–3

Myth of Economic Development, The (Furtado), 111–12

Phantom of Populism, The (Quintero), 213
Pinto, Aníbal, 90, 96, 140
Pipes, Richard, 194
Pirenne, Henri, 155
Pirovano, Ignacio, 55–56
plurinational state, 9, 16–17, 20, 77, 221, 225, 229–36, 240, 329
Polanco, Díaz, 74, 196
Polanyi, Karl, 263, 291
political ecology, 121–22, 330–34
Political Ecology Work Group, 121
political ontology, 266–67
Política y sociedad en una época de transición (Germani), 183–84
popular ecology, 123
populism: and Bonapartism, 187, 189; and capital accumulation, 186, 194–96, 199; and class, 203–4, 209, 309; criticisms of, 309–13; defined, 4, 179, 194, 305, 308; developmentalist, 187–89; and disarticulation, 186; discussion of, 177–82, 213–14, 301–27; the end of, 163; failures of, 133; high-intensity, 307–9, 320, 326–27, 338–39; and the integrationist model, 18–20, 48–54, 57–58; low-intensity, 307; and mass movements, 184–85, 187–89; and the media, 325, 327; and the military, 52–53; and modernization, 183–84, 190; and the national-popular, 201–9, 211, 309–10; neo-, 211–13; new, 306–7; peasant, 9, 195–200; plebeian, 189, 208–10, 314–20, 327; political, 185–86, 188, 190, 192, 200, 205–6, 308–12, 317, 323; rise of, 7, 184, 191; Russian, 194–200; and secularization, 188; and unanimism, 206; and Velasquismo, 190–93, 210–11. See also democracy (discussion of); eco-territorial turn; fascism (discussion of); mythmaking
Populism (Ionescu and Gellner), 194
Portantiero, Juan Carlos, 192, 202, 204–6, 310
Portes, Alejandro, 293
Porto Gonçalves, Carlos, 331–32, 351n2
positivism, 22–25, 29–34, 37, 45–46, 266. See also racism
postcolonialism, 5, 278, 343n3. See also decolonialism
postdevelopment, 118–19, 251, 329, 332–33
Postero, Nancy Grey, 69, 73
postextractivism, 248, 268–71, 333

postgrowth, 263
post-neoliberalism, 329
poststructuralism, 117–18, 207
Prada, Raúl, 233–34, 314, 333
Prado, Caio, Junior, 125
Pratt, Mary Louise, 100–101, 348n5
Prebisch, Raúl, 90–94, 125, 170
Pre-Capitalist Economic Formations (Hobsbawm), 194
Preciado Coronado, Jaime, 281
previous, free, and informed consent, 236, 239–43, 245. See also environmentalism; prior consultation
prior consultation, 221–22, 236–45. See also environmentalism
"Problemas y perspectivas de la teoría de la dependencia" (Cueva), 165–66
"Problem of the Races, The" (Mariátegui and Pesce), 42
productivism, 88–90, 111, 117, 248
progress (as an idea), 5–6, 9, 107
progressivism (discussion of), 217–18, 249–51, 287, 312–13, 320–21
protest, 35, 48–50, 54–55, 244, 248, 255, 261, 276–77, 294. See also social movements
Psychology of Crowds (Le Bon), 22–23
Pueblo enfermo (Arguedas), 24–25, 344n7
Puiggrós, Rodolfo, 135, 156–58
Puleo, Alicia, 335

Quijada, Mónica, 28
Quijano, Aníbal, 5–6, 11, 21, 134, 144–45, 148–50, 167, 278, 291–92, 330
Quilito (Ocantos), 27
Quintero, Rafael, 192–94, 210–11
Quintero, Rodolfo, 102, 104–5, 213
Quisbert, Pablo, 51, 340, 345n28
Quispe, Felipe, 64

race regeneration, 30–31, 48
racialization, 21–25, 29, 345n30. See also ethnicity
racism, 21, 25. See also genocide; positivism
Ramírez, René, 261
Ramona, Comandanta, 222
Ramos, Abelardo, 183
Razeto, Luis, 292
reciprocity networks, 291–92, 299

www.ingramcontent.com/pod-product-compliance
Lightning Source LLC
Jackson TN
JSHW021628160725
87746JS00001B/5